Issues in Software Engineering Education

Richard Fairley Peter Freeman
Editors

Issues in Software Engineering Education

With 34 Illustrations

Springer-Verlag
New York Berlin Heidelberg
London Paris Tokyo

Richard Fairley
School of Information Technology
and Engineering
George Mason University
Fairfax, VA 22030
USA

Peter Freeman
Department of Information
and Computer Science
University of California–Irvine
Irvine, CA 92717
USA

Library of Congress Cataloging-in-Publication Data
Issues in software engineering education : proceedings of the 1987 SEI conference / edited by Richard Fairley and Peter Freeman.
p. cm.
Proceedings of the 1987 SEI Conference on Software Engineering Education, held in Monroeville, Pa., Apr. 30–May 1, 1987, sponsored by the Software Engineering Institute of Carnegie-Mellon University.
Bibliography: p.
1. Software engineering—Study and teaching—Congresses.
I. Fairley, R. E. (Richard E.), 1937– . II. Freeman, Peter, 1941– . III. Carnegie-Mellon University. Software Engineering Institute.
IV. SEI Conference on Software Engineering Education (1987 : Monroeville, Pa.)
QA76.758.I58 1988
005.7'07'1—dc19 88-20195

Printed on acid-free paper

Softcover reprint of the hardcover 1st edition 1989

Camera-ready copy provided by authors.

9 8 7 6 5 4 3 2 1

ISBN-13: 978-1-4613-9616-1 e-ISBN-13: 978-1-4613-9614-7
DOI: 10.1007/978-1-4613-9614-7

PREFACE

This volume combines the proceedings of the 1987 SEI Conference on Software Engineering Education, held in Monroeville, Pennsylvania on April 30 and May 1, 1987, with the set of papers that formed the basis for that conference.

The conference was sponsored by the Software Engineering Institute (SEI) of Carnegie–Mellon University. SEI is a federally–funded research and development center established by the United States Department of Defense to improve the state of software technology. The Education Division of SEI is charged with improving the state of software engineering education.

This is the third volume on software engineering education to be published by Springer–Verlag. The first (*Software Engineering Education: Needs and Objectives*, edited by Tony Wasserman and Peter Freeman) was published in 1976. That volume documented a workshop in which educators and industrialists explored needs and objectives in software engineering education.

The second volume (*Software Engineering Education: The Educational Needs of the Software Community*, edited by Norm Gibbs and Richard Fairley) was published in 1986. The 1986 volume contained the proceedings of a limited attendance workshop held at SEI and sponsored by SEI and Wang Institute. In contrast to the 1986 Workshop, which was limited in attendance to 35 participants, the 1987 Conference attracted approximately 180 participants.

This volume contains 23 refereed papers. Forty–one papers were submitted. Eighteen were rejected and 23 were accepted, but not all 23 papers were presented at the Conference. Instead, a few papers were selected for presentation to stimulate discussions among the attendees. A synopsis of each presentation and the associated question and answer session are included in this volume. Five of the 23 accepted papers were combined with five papers from the 1986 Workshop and published in a special issue of the *IEEE Transactions on Software Engineering* in November, 1987.

In addition to presentation and discussion of selected papers, the conference featured three invited presentations and two panel sessions. The invited presentations are contained in Section I of this volume. They include the Opening Remarks by Peter Freeman, the Keynote address by Al Pietrasanta, and a Post–Mortem Analysis of Software Engineering Programs at Wang Institute by Richard Fairley. Summaries of both panel sessions, Models of Industry/Academia Interfaces and The Role of Ada in Software Engineering Education, are contained in Section III.

Section II of this volume contains the 23 accepted papers. This section is presented in four parts. Part 1 contains six papers that are concerned with issues in undergraduate software engineering education. Topics presented include undoing the sequential mindset; reviews, prototyping, and frequent milestones; using software tools in a workstation environment; a first course in computer science that emphasizes mathematical principles of software engineering; a support tool for teaching computer programming; and a survey of undergraduate software engineering courses. The paper "Undoing the Sequential Mindset: The Software–CAD Approach," was written and presented by Professor Ray Buhr of Carleton University. A synopsis of his presentation and the ensuing question/answer session can be found at the beginning of Section II, Part 1.

Part 2 of Section II contains six papers on teaching project courses. Topics covered include some observations on teaching a software project course; two complementary sequences on design and implementation of software products; the system factory approach to software engineering education; performing requirements analysis project courses for external customers; an academic environment for software engineering projects; and the myth of the real world in project courses. Four papers from Section II, Part 2 were presented at the conference. A synopsis of each presentation and a summary of the question/answer session are included at the beginning of Part 2.

Part 3 of Section II contains five papers on issues in graduate–level software engineering education. Topics covered include education for research in software engineering; accommodating the evolution in software engineering education; the evolution of Wang Institute's software engineering education program; teaching a software design methodology; and software engineering at Monmouth College. The paper, "Education for Research in Software Engineering," was written and presented by Professor Caroline Eastman of the University of South Carolina. A synopsis of her presentation and the question/answer session are included at the beginning of Part 3.

Part 4 of Section II contains six papers on industrially–oriented education and training for software engineers. Topics covered include synergism of industrial and academic education; the Israel Aircraft Industry programs in software engineering education; a computer science education program within AT&T Bell Labs; formal education in software engineering within IBM; and the challenge of technology transfer.

Section III of this volume consists of two parts that contain edited transcripts of two panel sessions held during the Conference. The first panel, contained in Part 1, presented four models of industrial/academic interfaces in software engineering education. The transcript includes presentations by four panelists and the associated question/answer session. The panelists were Mark Ardis of Wang Institute, Jonah Lavi of Israel Aircraft Industry, William Lively of Texas A&M University, and Doug Politi of General Electric. Priscilla Fowler of SEI was chair of the panel. The panelists' remarks were based on their papers, which are contained in Section II, Parts 3 and 4 of this volume.

Part 2 of Section III contains an edited transcript of a panel session on the role of Ada in software engineering education, along with the associated questions and answers. The panelists were Ben Brosgol of Alsys, Larry Druffel of SEI, Robert Firth of SEI, Nico Habermann of Carnegie–Mellon University, and David Lamb of Queen's University. Norm Gibbs was chair of the panel. Nico Habermann was interviewed by Jim Tomayko of Wichita State University. The interview was videotaped and presented to the conference attendees.

We want to express our thanks to the support staff of SEI for their help in planning and executing the conference, and for their help in preparing the proceedings. In particular, Allison Brunvand and Albert Johnson of the Education Division of SEI made chairing of the Conference and editing of the proceedings pleasant and rewarding experiences. Nancy Avila and Sue Hovey of Wang Institute helped organize the refereeing process for the papers. Our thanks to them. Elisa Bartell of the University of California, Irvine worked long and hard on preparation of this volume, and did the first–pass editing and synopsizing of the transcripts. Our strong thanks to her.

We concluded the preface to the 1986 Workshop proceedings with a quote from the preface to the 1976 Workshop proceedings:

> "We believe that these proceedings will be of interest to all persons involved in developing computer science and software engineering curricula, not only in universities, but also in industry. Furthermore, we hope that these proceedings can serve as the starting point for additional work in the development of coherent software engineering curricula."

We believe this quote is appropriate for the present volume, which documents one more step in the steady evolution of software engineering and software engineering education.

Richard Fairley
George Mason University

Peter Freeman
University of California, Irvine

December 31, 1987

Contents

ATTENDEES
(Affiliations as of April, 1987)

Prof. Evans J. Adams
East Tennessee State University

Mr. Alan A. Adamson
IBM Canada Ltd.

Dr. Dennis M. Ahern
WestinghouseDefense
and Electronics Center

Mr. Jim Anderson
Rockwell International

Prof. Mikio Aoyama
University of Illinois at Chicago

Prof. Clark B. Archer
Winthrop College

Prof. Mark Ardis
Wang Institute

Prof. Gordon Bailes
East Tennessee State University

Dr. Osman Balci
Virginia Tech

Prof. J. Eugene Ball
University of Delaware

Dr. Bruce H. Barnes
Software Productivity Consortium

Mr. Mitchell J. Bassman
Computer Sciences Corporation

Mr. Ernest Bauder
GTE Government Systems Corp.

Dr. C. Eugene Bell
Mercer University

Mr. Ray Bell
University of Texas, El Paso

Mr. Martin Ben-Ari
Eaton Command Systems
Division

Mr. David J. Besemer
General Electric

Mr. Fred L. Bierly
Penn State University

Mr. Roger Blair
Software Engineering Institute

Prof. Patrick O. Bobbie
The University of West Florida

Prof. John W. Brackett
Wang Institute

Mr. Ben Brosgol
Alsys

Mr. Brad Brown
Boeing Military Airplane Co.

Prof. Ray Buhr
University of California, Santa Cruz

Major Dan Burton
Software Engineering Institute

Mr. Ted Buswick
Addison-Wesley

Prof. Hubert Callihan
University of Pittsburgh,
Johnstown

Ms. Maribeth Carpenter
IBM Corporation

Prof. Carl K. Chang
University of Illinois at Chicago

Mr. Mike Christel
Software Engineering Institute

Mr. Robert L. Christopher
Software Productivity Consortium

Dr. Henry Chuang
University of Pittsburgh

Mr. J. Craig Cleaveland
AT&T Bell Labs

Ms. Rita Lorraine Coco
Raytheon

Prof. Fred Cohen
Lehigh University

Ms. Sally C. Collins
Monongalia Co.

Prof. Jim Collofello
Arizona State University

Mr. Robert A. Converse
Computer Sciences Corp.

Prof. R. James Dawe
Memorial University
of Newfoundland

Mr. Keith S. Decker
General Electric Corp.

Dr. Lionel Deimel
Software Engineering Institute

Prof. Rahul Dhesi
Ball State University

Prof. Verlynda Dobbs
Wright State University

Ms. Gretchen V. Douglas
Singer-Link
Flight Simulation Division

Dr. Larry Druffel
Software Engineering Institute

Prof. Caroline Eastman
University of South Carolina

Dr. Theodore F. Elbert
The University of West Florida

Prof. Charles B. Engle, Jr.
U.S. Military Academy

Prof. Richard E. Fairley
Wang Institute of
Graduate Studies

Prof. John Fendrich
Bradley University

Dr. Robert Firth
Software Engineering Institute

Prof. Yvonne Florant
New York University G.B.A.

Dr. Gary Ford
Software Engineering Institute

Mr. John Foreman
Software Engineering Institute

Mr. David Forejt
University of Pittsburgh

Mr. Thomas J. Fouser
Jet Propulsion Laboratory

Ms. Priscilla Fowler
Software Engineering Institute

Dr. Glenn B. Freedman
University of Houston-Clear Lake

Prof. Peter Freeman
University of California, Irvine

Mr. J. Fred Gage
University of Pittsburgh

Dr. Norman Gibbs
Software Engineering Institute

Mr. Terry A. Gill
Carnegie Mellon University

Mr. Mark B. Glick
Lamar University

Mr. Robert Glushko
Software Engineering Institute

Mr. Peter S. Gordon
Addison-Wesley
Publishing Company

Prof. Pankaj Goyal
Concordia University

Prof. David C. Haddad
Miami University

Mr. Harvey Hallman
Software Engineering Institute

Ms. Kathleen M. Hanson
IUPUI

Donnita Hatlestad
Boeing Computer Services

Ms. Vicki Heilig
IBM FSD

Prof. Sallie Henry
Virginia Tech

Mr. Carl P. Hershfield
GTE Government Systems Corp.

LtCol Ronald P. Higuera
Defense Systems
Management College

Prof. Daniel Hoffman
University of Victoria

Prof. James W. Howatt
Air Force Institute of Technology

Mr. Paul J. Howe
USA Information Systems
Engineering Command

Ms. Susan Hruska
Jacksonville State University

Prof. Robert N. Hutton
West Virginia College of
Gradute Studies

Ms. Margaret Iwobi
Watson School

Mr. Albert L. Johnson
Software Engineering Institute

Prof. Bruce W. Johnston
University of Wisconsin - Stout

Ms. Pauline R. Jordan
General Electric

Mr. Howard Kaplan
Vitro Corporation

Prof. Elizabeth E. Katz
University of Maryland

Prof. James Kiper
Miami University

Prof. Mieczyslaw Kokar
Northeastern University

Mr. Thomas M. Kraly
IBM Federal Systems Division

Mr. Robert E. Kubiak
Carnegie-Mellon University

Prof. David Alex Lamb
Queen's University

Prof. Jeffrey Lasky
Rochester Institute of Technology

Mr. Jonah Lavi
Israel Aircraft Industries Ltd.

Mr. Clifford Layton
Rogers State College

Dr. Robert J. Lechner
University of Lowell

Prof. Steven P. Levitan
University of Pittsburgh

Prof. Wiliam McCain Lively
Texas A&M University

Mr. Robert Marek
Syscon Corporation

Mr. Richard R. Marks
E-Systems

Mr. Charles R. Martin
Duke University

Prof. J. Peter Matelski
The Hartford Graduate Center

Mr. Robert A. Mathias
Westinghouse R&D Center

Ms. J.E. Mazzaferro
Pacific Bell

Dr. Martha McCormick
Jacksonville State University

Prof. Ed McCrohan
Monmouth College

Dr. Charles W. McKay
University of Houston, Clear Lake

Dr. Katherine McKelvey
Indiana University
of Pennsylvania

Mr. George E. McLaughlin, Jr.
Lamar University

Dr. Mary Micco
Indiana University
of Pennsylvania

Prof. Marlin H. Mickle
University of Pittsburgh

Mr. Freeman L. Moore
Texas Instruments, Inc.

Prof. Larry J. Morell
College of William and Mary

Mr. Philip N. Mullen
GTE Government Systems

Mr. John Nestor
Software Engineering Institute

Prof. Robert E. Noonan
College of William and Mary

Prof. Eugene M. Norris
George Mason University

Prof. Linda Northrop
SUNY College at Brockport

Prof. Tom Nute
Texas Christian University

Dr. Bill Nylin
Lamar University

Mr. Jim Perry
Software Engineering Institute

Prof. Charles Pfleeger
University of Tennessee

Mr. Richard W. Phillips
IBM

Dr. Keith R. Pierce
University of Minnesota, Duluth

Mr. Al Pietrasanta
IBM Corporation

Mr. Douglas W. Politi
General Electric

Prof. Bernard John Poole
University of Pittsburgh

Mr. David E. Priest
General Electric

Mr. Stan Przybylinski
Software Engineering Institute

Mr. Phillip Purvis
Texas Instruments, Inc.

Mr. R.A. Radice
IBM Corporation

Cpt. Clark K. Ray
U.S. Military Academy

Dr. Jacques Raymond
University of Ottawa

Prof. Stuart Reges
Stanford University

Prof. Karl Rehmer
Purdue University at Fort Wayne

Mr. Donald J. Reifer
RCI

Prof. Robert Riser
East Tennessee State University

Prof. Linda Rising
Purdue University at Fort Wayne

Prof. Edward L. Robertson
Indiana University

Prof. Edwin H. Rogers
Rensselaer Polytechnic Institute

Prof. H. Dieter Rombach
University of Maryland

Prof. Lawrence L. Rose
University of Pittsburgh

Prof. R. Waldo Roth
Taylor University

Ms. Gail L. Sailer
Boeing Computer Services

Prof. Antonio Salvadori
University of Guelph

Prof. Walt Scacchi
University of Southern California

Prof. Elwyn M. Schmidt
California University
of Pennsylvania

Mr. Joel F. Schnoor
General Electric

Mr. Roger W. Scholten
Boeing Aerospace Company

Dr. Mary Shaw
Software Engineering Institute

Prof. Robert C. Shock
Wright State University

Prof. Dan Shoemaker
Mercy College of Detroit

Prof. Charles D. Sigwart
Central Michigan University

Prof. Judith O. Silence
IUPUI - CPT

Dr. Thomas P. Sleight
The Johns Hopkins University

Ms. Suzanne Smith
East Tennessee State University

Mr. James Solderitsch
Unisys Defense Systems

Prof. James Spruell
Central Missouri State University

Mr. Robert Steigerwald
U.S. Air Force Academy

Mr. Scott Stevens
Software Engineering Institute

Ms. Sara Stoecklin
East Tennessee State University

Mr. Don Stone
Software Engineering Institute

Prof. Marek A Suchenek
The Wichita State University

Ms. Alice Sun
Software Engineering Institute

Prof. Jim Tomayko
Software Engineering Institute

Mr. James L. Tucker
US AMETA

Prof. A. Joe Turner
Clemson University

Dr. Hasan Ural
University of Ottawa

Prof. Gretchen L. Van Meer
Central Michigan University

Prof. Frances L. Van Scoy
West Virginia University

Dr. Laurie Werth
University of Texas, Austin

Dr. Ronald White
Jacksonville State University

Prof. Arthur J. White
Taylor University

Major Colen K. Willis
U.S. Military Academy

Mr. Thomas O. Winfield
Hughes Aircraft Company

Ms. Audrey B. Winston
Westinghouse Electric Corp.

Major Duard S. Woffinden
Air Force Institute of Technology

Mr. Keith Wollman
Addison-Wesley Publishing Co.

Prof. Kwok Wong
Fayetteville State University

SECTION I

INVITED PRESENTATIONS

Section I contains three invited papers that were presented at the Conference. They are the Opening Remarks by Peter Freeman, the Keynote Address by Al Pietrasanta, and A Post–Mortem Analysis of the Software Engineering Program at Wang Institute by Richard Fairley.

Opening Remarks

Peter Freeman[1]

It may come as a surprise to a few of you, that software engineering education is almost 20 years old. In the fall of 1968, Alan Perlis gave the keynote address at the first software engineering meeting at Garmisch Partinkirchen. In that talk, among other things, he stressed the importance of education in this new field.

When he came back to CMU and gave a small colloquium on the conference, a few of us who were graduate students attended. Our basic reaction, as I recall, was, "What's this stuff? Software engineering? What does it have to do with computer science? What does it have to do with education?" Since most of us were heading toward careers as professors, he said, "It's going to be very important. It's going to be something that will affect most of you throughout your professional lives." Well, it's almost 20 years later and it is, indeed still affecting the lives of some of us!

In 1976, we organized a one-day industry-university interface workshop at the University of California, Irvine, in which we tried to bring together equal numbers of people from both sides to discuss what was needed in software engineering education. Although it was only one day, that workshop has turned out to be one of the turning points in SE education.[2]

Another turning point in the history of SEE was the "first annual" SEE workshop held here at the SEI, just a year ago, 10 years after the workshop at Irvine. Norm Gibbs' attempt to make this into an annual interaction between peers is extremely important because it provides an interactive way to exchange information among those on the front line of SEE.

In our society, universities are supposedly the leaders in education. As I look back over the past 10 or 20 years in software engineering education, however, I have to admit that very often the leadership has not been in the

[1] Professor Freeman has been active in software engineering education (SEE) for a number of years, including co-authoring and co-editing several papers and a book, which have been instrumental in the development of SEE.

[2] A less public meeting sponsored by IBM the previous year was also focused on software engineering education and may well have been an important internal milestone for IBM.

universities. Indeed, as a university faculty member, and as an educator, I'm not very proud of that. It's something that some of us try to work on and that is extremely important—standing up to the responsibilities that we have as professionals in this field. Workshops like this have the effect of making us sit down and think about what we're doing, in order to write a paper or to attend. Even more importantly, they give us the opportunity to talk to each other, to find out what is happening, to get new ideas, to exchange ideas, and so on.

Before introducing the main speaker this morning, let me share with you a comment made by a colleague of mine in another field. All of us at UCI who are at the associate dean level, meet several times a year to exchange information. At the first meeting this year, we were discussing class size, student demand, and so on. The Associate Dean from Biological Sciences reported that they were adding extra sessions of their introductory courses, even though it meant an overload of work for their instructors. Afterwards, I asked him, "Stanley, why are you adding extra sections and overworking your instructors, when you don't have to? You have all the political power and money on campus. You don't need to do this." He replied, "We believe very strongly, that no educated citizen, no educated student should leave this campus, without a thorough understanding of biology; it would be irresponsible for us to help educate students and let them go out into the world, not understanding the principles and the basics of biological sciences."

I'm not sure we can yet make such a strong statement about computer science and software engineering, but we can certainly make a much stronger statement than we do—about the importance of computing, in general, and certainly about our specialty, software engineering. This is something that we simply must do and take the responsibility for doing, in all of our institutions, whether they are universities, colleges, community colleges, or industrial organizations.

With this brief sketch of SEE history to set the context, let me introduce our keynote speaker, Al Pietrasanta. Al has been doing and teaching software engineering for much longer than there has been an activity called that, and we are honored to have him with us today.

Software Engineering Education in IBM*

Al Pietrasanta

As Director of the IBM Software Engineering Institute from 1982 to 1985, I have a great deal of empathy, and even sympathy, for all of you who are providing, or considering providing, software engineering education. Based on my personal experience in industrial education and the massive IBM program in software engineering education over the past decade, I'd like to draw some lessons for you.

Background:

The story starts about a decade ago, around 1976, in our Federal Systems Division (FSD). The reason that we got heavily into software engineering education, at that time and that place, is very interesting. The Federal Systems Division, among other things, does military contracts involving a lot of software, and we were having trouble. We were finding it more and more difficult to compete. IBM has excellent salaries, excellent benefits and is desirous of nice–profit margins. You add all of that up and we were finding that in head–to–head competition with some other software houses, we were not cost competitive.

So, what do you do? Well, the president of FSD said, "We are going to start competing on some other parameters. We are going to start competing on high quality, on–time performance, within budget. We think those parameters are worth money. We think we can sell contracts. Now we've got to make sure that we can do it." So, the president turned to Harlan Mills and others in FSD.

Harlan had been touting, for a number of years, software engineering methodology, software engineering concepts, without too many eager listeners. But at this point, the motivation was there, so Harlan and others set up a lengthy curriculum in software engineering education. Over the next

*Edited version of conference keynote address.

five years, they trained virtually every programmer in the Federal Systems Division, about 2,400 in all.

What has the result been? The contract programming in the Federal Systems Division has not only survived, it has flourished. In IBM, the FSD programming centers in Gaithersburg, Manasses, Houston and elsewhere, are considered outstanding examples of the right way to do programming and software development. And, beyond IBM, I believe FSD has a well-deserved positive reputation. This is due, in large part, to the training and the application of software engineering.

There have been a series of design practices and development practices that have been documented and used throughout the Division. Rigorous process management disciplines have been established. Tools have been built to surround the software process and exploit the best characteristics of the methodology. Measurement and feedback mechanisms have been put in place. Add all of this together and you have software engineering in the large, which has contributed to the success of the activity.

For those of you who are interested, there is an issue[1] of the IBM Systems Journal that is still relevant. The theme was the management of software engineering, and Harlan Mills wrote the lead article, on the principles of software engineering. There are also articles on the educational program, design practices, development practices, and the management of software engineering.

The Importance of the Profit Motive:

There are a lot of lessons from what happened in the Federal Systems Division, but I want to highlight one: The tremendous importance of the profit motive. We deal with a very pragmatic language in industry—profit, revenue, cost, return on investment, and return on capital assets. No matter how technical a decision may be, there is a very large component of the decision-making process that's involved with these pragmatics. I sincerely doubt whether IBM would have plunged headfirst into software engineering education back in 1976, without a clear linkage to profit. FSD had to invest millions of dollars to make their educational program happen. And you don't do that, in industry, without a tremendously strong argument.

The argument was conceptually very simple: profit equals revenue minus cost. You either justify an action on increased revenue or decreased

[1] *IBM Systems Journal*, Volume 19, No. 4.

cost, or, if you're fortunate, both. In FSD, as a matter of fact, the justification of software engineering education was clearly to increase revenue and also, in the longer term, because of the anticipated improvement in quality and productivity, a justification of decreased cost. From my perspective, those arguments still hold as much today as they did 10 years ago.

The experience of some of my friends and colleagues, however, emphasizes that profit is a two-edged sword. You can use the argument both to start new projects and also to kill them.

Conversion of the FSD Techniques to Commercial Applications:

After the demonstrated success at FSD, we passed on to the next major phase —the world of commercial systems programming. Much larger than FSD, there are at least 10,000 systems programmers in IBM. And they're building all those operating systems that you know and love, MVS and VM, DOS and a lot of the mid-range and low-range systems and all the subsystems that go on top of them. Commercial systems programming does not work on fixed price contracts, like FSD, but it still has a very distinct linkage into the profit motive. It's essential to have high quality and high productivity in systems programming.

In the 1970's, the emphasis had been on defect detection, and tremendous progress had been made in improved quality via this route. But entering the 1980's, it was apparent that we were really running out of gas on defect detection technology and that we had to begin to exploit defect prevention. So we turned, with some degree of envy, to our colleagues in the Federal Systems Division, who were, at that point, well along in implementing their software engineering methodology and were correctly touting software engineering as an outstanding means of defect prevention.

A major task force was run about 1980, with Watts Humphrey[2] heading the process activities. Watts drew participants from all the major laboratories in IBM and the conclusion was something that I guess was obvious when we started: That the world of commercial programming should pick up the experience of FSD and apply it.

So that's what we did. We modified the education program, adapting it to the needs of the commercial world. We also picked up the formal design language, called PDL, that had been in use by FSD, changed the syntax a bit to conform to the commercial languages we were using, and changed

[2]Currently on the staff of CMU-SEI.

the name to CDL, Common Design Language. We set up the Software Engineering Institute at IBM out of that effort several years before CMU-SEI was established. It's still going strong. To date we have trained nearly all of the systems programmers in IBM, a massive education program.

Teaching SE is Difficult:

Out of that experience, I would like to convey a few lessons. First, teaching software engineering is very difficult. Let me give you the context. We are training (actually, retraining) professional programmers of five, ten, twenty years of experience. There's a whole curriculum, but the bread and butter course is a basic two-week course, called "The Software Engineering Workshop." It is a total immersion course. Students must pass three prerequisites to enter it: algebra, symbolic logic and set theory, and the design notation. During the course, there's homework, exercises and case studies, an exam after the first week, and a final after the second—a tremendously intense course. It covers conceptual models, both function and state machines, basic function and data structures, function commentary (which is used for precise expression and for verification), function and data abstraction, stepwise refinement, separation of concerns, encapsulation, and lots of other things, all wrapped up in one course.

Now, the question is, how do you get teachers to teach that? The instructors had to be experts in the development process. On average, the instructors at the Software Engineering Institute had about 10 years of development experience. Why was that necessary? Continually, throughout the course, the students would be saying, "But how do you apply it?" "But I'm doing it differently today." "But it doesn't work that way, in my laboratory...," etc., etc. In order to hold the class together, and to provide some credibility, the insructors had to be intimately familiar with the existing development process. Thus, the instructors were able to map the new software engineering methodology on top of the old—a very difficult task.

Now, it would also have been nice if they were experts in software engineering. But that's a contradiction in terms, because we really didn't have them. So, we had to train the instructors in the methodology. We put a training program together and it still surprises me today that it took an intensive year of training to reach the point where experienced development professionals could capably teach the two-week course. After several years of improving the efficiency of that training program, it's down to nine months. So, it takes a long while.

Student Resistance:

There's a corollary to this lesson. Not only is software engineering difficult to teach because of instructor qualifications, but it's difficult to teach because of student resistance. Those of you who work in universities have the advantage of dealing with uncluttered minds, students with no preconceived notions, who are sitting there gladly soaking up the wisdom that you're imparting. That may be a slight exaggeration, but the fact is, we are really at the opposite extreme in industry. We're dealing with students who are very experienced, very competent. They have been successful in their careers. Furthermore, they have been designing and developing very complex software products for a number of years, which have also been successful. So, we bring them into a classroom, sit them down, and say, "You haven't been doing design right. There's a different and better way to do it." Clearly, we don't come out and say those words, but believe me, the message is there. And it generates resistance, so that by the middle of the first week, there's almost a revolt going on. Fortunately, because of the caliber of the instructors, and the intrinsic value of material, we are able to turn that resistance around by the end of the second week, in virtually every case. Consequently, we have graduates who are strong advocates of the new methodology.

Design Bureaucracy:

There's another resistance point that I call the resistance point of design bureaucracy. What we're teaching is precise, complete design recording, using a formal, rigorous, mathematically-based design language. The experienced designers have been doing design on yellow pads, scribbling in an informal way. Even when they begin to buy the methodology, they say, "You've taken the fun out of design." The only answer, and perhaps the best answer is, "We may be taking the fun out of designing by the seat of your pants, but we're also taking the bugs out of that design." That's the reason we're doing it. The trade-off is well worth it.

SE is Difficult to Learn:

What I've been saying is from the perspective of the teachers of software engineering. Now, let me flip the coin over and look at the situation from the students' perspective.

If it's difficult to teach software engineering, it's even more difficult to learn it. After an intensive course, our graduates are far from experts. They go back to the laboratories and they try to apply the methodology. They run into all sorts of problems, difficulties, and roadblocks. A formal design language to express software engineering methodology is very powerful, but difficult to use.

I compare it to learning your first programming language, in a course, or out of a book. You left it and said, "Hah! Now I'm a programmer!" Then you started applying the language. You started programming. It might have been one, two, or three years later, when you reflected back and said, "Now I understand. Now I'm a programmer." It's the same thing in software engineering, applying a design notation; it takes a tremendous amount of application and experience, and trial and error to reach the point of proficiency. You can learn the syntax, you can learn the mechanics, but it takes a long time to apply it.

The Difficulty of Applying SE:

In the IBM Software Engineering Institute, we recognized this problem quite early and we expanded our mission, from strictly one of imparting education, to one of helping the graduates become practitioners. So, what we put in place was a software engineering notebook, where we collected together all of the technical reports, all of the experiences, and all of the evaluations by the practitioners. They were published and sent to all of the graduates. We ran software engineering symposia, where we brought the practitioners together to share their experiences. We set up a course, called the Software Engineering Application Laboratory[3], which brought together people who were about to implement major projects using the new methodology; they would bring real, live, large problems and, in a laboratory environment, we would analyze and solve those problems. That was desirable, because the basic course necessarily had relatively small programs and design problems in its content. Finally, we made sure that every programmer location had on-site consultants, so that anyone beginning to use the methodology and running into a problem could turn to a local expert and get over the roadblock to proceed. This was very, very important.

So, the message from this lesson is simply that formal education does not make a qualified software engineering practitioner; it is an essential first

[3]This course and the software engineering notebooks referred to were set up by Mary Beth Carpenter.

step, but much more is needed.

The Difficulty of Getting Management to Change:

I've talked about the difficulty in teaching software engineering and the difficulty of learning software engineering. There is yet one more difficulty, that perhaps masks the other two. The difficulty is getting programming management to apply the software engineering methodology on their projects and products. Every programming shop at IBM is overcommitted. We have much more work than we can do. We're short on resources. The management is staring many commitments and deadlines in the face, so when you say, "Why don't you start implementing all of this methodology?", the answer is, "Wait until next year. As soon as the smoke clears, as soon as I can see my way free, I will do what you say. But please, not now." Of course, next year never comes in that mode.

Another argument was, "But at the moment, all we are doing is modifying existing products. As soon as we have a new product, that's an ideal time to implement the new methodology." Well, it's not too often at IBM Systems Programming, that we have a totally new product. Virtually everything we do is modifying existing products. So, unless the methodology can be applied in that context, then it's a failure.

Once again, the Software Engineering Institute expanded its mission, from education, to helping the practitioners, to being a PR firm. We began to visit every programming site, every center manager, and over and over again, convey the necessity, the benefits, and the value of the new technique, and to discuss with them how to begin to implement the technical methods on real projects. Our recommendation was a very obvious one: "Start small. Pick a small project. Pick a relatively simple project. Pick an isolated project. Get the people on that project trained, make a consultant available, and start to get some real experience in your shop using the new methodology. Once you have that under your belt, expand to more projects and, over a period of time, get the whole place converted."

Now, that is an approach that takes a great many years. Anyone who wants this to happen overnight is really kidding himself. We had to take a realistic approach: Implementation would be evolutionary and evolutionary meant years. It is, in some senses, agonizingly slow to convert. Maybe there's a faster way, but we haven't yet figured it out. So, that's the approach we took, and I think, thus far, we've been pretty successful.

The Reward:

So far, I've been concentrating on the difficulties: The difficulties of teaching, the difficulties of learning, the difficulties of applying software engineering. Let me present one final lesson—a very positive one, and by far, the best lesson of all. That is, the immense satisfaction you'll experience when you begin to see the results, when you begin to realize that what you have been preaching and teaching for years really works.

You've all been involved in education. Many of you have been in front of a classroom, and I'm sure you've faced the same kinds of concerns and doubts that I have in front of a classroom: That is, are you really accomplishing anything? Are you really changing anything? You pour your heart and soul out to the students, in your course and you wonder, "Is anything going to change?" Well, if you have all passed through that dark night of the soul, then you can imagine the immense sense of accomplishment and achievement, when you begin to see the results of your work. All over IBM, in every programming laboratory, projects are using the methodology and the results are demonstrating that the investment is well worth it.

Let me give you one example as illustrative of what's been happening. On a large programming system, which has had a history of a defect injection rate of 60 defects per thousand lines of source code (which, by the way is average for us, not unusually high or low) a portion that operating system under development used the full range of function and data abstraction that we were teaching and their injection rate was reduced by a factor of 10, from 60 defects per thousand, to 6. Even better than that, their shipped quality level (the number of defects in code that was shipped) was reduced by a factor of 12. And this, by the way, is at a point in time when we do not really have full exploitation of the methodology, because we are still in the process of building support tools which will make the job much easier and faster for the designers and developers.[4]

[4]This experience has been documented in the *IBM Systems Journal*, Volume 24, in 1985. The theme of the issue was quality and productivity in our systems programming effort. The article referred to is "Quality Emphasis in IBM Software Engineering Institute," by Harvey Hallman [now at CMU-SEI]. It brings up-to-date, the previous Journal articles on software engineering education. There is an outstanding article on software process architecture, by Ron Radis, an article on formal requirements definition, by Dick Phillips, other articles on process automation, process productivity and so on. [All the authors mentioned above were present at the conference].

Conclusion:

So, there are some of our experiences, and some of the lessons we've learned. I very briefly covered a decade of experience in IBM. To net it all out, I would make two points. First, don't be complacent. It's not easy to convert individual professional practitioners and it's certainly not easy to convert whole development laboratories to a new methodology. But also, don't despair. When the conversion does happen, when the results do occur, you will realize, like us, that it was worth all the effort.

Questions from Audience:

Charlie Martin: I have two questions. First, is the software engineering notebook available to the public?

Al Pietrasanta: No. It's IBM confidential because the articles in it deal with a lot of unannounced products and the work that's being done on them.

Charlie Martin: Second, once you've taken somebody through this software engineering workshop and you send them back to their old shop, how do you integrate them back into projects that they were working on? How do you take them back to the farm?

Al Pietrasanta: Well, you certainly don't apply the methodology in the middle of the project. You don't—if you're in the middle of development or testing—all of a sudden say, "Let's flip over." The methodology can only be properly applied at the beginning of a project, although it can be applied to projects that are modifying products, as well as producing new products. But, nevertheless, you start at the beginning. What often happens, is that these students are coming to class between projects, so when they go back, they are about to start some new project. What we try to do, is fill a class with all of the programmers and designers from a project, so that when they leave the class, there is a critical mass of trained individuals at the start of a new project. That doesn't always work, but that's what we try to do.

Steve Woffinden: How much did you have to educate your supervisors before you started working with the workers?

Al Pietrasanta: Well, it wasn't before. It was during. We did it in parallel, rather than serial. We actually had more than one version of the workshop that I'm talking about. The total immersion, two-week version was for first-line managers and all the professional programmers. We had a one–week variant which was a software engineering workshop for managers, second–line and above, in which we introduced all of the methodology, the techniques, and the language. We concentrated very heavily in that course, on the value of the methodology, on experiences with it, and on the kinds of arguments needed to present to upper management in order to sell it. So, the course was a combination of technical and sales course, if you will, to upper management. Our intent was to put the whole population through either the basic software engineering workshop or the software engineering workshop for managers.

Steve Woffinden: Did you identify any things that you would like to have new people that you've hired out of the universities know or not know about software engineering before they came to you?

Al Pietrasanta: Boy, we could take all day on that question, not because universities are doing a bad job, but because the interrelationship between university education and industry training is a very tricky one. I will tell you, in general, we have hired, in the main, computer science graduates, into the programming profession, and they have been outstanding. The education that you university people are giving to computer science majors is, in general, excellent. As a matter of fact, the concern we have is that we bring these very well–trained, very sharp young people into IBM and they sit next to all of us old timers and we're going to brainwash them out of their new, young, excellent, creative ideas. I will say that in general, there are two roles. The role of the university, in computer science, is to provide a broad conceptual foundation, as deep as possible, and as detailed as possible. We can't do that. What we can do, is build on that conceptual foundation and give the precise, tailored training that we need, for our specific projects, for our specific work. So, I think there is a split between what universities can do and what industry has to do. I guess my message is to continue doing the excellent job you've been doing.

Gail Sailer: You've talked about the instructor needing a one–year preparation period. Can you discuss the preparation that went into getting ready to train the instructors? Do you have a rotating staff that does that?

Al Pietrasanta: At the moment there are, I guess, something like 50 certified instructors. The only people who are allowed to teach this particular course are those who have passed through the formal Certification Program. Initially, all that work was done at the central Software Engineering Institute. Now, because each laboratory has certified instructors and because the software engineering workshop is decentralized and taught in the individual programming laboratories, rather than at the central institute, a lot of new instructor training goes on at the local sites. What it consists of is going over every module of the course, practicing it, dry running it in front of experienced instructors, reviewing video tapes of other presentations and reviewing video tapes of your own work, getting general instructor training on how to be a good instructor, because a lot of the people have not had prior teaching experience. All of that takes about 9 months.

Judy Silence: Do you have a list of software tools that are used in each of the stages of the software life-cycle?

Al Pietrasanta: I would like to refer you to an article in the Systems Journal.[5] It is the best presentation of the tool stategy that we have to surround our commercial systems programming and to exploit the software engineering methodology.

Joan Mazzaferro: First, you mentioned that for your first go–round of instructors, that you took experts from the field, in order to help convince the people being trained that this stuff is good for them. That implies to me that you had a really strong commitment from your top management. Can you help me in understanding what you did to influence that commitment to show them the value, or did they send that message down?

Al Pietrasanta: Well, first of all, we had the benefit of building on the FSD experience. At FSD, that commitment started from the top. The Division President was totally committed to the program. When we got into the commercial world, the initial staffing of the Software Engineering Institute, for the commercial systems programmers, was done with several of the FSD certified instructors. So, the nucleus came out of FSD and then, we were able to build on that nucleus. We started with the highest level of support in IBM, for the commercial Software Engineering Institute, one level below the Chairman of the Corporation supported what we were doing. Having said that doesn't mean a whole lot, because in IBM, there is a surprising amount of autonomy. Even though the top of the corporation will say, "Go forth and do it," you still have to sell every level of management. That's what took a number of years.

Joan Mazzaferro: You mentioned a cost benefit study.

---

[5] "Software Automation," written by Huffnagel and Beregy.

Al Pietrasanta: Yes.

Joan Mazzaferro: Did that have an influence factor? A high one, medium, or low?

Al Pietrasanta: Well, the trouble 10 years ago, was that we were working on faith. We didn't have the cost benefit analysis. As a matter of fact, that, to me, indicates the tremendous decision that the FSD President made, back at that point in time. He was really betting his job on the possibility that software engineering could pay off. But we did not have any cost benefit analysis. We were praying, back then. Now, as the years have passed and experience began to come in, we could build on that experience and we could quantify more and more, that there truly was a benefit. Today, we really don't have an argument anymore.

Joan Mazzaferro: After the completion of the two-week Program, does the reward structure change for the people in the program that encourages them to use what they've learned by going through the training? If so, that implies that you've got your other lines of management agreeing that this is the way to go about doing things.

Al Pietrasanta: Oh, but the implication is the critical part, your last sentence. The rewards structure only changes, if when they go back to their laboratory and start dealing with their management, their management says, "Use it." If the management says, "I don't understand it," or "I don't want you to touch our project," or "I'm holding it together with band-aids and bailing wire, don't talk to me about software engineering methodology," you are in trouble. These people are very maze bright. They're going to learn very quickly that their reward structure comes from their manager. So, the answer is you've got to work from the bottom up and the top down. You've got to train the people, from the bottom up and get them qualified and capable in new methodology. You've got to work from the top down, through every level of management and train them and convince them that it's right. What I just said in two sentences, is a very, very hard job. I'm talking years, and it's still going on in our case at IBM.

Joan Mazzaferro: How long did it take for you to get that satisfaction that you talked about?

Al Pietrasanta: When I started running the Software Engineering Institute in 1982, it was not there and I would say maybe by 1984, when the election returns began coming in, it began to build up. So, it took a couple of years.

Dennis Ahern: My question is, you've presumably used a lot of different languages, computer languages, from the Federal Systems Division and in the commercial area. In your opinion, are some languages better or worse than others, in terms of software engineering methodology?

Al Pietrasanta: Well, first of all, as I'm sure many of you know, there are fundamental differences between a design language and a programming language. Everything that I've talked about this morning surrounding the software engineering design methodology, is the use of a design language. Now, as you cascade down through stepwise refinement using that design language, you ultimately reach the point where you have to interface with a programming language. The programming language in major use in IBM commercial programming, is a variant of PL1. That's why we changed the FSD design language because we wanted the interface into the programming language, to look more like PL1. But in the main, when you're doing the design, you are working at abstract levels, significantly above the programming language.

The design language has gone through several evolutions, from PDL, in the Federal Systems Division, to CDL, the Common Design Language that we started off with. We have recently put together a new design language, with all of the same syntactical power, but it's Ada based.

Understand, our programming is not in Ada, it is still in versions of PL1. But the design language is Ada-based, because we believe that the syntax of Ada is closer to what we needed in a design language, than any other programming language. We've been very pleased with that decision.

Peter Freeman: We're almost out of time for this session, but please let me exert the moderator's prerogative and ask the final question.

Al, the SE curriculum that you've been discussing this morning and the experience that you've been reporting, is clearly very valuable. Yet, it is, at the best, only a few weeks of instruction and admittedly covers only one aspect of the software engineering process. What's the next thing that IBM or someone building on that base of experience should be working on?

Al Pietrasanta: There are a lot of directions you could go. One thing that we are emphasizing very heavily is surrounding the concept and the theory and the methodology with tool support. We have never been able to have significant tool support of the design process, because if you are designing in English or native language, it's hard to have supporting computer tools. But, when you start designing with a formal design notation, then, all sorts of tool support opens up. That has been lagging the education, because tool development is very expensive and you don't do it overnight. We are investing a lot of money and a number of years to build a supporting tool kit surrounding the methodology.

In terms of the next world to conquer, I would step backwards and go to the requirements definition, the very front end of the process. A comment that comes out of our Software Engineering Workshop, over and over again, is "Terrific! You've now explained to me how to design. But don't you realize that designs are built on requirements and our requirements are lousy and therefore, we are building a very rigorous, formal design, on a pile of sand." And they're right. The answer that I always give them is, "Look, we're solving one problem at a time. We figured out how to solve the design problem. That's what we're teaching. As soon as we figure out how to solve the requirements problem, we will teach you that." We are working on that. So, I would say building the rigor and the formality into the very initial requirements definition, is the next major step.

A Post-Mortem Analysis of the Software Engineering Programs at Wang Institute of Graduate Studies

presented by

Richard E. Fairley, Chairman

School of Information Technology

Wang Institute of Graduate Studies

presented at the

Software Engineering Education Conference

Software Engineering Institute

Pittsburgh, Pennsylvania

May 1, 1987

Abstract

This paper contains the text of an invited presentation by the author at the Software Engineering Education Conference, which was held in Pittsburgh on April 30 and May 1, 1987. Topics presented here include an overview of the Wang Institute programs in software engineering, an analysis of the strengths and weaknesses of the Master of Software Engineering curriculum, and a discussion of reasons for termination of the software engineering education programs at Wang Institute of Graduate Studies.

Introduction

I thought it would be appropriate to do a post-mortem analysis of the software engineering programs at Wang Institute this morning. Wang Institute has been sold to Boston University, and BU plans to use the facility for continuing education activities. The School of Information Technology is being closed at the end of Summer Session. The Master's program in software engineering will be terminated then.

By continuing through the end of summer, 40 of our current students will be able to complete the Master's program. That will leave around 20 students in various stages of the program. We hope that we can arrange for five or six of those students to take their remaining elective courses at Boston University in the coming year and receive the Master of Software Engineering degree. Some of the other students may transfer into other Master's degree programs at Boston University.

Wang Institute of Graduate Studies was founded in 1979 by Dr. An Wang of Wang Laboratories. The Institute is totally independent of Wang Laboratories and operates as a non-profit institution of higher education. We have degree-granting authority from the Commonwealth of Massachusetts and accreditation by the New England Association of Schools and Colleges. Until recently, the Institute was supported almost exclusively by financial contributions from the Wang family.

I want to start by saying a few words about other software engineering programs at Wang Institute. We are best known for the Master of Software Engineering program, but we have done several other things that have been, I think, quite successful in bridging the gap between university and industry. We have a library of about 5,000 volumes and 300 journals in the areas of computing, mathematics, and management. I think it rivals anything in the New England region, including Harvard and MIT, within the admittedly narrow areas of our collection. It's been a great resource for local industry and other universities, as well as a resource for Wang Institute faculty and students. The fate of the library is unknown at this time. It will either be sold or absorbed into the BU library system.

We have run a distinguished lecturer series for the past several years. About once a month during the academic year we have invited various distinguished computer scientists and software engineers to spend a day with us. The distinguished lecturer meets with faculty and students and gives a lecture that is open to the public, followed by a wine and cheese reception. These lectures usually attract 150 to 200 people. You have probably received announcements of these lectures, and some of you may have attended some of them.

We had a Corporate Associates Program, in which we did special things for local companies, such as our annual symposia where we presented tutorials on topical issues, faculty research colloquia, and student projects. In return, they let us know what was going on in their organizations. Sometimes these affiliations resulted in consulting arrangements for our faculty members and adjunct faculty appointments at Wang Institute for our industrial colleagues. In general, the CAP program was an effective vehicle for technology transfer, both from academia to industry and vice versa.

Our Summer Institute program of one week short courses has also been quite successful. In the past five years, we have given approximately 50 short courses, with a total attendance of around 1500 people from industry. Some of these courses were taught by our faculty, but mostly they were taught by distinguished others. We always tried to find the best possible instructors for those courses. The quality of instructional support services, as well as the environment in which the courses were conducted, gave the program a good reputation with both the guest instructors and the industrial students.

Overview of the M.S.E. Program

The program for which Wang Institute is best known is the Master of Software Engineering (M.S.E.) degree program. I would like to give you a little background on the history and evolution of the curriculum and make some observations on the current status of the program.

Wang Institute was founded in the fall of 1979. I was invited, along with about a dozen other people, to meet with Dr. An Wang in Boston in October of '79 to talk about a Wang Institute. I was invited because of some previous work I had done on software engineering curricula, dating from the early to mid-70s. During that period, I had worked with people like Peter Freeman and Tony Wasserman, and we wrote papers, individually and collectively, about software engineering education.

In '77 and '78, I was chairman of a committee of the IEEE Computer Society to develop a Master of Software Engineering curriculum. We did good work and we produced a nice report. However, it was not well received by some of the people who were in powerful positions within the Computer Society at that time. This was partly because of political reasons that I was unaware of, and somewhat naive about, but largely because the proposed curriculum wasn't perceived as being real engineering. I'll never forget the quote by one hard-core engineer (pardon the pun) who said "I don't know what you guys have done, but it ain't engineering." He could understand the need for courses in design and implementation and testing, but customer requirements, project management, technical communication? "What are you guys talking about? That isn't graduate-level engineering education."

That experience, plus a few similar ones, have led me to think of software engineering as a discipline in search of a home. I have heard comments along the lines of "Is there a future for software engineering?" I think there is a future because of the overwhelming social and economic importance of the topic, as well as the intellectual challenges involved, but I'm not optimistic that software engineering is going to dominate the computer science departments (nor should it). We will probably have more success in separate departments or as professional schools or institutes - but that's another topic for another day.

So, the Wang Institute curriculum was designed in '79 and '80 by the National Academic Advisory Committee, which grew out of the group that met with Dr. Wang in the fall of '79. And as I said, I was invited to participate because I had previously done curriculum work in software engineering. I had a Master's curriculum in my hip pocket that I was glad to try out on the Committee. The MSE curriculum at Wang Institute is not identical to the IEEE report, but it is based on, and resembles, that earlier work.

I think there's an important lesson here, of being prepared and being ready when opportunities arise. It takes a long time to evolve a curriculum; and when management is ready to act, they want to do it in the next three months. We were able to do that at Wang Institute because of prior preparation.

I'm going to tell you, in a few minutes, about the Ph.D. program we had planned at Wang Institute, which will not happen now. But I do have a Ph.D. program plan in my hip pocket and someday, somewhere, someone's going to want one. I'll be ready. So, plan ahead, because opportunities arise suddenly and we must be prepared to respond to them.

Classes started at Wang Institute in January of '81. We received full accreditation in the Fall of '84. I want to come back and talk about that, at the end. A full-time president was hired in 1984 and he started in 1985. We are currently in the middle of a $5.5 million building expansion program, which started last summer. I was a member of the planning committee that worked with the architect to define the functional requirements for new offices, classrooms, and laboratory space. It is very strange to see our new building going up around us, and knowing that we won't be occupying it.

The M.S.E. program started with two faculty members and 15 part-time students. We now have 11 faculty members. We started the current academic year with 60 students, approximately 30 full-time and 30 part-time. The support staff has grown from 5 to 25. We turn away qualified applicants. We seem to be successful by every measure, except for the continued financial support of our benefactor.

The M.S.E. Curriculum

The structure of the Master's program is illustrated in Figure 1. Prerequisites for the program appear at the top in the shaded boxes. The prerequisite structure of the courses is indicated by the arrows. Over the years the content of the courses has evolved, but we've not felt the need to redo the structure. I think this structure has served us well and continues to do so.

Those of you who have only one or two software engineering courses on the books probably look at this structure and say, "Gee, imagine the luxury of 11 courses. Boy, could we do everything there isn't time to do!" But with the luxury of 11 courses comes the obligation of feeling that you must do everything. We continually confront the issue of breadth versus depth. How can a person graduate from Wang Institute without hearing buzzword X, Y, or Z? Fill in your favorite buzzword. And that is the way the program began. It was very survey oriented and broad brush in nature.

As time went by, we gained more confidence and began to understand what was truly important. We worried less and less about whether students had heard buzzword X, or Y, or Z and began to develop more depth and to do fewer things better. I think this is probably typical of every new academic program.

Let me give a brief description of the curriculum. Prerequisites for the program include knowledge of a modern programming language, data structures, discrete math, and assembly language/architecture. In addition, an entering student must have at least one year of work experience. We started with a requirement of two years work experience and changed it to one year to see if we were discouraging otherwise well-qualified students from applying to Wang Institute. In fact, our students have, on average, about five years of work experience. We have only admitted one or two students with less than two years work experience, and in each case they turned out to be some of our weaker students. So, we feel that the work experience is very important.

One of the most important things we do with respect to admissions is to conduct an oral admission interview with each applicant. I tell the students that the oral exam comes at the beginning of our program, rather than at the end. These interviews usually last for one or two hours. We try to determine the student's prerequisite knowledge in the various subject areas, and we also assess their communication skills and their ability to think on their feet. The procedure is quite time consuming for the faculty, but we are convinced that it is an extremely important aspect of our admissions procedure. Last year, we interviewed 80 applicants and admitted 32. The 80 applicants were selected from a pool of about 400. So you can see that we were quite selective in our admission procedures.

The M.S.E. program consists of 11 courses. Each is a three credit semester-length course. Six of the courses are core courses required of all students. Of the remaining five courses, three are electives and two are project courses. The six core courses are Formal Methods, Programming Methods, Software Engineering Methods, Systems Architecture, Management Concepts, and Software Project Management. The major topics in each core course are indicated in Figure 2.

Formal Methods is intended to cover formalisms that are important to software engineers. We look to Formal Methods to supply the theoretical underpinnings needed for the remainder of the curriculum. Mark Ardis, who has taught Formal Methods several times, refers to Formal Methods as Wang Institute boot camp. In the beginning, we tried to cram way too much material into the course. It is still very intense, as are all our courses, but we have pretty much settled on abstraction, specification, and verification as the main themes of the course. Formal languages/automata and analysis of algorithms get some coverage. I think we should have more coverage of those topics than we are able to give them, but there isn't time to do everything.

Programming Methods covers the pragmatic aspects of detailed design, implementation techniques, and testing. Formal Methods is a co-requisite for Programming Methods. The two courses are phased carefully so that students have been exposed to formal verification and testing theory in Formal Methods before they get to the testing segment of Programming Methods. Other topics are phased in a similar manner. For example, students learn the theory of regular expressions in Formal Methods and the applications of regular expressions in Programming Methods.

In Programming Methods, and in all of our courses, we place a strong emphasis on software tools. In fact, we employ two Master's level people (two of our own graduates) to acquire and install software tools, and to develop supporting materials for the software tools used in the courses. Even though our students have, on average, four to five years of work experience, they are usually not very familiar with software tools. It is not unusual for a student to learn three or four new tools in a course. I think the emphasis we place on software tools is a truly unique aspect of the Wang Institute M.S.E. program.

Software Engineering Methods is concerned with analysis and design techniques. We tend to think of Programming Methods as covering topics of interest to the individual programmer, while Software Engineering Methods covers topics that typically involve teams of programmers working on analysis and architectural design. In the beginning, Software Engineering Methods was the catch-all course where we covered topics that hadn't received adequate attention in the other courses. With passing time and more experience, we learned how to better integrate those left-over topics into the other courses. At the same time, we realized, and our students confirmed, that we were not spending enough time on analysis and design. So, we did a major modification to Software Engineering Methods. In fact, we were planning to rename the course Analysis and Design Methods to better reflect the content of the course.

Of all the successes we have had at Wang Institute, I would not claim that teaching our students to be great software designers is one of them. This is not for lack of trying or for lack of competent and talented instructors. I tend to think that Fred Brooks is correct when he says great designers are born and not taught [1]. Nevertheless, we continue to expose our students to what is known about software design in the hope that a few great software designers will emerge. At the least, our students understand the concepts on which different approaches to software design are based, and they learn the notations and software tools that support software design. As Bo Sanden (a Wang Institute faculty member) remarked, "It may well be that great designers are born rather than taught, but they do no grow into great designers by themselves. Without training, they may become great hackers instead." Our students are undoubtedly better software designers as a result of taking the Software Engineering Methods course, but I don't think we know how to train great designers, any more than we know how to train great programmers. It is interesting to observe that mechanical engineers, architects, textile specialists, and other industrial design educators say that they don't know how to develop great designers either. It is a very difficult problem.

Like all the other core courses, Systems Architecture has evolved with passing time. The original concept for the course was that it would be a capstone course sitting on top of a firm grounding in architecture and operating systems. Our plan was for the instructor of this course to spend a lot of time on hardware/software design tradeoffs, networking, distributing processing, and other advanced systems topics. In practice, we found that most of our students were not prepared for this advanced course. Many of them were competent in architecture or operating systems (at the graduate-level), but not in both. Given the diverse backgrounds and goals of our students, we decided to let students satisfy the Systems Architecture requirement by taking either a graduate level Operating Systems or Computing Systems Architecture course. This seems to work well. Some students take one of the courses to satisfy the core requirement and the other as one of their electives. They are then qualified to take the advanced topics course (that we originally envisioned as the core course) as one of their other electives, if they so choose.

Practically all of our students are educated and have work experience in science and engineering. Most of them have never taken a business course, other than the required Economics 101, in their undergraduate engineering program. The goal of Management Concepts is to expose them to the management side of software engineering. The course covers organizational structures, organizational behavior, finance and accounting, and topics such as the roles of personnel departments, marketing and sales, research, and manufacturing in a modern, high tech corporation. The students call it an MBA in 13 weeks. The course requires a lot of reading and synthesis. It is very intense. Students complain that, compared to their technical courses, the reading material is not very dense in concepts presented per page. The material also tends to be rather subtle. Like Formal Methods, this course has too much material for the time available. However, we have found it difficult to decide which parts to delete.

The Project Management course covers techniques for planning, monitoring, and controlling a software project. In addition, a fair amount of time is spent on the interpersonal aspects of leadership and team building. The course is targeted at project sizes of 10 to 15 people working for periods of 18 to 24 months. This is large enough that issues such as team structure, baselines, change control, documentation, and quality assurance become important, but not so large that the bureaucratic issues of large projects dominate the discussion. Most all of the core courses require the students to work in teams on term projects. In Project Management, the students work in teams of 3 or 4 to develop comprehensive project plans for software projects. Sometimes the projects are hypothetical, and sometimes they are projects that one of the students is involved in at work or has been involved in at some previous time.

The elective courses are predominantly from the areas of computer science and management, mostly from computer science because that's the background of most of our faculty members. So, the electives are courses such as database systems, transaction processing, knowledge-based systems, user interfaces, local area networks, compilers, and operating systems. But we try to put a software engineering flavor into those courses, and to have term projects that involve the students working in teams to build things and experiment with them. As a consequence, we have not been able to use adjunct faculty members to do elective courses in the way you might expect. We feel it is important for the full-time faculty to do the electives, because the full-time faculty members understand the core courses and the philosophy of our curriculum.

We do have two or three adjunct faculty members, who do specialized courses for us that they have developed over time in the Wang Institute environment. For example, we have a very nice course in technical communication, which is taught by a professional technical writer who works in the software industry. All of his examples center around requirements specs, design documents, user manuals, and other types of material appropriate for software engineers.

There is an interesting aside with regard to that course. It is a very effective course. Students improve their writing and presentation skills tremendously by taking the course. But there are those among our faculty who think that the material is not appropriate graduate-level material; the intellectual challenge is not particularly great. My response is that we should think of software engineering as a professional discipline rather than a traditional academic program. Certainly there are lots of things that happen in law and medicine, and in dentistry and business schools that are not academically challenging but are nevertheless important to the professional development of the students.

Before I move on, let me say a couple of words about the project courses. We require two project courses (six credit hours) in place of the traditional Master's thesis. Students are required to work in teams of 3 to 7 and to apply good software engineering practices to the development of a software product. They conduct milestone reviews, practice baseline control, and do a formal presentation of their work at the end of the semester. It took a long time for us to learn how to teach the project courses in an effective manner. Some of our wisdom about teaching project courses has been documented in Bill McKeeman's paper for last year's meeting and John Brackett's paper for this meeting (see references [2] and [3]). I think the main keys to success for project courses are up-front preparation of the project requirements and the software environment by the instructor, identifying and sorting out of the roles to be played by the students and the instructor, and recognition that teaching a project course for 3 to 7 students is an equivalent work load to doing a much larger lecture course. The factors that contribute to success for student projects are not all that much different than the success factors for "real world" projects, by the way.

It is possible for a student to complete the program in 11 months. That requires the student to take four courses in each of the fall and winter semesters and three courses in the summer semester. It is important for the industrially sponsored, full-time students to be able to complete the program in one year. However, this approach requires that faculty members teach year-round, which leads to problems of faculty burn-out and lack of concentrated time for research.

I want to make a couple of comments about the tailoring of this curriculum to local situations. That's a point that has not been addressed very much but has always been a strength, in my mind, of this particular structure. There are three methods courses: Formal Methods, Programming Methods, and Software Engineering Methods. Those courses concentrate on the technological aspects of our discipline. Depending on how you slant the program, the underlying concepts will be the same, but the examples used and the methodologies discussed might be quite different in different settings. So, the actual day-to-day content might differ in a business school teaching information systems applications from that in a EE Department specializing in embedded systems; however, the structure of the curriculum would be the same. Also, the two project courses and three electives can be tailored and moved in whatever direction you might choose.

Legacy

Figure 3 shows the number of graduates over the years. We were pretty much in steady state of admitting and graduating around 30 students per year. This year, we will graduate around 40 students because some students have accelerated their programs in order to graduate before the School disappears. If everyone performs as expected through the summer, we will have graduated a total of 121 students. Then there are the 5 or 6 I mentioned who may finish up in a semester or two. So, Wang Institute will have produced around 125 Master's of Software Engineering during its lifetime.

Figure 3 illustrates the five year plan that was done in 1985. We have already seen a trend to more full-time students than we anticipated. That's because industry is sending more and more full-time sponsored students. We take that to be a testimonial that we are doing something of value. So, I think by 1990 the numbers of full-time and part-time students might have flipped to be more like 45/25 full-time/part-time, rather than the other way around.

We have had numerous discussions among the faculty about the desirability of having part-time students. We offer no evening courses at Wang Institute. We want the students to be awake and attentive when they come to class. Also, we want them and their managers to recognize that attending Wang Institute is a serious commitment of time and energy. Even so, part-time students have more demands on their time than do the full-time students, and their educational experience is undoubtedly less fulfilling than that of the full-time students who spend considerably more hours per semester at the Institute. However, the part-time students often have a pressing need to cut to the heart of an issue, and they usually try to relate the material they are learning to their immediate work situation. This results in some very interesting discussions and brings a strong dose of reality to the classroom. On balance, I think most of the faculty are convinced that the part-time students are a positive influence on the program, although there are differing opinions on this issue.

The Ph.D. Program

I want to say a few words about our planned Ph.D. program (see Figure 5). For breadth, we planned 12 graduate courses, including the six MSE core courses, which map into four areas of study. We expected that the 12 courses would be spread among the four areas of Software Engineering Methods, Software Engineering Management, Quantitative Methods, and Computing Technology. A minimum of two courses in each of the four areas would have been required, with the remaining four courses concentrated in one area or spread across the areas as determined by the student and the faculty advisor. The six MSE core courses plus three well-chosen electives in the MSE program would leave three courses to be completed beyond the Master's degree for the Ph.D. breadth requirement.

We expected that depth of knowledge would be obtained, as it usually is in a doctoral program, through a combination of courses, seminars, directed studies, and individual study. We saw a wide range of possible topic areas for dissertation work, including theoretical studies, development of exemplar software artifacts, experimental work (perhaps involving human subjects), and analyses based on comprehensive case studies.

We went through a long series of discussions about the proper title for the doctoral degree. Should the graduate be called a Ph.D.? a Doctor of Software Engineering? a Professional Software Engineer? In the end we decided that in time we might have more than one doctoral degree, but that the first one should be a Ph.D. because we believe that software engineering is a credible intellectual discipline. To do anything else would imply that our discipline is not on par with other disciplines. I think there is a need for the traditional, research oriented Ph.D. and also for the professional engineer or doctorate degree. But we decided our first doctoral program should be a Ph.D.

What Went Wrong?

What went wrong? Academically, I think nothing. I, and a lot of other people (including our Academic Advisory Committee), thought we were right on target. We had recruited and built an excellent faculty. We had reached steady state with the Master's program. We were ready to start the Ph.D. program.

What went wrong financially? Again, I think nothing was wrong within the Institute. Dr. Wang, from the very first meeting of the Advisory Committee, understood the likely cost of the Institute. We made it clear that the Institute would be a very expensive undertaking and that it would probably never be a self-sustaining operation. In 1979, he said words to the effect, "I want to build it fast and I want it to be of high quality." You don't have to be an experienced administrator to understand that building a new academic institution and a new educational program rapidly, and of high quality, is an expensive undertaking. He told us that cost was not a constraint. I think we used the resources available to us in a responsible and responsive manner.

We have received no statement from Dr. Wang concerning his reasons for selling the Wang Institute facility to Boston University, other than a brief press release that said the original goals in founding Wang Institute had been achieved and that the Wang family now wanted to spread their philanthropy over a broader range of areas. The announcement that the School of Information Technology would be closed was contained in the press release. So, we can only speculate as to his real reasons. It is no secret that Wang Laboratories has fallen on hard times in the past couple of years. The Lab has undergone several layoffs and salary reductions. Although Wang Institute was an independent, non-profit corporation, our resources were ultimately tied to the fortunes of Wang Labs.

In December, 1986 we were asked to reduce our operating budget by 10 percent, for the remainder of the fiscal year, which ends on June 30. We did so, without too much pain. On February 25, 1987, Dr. Wang convened a meeting of the faculty and staff. I thought we were going to get a pep talk. I thought it was going to be "Times are hard. Hang in there. We appreciate everything you're doing. We'll pull through this together." Without any forewarning, an aide to Dr. Wang read the above-mentioned press release stating that the facility had been sold to Boston University and that the School of Information Technology would be closed and the Master's program in software engineering terminated. The announcement was greeted with stunned silence.

The president of the Institute found out the night before the meeting exactly what was to be announced. He knew something was afoot, but he learned the exact details the night before. I was out of town the day before the meeting and was told by the president the next morning, two hours before the general announcement. So, it was totally unexpected, and totally inconsistent with Dr. Wang's past behavior. Dr. Wang is a well-known philanthropist and patron of the arts in Boston. He has been a long-term contributor to Harvard. He made statements about Wang Institute being one way in which he could repay the New England region for his good fortune. He often, until recently, talked about what Wang Institute might be in 100 or 150 years.

Summary Comments

On a personal note, the hardest part for me is the break-up of our faculty team. It was a long, slow process to put together a faculty who enjoy working together and who are extremely effective at what we do. We determined the content of the core courses by a consensus process, and once we came to an agreement, we were pretty rigid about the content of those courses. But there were also the elective and project courses which gave faculty members an opportunity to pursue their other teaching and research interests. It was a nice combination. The core gave us a focal point for common interests and provided common goals while the electives and projects gave each of us an opportunity to pursue our own interests and exercise our academic freedom in choosing additional areas for teaching and research.

Speaking of research, I want to say a word or two about that. People have said that Wang Institute is a teaching institution, and certainly that is true. We valued and rewarded good teaching. But it is not true that we did no research. You could not evolve a program like ours and develop the course materials to the depth we did without being involved in a lot of primary, as well as secondary, research activity. We haven't published a lot because we were up to our ears in alligators during the start-up phase. With the planned Ph.D. program, most of the faculty were anticipating the opportunity to reap the benefits of the investment we had made and to clear a backlog of planned research and publishing.

What are the prospects for similar institutes? I doubt that there will ever again be a situation so amply endowed as we were to offer a professional degree program in software engineering. But I'm confident that professional degree programs in software engineering can and will flourish, probably with higher student/teacher ratios and with emphasis on externally funded research. I think there is great potential for industrial support for programs such as this one. I'm confident that we will see other programs and that there is a future for software engineering education. I hope to be part of that future.

I think I'd better stop here. Time for a couple of questions?

Questions and Answers

Q: You have a good reputation and there are probably enough businesses around to support you. It seems to me you could say to Boston University, "Why don't you let us continue with the reputation we've built, get some financial support from local industry, and continue what we're doing?"

A: There are a couple of answers to that. The first is that this transaction occurred at the level of Dr. Wang and President Silber of Boston University. Neither of them know anything about software engineering education. It was a business deal. BU bought our facility as a satellite campus for continuing education programs. They have other plans for the facility, and our program is a liability to them. Second, there was no opportunity for any academic person inside BU to say, "Yeah, I think that's a viable operation." We had no champion to argue for us. The deal was done before anyone at Wang Institute or Boston University had a chance to react. So, the software engineering program is dead in the Tyngsboro location.

Q: You spoke of accreditation. How did you find your curriculum to be received by people like ABET?

A: Thanks for reminding me about accreditation, because there are a couple of points I want to make about that. But first, let me answer your question. Graduate programs are not accredited by the professional societies, and the regional accrediting agencies accredit institutions rather than particular programs. Our accreditation was from the New England Association of Schools and Colleges (NEASC). Because there was only one degree program in our school, it was pretty hard to accredit the institution without examining the MSE program. Nevertheless, NEASC was primarily concerned with issues such as the quality the library, the qualifications of the faculty, the financial stability of the institution, and not so much with the content of the Master's program.

But the point I want to make, and I'm glad you reminded me, is that I feel the ultimate responsibility for our situation lies with the accrediting agency. The accrediting team that visited the Institute produced a report listing seven major things that should be done in order for us to receive accreditation. I don't remember all of them, but they were things like hire more faculty members, which we did; hire a full-time president, which we did; and provide for the long-term financial stability of the Institute, which didn't happen. Until the time of the accreditation visit, Dr. Wang was the president of Wang Institute. As a result of the accreditation report, he hired Ed Cranch, who was the president of Worcester Polytech and before that Dean of Engineering at Cornell, to be our president.

The capital and operating funds for the Institute came directly from the Wang family; we had only a small endowment, although it was understood that Dr. Wang would leave his personal fortune to the Institute upon his death and that it would provide the long-term endowment. Dr. Wang did not follow the NEASC recommendation concerning financial stability of the Institute. It was the only one of the seven recommendations that did not receive a prompt response. Dr. Wang chose to ignore it, and NEASC chose to let it go. In retrospect, that was a mistake. NEASC should have insisted on financial stability. But, on the other hand, Dr. Wang is a former member of the State Board of Regents in Massachusetts; he is a long-term benefactor of Harvard University; and he had his personal reputation as well as his considerable fortune behind the Institute. No one, including me, was terribly concerned that he hadn't made long-term provisions. But we sure wish now that NEASC had been tougher on this issue. And I think NEASC does too, as a matter of fact.

Q: Two questions: Where does your library go? And secondly, do you think it would be a good way to go in the future, to have schools of software engineering, like business schools or schools of social work, that is, separate professional schools within academic institutions?

A: Concerning the library, it is uncertain whether it will be sold or absorbed into the BU library system. The cost of developing the library to its present point is about $250,000. Of course, it would cost much more to recreate it at today's prices. So, it is a considerable asset for Boston University; but I don't know, and I don't think they know what will become of it at this time. It's a great resource. It would be sad to see it split up or diffused into another collection.

As for the issue of professional schools, I think that's exactly how software engineering education should go. We are a discipline in search of a home. We are not computer science. We are not business. We are not engineering, at least in the traditional sense. But certainly, we draw on each of those camps, as well as several others. I also think the emphasis on professional practice, staying in touch with industry, technology transfer - all those issues do not fit under the traditional academic umbrella. I truly believe that professional schools are the way to go in the future.

Q: It seems to me that you should have been able to justify your existence on the basis of benefits provided to industry. You should have been able to translate that into direct support, through tuition fees and from the corporate sponsors of the individual students. Did you ever try that, or do you think it might work again?

A: When times were good, Dr. Wang was giving four million dollars to the Performing Arts Center in Boston, five million to Harvard, and four million to operate Wang Institute. It was pretty hard to go to other people and say, "Dr. Wang needs help with this program." We didn't see the need for it. And then, in the end, the time was too short. Now, we are all out looking for jobs. There just isn't time enough to hold the faculty together and put together a base of support that would allow us to continue. With six months or a year lead time, I'm confident we could have done it. But not under the present conditions.

Thank you very much for your attention.

Acknowledgements

The quality of an academic program is directly proportional to the quality of the faculty that offer that program. The opinions expressed herein are mine, but the factual account is based on the accomplishments of Mark Ardis, Phil Bernstein, John Brackett, Billy Claybrook, Dick Fairley, Hassan Gomaa, Dave Lomet, Bill McKeeman, Gary Perlman, Sri Raghavan, and Bo Sanden. Former faculty members Jim Bouhana, Susan Gerhart, and Nancy Martin made significant contributions to the software engineering programs at Wang Institute.

References

[1] Brooks, F.P. Jr. "No Silver Bullet: Essence and Accidents of Software Engineering." *COMPUTER*, Vol. 20, No.4, April, 1987.

[2] McKeeman, W.M. "Experience with a Software Engineering Project Course." *Software Engineering Education: The Educational Needs of the Software Community*, N. Gibbs and R. Fairley, Eds., Springer-Verlag New York, 1987.

[3] Brackett, John "Performing Requirements Analysis Projects for External Customers." *Educational Issues in Software Engineering*, R. Fairley and P. Freeman, Eds., Springer-Verlag New York, 1988.

Appendix

Several relevant events have occurred since this paper was delivered in May, 1987. Forty students did in fact graduate with M.S.E. degrees on August 9. It appears that six additional students will be able to complete their M.S.E. degrees by taking their remaining elective courses at Boston University. Three faculty members moved to George Mason University in Fairfax, Virginia, to start a graduate-level software engineering program in the School of Information Technology and Engineering. One faculty member joined the School of Engineering at Boston University and is developing a software engineering program there. Another faculty member is at Bentley College, where he is developing courses in software engineering. One faculty member joined the Software Engineering Institute of Carnegie-Mellon University, where he is working on software engineering curricula. Another faculty member is at Harvard University on a visiting appointment. The remaining faculty members are working in industry. The library has been transferred to the School of Engineering at Boston University.

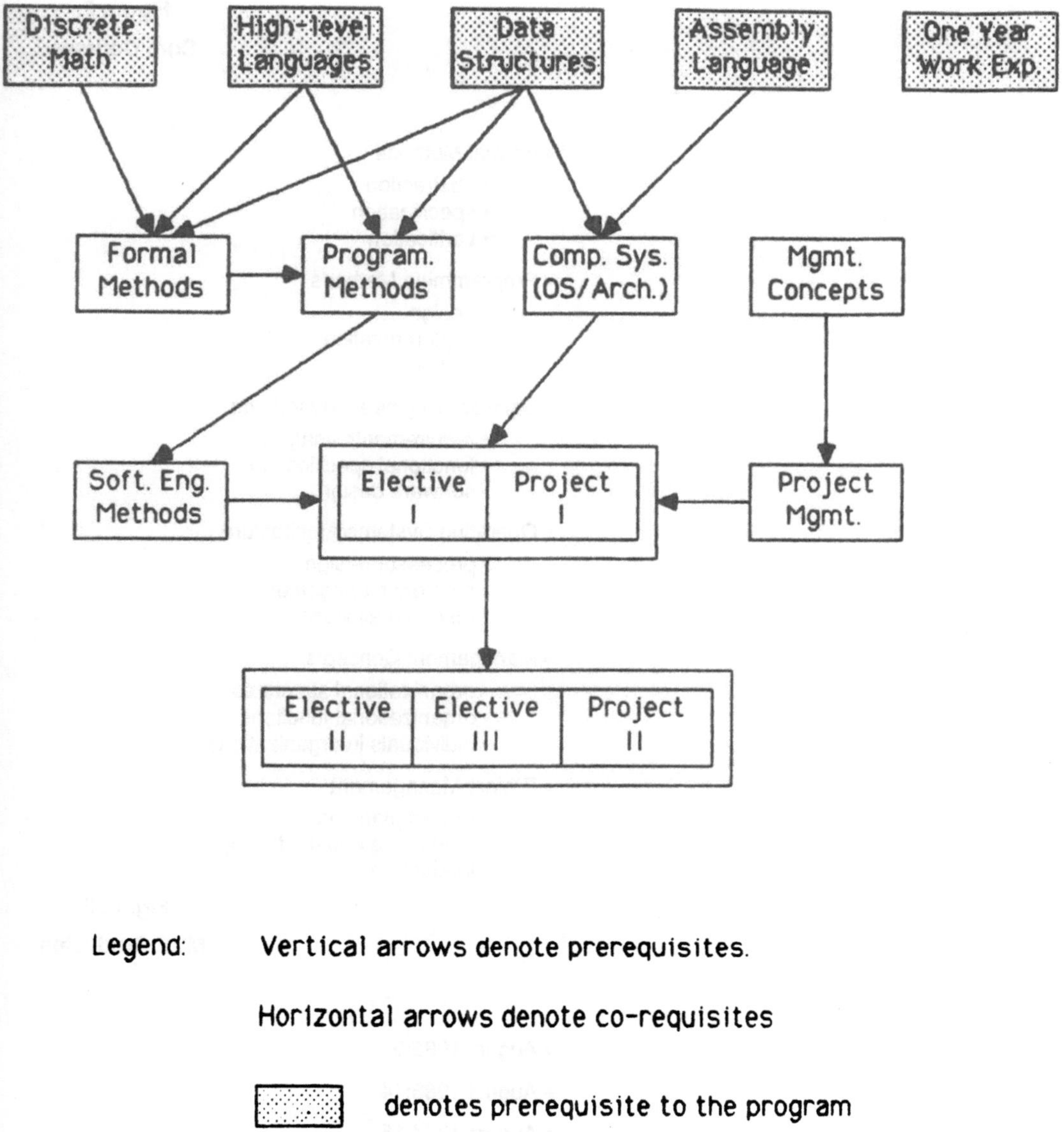

Figure 1. Course Prerequisite Structure

Figure 2.

Core Courses

- Formal Methods
  - abstraction
  - specification
  - verification
- Programming Methods
  - design
  - implementation
  - testing
- Software Engineering Methods
  - requirements analysis
  - functional specification
  - software design
- Operating Systems/Architecture
  - processor design
  - memory management
  - resource allocation
- Management Concepts
  - organizational structures
  - organizational functions
  - individuals in organizations
- Project Management
  - project planning
  - monitoring and controlling
  - leadership

Figure 3.

MSE Graduates

- August 1982:5
- August 1983:14
- August 1984:15
- August 1985:17
- August 1986:30
- August 1987:40
  - Total: 121

Figure 4.

Five Year Plan (1985-1990)

1990 Goals:

- 25 full-time MSE students
- 45 part-time MSE students
- 10 full-time Ph.D. students
- 15 regular faculty
- 3 visiting faculty

Figure 5.

The Planned Ph.D. Program

- Breadth
    - 12 graduate courses
    - 6 from MSE core
    - 4 areas
        - SE Methods
        - SE Management
        - Quantitative Methods
        - Computing Technology
- Depth
    - courses
    - seminars
    - directed studies
- Dissertation Areas
    - case studies
    - exemplar artifacts
    - experimental studies
    - theoretical studies
- Research Orientation
    - software technology

SECTION II

REFEREED PAPERS

Section II contains 23 refereed papers presented in four parts:

- Part 1: Undergraduate Software Engineering Education
- Part 2: Teaching Project Courses
- Part 3: Graduate Level Software Engineering Education
- Part 4: Industrial Education and Training

An introduction to each Part is presented at the beginning of the Part.

SECTION II

PART 1

UNDERGRADUATE SOFTWARE ENGINEERING EDUCATION

The six papers in this Part are concerned with teaching software engineering concepts to undergraduate students. Emphasis is primarily, but not exclusively, on teaching software engineering concepts to students majoring in computer science. Topics presented in Part 1 include undoing the sequential mindset; introducing reviews, prototyping, and frequent milestones; using software tools in a workstation environment; a first course in computer science that emphasizes mathematical principles of software engineering; a support tool for teaching computer programming; and a survey of undergraduate software engineering courses.

The paper, "Undoing the Sequential Mindset: The Software–CAD Approach," was written and presented by Professor Ray Buhr of Carleton University. A synopsis of his presentation and the ensuing question/answer session are included at the beginning of Part 1.

Synopsis of Presentation

Prof. Ray Buhr

Professor Buhr presented the main points in his paper, tied them into some of the other presentations at the Workshop, and provided some of the background and rationale for the ideas presented in his paper. Among the points he made in his presentation were the following:

- Agreement with Al Pietrasanta on the difficulty of teaching software engineering to practitioners. Seems to be a matter of mindset, found even in young programmers after the first few courses.

- Paper describes an approach, Software CAD, to overcoming the mindset. Professor Buhr has been experimenting with the approach in his teaching.

- A key problem is the "sequential mindset" that stems from first introducing students to older, sequential languages. This leads to "program carpenters" who think only in terms of monolithic, sequential programs that have little or no significant architectural context.

- The essence of Professor Buhr's approach is to introduce students at an early stage to an architectural way of viewing software which is compatible with both sequential and concurrent models of computing.

- Another important stumbling block is the difficulty of thinking about concurrent programs on the basis of sequential concepts only.

- His approach is based on introducing beginning students to what he perceives as the three aspects of software: Structure, interaction, and function.

- Traditional programming ("carpentry") only really addresses the functionality aspect. His approach advocates starting students out by teaching them on the basis of a model of interconnected machines.
- The approach also requires a good graphical notation.
- A programming language must be used which incorporates the notions of interconnection found in the graphical language and the underlying model of interconnected machines.
- The final aspect of his approach requires support for these notations – this is the Software CAD aspect.
- The approach fosters a total system viewpoint, encourages learning good software design principles, prevents formation of the sequential mindset, and fosters a mindset appropriate for the real world of concurrent systems.
- The approach casts programming in an engineering framework.
- After students' intitial reaction, they usually become *very* strong adherents to it and even advocates for it.
- This approach treats software somewhat like hardware. Professor Buhr disagrees with the view that software is fundamentally different from hardware, citing examples such as concurrency.
- Several examples and illustrations of the approach, taken from his own teaching, were provided by Prof. Buhr.
- Modula 2, picked initially because it was the closest available substitute for Ada, has turned out to be a very good teaching language.
- Additional work is needed on the approach—methods, textbooks, support tools, etc.

Questions for Ray Buhr

Peter Freeman: Could you elaborate on your comment about a forthcoming software CAD support system?

Raymond Buhr: Only very briefly. First, there is some work going on, to port CAEDE to a PC, so that hopefully something will happen within the next six months to a year. There are a surprising number of graphical-based tools for Ada popping up. At ICSE 9, I spent quite a bit of time sitting in front of screens, looking at products that people had or that were about to come out, and it looks like there's been a ground swell of enthusiasm for the use of graphics and CAD approaches to software. Also, I am working with a company, which has an environment for building graphics interfaces or graphics–CAD tools to get some of my new ideas into the PC world—which is what universities can afford at the introductory level.

Peter Freeman: Of those tools that were available, are they sufficient to support the kind of approach that you've been using or are they just the first step and not really there yet?

Raymond Buhr: Well, some of them look to be almost there, but others are still in the development stage. Within a year or so, there should be some systems that are candidates, but it depends on whether people can fulfill their expectations of development times or not.

Dan Hoffman: In your paper and talk, you say that programs written in Basic or Fortran or Pascal or C are sequential and monolithic. I'm completely confused by that, because I've seen programs written in those languages, that are divided into the kinds of modules you talked about, and I've seen programs written in Modula 2 and Ada that are sequential and monolithic.

Raymond Buhr: I absolutely agree. You can certainly build modular programs in Pascal or C, but you have to have learned something about software engineering first. The people who write those programs are usually at a higher level. They've learned how to program. Moreover, they have taken courses in software design or have learned it somehow, and then, they eventually write good modular programs. The whole point is the interfaces and the interactions, rather than the algorithm or the way that you write the functional aspects.

The issue is that students are under pressure to write programs in introductory courses in languages like Fortran, Pascal, and C; they form a model of computing, which doesn't include these nice attributes, because they don't know about them yet. In introductory courses, you are taught that flowcharting is the way of designing programs. I'm presently teaching a software methodology course now, to a group of 4th year students at UC Santa Cruz, and we were talking about this business of partitioning systems into modules and the design issues involved and all that kind of thing. I presented two views of a program to some of my students; one was a very sequential shared data design and the other was a highly modular design. Then, I asked students how many would have come up with the highly sequential shared data design as a result of the way that they had learned programming. Almost everybody said they would have. They thought in flow chart terms. Those languages simply do that. Unless you've got a construct in the language that has a notion behind it, beginning students do not pick it up.

Dan Hoffman: It sounds like what you're saying is that it wasn't the choice of language that was wrong, it was the choice of pressures that was wrong; the students should have been pressured to split it into modules.

Raymond Buhr: That's certainly a part of the argument that I'm advancing. They should be pressured to put things into modules. However, I'm a great believer in languages, as thought–structuring artifacts. People argue that you can say anything in French that you can say in English, but they are very different languages; they have different cultural connotations to them. Modula 2 and C are very different languages; they have different cultural connotations to them as well. A language defines a cultural framework in which you think. My experience with many students is that those who learn in languages like Basic, Fortran, and C have a mindset, which does not make it easy for them to acquire design notations.

Undoing The Sequential Mindset: The Software-CAD Approach

Raymond J.A. Buhr
Systems and Computer Engineering,
Carleton University, Ottawa, Canada

February 12, 1988

Abstract

This paper proposes a non-traditional approach to teaching programming, characterized here as the "Software-CAD" approach, which is particularly appropriate for students in professional computing programs, such as computer engineering, who need to acquire as early as possible a "total systems" view of computing embracing both hardware and software, and which can help to instil in any type of student good notions about program design. In this approach, programming is taught from the start in terms of a model of interconnected machines, using a graphical notation rooted in a an appropriate programming language (e.g., Modula2 or Ada) and supported by Software-CAD laboratory tools. Such an approach helps to undo the "sequential mindset" which traditional ways of teaching programming in languages such as Fortan, Pascal and C tend to impart. The paper outlines a set of courses following the approach and points to successful experience with prototypes of some of the courses at Carleton University and U.C. Santa Cruz, using both Ada and Modula2 (though not yet with supporting CAD tools), to indicate that the approach is feasible and promising and that students accept and like it. Although the approach can be followed without CAD laboratory support, such support is desirable for reasons of self-motivation and efficiency; appropriate support is expected to be available soon.

1 Introduction

I propose a non-traditional way of teaching programming, which I call the "Software-CAD Approach". My experience suggests this approach may have advantages over more traditional ways, at least for certain classes of students. The approach is particularly appropriate for students in programs such as computer engineering, who need to develop mental models of computing embracing both hardware and software. For brevity, I shall refer to this viewpoint as the "total systems viewpoint". The novelty of the approach lies in its use of programming courses to instil the total systems viewpoint, starting from the first introductory programming course.

Although my motivation in developing and promoting the approach has been primarily my perception of the need for it in Computer Engineering programs, it seems likely that it may also be a good, general approach to teaching programming in a way that will prepare students faster than traditional approaches for the world of large programs, multi-person projects, embedded systems, distributed systems, software/hardware codesign and silicon compilation.

The purpose of this paper is to convince readers of the desirability and feasibility of teaching programming via the Software-CAD approach, and thereby to encourage further development of the approach. The paper motivates and then describes the approach, recounts experience indicating it is desirable and feasible, suggests the outlines of a series of courses to teach it, and indicates the nature of the laboratory support and teaching materials required.

These proposals are rooted in my experience developing and teaching the CAD approach for Ada (Ada is a trademark of the U.S. Department of Defense) [1,2,3,4,5,6]; designing and teaching courses for a BEng program in Computer Systems Engineering at Carleton University, which has produced two graduating classes whose members have found strong acceptance in industry; participating in planning software engineering courses for the new Computer Engineering program at the University of California at Santa Cruz; and teaching an introductory course there following these ideas, using Modula2.

2 The Central Ideas

2.1 An Analogy

A good way of characterizing the difference between my proposed approach to teaching programming and the traditional one is to draw an analogy between programming on the one hand and the activities and training of architects and carpenters who design and construct buildings on the other. An architect draws plans; a carpenter implements the plans at the level of boards and nails. An architect thinks in terms of form and its relation to function; a carpenter thinks in terms of cutting boards and nailing boards to other boards. An architect has to be a total systems thinker; a carpenter does not. An architect is a professional; a carpenter is a tradesman. Architects are not trained by starting them out as carpenters, because this would not foster an architectural viewpoint. Carpenters may become architects, but much additional training would be required.

Traditional approaches to teaching (and often to doing) programming are closer in spirit to program carpentry than software architecture. Yet software architects are needed, who think in terms of form and its relation to function in software, just as architects do for buildings.

I am not suggesting that this notion of software architecture as distinct from program carpentry is new or that software architects do not exist in the professional community. What I am suggesting is that the time is ripe to start training software architects as such from the beginning, starting with the first programming courses.

2.2 Software Architecture

Figure 1 conveys the idea of software having three aspects: structure, interaction, and function. The aspects of structure and interaction correspond roughly to what I have referred to as "form" in building architecture. The aspect of function is concerned with the details of the work the program has to do.

Software architecture is primarily concerned with form and its relation to function. Program carpentry is then concerned primarily with implementing function.

If we are to teach software architecture in a way that fosters total systems thinking, we need notions of form embracing both hardware and software. Fortunately, such notions exist and are intuitively natural. The central idea is of black boxes with interfaces, which may interact with other black boxes with compatible interfaces. The notion of a black box conveys the idea that its inside is invisible at the interface level. The notion of interface needs to include the possibility of multiple interaction points with well-defined connection properties and interaction semantics , like the multiple connectors on chips and boards. Procedures are not enough. Fortunately, newer programming languages include black-box-like objects of exactly this kind (for example, packages in Ada and modules in Modula2).

As in building architecture (and hardware design), form is naturally expressed graphically. However, the specific requirements above eliminate from consideration many traditional graphical methods of describing programs, such as flow charts, Yourdon-type structure charts, HIPO diagrams, Jackson diagrams, and so forth. Further discussion of this issue will be found in [6]. Examples of a suitable notation are given later.

Thus, teaching tools for software architecture include appropriate graphical notations and appropriate programming languages. However, although these can be used to introduce more advanced students to software architecture, they are not sufficient at the introductory level.

2.3 The Software CAD Approach

The feasibility of teaching software architecture from the start depends on being able to reduce the program carpentry aspect to manageable proportions. Program carpentry tends to dominate students thinking and activity in traditional programming courses. Needed are laboratory support tools which take over some of the carpentry aspects, freeing the students to think in terms of form, draw their thoughts on a workstation screen and have a program framework automatically produced into which functional fragments can later be inserted by traditional program carpentry methods. This is what I call the Software-CAD approach.

Recent developments in programming languages, personal computers and Software-CAD environments appear to be converging to make the Software-CAD approach feasible soon in a university teaching context.

2.4 The Sequential Mindset

The lack of a software architectural viewpoint in traditional ways of introducing programming makes it difficult for students to form broad enough mental models of the nature of computing.

I use the term "sequential mindset" to characterize the limited mental model of computing that tends to form naturally and spontaneously when learning to become a program carpenter with older languages like Basic, Fortran, Pascal and C. Programs in these languages are monolithic, sequential artifacts, without significant architectural content in the sense defined earlier. Preoccupation with the details of their carpentry tends to embed in the students' minds a mental model of all software as like these programs and fails to provide a mental model of computing appropriate for a total systems viewpoint.

A key in undoing the mindset is to provide an architectural view of software compatible with both sequential and concurrent models of computing. This can be done at an advanced level, as is usually the case in current teaching practice, or it can be done from the start, as proposed here.

2.5 Programming Can Provide the Mental Models for a Total Systems Viewpoint

The basic idea is to lead students naturally towarding thinking about software and hardware in a unified fashion by starting them programming from the beginning in a software language which has the capability to define hardware-like components and then later to treat design of software, hardware and systems in a unified fashion at a higher level of abstraction by analogy with things they have already seen in this software language.

The two requirements of the software language are (1) the ability to define black-box-like components and (2) the ability to have concurrency among components (including both synchronous and asynchronous concurrent behaviour). These are two key characteristics of hardware which students encounter immediately in introductory courses on digital logic, but which are deferred till much later in software. Often they are never treated in a unified manner on the software side until graduate school. To avoid prejudicing the discussion towards a particular language, I shall refer to the class of such languages as Black Box Concurrent, or BBC.

The concurrency aspect would not be taught in the first programming course, but it is important to have the ability to move naturally from programs in which black boxes execute sequentially to ones in which they can be concurrent, without having to unlearn anything already learned.

Unfortunately, none of the common teaching languages are of much use for this purpose, because they contain neither good facilities for defining black-boxes nor any direct means of expressing concurrency.

Although the idea of black-boxes can be introduced in a conventional programming course, without language support they have little practical reality to students interested in getting assignments done quickly.

As for concurrency, the use of a language supporting it provides the only reasonable pedagogical tool for introducing it early. Concurrency is usually regarded as complex subject. However, much of its complexity lies in the traditional tools for implementing it, not the essential material. The usual ad-hoc combination of an ordinary programming language and an operating system or real time executive confronts the student with a bewildering array of mechanisms and manuals which appears to be, and is, very complex.

In any case, operating systems courses, where this kind of material is usually introduced, do not provide the right kind of background in concurrency early enough to serve the purpose. Postponing treatment of concurrency in software until the study of operating systems is surely putting the cart before the horse. Concurrency should be treated as a basic issue early in software courses, just as it is in hardware courses, to avoid a sequential mindset developing. Operating system courses can then build on this background.

2.6 The Importance of an Early Start

There are two reasons for starting early in the educational process with this approach.

The first reason is the shallow rooting of the sequential mindset in first and second year students. My research and teaching experience with the Software-CAD approach for the Ada language [1,2,3,5,6] and more recently with Modula2 has convinced me that students in which the sequential mindset is not too deeply rooted find it very logical and natural to view software in this way and quickly become enthusiastic about it. The deeper rooted the sequential mindset, the more difficult it is to get this view across.

The second reason is leverage. To affect the way things are done in industry, one must send to industry students who are missionaries for change. The Unix/C combination provides an example; its move into the industrial world was triggered by university students taking their enthusiam for it into industry.

This obviously requires that the Software-CAD approach be one about which students can and will become enthusiastic. Experience with my own students who have become missionaries for the introduction of this approach into industry even before any CAD tools are available suggests that it is one about which students will become enthusiastic.

3 Experience Using Elements Of The Software CAD Approach

3.1 Experience With A Prototype Introductory Modula2 Course

A prototype introductory programming course for computer engineering students using elements of the Software-CAD approach was tested in the winter of 1987 on a small group of students at U.C. Santa Cruz. The course used the Modula2 language and a graphical notation called "machine charts" which is a simplification and modification of an earlier notation I developed for design of concurrent Ada programs [1,6]. Some examples of material from this course will convey the flavor of what I propose.

Figure 2 shows a machine chart given to the students as an example of the external representation of a program module. It represents a simple counter as a module machine with multiple, push-button-like action machines (procedures) to perform counter functions. In the course, the evolution of the counter design proceeds through a number of intermediate diagrams not shown here to the final diagram shown in Figure 3. Normally, all this detail would not be shown in a single diagram and some of it would not be shown at all, because it unecessarily displays information which is implicit; all of it is shown here only to illustrate the notation. The resulting Modula2 program is shown in Figure 4, to illustrate the correspondence between the notation and the program text. Note that this example does not illustrate the principle that a "picture is worth a thousand words", because this very simple program is almost all structure and interaction, exactly those aspects which are conveyed in the picture. In more realistic examples, the structure and interaction aspects are often buried under much functional detail in the program text.

Figure 3 illustrates some notions which are useful for imparting an easy to understand architectural viewpoint of sequential programs, and which also pave the way for treatment of concurrent programs in a similar fashion. The central notion taught is of machines with interfaces and engines. Engines are sequential machines, which are the only active parts of programs. Sequential programs are presented as compositions of machines which interact with each other in such a way that only one engine at a time can run. Briefly, the explanation is as follows: engines of server module machines run only at initialization; the engine of the (necessarily) single master module machine starts running after that and henceforth controls program behaviour; the engines of procedure machines run only when triggered by an interaction; and interactions are interlocked, such that the engine at the calling end pauses while the procedure machine's engine performs a requested action. Procedure machines are introduced in their interface aspect first as pushbutton-like objects which can be used to perform actions. Concurrency is easily included in this model by relaxing the constraint that there be only a single master machine.

The prototype course using these notions was taught without software CAD tools, so machine charts were drawn by hand on the blackboard and on paper and manually converted into Modula2 programs (the figures reproduced here are from a diagram-drawing system used by the author rather than a software-CAD system used by the students). This manual approach did not relieve the students of any program carpentry responsibilities, as advocated earlier, and there was no suitable textbook to get the viewpoint across at an introductory level, so it was not possible to accept students without any programming preparation; some facility in Pascal was required as a prerequisite, to free the course from having to teach the Pascal-like parts of Modula2. Experience showed that this Pascal background had already given some students a sequential mindset which was hard to undo; it was very difficult to persuade these students that programs should not be monolithic artifacts and that every new module introduced in a design should not include the functionality of the entire program. In such cases, great persistence is required by the instructor to get the ideas across. However, most students were able to overcome their sequential mindsets by the middle of the course and to gain some significant software architecture experience during the latter half. Some students became quite adept at design by the end of the course.

The idea was introduced early that it is important to specify and test the external behaviour of machines before attempting to fit them into a system or implement their internals. A variety of methods for doing so were covered, including narrative text, timing charts, state machines and pseudo-code. The idea of test harnesses was central to the course (as illustrated by the test harness in Figures 3 and 4).

The initial introduction to the ideas relied on library modules. Students used standard modules like InOut to interact with the console, made modifications to increase the functionality of modules specifically written for the course, like the counter module of Figures 2 to 4, and in general built programs from canned or slightly modified modules. Only later were they asked to design and implement their own modules.

A Software-CAD laboratory would have greatly speeded up the learning process and would, I think, have made it possible to give the course as a first programming course (although the latter supposition remains to be tested). Needed for this purpose would be a textbook treating the language from the viewpoint of the course. Also needed, because a crucial part of the learning process in such a course is the criticism and discussion of trial designs, is a group of teaching assistants trained in the approach.

3.2 Ada-Related Experience

My iconic notation and Software-CAD approach for concurrent Ada programs is described and illustrated in a textbook and several papers [1,2,3,6]. The approach has been successfully taught in a number of senior undergraduate and graduate courses in the Department of Systems and Computer Engineering at Carleton University (e.g., [4]).

Recently [4] I demonstrated to my satisfaction that a relatively small "real time subset" of Ada which included only the basics of packages and tasks could be quickly learned and used in a real time programming course by a group of senior and graduate computer engineering students who had never seen Ada before. One of the keys to success was the use of a graphical design notation [6] to talk about concepts in class and for program design purposes. The proof of the pudding was the the students became enthusiastic about both Ada and the graphical design approach. Although this experience was with a class of relatively advanced computer engineering students, it convinced me that it would be possible to teach a "black box subset" of Ada in first year and a "concurrent black box subset" in the second year of an undergraduate university program, based on a graphical notation and a supporting Software-CAD teaching laboratory.

4 Feasibility Of The Software-CAD Approach For University Training

While the idea of the CAD approach to software is hardly new, the ability to support it for teaching purposes in a university setting at a tolerable cost is new. Relatively inexpensive personal computers are available with adequate graphical support for Software-CAD.

Environments to support a CAD/CAM approach to programming are emerging in the laboratory for relatively expensive CAD workstations [1,2,3] and similar systems should soon be appearing for less expensive personal computers. Therefore it should be possible soon to assemble a suitable teaching laboratory for the Software-CAD approach using essentially the same personal computers as are already becoming ubiquitous in university environments.

Furthermore, appropriate BBC languages are available for these same personal computers.

5 Choice Of A BBC (Black-Box-Concurrent) Language

The BBC language should be available for the entire range of teaching computers in a program, from microcomputers to mainframes and should be a supported product. This, taken together with the requirements for a BBC language stated earlier, severly limits freedom of choice. Modula2 is a candidate. With recent announcements of full Ada compilers for a popular personal computer, Ada has become a candidate.

5.1 Modula-2 -

Modula-2 is a candidate - it has "modules" for black-boxes - but its main disadvantage is that it lacks features in the language itself for expressing concurrency in a sufficiently general manner. One must go outside the bare language to consider general multitasking or distributed computing. However, it is possible to write a module in the language to implement a suitable multitasking model, say Ada's, which could be used by students.

Recent experience with Modula2, recounted earlier, leads me to conclude that it is an excellent language for teaching this material. It is small enough not to be daunting to students and yet complete enough to be useful. Perhaps an Ada subset is not needed for teaching Ada concepts; Modula2 could serve the purpose nicely.

5.2 Ada -

Ada has the right stuff - "packages" for black-boxes and "tasks" for concurrency - but its size makes it daunting for a beginner. Its viability as a teaching language in universities at the introductory level remains unproven and may depend on the availability of subset compilers, subset development systems and subset textbooks specifically for this purpose. However, subset compilers for the language have been specifically discouraged by its sponsor. Universities remain wary; Ada has not yet been widely accepted as a teaching language in the academic community.

An advantage of Ada is that its concurrency mechanisms provide natural models for distributed computing, thereby avoiding the need to explain how a more limited model like Modula-2's might be extended.

Enthusiasts of Modula-2 may also be surprised at how well Ada fares in comparisons with Modula-2 [7].

Ada has also been shown to be a feasible language for hardware design [5], so it clearly does provide an appropriate framework for total systems thinking.

5.3 Other Languages -

Other languages which might be desirable but which have the disadvantage of being less widely accepted or supported are NIL [8], Concurrent Pascal [9], and Concurrent Euclid [10]. No doubt readers will have their favorite candidates.

6 Towards The Goal Of Acquiring A Total Systems Viewpoint

Approaches to teaching software architecture like that described earlier can help students to acquire a total systems viewpoint in at least two respects: familiarity with architectural issues and familiarity with concurrency.

Architectural issues in software are similar to those arising in hardware. In hardware, physical packaging may not necessarily correspond to functional packaging, thus violating logical modularity. In software, the possibility also exists of packaging violating logical modularity. The issues are similar, although the reasons for adopting particular solutions will be different.

Concurrency issues are similar - races, critical races, deadlocks, and starvation are examples of concurrency issues which arise in both hardware and software.

However, software architecture is not the only component of a total systems viewpoint.

Personal experience with many students at Carleton has convinced me that the most effective way for students to acquire the early insight into hardware/software issues so essential for the total systems viewpoint is for them to do low-level interface programming, including experimenting with interrupts, device status registers, i/o ports, and so forth.

There is often difficulty squeezing an early laboratory course for such a purpose into already overcrowded programs. However first year, or the first term of second year, is the best place for it pedagogically, nicely complementing an introductory, software architecture oriented, programming course.

Is this too early to introduce such complex material? I do not think so; not only should the students be well motivated by the general technological climate and their own choice of program, but also they do not have to learn everything in this course, or even learn it in a particularly organized fashion. The same material can be tackled again later from a higher level viewpoint.

The existence of a laboratory course in this area is more important than the software language used to do the programming. It might be desirable to do the programming in a BBC language, particularly as a prelude to the idea that such languages are probably the "assembly languages" of the future. However, some actual assembly language experience is desirable in its own right, to give insight into the hardware/software interface and to pave the way for study of compilers.

7 Some Suggested Courses

Here are some suggested courses which might be used to implement this approach in an undergraduate computer engineering program. This list is not intended to be complete nor are the descriptions intended to be comprehensive. For example, it does not include traditional courses like data structures, which would be largely unaffected by Software-CAD approach. Nor does it include detailed descriptions of the more advanced courses. However, these sketchy outlines of courses convey the flavour.

Where appropriate, comments on experience with a course are given in brackets following the course description.

Programming 1 (First Year)

Programming from a black box viewpoint in a BBC language, focusing on non-concurrent systems. Black boxes as machines with interfaces, engines and stores. Machines for encapsulation (modules, packages) and action (procedures). Programs as compositions of machines, focusing on structure and interaction (examples drawn from console i/o). Data flow as a component of interaction. Reasoning about behaviour: interlocking of interactions; constraints for sequentiality; timing charts for understanding sequencing. Machines for data encapsulation, data manipulation (abstract data types), interaction control (state machines). Design methodology for modular programs based on machine notions; criteria of coupling and cohesion. Implementation methodology: specifying interface behaviour and testing it using test harnesses; starting with partial implementations. Case studies and assignments include programs to store and search for words, to play board games, and so forth.

Prerequisite - Nil; Corequisite - Software-CAD Laboratory 1

(This material is distributed through several third and fourth year courses in Carleton's Computer Engineering program. As described earlier, a prototype version of it has been tried with encouraging results, without the supporting Software-CAD laboratory, in an introductory Computer Engineering course at U.C. Santa Cruz. Instead of a single semester course, it may be desirable to have this as a two-semester course, to make sure the notions sink in.)

Software-CAD Laboratory 1 (First Year)

A laboratory course paralleling Programming 1 using a graphics workstation with appropriate software tools to prepare "wiring diagrams" and temporal behaviour descriptions of software graphically, analyze the designs, generate some code automatically, augment the generated code manually and compile/run/test the result.

Prerequisite - Nil; Corequisite - Programming 1.

(I expect suitable tools for Ada for personal computers to be available soon. Versions would have to be developed for Modula2).

Microprocessor Laboratory (First or Early Second Year)

Introduction to the organization and programming of a typical microprocessor system. Laboratory experience with low-level interface programming, including experimenting with interrupts, device status registers, i/o ports, and so forth. Intended to give the student insight into how a combination of hardware and software is formed into a computing system.

Prerequisite - A high school or makeup course in programming in any language.

(This course is present in many programs, but usually much later than this).

Programming 2 (Second Year)

Thinking about and designing software as collections of concurrently operating black boxes. Making the mental leap from sequential programming. Assignments include the programming of hardware-like components, e.g., shared resource arbiters analagous to bus arbiters.

Issues illustrated include deadlock, starvation and critical races. Comparisons to hardware are drawn continually. Standard data structures such as arrays, lists, queues and stacks are introduced as black boxes in a manner that illustrates their place in both software and hardware. Teaching is done by instructors with enough total systems background to illuminate the material with this viewpoint.

Includes concurrent programming material traditionally handled in courses on operating systems.

Prerequisite - Programming 1, Software-CAD Laboratory 1 and Microprocessor Laboratory; Co-requisite - Software-CAD Laboratory 2.

(The material of this course is distributed through several different courses at Carleton University, on real time programming and software engineering. The availability of a Software-CAD laboratory would enable it to be consolidated.)

Software-CAD Laboratory 2 (Second Year)

A laboratory course taken concurrently with Programming 2 and supporting it.

(The laboratory environment is the same as for Software-CAD Laboratory 1, except that now concurrency must be supported in the tools. Appropriate tools have been developed in research laboratories to support Ada design (e.g., [1,2,3]) and versions are expected to be available commercially soon for personal computers. Support of Modula2 would require additional work.)

Corequisite - Programming 2

Languages And Systems Laboratory (Second Year)

This course is aimed at broadening the student's knowledge. Hands-on familiarization with two other very different high level languages (e.g., C and Prolog) and two operating systems (e.g., Unix and a real time OS). Intended to give students insight into other languages and operating systems, corresponding to the insight they developed into microprocessor sytems in the first year Microprocessor Laboratory course. A later course will give more thorough coverage.

Prerequisite - Programming 2 and Software-CAD Laboratory 2 (not so much for content as for maturity and to give the Software-CAD approach time to take root before tackling other approaches).

(This course is untried. I see the need for it arising from the early focusing on the Software-CAD approach for both architecture and concurrency. By this time the students should have a solid enough grounding in these areas to be ready to broaden their perspectives. This course, together with other proposed courses, eliminate the need for a separate operating systems course.)

Real-Time Systems (Third Year)

Deals with advanced level BBC programming on the microprocessor for devices and interprocessor communication. Considers matters like real time response, deadline scheduling, tradeoffs between asynchronous and sysnchronous designs, resource management and allocation, reliability, quality, testing, debugging.

Covers many topics traditionally handled in courses on operating systems, but with a different slant.

Prerequisite - Programming 2, Software-CAD Laboratory 2, Languages and Systems Laboratory

(Material like this is covered in a third year course in Carleton's Computer Engineering Program. However, this course can be more ambitious, because more of the principles have been covered earlier. At Carleton, this is the place where architectural ideas about programming are first introduced.)

Real-Time Systems Laboratory (Third Year)

The laboratory for Real Time Systems. Uses the same hardware as the first year microprocessor laboratory course.

Corequisite - The Real Time Systems course

(Laboratory work like this supplements real time systems lecture material at Carleton.)

Computing Project (Third Year)

A project resulting in a major report. Placed in third year to give students a head start in attacking an area of specific future interest and to take some pressure off fourth year.

Prerequisite - third year registration

(This is usually a fourth year course. However, there are advantages to placing it in third year, as described.)

Languages and Systems (Fourth Year)

A comparative course to cover in a more systematic manner than was possible in the corresponding second year laboratory course the relation between what has been learned and a range of programming languages and operating systems. Treats one conventional programming language (e.g., C), one declarative programming language (e.g., Prolog), one conventional operating system (e.g., Unix) and one real time operating system. Emphasis is on constraints imposed by different languages and systems.

Prerequisite - fourth year registration

(This is an untried course.)

Computer System Design (Fourth Year)

Deals from an integrated viewpoint with the design of software/hardware systems for real time applications.

Prerequisites - Real Time Systems - Course and Laboratory

(A course along these lines is an important component of the fourth year of Carleton's Computer Engineering program.)

Computer Systems Design Laboratory (Fourth Year)

The laboratory for Computer Systems Design

Corequisite - The Computer Systems Design course.

(At Carleton, a laboratory like this complements the design course).

8 Issues

8.1 The Need for More Formal Prerequisites

Some colleagues who have studied these proposals and substantially agree with them have pointed out what they see as the need for more formal prerequisites in the areas of mathematics, logic, boolean algebra and switching circuits. While acknowledging the importance of these subjects in professional programs, it seems important to observe that (1) they are not necessary to study software in the way being proposed and (2) there is actually an advantage to be gained by approaching software composition from an informal viewpoint. Therefore, while such courses may be required in an overall program, I believe it would too constraining to insist on them as prerequisites for particular courses.

More prerequisites are unecessary, because the view of programs as compositions of machines does not need a theoretical basis to be teachable. The teacher can draw on common sense and intuition about the modularity of everyday objects to get the points across.

More prerequisites may be undesirable, because there is a need to develop early some basis for the use of common sense in engineering design and it seems inappropriate to postpone unecessarily the courses which can do this. Software courses provide an opportunity to do this, because there is so little constructive theory available for shaping software.

For example, I consider that it would be a mistake to insist on a course in digital logic as a prerequisite to the introductory microprocessor laboratory. The purpose of this laboratory is to give early insight and such a prerequisite would push the course too late in the program. There is no reason why a digital logic course and a microprocessor programming laboratory course cannot proceed in parallel; one does not need formal digital logic to write programs to control chips or to understand a microprocessor board, any more than one needs programming to study digital logic. The two can be advantageously studied in parallel.

8.2 Where Does Traditional Software Material Fit?

I do not mention courses on data structures, compilers, algorithms, operating systems, software engineering, and so forth.

With respect to data structures, very little change is needed to traditional methods of teaching them to fit in with this approach, although there is obviously a challenge to develop a compatible CAD-based approach. My proposed approach provides early motivation for studying data structures, because data abstraction is an inescapable aspect of the approach from the beginning; the earliest black boxes studied in the approach are used to encapsulate data. A traditional course on data structures naturally follows Porgramming 1, with very litte modification; I have not included a description because I do not at this time propose anything new in this area.

With respect to compilers and algorithms, much the same is true. Traditional courses are unaffected by the approach. The only difference is that the students' perspective of algorthms will be slightly different; they will be perceived as sequential program fragments to implement the function aspect of the Y-Chart (Figure 1).

With respect to operating systems, I have distributed traditional material over several courses, thus dispensing with the need for a specific operating systems course.

With respect to software engineering, the design aspect pervades the earlier programming courses, providing a solid basis for further study of life cycle issues.

9 Conclusions

I have presented proposals for teaching programming using a Software-CAD approach. Although the approach has not yet been fully realized in a specific university program, experience with aspects of it leads me to believe it both feasible and very promising. Much work remains to be done to make the approach a practical reality: methodologies need refinement; tools must be developed; supporting textbooks must be written. A purpose of this paper is to stimulate work in this direction.

Acknowledgments

Thanks are due to many students at Carleton university who contributed to the development of these ideas by suffering through prototypes of courses which tried them out; to Pat Mantey at U.C. Santa Cruz, who provided the opportunity to try the ideas out for the first time in an introductory course; to the small group of students at U.C. Santa Cruz who took the protoype version of Programming 1; and to the reviewers and editor who helped to focus the arguments of this paper.

References

[1] Buhr, Karam, Hayes, Woodside, "Software CAD: A Revolutionary Approach", IEEE Trans. Software Engineering, Special Issue on Ada, Spring 87.

[2] Buhr, Woodside, Karam, Van der Loo, Lewis, "Experiments with Prolog Design Descriptions and Tools in CAEDE, an Iconic Design Environment for Embedded, Multitasking Systems", Proc. 8th International Conference on Software Engineering, London, Computer Society Press, Sep. 85.

[3] Buhr, Woodside, Karam, "An Overview and Example of Application of CAEDE: A New Design Environment for Ada", Proc. International Ada Conference, Paris, "Ada in Use", Cambridge University Press, May 85.

[4] Buhr, "Lessons from Practical Experience Teaching Hands- On, Real Time, Embedded System Programming With Ada", Proc. International Ada Conference, Paris, "Ada in Use", Cambridge University Press, May 85.

[5] Girczyc, Buhr, Knight, "Analysis of Ada as a High Level Hardware Description Language", IEEE Trans. on CAD of Integrated Circuits and Systems, Vol. CAD-4, No. 2, Apr. 85.

[6] Buhr, "System Design With Ada", textbook, Prentice Hall, 1984.

[7] Feldman, M.B., "Ada vs. Modula-2: A Response From the Ivory Tower", ACM Sigplan Notices, Vol. 21, No. 5, May 86.

[8] Strom, Halim, "A New Programming Methodology for Long-Lived Software Systems", IBM Jour. Res. Dev., Vol. 28, No. 1, Jan. 84.

[9] Brinch Hansen, "The Architecture of Concurrent Programs", Prentice Hall, 1980.

[10] Holt, "Concurrent Euclid, Tunis and Unix", Addison-Wesley, 1984.

FIGURE 1

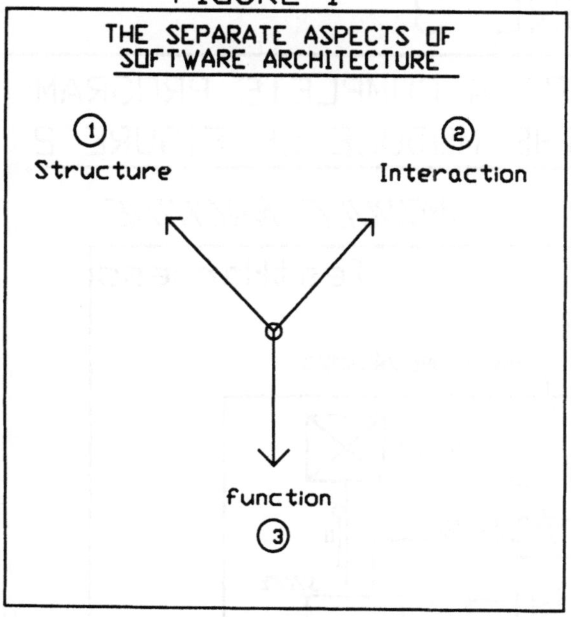

FIGURE 2

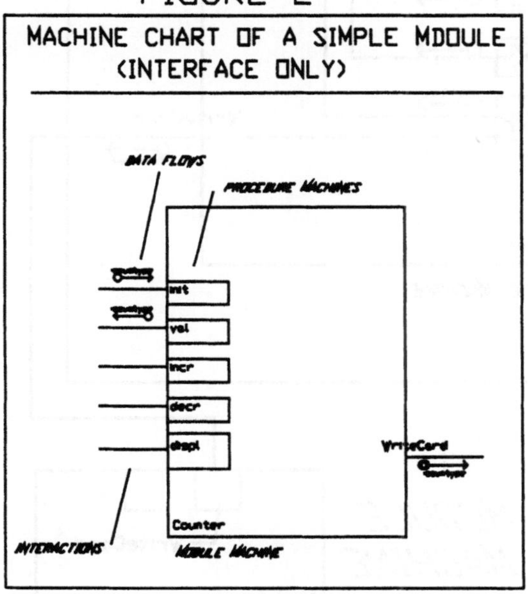

FIGURE 3

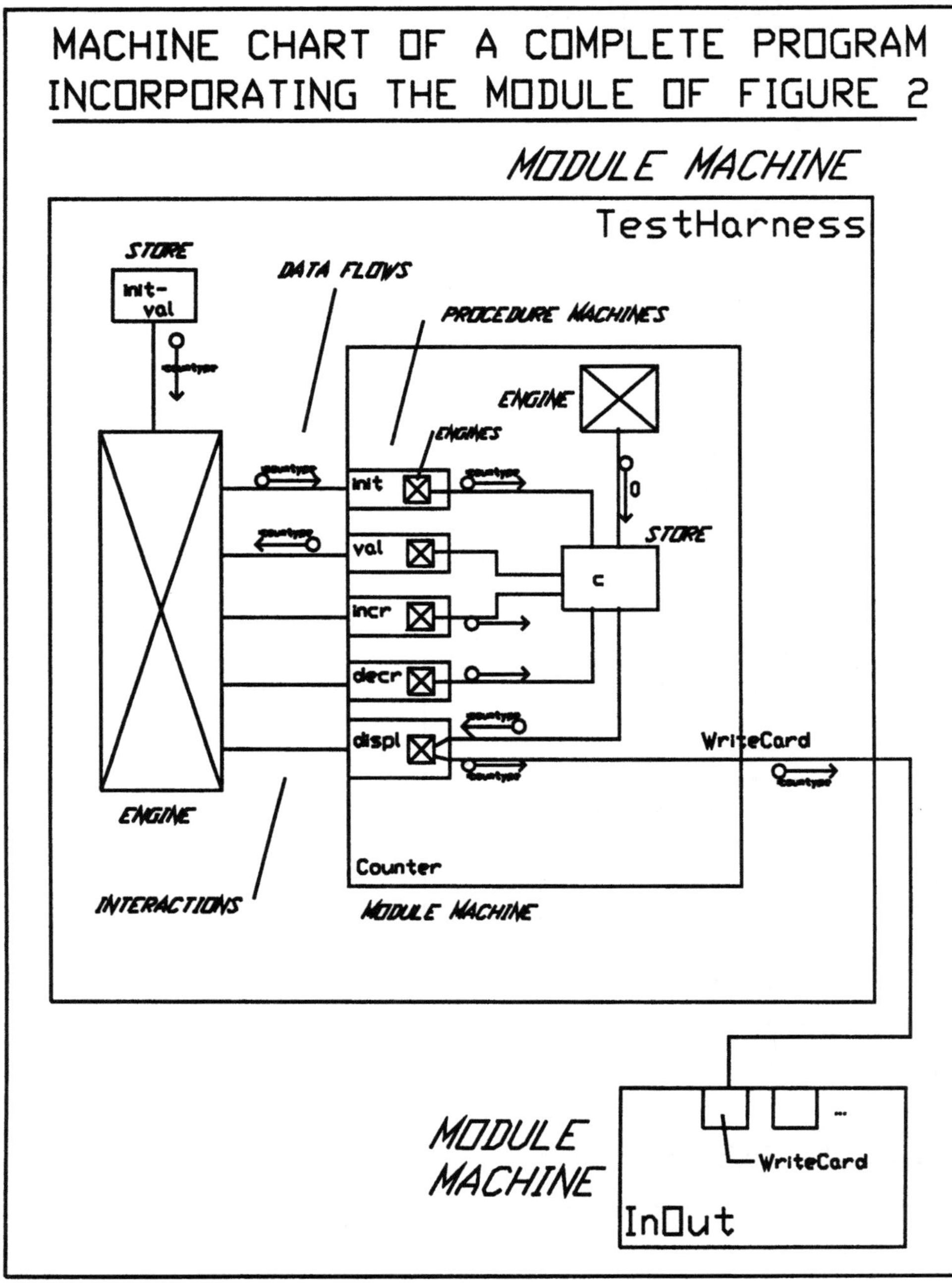
MACHINE CHART OF A COMPLETE PROGRAM
INCORPORATING THE MODULE OF FIGURE 2
MODULE MACHINE
TestHarness
STORE
int-
val
DATA FLOWS
PROCEDURE MACHINES
ENGINE
ENGINES
init
val
incr
decr
displ
0
STORE
c
WriteCard
ENGINE
Counter
INTERACTIONS
MODULE MACHINE
MODULE
MACHINE
WriteCard
InOut

FIGURE 4

```
(*
COUNTER EXAMPLE WITH PROGRAM SOURCE LINES CATEGORIZED BY Y-CHART
   (*S*) - STRUCTURE
   (*I*) - INTERACTION
   (*S*) - FUNCTION
*)

(*S*)    MODULE TestHarness ;             (* master machine *)
(*S*)     IMPORT InOut ;

(*S*)      MODULE Counter ;      (* internal module machine *)
(*S*)       IMPORT InOut ;
(*S*)       EXPORT
(*S*)        countype , (* type *)
(*S*)        init , val, displ , incr , decr ; (* procedures *)
(*S*)       TYPE
(*S*)        countype = CARDINAL ;
(*S*)       VAR
(*S*)        c : countype ;
             (* local store *)

(*S*)       PROCEDURE init ( initialcount : countype ) ; (* action machine *)
(*S*)        BEGIN (* init engine *)
(*F*)        c := initialcount ;
(*S*)        END init ;

(*S*)       PROCEDURE val () : countype ; (* action machine *)
(*S*)        BEGIN (* val engine *)
(*F*)         RETURN c ;
(*S*)       END val ;

(*S*)       PROCEDURE displ ; (* action machine *)
(*S*)        BEGIN (* displ engine *)
(*I*)         InOut.WriteCard ( c , 1 ) ;
(*S*)        END displ ;

(*S*)       PROCEDURE incr ; (* action machine *)
(*S*)        BEGIN (* incr engine *)
(*F*)         c := c+1 ;
(*S*)        END incr ;

(*S*)       PROCEDURE decr ; (* action machine *)
(*S*)        BEGIN (* decr engine *)
(*F*)         IF c > 0
(*F*)          THEN c := c-1 ;
(*F*)         END ; (* if *)
(*S*)       END decr ;

(*S*)       BEGIN (* Counter engine *)
            c := 0 ;
(*S*)      END Counter ;

(*S*)      CONST
(*S*)       initval = 10 ;

(*S*)      BEGIN (* TestHarness engine *)
(*I*)       init ( initval ) ;
(*I*)       WHILE val () > 0 DO
(*I*)        displ ;
(*I*)        decr ;
           END ; (* while *)
(*S*)     END TestHarness.
```

Adding Reviews, Prototyping, and Frequent Deliveries to Software Engineering Projects

Connie U. Smith
Performance Engineering Services Division
L&S Computer Technology, Inc.
P.O. Box 9802 Mail Stop 120
Austin, TX 78766

Charles R. Martin
Department of Computer Science
Duke University
Durham, NC 27705

May 20, 1987

Abstract

Program Design and Construction is Duke's introductory software engineering course. Until spring semester of 1985, this has been a fairly conventional project-oriented course. At that time, we added critical evaluation of other software systems, more frequent intermediate deliveries, and human-interface prototyping to the project assignments.

These additions to a previously-successful course produced a positive result far out of proportion to what we expected. This was surprising enough that we thought it should be reported; the first part of this report describes the original course and our changes to it.

In addition, we think we have learned something more general about teaching software engineering principles, and improving software engineering practices. What we have learned, and ideas and speculations based on this, make up the second part of the report.

Index Terms: Software engineering education, prototyping, reviews, deliverables, specification, classroom methods.

1 Introduction

CPS155 (Program Design and Construction) is an undergraduate course in which computer science students are exposed to basic software engineering principles. This is done in two stages: first, independent programming assignments to introduce "programming-in-the-large" and software maintenance concepts; second, a team project in which a small, useful system is taken from an informal specification to a working product, including all associated documentation.

The course has been quite successful: user manuals and other documentation are produced; the group dynamics simulate project management aspects of larger development teams (which convinces us our simulation is a good one); feedback from students after their first industrial experiences has been favorable; and feedback from industrial representatives who interview and hire these students has been positive.

With this success, there were also frustrations: the quality of the documentation was marginal, and we had trouble communicating what was wrong; the usability of the human interface, and thus of the project software, seemed to vary widely from group to group; and the presence of egregious bugs in the final product made us feel our discussions of testing were wasted.

This frustration caused us to try some changes we felt would make the students more aware of what we expected, and give them useful skills with which to evaluate their own work. These skills were based on the ideas of prototyping, incremental development, and reviews which are widely described in the software engineering literature. The results suggest these are useful additions to computer science courses and industrial training; our experience with these changes also suggest that these methods are important in general. In order to put these changes in perspective, we will also give a general description of the course and how we teach it.

2 Related Work

Software engineering deals with problems beyond the scope of conventional computer science. As with all engineering disciplines, software engineers must make decisions based not just on the mathematical properties of the problem in question. Instead, the software engineer must capture and define requirements and organize that information into a design. It is then that real "engineering" takes place — decisions must be made not only on the theoretical ability to perform the function desired, but also attempting to optimize among parameters such as cost, efficiency, and maintainability.

Mills[16], Sommerville[17] and Fairley and Martin[8] discuss how project laboratories are a necessary part of software engineering education, in order to expose the student to realistic simulations of the project environment. As will be seen below, our course is similar in outline to those described in [3], [10], [21], and others.

Particular problems with project-oriented courses lie in the area of grading and assessing students' projects. This difficulty has been noted by many authors. One interesting solution to this problem was in the "Software Hut" method developed by Horning and Wortman [11][12], further experience with which was reported for example by Woodward and Mander[13]. In Software Hut, the projects are evaluated (at least in part) by their place as products in a simulated market. Thus the evaluation was competitive.

We did not use so competitive a method of evaluation for several reasons. First, Wortman and Mander found that in order for the pricing and quality measures in the Software Huts to reflect the quality of the actual software delivered, the instructors must "make a[n] ... effort to assess software quality and penalize students heavily for poor-quality software,...."[13] This means that the instructors must spend a lot of time in this evaluation; this would not be practical in our larger classes. Second, our project time was quite limited (about seven weeks), due to the assignments we use to explore the basic software engineering skills in the beginning of the semester: there is no time to spare for marketing and evaluating the software during the progress of the course. Finally, we found that — especially after the changes we describe in this paper — the quality of all the projects was closely enough comparable that competitive evaluation seemed likely not to be very informative.

However, some grading method is necessary. When working on the class projects, co-worker's inputs are a major factor in determining each student's grade; thus the desire to be perceived as doing a good job and working hard replaces to some extent the salary and performance reviews they will receive in practice. We feel that our grading method actually improves the simulation of a project environment for two reasons.

The major differences between our course and other project-oriented courses lie in the fact that we made reviews of software from outside the class and prototypes of the student systems part of the projects. While we also increased the number of deliverables, it is not clear from the literature that the number of deliverables we require is very much different from other's courses; differences in the courses and the time available for projects make them hard to compare in this respect.

We found no references to experiments in which reviews of programs were used to teach programming practices; however, it has often been suggested as a good way in which to teach programming, e.g. in Brian Kernighan and P. J. Plauger's books[14][15].

Boehm *et al.* performed an experiment to compare prototyping with specification in projects.[4] His experiment was conducted using a software engineering project class, and was therefore somewhat similar to our class after we made the changes described in this report.

In Boehm's experiment, prototyping was defined to be constructing a sample system, then modifying it until it received customer approval, whereas the specifying approach was the more conventional one of writing a specification, then constructing the system to meet this specification. They found the prototyping approach gave a large increase in productivity (and thus a lower cost), and that the systems produced were more satisfying to the users.

However, they also reported that the prototype systems were judged to be less maintainable.

There are several differences between the method reported by Boehm *et al.* and our method. First, Boehm's groups were composed of only two or three people, rather than the four or five people in our groups. This means that the group interaction in Boehm's groups would be much less complex, and the corresponding group dynamics much different — for example, scheduling group meetings would be much easier.

Second, the people in Boehm's project course were graduate students with industrial experience. Thus they brought into the course skills that our students could not have developed. In particular, Boehm's students would have had some experience with arriving at an understanding of the user's needs, as well as greater programming skill.

Finally, several of the project standards Boehm's students had to meet were quite different from ours, especially in documentation. We look on prototyping not as a replacement for specifying a system, but as a tool for deriving the system specifications. A large part of Boehm's productivity increase seems to have been due to the smaller amount of documentation that the prototyping groups needed to produce, so we would not expect to see a corresponding increase in productivity in groups working within our prototyping paradigm. Together, these differences cause us to believe that the working environment overall must have been quite different in Boehm's experiment and in our classes.

We chose to add prototyping to *Program Design and Construction* because of our general agreement with the method of prototyping and incremental development, rather than responding to the Boehm paper in particular. The fact that the addition of prototypes in two courses that differ in many respects has been successful leads us to believe the technique is more generally applicable.

3 Overview of *Program Design and Construction*[1]

CPS155 (Program Design and Construction) is an elective course for juniors and seniors majoring in Computer Science. In their introductory courses, we expect the students to have developed basic programming skills, to have been exposed to programming using the usual data structures such as queues, linked lists, stacks and trees, and to have been exposed to some of the issues of the underlying computer architecture. In addition, they normally have had several math courses, and will have completed at least one course in composition. The composition course is quite important, as the students will spend a large part of their time and effort writing documentation.

The primary purpose of *Program Design and Construction* is to supplement the teaching of programming with exposure to the problems of system design and implementation, and to fundamental concepts of programming-in-the-large. We have concluded, as have others, that the best way to do this is by a project-oriented course. Since the students have been taught programming, we would ideally begin the project immediately; however, there are a few fundamental concepts of programming-in-the-large in which we feel the preparation afforded by other courses is insufficient. Therefore, we have added the topics shown in Table 1.

In order to stress the importance of planning and scheduling tasks, we encourage them to start the assignments early, and late assignments are not accepted. We encourage an "incremental build" approach similar to that advocated by Brooks and Basili.[5][2] Students are to create a working version of a subset of the assignment, then add subsets one at a time. Students receive a much better grade of they submit a program that works successfully on a subset of the assignment than if they have coded everything but nothing runs.

[1]This describes *our* version of CPS155 — other instructors at Duke have used other approaches and pursued other goals.

[2]Studies have shown that breadth of experience in programming languages is a key to productivity and proficiency in programming[7].

Algorithms for Programming-in-the-Large	Large problems, and algorithms suitable for processing millions of data records. These are not solvable using the in-core algorithms that are commonly taught to undergraduates.
File Structures	The undergraduate data structures courses usually cover in-core data structures where device access time is not an issue. We cover sequential, indexed-sequential, and random-access files, as these seem appropriate for a basic understanding of the problems of dealing with very large data stores. (A data-base course covers additional concepts.)
Program Documentation	Program documentation is stressed in other undergraduate courses; but class assignments are still "write-only" programs that are written, submitted for a grade, then discarded. Since the value of documentation is in program maintenance, we reinforce this by asking students to modify an existing program from a previous year.
Programming Languages and Systems	Most courses at Duke are taught in Pascal using microcomputers. We use PL/I under MVS, as this is closer to most production environments.[2]
Peripheral Problems	Assignments in other courses leave students with the impression that selecting the algorithms and data structures are the only problems to be solved. Our assignments expose them to new operating systems, and large environment problems that affect project management.

Table 1: Topics Added to CPS155

In addition to the programming-in-the-large concepts in Table 1, the software engineering concepts that we emphasize are:

- the necessity of good specification and design to successful large system projects.
- the importance of creating good user manuals early in the design stage.
- basics of human interface design.
- good organization of designs and documentation.
- scheduling and manpower allocation.
- system integration and test techniques.

We use a preliminary sequence of about six assignments to reinforce these topics. At about mid-term we assign the term project. Term projects have the following characteristics:

- The *minimal* version of the project is something that a three or four person group can readily complete in six to eight weeks.
- The scope of the *complete* project as the students originally see it is more than we expect can be implemented. This forces the students to make some engineering decisions on the scope and ambition of the project.
- The project is not one that has been recently used, so no previous solutions are easily available to the students.
- The human interface is a major part of the system, and it has some parts in which well-chosen algorithms can give large performance advantages.
- The project has a loose enough set of requirements that there are ambiguities and room for interpretation. (Needless to say, we have had little trouble finding projects with this characteristic.)

Some examples of projects we have chosen are: a comprehensive small business management system; an "office manager" system for small consulting firms; an income tax-advisor system; a kitchen inventory system with menu-planning functions; and an appointment and time accounting system for Duke's internal microcomputer repair facility. (The alert observer might guess that one of our ways of devising a project is to look for something we'd like to have ourselves.)

Once we have determined the course project, we must then arrange the teams that will work together for the duration of the course. Others have allowed the teams to be chosen by the students themselves, or allocate people to teams arbitrarily. We feel this complicates the problem of grading the projects unnecessarily, in that we must then find a way to normalize the effects of variation in talents or skills as distributed among the groups. We are also interested in the groups' dynamics being similar, for reasons which are discussed below.

We feel team selection is very important to the success of the course, so we instead assign people to project teams. We do so by using the scores on the preceding assignments to allocate the students evenly among the project teams. We try to allocate only one "star" and only one student from the other end of the curve to each group. We then assign remaining people to the groups working by cumulative numerical score. The result is usually that each group's cumulative score is about equal.

All teams compete on the same project.[3] It is presented to them in a single class session by someone who has volunteered to act as the customer for the project. Usually, we also give the students the informal specification at that time. This informal specification takes the form of a "wish list" which

[3]Once we tried assigning a special project to a group of experienced students to provide them with a more challenging problem. The results were disastrous: they ignored delivery deadlines; they did not have the same group dynamics, so their project-management experience suffered; and they failed to complete the assignment. The illusion of "special treatment" was still resented by the other students, who felt like theirs was not a "real project" — just a toy. We *strongly* discourage special projects.

contains everything the user would ever possibly want in such a system. (One example of a project wish list is given as an appendix.)

It is the students responsibility to organize the teams once we have assigned the people. We recommend the producer-director organization in Brooks[5]. We require them to choose a team leader for each team who is responsible for the team's schedule and progress, and acts as the main interface to the instructor and the customer.

Our grading methods for the initial assignments result in grades that usually have a roughly Gaussian distribution. Those at the high end are talented, highly motivated students, while those at the low end generally are capable but do not invest as much effort in the course as others. (Those who are simply incapable usually drop the course before the project begins.)

When we assign students to the teams, we assign one "star" to each group, and one student from the other end of the curve, with the others from somewhere in the middle. This introduces a project management challenge: the team manager must effectively schedule team efforts, delegate some parts of the effort, monitor the team's progress, and motivate the under-achiever in a (relatively) diverse group.

As we originally organized the course, we required four deliveries: a preliminary project plan, a user's interface specification, user's interface screen layouts, and a final delivery. Beginning with Spring Semester 1985, we required five deliveries: a review of another CPS155 project system, a preliminary project plan, a user's interface specification, an executable user's interface prototype, and the final delivery. The details of these deliveries, both before and after the change, are included in Table 2.

Each delivery is graded, and grades are returned to the students as soon as feasible (ideally at the next class meeting.) At the end of the term we collect the projects, which are then graded for inclusion in the final grade for the course. At this time, we attempt to correct for the effects of individual effort in translating from the team grades for the project to the individual grades used in calculating the students' final grades.

Old Assignments		New Assignments	
Deliverable	**Description**	**Deliverable**	**Description**
		Project Review	Written report.
Preliminary Project Plan	Proposed schedule and preliminary requirements.	Preliminary Project Plan	Same as old assignment.
User Interface Specification	User's manual: functions, screen descriptions, and operations invoked by each action.	User's Manual	Same as the old assignment, except screen layouts not included.
Screen Layouts	Drawings of all screen layouts.	Screen Layouts	Same as old assignments.
		User's Interface Prototype	All screens as described; data entry and changing displays. No calculations or other output required.
Final Delivery	Final (as delivered) requirements description; Final User's Manual; Programmer's Reference Manual; Code listings; Test data and test plans; Example scenario; Tutorial; Executable system.	Final Delivery	Same deliverables as previously.

Table 2: A Comparison of Old and New Assignments in CPS155.

We have found a useful way of handling this problem which we adapted from Dr. Frederick P. Brooks, Jr. at the University of North Carolina: each student turns in a personal evaluation of the effort and contribution of other members of his or her team. In this evaluation they allocate points to each member of the team (including themselves), according to their perception of the level of effort and effectiveness of that person. We set the total points that may be allocated to be $10m$ where m is the number of team members, but then allow these points to be allocated in any way that results in this total — so for example, a four member team has a total of forty points that may be allocated, but the allocation may be $20, 10, 5, 5$.

Our experience with this method has been that it is quite effective — the allocations within a team almost always agree within a few points, and they usually correspond to our own subjective evaluation of performance.[4] Surprisingly, this is even true of students who receive dramatically low evaluations — although their own evaluations of themselves are often a few points above the others.

This method has a particular advantage for us. We feel it necessary to grade in part on a student's participation; however, in most classes this kind of grading requires a subjective judgement on the part of the instructors. While we feel these judgements are qualitatively correct, the evaluations turned in by the students give us a quantitative evaluation that is not based only in our own perceptions.

The individual grades are combined with the group project grades for the final assessment. This approach is used by Brooks to normalize group and individual efforts: a hard-working individual on a mediocre teams gets some compensation for extra effort; a mediocre effort on a successful team is appropriately downgraded.

[4]Occasionally, students point out subtle differences in performance that we would not have noticed.

4 Additions Made to the Course

As we mentioned above, although the course as a whole was successful, we still felt some aspects of the course were not as effective as they might have been. In particular, we felt that the quality of the documentation was simply not sufficient, and the design and implementation of the human interfaces needed improvement.

We observed that the documentation provided by the teams had three major problems. First, the documentation was vague and imprecise. Second, the documentation (and the design being described) was inconsistent: it often gave the impression that each section was a separate document, and the complete manual simply a collation of these documents. Third, there was almost never sufficient overview information about the systems, resulting in a manual which one must completely absorb in order to understand any section.

We originally made samples available for all of the types of manuals we would require. We found that this alone had no effect; just reading the manuals was not sufficient to make any change in the quality of the results obtained.

We also found that the user interfaces developed by the students were not well designed. In particular: user interfaces were often designed to be easy to *code* rather than easy to *use*; the user interfaces often were not consistent across all functions; and the dialogue with the user often required too many responses.

We decided to make some changes in the course starting in hopes of improving the students' performance in these areas.

4.1 Adding Prototypes

Another problem that we had observed was that the human interface was simply not very good. We had emphasized human factors in class, but this was apparently not enough. Our hypothesis was that the students were not skilled enough to recognize those times when their human interface designs were not going to be sufficient.

In addition to the reviews, we made the construction of a human-interface prototype an early deliverable in the project plan. We made it clear that this need not be deliverable code, and need not meet coding or performance constraints — it simply must simulate the barest skeleton of the human interaction with the system.

4.2 Adding Intermediate Deliverables

To allow us to better track and understand the process the students were going through, we added deliverables to the projects so there was a delivery of some sort to be made about every two weeks. This would have two effects: we could examine the changes in the systems and the associated designs, which would give us feedback about what changes occurred because of each of the other changes we were making; and deadlines would become part of day to day life by making sure that there was a deliverable within the two-to-three week "horizon" that has been widely reported.

4.3 Adding Reviews of Other Projects

Our basic hypothesis about the documentation was that the quality of the students' project documentation was poor because they had no examples from which to learn. We found it hard to find good examples for the students, because first, much system documentation is tied to systems so large they are simply infeasible for short-term examination; and second, there wasn't much we wanted to expose an impressionable young programmer to anyway.

We decided to try something suggested by Robert Persig's *Zen and the Art of Motorcycle Maintenance*[19], in which Persig describes an attempt to teach Quality to composition students by having them compare different examples of writing. We adapted this by having the students review a project from an earlier semester; this was one of the last assignments before the term project. The guess was that seeing an example of another project would have two effects (at least): they would see the areas in which the quality of the result was not high enough, hopefully learning from the mistakes of others; they would realize that the results of their project would have a life beyond the end of the term — would their project be an example next term?

This review was not simply to read the manuals; the actual software produced by previous teams was made available to the students for testing by putting the software on reserve in the library. This software was then to be executed and evaluated by the students.

The review assignment is included in the appendix. Note that the documentation lesson is disguised; the assignment is to evaluate the user interfaces of several different projects. By using the software, the students *experience* several different approaches to the same problem. There is always room for improvement in user interfaces — as is discussed in greater detail in [20] — so the students get experience with features that are effective, and others that are awkward.

5 Results

Our results were invariably good — surprisingly so. In fact, we feel that the worst of the projects since we have made this change are of the quality we associated with the best projects before the change. We observed similar effects in two different semesters and are confident that they represent a positive, fundamental effect which was not due to unusual talent in one class.

We feel this improvement was concentrated in certain areas. First, the quality of the documentation and of the human interface was considerably better. Second, the distribution of student hours over the life of the project was better; there were fewer dark circles under the student's eyes at the end of the semester, even though our suspicion is that the time spent on projects are nearly the same as before (we collected no data on total hours to support this). Third, the groups seemed to be more successful at selecting a set of functions to be implemented in the available time. Finally, the project management seemed much improved — the project managers were better able to control the projects.

In the next section, we describe these results, considering them both from our own perspective and from our understanding of the student's perception of the result.

5.1 Added Deliverables

Adding deliverables to the projects is one area in which we are not easily able to determine the effect. In retrospect — had we intended this as a formal experiment rather than simply trying to improve an existing class — we might have attempted adding more deliverables to the projects without making any of the other changes.

However, we feel we can draw some tentative conclusions from the results we have already had: suppose the good effects we saw are attributable only to the more frequent deliveries. Then we would have expected that all deliveries and all products would have improved, since they were all affected by this change. As reported in the next sections, the improvements we saw seemed to be preferentially in the human interface and documentation sections, which would then not support this hypothesis.

We did, however, observe that the project management improved. In previous years, frantic project managers appeared the week before the final delivery date complaining about under-achievers. Unfortunately, then it is too late to correct the problem. After we made these changes, the same phenomenon occurred — but very much earlier! (Usually in the week before the *prototype* was to be delivered.) It was then still possible for the project managers to learn the necessary leadership skills for them to motivate the under-achievers.

Another (less dramatic) improvement attributable to the effects of more frequent deliveries was that the teams seemed more likely to propose systems which were achievable subsets of the wish-list. This could be attributed to either the increased horizon effect — the deadlines were always close enough to be worrisome — or it could be attributed to improved organization.

Our students' perception was that (with the exception of the prototype) the many deliveries were simply a lot of trouble — they were not helpful. We can sympathize, because the many deliveries were a lot trouble for everyone. Further investigation would be worthwhile in order to determine the particular effect of frequent deliveries.

5.2 Reviews

As we noted above, we felt that the quality of the documentation was one of the areas which improved most after the change. In particular, the user's manuals included an effective system overview section, and the manuals were better integrated. We believe this is due to the students' experiences with poor overview and documentation in the systems they reviewed. Also, the need for a system overview was subtly reinforced by the assignment question asking for the purpose of the software. In their reviews, the students were forced to derive the overall purpose by experimenting with commands — a frustrating experience. System manuals after the change invariably contained a concise statement of the system's purpose.

We offered two possible ways in which reviews would lead to better systems and documentation; learning from other's mistakes, and the worry that their projects might be a (bad) example next term.[5] We believe the improvement we saw was due almost entirely to the students having learned from the previous systems' painful properties. This supposition is supported by interviews with the students after the class was over.

[5]Names were deleted from the projects used for review, to protect the privacy of the students who implemented the projects. However, the students were aware that these examples were from earlier semesters. We feel this at least leads to the recognition that their projects would have a life beyond the end of the semester.

5.3 Prototyping

The other area of dramatic improvement was in the human interface, and we believe this improvement to be due almost exclusively to the human-interface prototype.

This conclusion is arguable — one could just as easily say that the reviews had as good an effect in the human interface as in the documentation. There were a few ideas the students obviously learned from the exercise[6]; However, we (accidentally) had a chance to eliminate this effect in the most recent semester. This system had a secondary communication section that was not required in the prototype; upon completion, the quality of the human interface of this section was dramatically lower than other parts of the system. This supports prototyping as the main reason for the improvement.

5.4 Overall

We noticed several other improvements in the overall projects. The conceptual integrity of both the software and the documentation was greatly improved. That is, all facets of the system appeared to be a "unified whole" rather than unrelated pieces that were combined at the last minute. The user interfaces had consistent rules of discourse throughout. This we attribute primarily to the prototype, but we believe the different systems used for the reviews reinforced this idea. We believe team members cooperated on the development of the user interface prototype, integrated the pieces early, and then modified them to improve consistency. In previous years integration was done too late to allow these improvements.

We mentioned in section 5.1 that the students were better able to judge the project scope. On many projects though, the students actually implemented *more* than they originally thought possible. It appeared this was

[6]For example, one early project required a carriage return following each field when entering a date, i.e. *mm⟨cr⟩dd⟨cr⟩yy⟨cr⟩*. All students recognized that the carriage returns should be eliminated.

partly due to better project control. The *students* attributed it to having the user interface prototype working early; it served as scaffolding and made testing much easier.

It is interesting to note that since we have made these changes, we find we must use pre-change projects for class evaluation. The deficiencies in the documentation and user interfaces are no longer as obvious as before.

5.5 Analysis of Results

One of our colleagues suggested that perhaps we were giving post-change students more attention and direction than their predecessors. We had an (accidental) opportunity to evaluate this effect. In the most recent class project, the customer for the project volunteered to meet with the teams regularly to provide direction. Two of the four teams met with him weekly; the other two teams never met with him (other than during two in-class sessions that all students attended.) If these effects were the result of receiving more attention and direction, one would expect better results from the two teams that met regularly with their customer; however, there were only minor differences in the results. The documentation was not affected. The user interfaces of the two "supervised" groups had a few minor features to make data entry easier, but the other groups had as many other features that improved usability (that the customer had not thought of.) The customer liked the other features and said "all projects were good, and he wished that he could combine some features from each of them rather than selecting just one." During the last week of the semester, we were surprised to discover that there had been differences in supervision; we had not noticed a difference in earlier deliverables, nor could the grader identify from the products which of the groups had closer supervision.

As we mentioned earlier, Boehm reported several positive effects of prototyping in software engineering courses[4]. Our method of prototyping in this class is rather different from his method. In Boehm's experiments, the prototype is used in lieu of a specification for the systems — no prose specification is written or delivered. In our classes, the prototype was part of the specification process; written specifications of the system were still required.

Boehm's paper concluded that the systems developed from a prototype took fewer staff-hours and provided better function to the user, but (on inspection) seemed not as maintainable. The systems constructed by our students seemed to us to be at least as maintainable as the systems built before prototyping.

Building and experimenting with a prototype is a process of developing an exact understanding of what the system is to do. This is the important part of specifying a system in any case, and in those functions which are difficult to describe formally — as are human interfaces — a prototype may be the most effective way in which to do so.

But once this understanding is achieved, it is still necessary to *organize* this information. Prototyping with an intervening requirements-description and design step allows this information to be drawn together and organized. Systems developed without this intervening step are likely to have an *ad hoc* organization with little conceptual integrity — and this leads to systems which are hard to understand and therefore hard to maintain.

6 Discussion and Conclusions

The paper describes a limited experience with the addition of prototyping and reviews of similar projects, along with more deliverables, in an introductory software engineering course. This experience was not a properly controlled experiment, but the effects we observed are so dramatic that we feel they indicate that the addition of prototyping and reviews can have very good effects.

Boehm's experiment replaced a written specification with prototyping, while our experiment added prototyping as part of the process by which specifications are derived. We conclude that combining prototyping with specifying results in better specifications with greater conceptual integrity. Our approach advocates first writing specifications for the system architecture in the form of a preliminary user manual, then implementing the prototype, and finally revising both the software and the user manual to incorporate improvements. Developers do not spend too much time specifying since the prototype deadline is imminent, but they do have a unified plan before starting the prototype.

Since much of the prototype code is in the final product, we could also consider these steps as increments in an incremental build approach. On the other hand, we specifically instructed the students to consider the prototype code as disposable, to be used in their final product only if it fit their other goals of maintainability and clarity. Our experience yields additional support for the usefulness of this approach to prototyping.

We conclude that adding reviews of other's documentation in a context in which realistic evaluation is encouraged — that is, in a situation where the people involved have no particular relationship with the other project — improves the quality of the documentation those students write. Our conclusion is that this is due to the students having an example of "what not to do." We conclude that these examples are at least as effective as examples of what they should do; these examples are also easier to find.

We conclude that adding more frequent deliverables and human interface prototypes has a good effect on student projects in general. In particular, we feel the dramatic improvement in human interfaces was the result of the addition of prototypes; prototypes were the only addition to the project assignment that followed the preliminary specification. As we noted above, we had a chance to observe a subsection of a human interface that was *not* included in a prototype even after we added prototyping to the general assignment, and observed that this subsection was consistently of lower quality. Thus we feel that prototyping and adaptive design are very helpful (especially for novices) when designing human interfaces.

We do not feel that these conclusions apply to introductory software engineering courses alone.

The method we have used in *Program Design and Construction* can easily be adapted to industrial training. A training program that began with reviews of already-finished projects would have two good effects: first, it would help assimilate the students into the corporate culture; second — and perhaps more important — it provides experience in software engineering in a sheltered "hot-house" environment. Our class experiences strongly suggest that reviewing systems provides the students with many of the benefits of experience by exposing them to the successes and failures of others.

Designing and prototyping human interfaces for complex systems would be an especially useful addition to such a training program. Human interfaces are among the hardest parts of a system to design, and as we have noted, are one of the areas of design which most benefits from experience. We have seen that this kind of experience comes at great cost on the job: the delay between design and realization of a human interface in a system may be years. By adding prototyping in projects of reasonable size, the students have the opportunity to develop and experiment with a number of designs (their own, and those of systems chosen for review) in a short time.

The course we describe has certain limitations, most being the result of the limited time available in the semester. In a two-semester course we could include certain things which are simply not possible in the time we have: an assignment in maintenance that requires changing an existing student system; project presentations, which we gave up when we made the changes described here; and a deeper exploration of testing and of various different methodologies. We would also like to give some time to the concepts and use of separate compilation, which is not easy to do with our current undergraduate programming environment. But we are happy on the whole with the course as it now stands; we feel that after completing *Program Design and Construction* our students have developed useful skills that will ease the transition into the industrial world.

References

[1] Anderson, D. E. "Software Engineering: an Art Searching for Scientific Recognition?" *Software Engineering Education*, Anthony I. Wasserman and Peter Freeman, eds., Springer-Verlag, New York NY, 1976.

[2] Basili, V. and A. J. Turner, "Iterative Enhancement: A Practical Technique for Software Development," *IEEE Transactions on Software Engineering*, Vol. 1, no. 4, pp. 390-396, December 1975.

[3] Bickerstaff, Douglas D., Jr. "The Evolution of a Project-Oriented Course in Software Development", SIGCSE Vol 17 No. 1 1985.

[4] Boehm, Barry W., Terence E. Gray, and Thomas Seewaldt. "Prototyping vs. Specifying: a Multi-Project Experiment", *IEEE Transactions on Software Engineering*, Vol. SE-10, no. 3, pp. 290-302.

[5] Brooks, Frederick P., Jr. *The Mythical Man-Month*, Addison-Wesley Publishing Inc., Reading, MA, 1975.

[6] Busenberg, Stavros N., and Wing C. Tam. "An Academic Program Providing Realistic Training in Software Engineering", CACM Vol. 22 No. 6, pp. 341–345, June 1979.

[7] Curtis, Bill. "Fifteen Years of Psychology in Software Engineering: Individual Differences and Cognitive Science," *Proceedings of the 7th International Conference on Software Engineering*, pp. 97–106, IEEE Computer Society, New York NY 1984.

[8] Fairley, Richard E., Nancy Martin, "Software Engineering Programs at Wang Institute," *Proceedings of the ACM National Conference*, pp. 240–250, ACM New York, 1983.

[9] Freedman, Daniel P., Gerald M. Weinberg. *Handbook of Walkthroughs, Inspections, and Technical Reviews* Third Edition, Little Brown and Company (Inc.), 1982.

[10] Henry, Sallie. *A Project-Oriented Course in Software Engineering* SIGCSE Bulletin Vol 15 No. 1 February 1983.

[11] Horning, James J. "The Software Project as a Serious Game," *Software Engineering Education*, Anthony I. Wasserman and Peter Freeman, eds., Springer-Verlag, New York NY, 1976.

[12] Horning, James J., D. B. Wortman. "Software Hut: A Computer Program Engineering Project in the Form of a Game," *IEEE Transaction on Software Engineering*, Vol. SE-3, no. 4, July 1977.

[13] Woodward, Martin R., Keith C. Mander. "On Software Engineering Education: Experiences with the Software Hut Game", *IEEE Transactions on Education*, Vol. E-25, no. 1, pp. 10–14, February 1982.

[14] Kernighan, Brian, P.J. Plauger. *The Elements of Programming Style*, Second Edition, McGraw-Hill Book Company, New York 1978.

[15] Kernighan, Brian, P.J. Plauger. *Software Tools*, Addison-Wesley Publishing Co., Reading MA, 1976.

[16] Mills, Harlan D. "Software Engineering Education", *Proceedings of the IEEE*, Vol. 68, No. 9, pp. 1158–1162, September 1980.

[17] Sommerville, Ian. "Software Engineering — an Educational Challenge", *Information Processing 83*, R.E.A. Mason (ed.), Elsevier Science Publishers B.V. (North-Holland) pp. 193–197, 1983.

[18] Page-Jones, Meilir. *The Practical Guide to Structured Systems Design*, Yourdon Press, New York NY, 1980.

[19] Persig, Robert. *Zen and the Art of Motorcycle Maintenance*, pp. 198–203, Corgi Press, London, 1979.

[20] Smith, Connie U. "Experience with Tools for Software Performance Engineering," *Modelling Techniques and Tools for Performance Analysis 85*, pp. 29–40, Elsevier Science Publishers, New York 1986.

[21] Woodfield, Scott N., James S. Collofello, and Patricia M. Collofello. *Some Insights and Experiences in Teaching Team Project Courses* SIGCSE Vol. 15, No. 1, February 1983.

[22] Wood-Harper, A. T., D. J. Flynn. "Action Learning for Teaching Information Systems", *The Computer Journal*, Vol. 26, No. 1, pp. 79-82, 1983.

A Project Assignment

This is the text of one project-review assignment we have given.

A.1 Assignment

There are two system packages on reserve in the Engineering Library. You have been assigned to evaluate them. For each package, you should do the following:

1. Get the documentation and the diskettes.

2. Familiarize yourself with the system functions, and procedures for using the system.

3. Locate a PC and test each package.

4. Prepare a report containing the following information:

   - A brief summary of each package's capabilities.

   - At least *five* good features of each user interface.

   - At least *five* features of each interface that could be improved to make it more "user friendly."

   - At least *five* things you wish had been in the documentation.

There are a few ground rules:

This is to be a two-person team project.

There are a limited number of copies of each package. Try to maximize sharing. *DO NOT* put off the usage part of the evaluation until the last minute. Also, be careful with the packages' software — it *is* possible to clobber the floppies if you are not. This will slow both you and others down.

B An Example CPS155 "Wish List"

For this term project, one of the authors (Martin) acted as the customer for the class. This is the project wish-list, with only slight editorial changes.

B.1 Introduction

In addition to the work I do at Duke, I do a certain amount of consulting. I would like to have a way to automate some of the awful things the IRS call on me to do, and I would also like to take care of some of the home and office chores that pile up.

Besides the simple bookkeeping, I am not very good at keeping the figures straight or doing some of the things that need to be done — like balancing my checkbook. So I would like a system that will take over some of that work for me.

What I need is a system that I can run every so often to take the information I have been keeping, file it, and be prepared to figure out the answers I need.

B.2 Wish List

These are the functions I would like to have:

1. Record bills as they come in.

2. Record the amounts of checks I receive.

3. Record the amounts of checks I write (preferably for both my business account and my personal account. Also, I might want to add my wife's checking account into the system at some time. Also the house account we use for expenses connected to our house, and investment accounts, like money-market accounts.)

4. Keep track of the regular bills, and tell me what I have to expect to pay in a month.

5. Keep track of my regular income, and use this along with the item above to tell me if I am going to be broke this month.

6. Keep track of expenses I can allocate to clients, so they can be billed back to the clients.

7. Let me record hours spent for my various clients or working for the department, so I can bill for them.

8. Sometimes, someone wants me to do a job, and I can't say for certain if I have enough time to finish it before its due date. Let me have the system figure this out for me.

9. Make up bills for my clients.

10. Sometimes I know my client can't pay as much this month as I should really charge: for a good client, I will sometimes spread my charges over a number of months. Let me review billings before they are sent, so I can make this sort of arrangement if needed.

11. I often have to make long-distance phone calls that should be charged to clients. Let me record these calls and keep track of their costs. (Ideally, I would like to do this without having to get time-and-charges from the operator, since that is usually more expensive than a regular DDD call.)

12. When I work for my consulting clients, I need to keep track of both the hours worked and what I was doing.

13. Make the user interface as easy to use as possible: otherwise, I probably will just put off doing the work with the system.

14. Remember that I will probably not be using this system every day. Make the system easy to learn, and suit it to occasional users.

15. We keep a calendar in which we write the following things:

- What bills we should get in the month.
- What day to expect these bills.
- What day these bills will be due (which is often but not always about 30 days after they come in.)
- What day to mail these bills on to make sure they get in on time.
- How much each bill will be.
- When we can expect to get paid.
- Whether or not the amount of money coming in will be enough to cover the bills we have (remember this depends not just on the sums, but on the time relationships between the bills and the paychecks.)

16. Remind me of things I need to do, like send flowers for anniversaries or turn in a report.

17. At the end of each quarter, I must send the IRS money to cover my tax witholdings for that quarter. How much should I send, and where do I send it?

18. Besides the usual monthly bills, there are some bills (water bills) that come every two months, some that come every quarter, and some that come every six months. Remember these for me too.

19. My wife gets paid every two weeks, I am paid weekly by Duke and monthly by my consulting customers. Every three months, we get a stock dividend.

Producing Software Using Tools in a Workstation Environment

Mark Sherman
Robert L. Drysdale III

Information Technology Center
Carnegie-Mellon University
Pittsburgh, PA 15213

and

Department of Mathematics and Computer Science
Dartmouth College
Hanover, NH 03755

Abstract

We discuss how we taught students to build and use translation, interpretive, editing and monitoring tools in an undergraduate software engineering course. Students used these tools on low-cost workstations (Macintoshes) to build large, group projects. The students' projects used all available features of workstation environments, including graphics, windows, fonts, mice, networks and sound generators. We found that 1) the use of tools increased student productivity, 2) a shift in data structure and algorithm topics is needed to cover material relevant for workstation environments, 3) new topics in system design are required for a workstation environment, 4) traditional material can be easily illustrated with a workstation environment and 5) students enjoyed being able to manipulate the advanced features of workstations in their work, which in turn increased their motivation for and concentration on the course material.

I. Introduction

Dartmouth College has continually reformulated its undergraduate software engineering course to give students experience with designing advanced systems using modern architectures. Our course is oriented towards the technical aspects of building a large system rather than the managerial aspects, and as such, tries to incorporate the principles and applications of current technologies and trends.

One recent decision was to emphasize the construction of systems using tools in a workstation-oriented environment. Our decision was based on two beliefs about the nature of future software systems. First, construction of large systems will be done by the integration of many pieces, each possibly built in a different way. Many pieces will not be programmed in the traditional sense but will be developed through the use of tools, specified via "very high level languages" or simply taken off the shelf. Second, workstations provide a richer and more sophisticated set of facilities than conventional computers. For example, workstations usually provide substantial graphics facilities (both vector and bit-mapped), network facilities, sound facilities and pointing devices, e.g., a mouse. Although no single facility is unique to workstations, for example, networks existed before widespread deployment of workstations and not all workstations are on a network, the combination of features affects the kinds of decisions that are needed when building a large system.

We believe that we have succeeded in teaching our students how to build and use tools, how to build systems out of pieces developed in heterogenous ways, and how to exploit the features of a workstation environment. The resulting systems are straightforward to build, easy to use and accomplish their intended functions. Through this article, we wish to share our experience with the novel aspects of our course.

We start with a general discussion of our course. We use section 3 to describe some workstation features that students used. In section 4, we elaborate on some of the tool and system building technologies that we used. The next section contains a discussion of the program organizations we taught students. In section 6, we briefly list the kinds of computer-user interactions that we covered in class. Section 7 discusses how we shifted our traditional presentation of data structures to accomodate workstation environments. Our experiences with the revised course are given in section 8. We present our conclusions in section 9.

II. General Outline of Course

Our course is officially titled *Programming System Design and Development.* We give a series of lectures on system specification and design, project team organization, project construction, and data structure selection and evaluation. Weekly homework assignments illustrate how the principles discussed that week in lecture can be applied in a specific situation. During the latter half of the ten week course, students design and build a project. Our intention is to provide students the opportunity to synthesize and apply the material they learned to a real system. To assist students with selecting a project, we occasionally circulate "requests for proposals" to the general faculty for appropriate projects. Students may select a project from this list or may choose one of their own (subject to our approval on scope and feasibility). About one third of the projects are selected from the returned suggestions. Either the faculty member who made the project request or one of the course instructors serves as the target user who must be satisfied.

Our course is required for all majors in computer science, and a number of nonmajors take the course as well. The prerequisite is a course covering programming and an introduction to computer science. We typically have 25 students per section, most of whom are sophmores. Four sections of the course are offered each year.

III. Substantial Architectural Features

Students use Apple Macintoshes [Williams83, Apple86] in a variety of configurations in our class. The Macintosh provides many of the sophisticated facilities associated with workstations: graphics, sound synthesizers, networks and a pointing device. We chose the Macintosh over alternatives, such as a Sun workstation, because the Macintosh is relatively inexpensive. In this section, we wish to describe the available facilities to give a feeling of the breadth of possibilities. In later sections, we illustrate how each facility was used as a teaching medium in the course.

The Macintosh provides a bit-mapped display along with a substantial graphics library (Quickdraw). These facilities allowed students to write programs that produced charts, pictures, graphs and other visual results in addition to the typical text and numeric outputs. Further, the conventional graphics features of the Macintosh provide a basis for several other libraries that manipulate higher-level graphics. Such higher-level facilities, such as fonts, windows and menus, provide a basis for sophisticated user interfaces.

A second facility provided by the Macintosh is a sound generator. The generator can be used to produce simple tones or a free-form wave. Like the graphics facilities, the sound generator has an additional layer of software that permits higher-level interactions, such as a speech synthesizer.

Like most workstations, the Macintosh provides network software for both point-to-point and broadcast communication. The machines used by the students in our course were connected together on an AppleTalk network, as were a laser printer and a file (disk) server. Thus students had the opportunity to use network services, to create new network services and to write distributed applications.

A fifth facility is an analog pointing device, i.e., a mouse. In combination with the graphics facilities, a mouse allows for several kinds of user input that are unavailable with conventional terminals.

The students also worked with several implementations of the Macintosh architecture. The Macintoshes provided to the students had differing amounts of memory, secondary storage and screen size. Slightly different releases of software were also used. The Macintoshes produced output for several kinds of printers and could get information from several kinds of pointing devices.

The combination of these facilities provides a large space of alternative methods of computer-user interaction and an immense amount of available software for system development. Therefore the facilities allow a student to experience the need to *engineer* a reasonable system instead of building every piece from scratch. One key to manipulating the vast array of possibilities is the use of tools for specifying and manipulating higher level abstractions that are used by a working system. Without tools, students could only begin to use small subsets of the features. In the next section, we discuss some of the tools used and built by our students.

IV. Use of Tools

Our course placed a heavy emphasis on the use of tools to speed the development process and to aid the maintenance process. We acquired a large set of commercial tools for use by the students, built several more, and taught several techniques for building tools so that students could augment our facilities. Students used two kinds of tools, general-purpose tools and application-dependent tools. The general-purpose tools include a text editor, compiler (TML Pascal), interpreter (MacPascal), linker and low-level debugger. If we had been able to acquire them, we would have had several additional system development tools, such as a source-level debugger for the compiled code, a syntax-directed editor and a source control system. Most of the basic system development tools are well known and students had previous exposure to them in an earlier class.

Although programs like compilers really are tools that increase productivity, most students did not view these programs as tools that aided them in their work. Their view was simply that Pascal was the language of the machine; one used the editor/compiler to run one's program. When they wrote a Pascal program, the Pascal code was a running part of the final system. They resisted the idea of building programs that were not part of the final system -- anything a program could do they could do as well, they thought, by hand. To overcome this resistance, we had the students use a variety of application-specific tools, we instructed them on how to build other kinds of tools, and ultimately, we made them build a tool for a homework assignment.

We emphasized four general classes of tools: interpreters, translators, editors and monitors. The taxonomy is our own. One could separate tools into those that are used by a human (e.g., a text editor) versus those that are used by a program (e.g., a window manager). Our taxaonomy is intended to describe function rather than method of application, since we feel that an implementation of the same tool can vary from system to system. Although we do not believe that the space of possible programming aids sharply breaks into these four categories, it was a convenient way to discuss and illustrate a variety of tools. Below, we describe each class of tool and give examples of some application-specific tools that we had students use.

Interpreters

We described an interpreter tool as one that took a specification of an activity and used that specification to perform the desired action. We did not require the specifications to be free-format text, but allowed specifications to be given as templates and encoded descriptions (such as integers). The three most used interpreters were the window manager, the dialog manager and Quickdraw picture interpreter. The window manager [Apple86] can accept the template of a window and perform the necessary manipulations of the template to provide the desired window. The dialog manager [Apple86] provides a stylized way of collecting input from the user. Like the window manager, a template describes how information should be presented to the user and what inputs from the user are acceptable. A Quickdraw picture is a specification that encodes a picture that can be scaled, translated and displayed [Jernigan85]. Naturally, we covered conventional interpreters as well, and students built a simple interpretive calculator as one of their assignments.

Translators

We described a translator as a program that takes a description of an object or activity and converts it into another description of that object or activity. The latter description might be run directly on the machine, it could be given to another translator for further conversion or it could be interpreted.

Students used two translators. One, a program provided by Apple called *RMaker*, translates a textual description of Macintosh resources into a binary form [Hertzfeld86]. Most of the resources are templates to be used by various interpreters, such as a window template described above. A second system is called *Thunderscan* which is a video digitizer and image manipulator [Thunderware86]. The system can perform two kinds of translation. First, it can take a picture drawn on a piece of paper and translate it (via hardware) into its own special representation that it can later interpret for display. Second, the system can translate from its own representation to a form usable by other Macintosh software, such as the picture interpreter mentioned above.

Editors

We described an editor as a program that manipulates the description of an object or activity without changing the description language. The students were already familiar with a text editor for manipulating their program text. Because the Macintosh has more than text facilities, there naturally exist editors for more than text. Students used four additional editors during the course.

Three related editors were *REdit, ResEdit* and *Dialog Creator.* All three programs are similar in that they allow the programmer to manipulate objects such as windows and dialogs as those objects would appear on the screen. When editing a window description, for example, the window is displayed on the screen. To change where the window should appear, the programmer repositions the window on the screen using the mouse. When the editing is finished, the current state of the window description is stored. The first two editors alter the binary template (Macintosh resource) that can be directly interpreted by the appropriate Macintosh manager. The last editor manipulates the textual template that can be translated by RMaker.

A fourth editor was developed by one of the course staff [Grosz85], and was used to edit simple songs using an interface that resembles a piano keyboard. One could create, edit and save songs built with this editor, and later have a program play them by giving the saved description to the sound facility in the Macintosh.

Monitors

We described monitors as programs that control or describe the concurrent operation of a system. Many students had experience with debuggers, either the low-level kind used for assembly language programming or with a source-level debugger used in an interpreter, and therefore understood the basic idea of a monitor. Thus students felt comfortable using other monitors that provided information about the correct operation of their system. For example, students who built distributed systems on the network used the network spy program to observe how parts of their system were communicating. Similarly, we had a program that could record and playback user interactions in a system along with a real-time clock. Students used this system to measure the speed of alternative implementations as seen by the end-user.

However, students were less comfortable with the idea of using a monitor tool as a part of their final system. Because most projects could be cast as one large application, students did not view a monitor as a part of the final application. But monitors can be used to coordinate several separate programs into a unified system. To let students experiment with "coordinating" monitors, we gave them two examples: *Switcher* [Towner86] and *Guided Tour Builder* [Seropian85, Clark86].

The switcher program is a poor-man's multitasking system. It allows several programs to be running at the same time in the Macintosh (although only one can use the screen, mouse and keyboard at a time). Thus one can have a word processor, a terminal emulator and a drawing program running at the same time. To use it effectively as a systems building tool, one must be able to write several cooperating programs. One project group used this tool to integrate graphical input, text input and examination creation. They wanted to build a system that allowed both text and graphics to be attached to examination questions, but they did not want to rebuild complete text and graphics editors. So they built the question editor and, via switcher, combined it with a drawing program and a word processor. Thus they produced a reasonably high quality system with only moderate investments of time.

A second monitor program was the guided tour builder. Guided Tours are collections of programs, documents (files) and a monitor program (called the Tour Guide) that can record and playback sessions of user interactions. The intention behind the software is to provide an inexpensive teaching aid -- one provides a guided tour showing how to use the system. Only one project produced a guided tour of their system, but as mentioned before, other projects used the same piece of software for other purposes, namely recording and analyzing user actions.

V. Use of System Organizations

Because future systems will be built out of small parts, whether hand crafted or generated by tools, a system needs an overall structure for defining what the pieces are and how they should fit together. Because the workstation facility provides so many pieces from which to choose, the need to pick an appropriate system organization is acute. Therefore, we discussed several system organizations that could be used: some conventional, some unconventional.

Many of the conventional organization and refinement technqiues that apply to the construction of conventional systems, such as step-wise refinement, top-down design, and layers of abstraction, apply as well to the construction of systems that use tools in a workstation environment. However, the use of workstation facilities greatly increases the number of examples of standard techniques to which students have direct experience. Consider two examples: data abstraction and layered abstractions.

Students frequently are unconvinced about the utility or application of data abstraction since the usual examples are simple and transparent. Typically, one uses stacks, sets, queues, lists or deques to illustrate an object and operations on those objects. Unfortunately, the notion of information hiding is frequently lost because the same examples are immediately used to illustrate pointers or similar implementation techniques. Further, a list is usually a minor part of an entire system. Thus the students do not really appreciate the value of information hiding, nor how the idea can be applied beyond the textbook data structures. However, most workstation systems provide a large number of data abstractions for use by the students. For example, the Macintosh provides windows, dialogs, fonts, menus and a variety of graphics objects. These objects are more substantial and obviously useful in a system than a stack of integers. Further, most students do not know how the window system is implemented, and so must take the specification at face value. They experience the leap of faith that data abstraction requires. As a result, students appreciate the value of data abstraction and begin to design their systems using the same ideas.

A second example of how workstation facilities illustrate conventional concept concerns layered abstraction. Especially when using languages that do not support Smalltalk-80-like objects, a discussion of layered abstractions is an exercise of unspecified virtual machines and interpreters. However, most workstation environments provide two natural sequences of abstraction layers: graphics and networks. Using the Macintosh as our example, the most abstract facility used by students are dialogs, which are built on windows, which are built on graphics ports, which are built on bitmaps which are built on bit images. Another example is provided by the layering of network protocols: the unreliable, local datagram is used by the unreliable internetwork datagram, which is used by the reliable datagram which is used by the reliable byte stream. At each layer, one can clearly identify those details that are being suppressed and those higher-level functions that are being provided. Because students use different layers for different purposes, they get tangible evidence for the usefulness of layered abstractions.

The use of a workstation system allowed us to teach alternative program organizations besides the conventional ones. Two additional topics that we discussed were event-driven programs and window management [Apple86, Rosenthal86]. We feel that these topics need to be understood to develop future systems but are difficult to teach using non-workstation facilities.

When we discuss event-driven programs, we refer to programs that are able to receive any of a number of circumstances and process it accordingly. By contrast, most programs reach a point during their execution where they prompt the user (or file system) for some input and block awaiting an answer. An event-driven program makes no demands on the user -- it waits for some asynchronous action and then processes the event as required. The events could be hardware related: a key on the keyboard being pressed or released, a timer expiring, a packet arriving on the network or a mouse moving. The events could be software related: a window has been uncovered or some task is ready to run. In either case, the event is passed to an appropriate handler for that event and the program as a whole waits for the next event.

The techniques needed for window management are also new to most students, especially where multiple, overlapping windows are the primary output medium for a program. The key difference is one of history. Typical programs on time-sharing systems send a stream of information to a terminal (or file), and once written, never need to reproduce that stream. On the other hand, a window contains a variety of information that represents the state of the program. It is a status display rather than a stream and needs to be reproduced when needed. There are three common times when the information in a window must be regenerated: when a window is reopened after being closed, when a window is uncovered and when a window is scrolled. When a window is opened, it is usually blank, but many applications allow windows to be temporarily closed and reopened as a way for the user to control screen clutter. The display that used to be in the window must now be regenerated. Similarly when an obscuring window is removed, the underlying window usually needs its contents redrawn. Finally, when a window is scrolled, the contents that were previously hidden must now be drawn. (We assume that the window system does not keep a complete bitmap image of the window's contents.)

To provide the information about how to draw a window, the programmer must keep a data structure with enough information to regenerate the display. This is a foreign concept to many students. They are used to immediate output, even in a graphics system. For example, when their program needs to draw a rectangle, they draw a rectangle in the appropriate window. In a single window (or graphics terminal) system, this approach works fine. But in a workstation environment, the corresponding window could be partially or completely obscured and the need to display the rectangle postponed until far in the future. Therefore students are encourged to separate the manipulation of the program's state (or internal data structures) from the actual drawing on the screen. We teach an approach where programs just manipulate their internal state as necessary, and provide a way to display that internal state at any time. To return to our previous example, drawing a rectangle is a three step process. First one changes the internal data structure to reflect the fact a rectangle has been added to the window. Second, one informs the window system that certain parts of the window no longer show the correct image. Third, on demand, the window is redrawn with the new rectangle. Note that the rectangle might not be drawn right away if the window is covered. Naturally, there are many optimizations that can be made, but such optimizations should be introduced only after the general model is comprehended by the students.

VI. User interaction issues

Our collection of workstation features opens the door for many possible methods of computer-user interactions. Typically, courses in software engineering assume a simple conversational interface with users via a line-at-a-time interface or via a screen-terminal menu system. Because of their graphics, window facilities, dedicated processing, and picking devices, a workstation provides many more modes of interaction. We believe many should be covered in modern software engineering courses so that designers of systems can provide alternatives to users. We cover nine different approaches in our course.

We do not make the claim that we are exhaustive, only that we provide a wide exposure to possible techniques.

Our nine approaches are simple line-at-a-time text, forms, button picks, menu selection, command keys, static pictures, animation, sound effects and speech synthesis. Because students are familar with the simple read-a-line, write-a-line types of interactions, we spend little time discussing those in class. The fill-in-the-form approach is familar to the students who used the Macintosh since the commonly-used dialog facility implements the technique directly. Because several tools mentioned above allowed easy creation of forms, students could trivially provide such facilities in their systems. We force the students to experiment with "button picks" by requiring an assignment to use that technique: the available commands for the program are to be displayed in rectangles on the screen and executed when the mouse is pressed in that rectangle. Similarly, we require students to experiment with various kinds of graphical output in some assignments. In assignment four, for example, students have to show the area of the screen they are examining while they perform a search for a particular point. An example done in class demonstrates how animation can be implemented and the value it has in illustrating the changing state of a system [Glenn85]. Through the use of commercial software, we also illustrate how sound effects can provide qualitative effects [Fenton84, Fenton85] and finally, we show how speech synthesis can be used as an alternative to text for simple messages [Apple85].

A related, but different topic concerns how input information can be obtained. Again, the facilities provided by a workstation environment enlarge the design space of system interactions. We mentioned how a pointing device can be used to pick an object on the screen, but a pointing device can provide other information. For example, one can record the trace followed by a mouse in free-hand drawing, or use derivatives of mouse movement for velocity or acceleration information. One common application of this information is to control the speed of scrolling in a text window.

When we designed the latest revision of our course, we had in mind several other kinds of user interactions, including the use of touch screens, track balls, tablets and head-mounted infra-red tracking devices. Unfortunately, we could not acquire all of the necessary hardware and software in time for use in our course. We do believe that students should be exposed to these technologies so they can better experiment with new kinds of user interfaces.

Because we wanted our students to evaluate alternative user interfaces, we needed some aids to allow students to design alternatives and let users see them. We already mentioned one tool that students applied, the *Guided Tour Builder.* Students were able to record the actions of users working on a certain set of tasks and see how much time was spent trying to reach a goal. A second tool was a screen layout package that allowed students to easily simulate screens of proposed systems without building the interface. A collection of alternatives could be shown to prospective users for their evaluation and feedback. Students used these tools when writing their project specifications. Several students told us that having this kind of precise image of the system helped them design and build it.

VII. Supporting Data Structure and Algorithms

Students in our course are taught advanced data structures as they apply to building large systems. In the prerequisite course, students learn about stacks, binary trees, sorting and other elementary data structures and algorithms. When shifting to a workstation environment, a subtle shift of the important algorithms and data structures takes place, from special cases to more general cases. For example, one shift was from one dimensional to two dimensional techniques. One dimensional techniques work well if a single datum is presented and processed with a list of other data. For example, in keeping a dictionary of keywords, one takes a single word and compares it against other single words in the dictionary. However, the graphics and window facilities of a workstation use rectangles and points rather than a single datum in a list. For example, to see which point is closest to another point, one needs to search a two dimensional space. Thus we presented the multidimensional version of binary search trees: KD trees (K dimensional). Similarly, we expanded the interpretation of boolean connectives (e.g., and, or, xor) into interpretations on a display, relaxed the assumption of reliable interprocess communication, and showed how iteration can be unrolled onto a collection machines by spliting and joining.

We feel this is an important shift that must take place in courses that teach student useful algorithms and approaches for designing systems in and for a workstation environment. Just as certain topics in operating systems have changed in response to technology (for example, drum scheduling methods are not emphasized but huge memory allocation techniques are discussed), so too the focus and examples used for teaching the underlying algorithms and data structures must include discussions of bitmap models of computations, operations on a plane instead of a line, and distribution of function.

VIII. Experiences in the course

This course has been taught nearly twenty times over the last six years, though recently we shifted the emphasis of the course to development of systems on workstation environments with tools. Many of the students' experiences have not changed much from our shift: the course still takes a lot of time, the material is quite technical and the pace is very fast. However, we noticed four aspects of the course that convince us we made a good choice in shifting its focus.

First, students claim to have a lot of fun. As Alan Perlis has noted, a prime motivating factor in computer science is to have fun [Perlis77]. Students clearly enjoyed the ability to use sophisticated graphics, sound generators and the mouse. Thus the students concentrated on what they were doing and, we believe, more efficiently learned what we were presenting.

A second phenomenon we observed is that the students' projects were more aggressive or sophisticated. For example, card game programs were always a popular project, but in the past, one person on such a project was assigned the task of writing the software for displaying cards on a simple graphics terminal. After a lot of effort, an arguably recognizable deck of cards was usually implemented. During our latest offering of the course, a student used a digitizer to read a deck of cards for use in their program. In both the previous version and the current version of the course, students had to design an appropriate interface between the abstract cards and the rest of the system. But in the older version, a lot of manpower was wasted on mastering some very low-level command codes that control our graphics terminals. In the current version, the student was easily able to present a realistic visual presentation for the project in a minimum of time. Thus this student now had additional time to work on other aspects of their system, such as a better algorithm for automated playing. The result: the final system looked better and provided more functionality than equivalent systems in previous years. In general, most projects we saw had more sophisticated user interfaces and performed more complicated tasks.

A third phenomenon was not unexpected: the method and scope of project construction changed substantially. In particular, we saw a marked increase in tool use and generation, and we saw a decline in the total code size of projects.

Since we emphasized the building of systems by reusing existing facilities and applying tools, it came as no surprise that students took this advice to heart. Every tool we were able to find was used by at least one project group. Several project groups built tools of their own. For example, one group built a translator that took a description of a map and countries, and generated the necessary tables for using that world in a strategic game. Another group designed a facility for adding windows of documentation and help to an arbitrary system. A third group built a tool as their project: a sound wave editor. The idea was similar to the music editor we provided, but allowed manipulation and mixing of sounds based on their Fourier representation.

Perhaps a corollary to the increased use of tools and libraries is that projects also required carefully thought-out communication between the pieces. In past years, projects could be patched at the last minute by one part of the system reaching into another part and modifying some data structure that was supposed to be hidden. Since many of the facilities used by students in these projects were truly opaque to the students, the designs of their project had to delineate clearly how various pieces of information were being generated and distributed.

Because of the increased efficiency of system construction, the projects written by the students were substantially smaller than in previous years. A typical project in past offerings of the course required about 200 pages of PL/1 code. Projects using the techniques and facilities in our version of the course required about 50 pages of source code (mostly Pascal, but some of the code was specifications given to tools).

Our fourth observation concerns a phenomenon that did not happen. When we shifted the emphasis of the course, we were concerned that the general algorithms would be too abstract to grasp at the pace we were presenting them. Normally when one shifts from one dimension to n dimensions, one loses a certain fraction of students. However, we thought that the algorithms from computational geometry were crucial for effectively using the newer technologies. We are happy to report that we saw no substanative difference on the students' part in learning the different methods.

IX. Conclusions

We feel that learning how to build systems using tools in an environment that supports good quality graphics, networks, sound and a pointing device is a necessary part of good undergraduate computer science education. We are pleased that we were able to present this material by modifying our current software engineering course. The students who took the revised version of the course enjoyed the material that was covered and were able to apply it when building their own projects.

We believe that the design and offering of a course like ours is a straightforward task, but one that requires a conscious decision on the part of the relevant faculty. We believe that most universities do not have the infrastructure or campus-wide facilites to support a workstation-based project course. Appropriate faculty members need to specify and acquire new facilities and software for a course like ours to succeed. We do not know of any good substitute: the only effective way for students to appreciate the design and use of workstation environments is to use and build them. Providing a course such as ours requires extensive equipment (we had a 2:1 ratio of students to Macintoshes, 3:20 ratio of Imagewriters to Macintoshes, 1:20 ratio of LaserWriters to Macintoshes, and 1:15 ratio of file servers to Macintoshes), a capable corse staff (we had a 8:1 ratio of students to course assistants) and large library of software (a partial list of our materials is given in appendix II).

X. Acknowledgements

Our course has been evolving to its current state over the last two years, with its final jump onto a workstation (the Macintosh) in the winter 86 offering of the course. People who have taught the course in the recent past have helped in this evolution and include Paul Chew, Tom Kurtz, David Levine and Vivian Sewelson. To make this kind of course work successfully, one needs a large complement of qualified staff. Our able undergraduate course staff, Rob Collins, Larry Gallagher, Jerry Godes, Ed Grosz, Robert Munafo, and John Scott, created a number of the tools, libraries and demonstrations that students used in the course. Funding for the development of the Macintosh version of the course was provided in part by the Interuniversity Consortium for Educational Computing and in part from the Keck Foundation. Apple provided some of our equipment through a grant to Dartmouth College and assisted us in getting several tools they developed. Naturally, the students on whom *we* experimented deserve our thanks for being cheerful participants.

XI. References

[Apple85] Apple Computer Co, Inc., "MacInTalk 1.1: The Macintosh Speech Synthesizer," *May 1985 Software Supplement Update*, (Apple Computer Company, Inc.,) June 13, 1985.

[Apple86] Apple Computer Company, Inc., *Inside Macintosh*, Addison-Wesley, Reading, MA., 1985, 1986, Volumes 1-4.

[Clark86] Cary Clark, *Tour Tools*, Apple Computer Company, Inc., February, 1986.

[Hertzfeld86] Andy Hertzfeld, *Macintosh Resource Compiler*, Version 2.0, (Apple Computer Company, Inc.,) July 10, 1986.

[Fenton84] Jay Fenton, Marc A. Canter, Mark S. Pierce, *MusicWorks*, MacroMind, Inc., Chicago, IL., 1984.

[Fenton85] Jay Fenton, Mark Pierce, Marc Canter, Dan Sadowski, *VideoWorks*, MacroMind, Inc., Chicago, IL., 1985.

[Glenn85] John Glenn, *Binary Trees*, Technical Report DCS-TR86-127, Department of Mathematics and Computer Science, Dartmouth College, Hanover, NH. 03755,

September 21, 1985.

[Grosz85] Ed Grosz, *Music Editor*, Technical Report DCS-TR86-114, Department of Mathematics and Computer Science, Dartmouth College, Hanover, NH. 03755, January, 1986.

[Jernigan85] Ginger Jernigan, "Quickdraw's Internal Picture Definition," *Macintosh Technical Note*, Number 21, (Apple Computer Co., Inc.,) Cupertino, CA. April 24, 1985.

[Perlis77] Alan Perlis, "The Keynote Speech," *Perspectives on Computer Science: From the 10th Anniversity Symposium at the Computer Science Department, Carnegie-Mellon University*, Academic Press, 1977, Anita Jones, Editor, p. 1-6.

[Rosenthal86] David S. H. Rosenthal, *Window System Implementations: Denver Usenix Course Notes*, Tutorial Materials, Usenix Technical Conference, Denver, CO. January 15-17, 1986.

[Seropian85] Hasmig Seropian, *A Guide to Making Guided Tours*, (Apple Computer Company,) Inc., March 22, 1985.

[Thunderware86] Thunderware, Inc., Thunderscan Digitizer for the Macintosh, Orinda, CA.

[Towner86] George Towner, "Inside Switcher," *The Software Supplement*, (Apple Computer Company, Inc.,) Vol. I, Issue 3, June 27, 1986.

[Williams84] Gregg Williams, "The Apple Macintosh Computer," *Byte Magazine*, February, 1984, p. 30-53.

Appendix I - Course Assignments

This appendix gives a brief description of each weekly programming assignment. All of our assignments, examinations, handouts, sample solutions, example programs and supporting libraries are available on five double-sided 3 1/2 inch disks (HFS format) from the authors and from the technical report librarian (see Appendix II).

Assignment 1: Learning Pascal

The first assignment introduced the students the Pascal development system they were using. Students wrote 10 exercises requiring them to read a file, parse a sequence of characters into words, do some array manipulation and perform some simple graphics operations. Each exercise required about 10 lines of Pascal.

Assignment 2: Calculator

The second assignment required the students to implement a desk calculator (infix notation with parentheses and precendence). Students used a line-at-a-time interface provided by the Pascal run-time system to read a line of text, which they parsed and evaluated using a recursive descent design. Students were given routines to convert strings to numbers.

Assignment 3: Linked Lists

The third assignment required the students to build a linked-list package that supported appending a datum to the end of list, inserting a datum in the front of list and deleting a datum from anywhere in the list. All operations but delete-an-element were done with a line-at-a-time interface. Deletion was done by displaying the list as a series of boxes and lines, and selecting the box to be deleted with the mouse. The changed list was then displayed. Students were given the Pascal code for getting access to the graphics facilities.

Assignment 4: KD-Trees

The fourth assignment required students to create and manipulate a 2-dimensional binary-search tree. A user could place points on the screen using a mouse. The points were added to the 2D tree as they were entered. The user could draw a rectangle with the mouse and the program was to perform a search of the 2D tree to locate the points within the rectangle. The state of the search was to be recorded by drawing lines enclosing the parts of the screen that were being searched. Program commands were denoted by selecting a button with the mouse from a palette on the side of the screen. Students were provided a program outline that provided the palette and command dispatch.

Assignment 5: Window Manipulation

The fifth assignment required students to create a simple window application. The program provided two windows that could be overlapped and resized. Each window could display a collection of rectangles that the user drew. When a user drew a rectangle in a window, the program had to track the mouse and provide visual feedback about the rectangle. The pattern of the rectangle could be changed through the use of a dialog box. The windows could be reshaped and moved about the screen. Desk accessories had to be supported. Menu items for clearing the current window and deleting a rectangle in the window also had to be supported. Students were provided with a skeleton program that provided the all of the standard interface to the operating system and toolbox, recognized and dispatched all events, and maintained a single window with a gray background.

Assignment 6: Graphs

The sixth assignment required students to use a provided map, place nodes at cities, bridges and other landmarks, connect the landmarks with edges, determine the shortest path between two selected nodes, and display the result by highlighting the shortest route. All interactions with the program were with a mouse. Modes were selected by using a command palette (like in assignment 4); modes were indicated by changing the cursor shape. Students were provided with a skeleton program similar to the one in assignment 4.

Assignment 7: Enhanced Dialog Manager

The seventh assignment required students to build another toolbox manager called the Enhanced Dialog Manager. The new manager would provide easier access dialogs by automatically managing radio buttons and check boxes as well as editable text fields. Students were given several programs that used the new manager for testing.

Assignment 8: Backtracking

Students wrote a Pascal program to generate a solution to the 8-queens problem using recursion and backtracking. No special user interface was specified. This assignment was intended to be simple to allow students time to work on their projects.

Appendix II - Course Materials

We used two kinds of course materials: printed materials such as articles and book, and machine materials, such as programs, libraries and files. We describe each collection below.

II.1 Printed Materials

Most of our printed materials are readily available.

Aho, Hopcroft, and Ullman, *Data Structures and Algorithms*, Addison-Wesley, 1983.

Jon Bentley, "Multidimensional Binary Search Treees Used for Associative Searching", *CACM* , vol. 18, no. 9, Sept. 1975, pp. 509-517.

J. C. Enos and R. L. van Tilburg, "Software Design," *Computer*, Vol. 14, No. 2, February 1981, p. 61-83.

Jerome Friedman and Jon Bentley, "An Algorithm for Finding Best Matches in Logarithmic Expected Time", *ACM Trans. on Mahtematical Software*, Vol. 3, No. 3, Sept. 1977, pp. 209-226.

Leo Guibas and Robert Sedgewick, "A Dichromatic Framework for Balanced Trees", *19th Symp. on the Foundations of Computer Science*, Oct. 1978, pp. 8-21.

Butler Lampson, "Hints for Computer System Design," *IEEE Software*, January 1984, p. 11-28.

David L. Parnas, "On the Criteria to be in Decomposing Systems into Modules", *CACM*, Vol. 15, No. 12, December 1972, p. 1053-1058.

Robert Sedgewick, *Algorithms*, Addison-Wesley, 1983.

N. Wirth, "Program Development by Stepwise Refinement," *CACM*, Vol. 14, No. 4, April 1971, p. 221-227.

II.2 Machine Materials

Our collection of materials for the Macintosh came from a variety of sources, including commercial software houses, user groups, commercial data services, various computer-network mailing lists, visitors and companies. Many of our sources no longer distribute their materials. Therefore, we have provided a list of materials by the most common name we could determine, and have indicated where we think one can obtain these materials as of this writing (see key code at the bottom of the list).

Program Name	Description	Where to Get
3-D Edit	3-D object editor	BCS (49)
ADEdit	Alert/Dialog editor	EDUCOMP (222)
Animation Toolkit	Animation frame editor	AAS
Asm	68000 Assembler	Apple (part of MDS)
ASCII chart	(obvious)	BCS (Dev 2)
Atlas	Picture database manager	Kiewit
Base to Base	Hex/Octal/Dec converter	BCS (DA 4)
Bases	Hex/Octal/Dec converter	BCS (Dev 2)
Binary Trees	Binary tree illustrator	Kiewit
Boot Configure	Configuration editor	BCS (Util 3)
ConCode	68000 programming aid	BCS (DA 2)
Copy Disk	4 swap disk copier	Apple
CopyIIMac	General disk copier	Central Point
Coroutine package	Pascal library	Math & CS
Crash Saver	Crash recovery library	BCS (Util 4)
Cursor Designer	Cursor editor	BCS (Dev 3)
DeRsrc	Resource decompiler	BCS (Dev 1)
Dialog Creator	Dialog editor	BCS (24)
Didler	Text file manipulator	BCS (Util 2)
DisAsm	68000 disassembler	BCS (Dev 4)
Disk Info	File manipulation	BCS (DA 1)
DiskUtil	File manipulation	BCS (Util 2)
Dissbits	Graphics package	Kiewit
Drill	CAI interpreter	Kiewit
Dynamo	Animation constructor	BCS (Games 6)
EDialog	Dialog manager replacement	Math & CS
Edit	Text editor	BCS (Util 2)
Event Tutor	Demonstrates event handling	Kiewit
Exception Edit	Speech macro editor	BCS (Dev 2)
Extras	File manipulator	BCS (DA 1)
FEdit	Disk editor	BCS (Util 3)
Fat Bits DA	Mouse tracker	BCS (10)
File Tools	File manipulation	BCS (DA 4)
Font Blaster	Animation-to-font converter	AAS
Font/DA Mover	Resource installer	BCS (DA 1)
Font Display	Font illustrator	BCS (29)
Font Doubler	Font manipulator	BCS (Util 2)
Font Editor	(obvious)	EDUCOMP (42)
Font Librarian	Font manipulation	BCS (Font 3)
Graph Illustrator	Example graph program	Math & CS
Guided Tour Constructor	Demonstration creator	APDA, Mac. Journaling & Guided Tour
Help unit	Library package	Kiewit
Hex Calc	Hexadecimal calculator	BCS (Dev 2)
Icon Editor	(obvious)	EDUCOMP (223)
Icon Maker	Icon editor	BCS (DA 2)
IEdit	Icon editor	BCS (Util 2)
KD Tree Illustrator	Example KD program	Math & CS

KNet	Network stream library	Kiewit
Launch	Program execution tool	BCS (DA 3)
Localizer	Resource editor	BCS (Util 2)
Logic	Example object program	Math & CS
Link	68000 Linker	TML
MacDB	68000 assembly debugger	Apple
MacDraw	Object-oriented graphics editor	Apple
Macintalk	Speech synthesizer	BCS (Dev 2)
Macintosh Toolbox	Libraries	Part of Macintosh Computer
MacPaint	Bit-oriented graphics editor	Apple
MacWrite	Word processor	Apple
Macsbug	68000 assembly debugger	Apple
MacTools	File and disk manipulator	Central Point
Mass Initializer	Disk utility	BCS (Util 2)
Maze	Example network program	Math & CS
Menu Edit	Menu resource editor	BCS (Util 2)
MEdit	Macro text edtior	BCS (Util 6)
Menu Clock	Timer	BCS (Util 3)
MiniFinder	Command shell	APDA (Macintosh System Software for Developers)
Mousometer DA	Mouse measurements	BCS (10)
Multi-scrap	Graphics filer	BCS (DA 1)
Music	Sound editor	Math & CS
New Key Caps	Keyboard mapping tool	BCS (DA 1)
Other...	Desk Accessory test tool	BCS (DA 2)
Overlay	Graphics integrator	Kiewit
Paint Mover	Graphics integrator	BCS (Graphics 2)
Painter's Helper	Object-oriented graphics editors	(BCS 15)
Pascal	Pascal compiler	TML
Peek	Network packet spy	BCS (Dev 1)
Poke	Network packet injector	BCS (Dev 1)
PurgeIcons	Desktop file utility	BCS (Util 6)
RamStart	Memory utility	BCS (Util 1)
RasNix	Command shell	BCS (DA 2)
Read Lisa	Disk utility	BCS (Util 2)
REdit	Resource editor	BCS (Util 1)
ResEdit	Resource editor	BCS (Util 1)
Resume	Crash recovery library	Math & CS
RMaker	Resource compiler	TML
RMover	Resource manipulator	EDUCOMP (222)
Screen Layout	Screen design package	Kiewit
ScrnEdit	Configuration editor	BCS (Dev 1)
Set File	File utility	EDUCOMP (222)
SetFileInfo	File utility	BCS (Util 5)
Skel	Example program	Kiewit
Screen Maker	Graphics translator	BCS (Dev 1)
Skip Finder	Command utility	BCS (DA 1)
Slide Show	Graphics demonstrator	BCS (Graphics 3)

Speech Lab	Speech editor	BCS (Dev 2)
Squeeze File	Text manipulator	BCS (12)
StrCvt	String conversion library	Math & CS
Switcher	Command shell	APDA (Switcher Developer's Kit)
Tasking package	Programming library	Math & CS
Thunderscan	Video digitizer	Thunderware
Uriah Heap	Memory monitor	BCS (10)
Utils	File manipulation	BCS (DA 4)
VideoWorks	Animation editor	Macro Mind
XL/Serve	File (disk) server	InfoSphere

Keys:

APDA (name of the product followed in parentheses):

Apple Programmer's and Developer's Association
290 SW 43rd St.
Renton, WA 98055

AAS (name of program is the name of the product):

Ann Arbor Softworks, Inc.
308 1/2 S. State Street
Ann Arbor, MI 48104

Apple (name of program is name of product, except for debuggers and assembler, which are part of the MDS product):

Local Apple dealer

BCS (the name or number of the disk followed in parentheses):

Boston Computer Society
BCS-Mac 1
Center Plaza
Boston, MA 02108

Central Point (the product is CopyIIMac, which includes MacTools):

Central Point Software, Inc.
9700 SW Capitol Highway, #100
Portland, OR 97219

EDUCOMP (the number of the disk followed in parentheses):

EDUCOMP
2431 Oxford Avenue

Cardiff, CA 92007

InfoSphere (product was XL/Serve, updated now to MacServer):

InfoSphere
4730 SW Macadam Avenue
Portland, OR 97201

Kiewit:

Courseware Development Group
Kiewit Computation Center
Dartmouth College
Hanover, NH 03755

Macro Mind (name of program is the name of the product):

Hayden Software
600 Suffolk St.
Lowell, MA 01854

Math & CS:

Technical Report Librarian
Department of Mathematics and Computer Science
Bradley Hall
Dartmouth College
Hanover, NH 03755

Thunderware (name of the product is Thunderscan):

Thunderware, Inc.
21 Orinda Way
Orinda, CA 94563

TML (name of the product is MacLanguage Series Pascal):

TML Systems
PO Box 361626
Melbourne, FL 32936

A First Course in Computer Science: Mathematical Principles for Software Engineering

H.D. Mills, V.R. Basili, J.D. Gannon, R.G. Hamlet

Abstract

The discipline of software engineering has transferred the common-sense methods of good programming and management to large software projects. It has been less successful in acquiring a solid theoretical foundation for these methods. We have developed an introductory computer science course, much as calculus is a basic course for mathematics and the physical sciences, concerned primarily with theoretical foundations and methodology rather than apprenticeship through applications. This paper describes the principles taught in the course and gives part of a small example illustrating them.

Authors' addresses: Drs. Mills, Basili and Gannon, Department of Computer Science, University of Maryland, College Park, MD 20742; Dr. Hamlet, Department of Computer Science, Oregon Graduate Center, Beaverton, OR 97006. Research of Drs. Basili, Gannon, and Hamlet was partially supported by the Air Force Office of Scientific Research under contract F49620-83-K-0018.

1. Introduction

Software engineering is the name given to the art of programming (and surrounding activities) when art is replaced by a discipline using well defined methods and formal skills. During the last two decades, a great deal has been learned about good programming practices: structured programming [Dijkstra 72], [Wirth 71], information hiding [Parnas 72], data abstraction [Hoare 72]. The spread of this knowledge beyond expert programmers can be credited to software engineering. The transfer of knowledge to routinely trained technicians, the codification of common sense, and the introduction of management control are certainly functions proper to engineering, and software engineering has accomplished these things for programming.

The success and growth of any engineering discipline has never rested entirely on organization of trial-and-error knowledge, however. Application of deep theoretical results is also required to progress beyond the initial success that spreading common sense brings. The role of the engineer is sometimes to invent the required theory; more often it is only to apply an idea from a more abstract discipline to a problem the engineer understands. Furthermore, the application must meet a requirement peculiar to engineering: it must be in a form that can be used to solve practical problems.

The work of [Naur 66], [Floyd 67], [Hoare 69], [Hoare 71], [Mills 72], and [Dijkstra 76] comprise a theoretical framework for programming based on mathematical foundations. This work continues to inspire advances in formal specification, programming language semantics, and program verification. Because our understandings of these topics are quite recent, people regard them as subjects fit for graduate classes. Our belief is that the time has come for computer science students to start out with these ideas, not end up with them. At their roots, these deep simplicities can be formulated in classical mathematics, discrete mathematics. This is material that undergraduates can learn easily, because understanding it does not require a wide context of programming experience. And by teaching objective principles of syntax, semantics, correctness, and abstraction, we arm the student with solution patterns so that program design becomes a familiar problem-solving process with new-found mental tools in a new domain.

We have developed a two-semester, eight-credit basic course for computer science [Mills 86] much as calculus is a basic course for mathematics and the physical sciences, concerned primarily with methodology rather than subject matter. In fact we introduce a "program calculus" that deals with the functions computed by programs. Just as for ordinary calculus, there are two main problems in the program calculus. First, given a program, find its meaning (its derivative), and second, given a meaning, find a program with that meaning (its integral). This ability to derive functions from programs in the program calculus is of great value in computer science and engineering as well. First, it permits a mathematical treatment of program correctness, namely whether a program specifies correct behavior of the computer for every possible input. But even more importantly, it leads to a systematic design discipline for writing programs that are correct to begin with, and which do not require debugging.

2. Topics

In this section we outline the major principles covered in the course. They represent a synthesis of an integrated theoretical foundation for programming. They can be characterized by a mathematical formalism, simplified to the level necessary for the problem at hand, covering a large piece of the programming domain in a consistent way and permitting the process to be scaled up to deal with larger problems.

The simplicity and generality of the formalism permit the material to be taught to beginning college students. It forms a basis for their understanding of the programming process and product, and acts acts as a mechanism for communication.

2.1. Programming Methods

During the first semester, programs are developed using stepwise refinement, while in the following semester systems of programs and data are constructed using data abstraction. Programming has two distinct phases:

(1) *Design* —thinking out what the program should be in order to solve the problem.

(2) *Development* —putting the program text in execution form.

In the stepwise refinement of a program, text designed to carry out a task in more detail is called a ***design part***. A design part may itself contain more detailed task descriptions (in the form of comments) to be carried out by additional design parts. The result of the design phase will be a hierarchy of design parts which collectively solve the problem at hand. Each design part is a statement typically with 5 to 15 lines, perhaps with two to four tasks left to be designed at the next level.

After the program has been entirely refined into a hierarchy of design parts, the translation into machine-readable form begins. A sequence of executable programs, each reflecting a larger part of the design, can facilitate orderly and systematic translation into Pascal. Each program in such a sequence is called a *development program*. Development programs are accumulations of design parts, which grow in size until the entire design has been turned into Pascal. Each development program is defined so that it can be executed and tested to verify correct translation at each step of development.

In practice, the translation of a design into Pascal can be done in chunks larger than one design step, typically 15 to 50 lines at a time. That is, each successive development program is created by combining a few more design parts with the last tested development program. In order to verify correct execution, it may be necessary to include temporary WRITE statements to create visible output.

In data abstraction a system of procedures and data declarations are defined in such a way that these procedures provide the only means of access to this data. Since users of the abstract data access it through procedures rather than directly, their programs are unaffected by changes to the abstraction's data declarations (which might be made to improve functionality or efficiency).

During program integration, a top-down, functional approach to testing was adopted, integrating higher level design parts of the program a step at a time during the development. Abstract data types represent potentially reusable modules, and should be tested independently of their uses in programs. To test an abstract type functionally, the legal combinations of the operations should be applied to representative abstract objects (e.g., an empty object, a full object, etc.).

2.2. Programming Languages

Programs are written in three increasingly complex subsets of the programming language Pascal. In the simplest subset, CF Pascal, there is but a single kind of data (characters) and a single data structure (files of characters that can only be accessed sequentially). Restricting our attention to so simple a language emphasizes program design rather than programming language features. The character and file serve as the ruler and compass of programming.

Small, but classical, problems lead to interesting program design problems in CF Pascal. For example, breaking a text file into lines of a given length (given by the length of a file of blanks -- there are no integers!) takes quite a bit of programming. It simply cannot be done without a working sense of abstraction. Sorting and reversing files in $n \times \ln(n)$ rates are also challenges. And motivations are not hard to develop. Consider adding two hundred-digit numbers in different files and writing the result to a third file. The input files are read left to right, but digits must be added and carries computed from right to left. It is easy to see that the problem requires one pass over the two files for the add and carry logic but three file reverses. With an n^2 reverse, the solution will execute in $n + 3n^2$ time where it only takes n for what seemed the hard part. So reducing $n + 3n^2$ to $n + 3n \times \ln(n)$ by finding an $n \times \ln(n)$ reverse becomes an interesting problem. CF Pascal is a teacher's helper in a real sense -- an austere tool that rewards good programs in a visible way.

The second language subset, D Pascal, permits the same functions to be created with smaller and simpler programs than is possible in CF Pascal. D Pascal also contains language features (type declarations and records) needed to implement data abstractions. Prior data abstractions become concrete language features in D Pascal. The final Pascal subset, O Pascal, introduces powerful control structures and data types to help optimize programs by providing random access to statements and data. O Pascal language features such as goto statements, arrays and pointers should be used only when they are needed for algorithm optimization and when their functions can be determined and verified at least informally.

2.3. Mathematical Basis

The entire mathematical basis for the program calculus rests on just five discrete mathematical structures of character data: strings, lists, sets, relations, and functions. These five structures are not only sufficient to deal with program correctness and program design, but also admit treatment at various levels of formality with a mixture of English and mathematical notation.

Some sets are more easily and precisely described in English than in mathematics, but are sets no less because of the mode of their description. Many programming problems are better stated in English than mathematics, and we need to be able to treat questions of program correctness and design independent of the mode of description. It may seem surprising at first to discover that a mathematical discipline is possible for dealing with English as well as mathematical descriptions, but we will see that is so.

The mathematical property we study in programs is their effect on computer behavior. The functional behavior of a program that sorts strings will be independent of the programming language and the exact form of the program itself. That is, understanding a program as a mathematical object is understanding the functional behavior it induces in a computer.

An execution state is a relation or function whose domain is the identifiers of a program and whose range is the values attached to those identifiers. The semantic meaning of a program will be a mathematical relation or function, a set of ordered pairs that defines a correspondence between one state (the inputs) and another state (the outputs). The meaning of a program will be taken to be the transformation implied by this correspondence; certain outputs are paired with certain inputs because given any such input, the program instructs the Pascal machine to compute that output.

2.4. Meanings of Program Parts

It is convenient to have a notation for meaning relations or functions, and we adopt a convention similar to one used by Kleene: the meaning function corresponding to a program object is denoted by a box around that object. The meaning of an identifier V1 in execution state s is simply the value of V1 in the state.

$$\boxed{\text{V1}}\,(s) = s(\text{V1}).$$

Values of literal character expressions do not depend on the execution state at all. The meaning of an assignment statement is a function from execution states to execution states. The intuitive meaning of the assignment statement as an execution state transformation is that the identifier on the left side ceases to be associated with an old value, and becomes associated with a new value, obtained from the expression on the right side.

$$\boxed{\text{V1 := V2}} = \{<r,s> : \text{s is the same as r except that } \boxed{\text{V1}}\,(s) = \boxed{\text{V2}}\,(r)\}$$

The meaning of an IF statement with Boolean condition b and statements t and e is:

$$\boxed{\text{IF b THEN t ELSE e}} = \{<s, \boxed{t}\, s>: \boxed{b}\,(s)\} \cup \{<s, \boxed{e}\, s>: \neg \boxed{b}\,(r)\}.$$

The first set contains all state pairs in which the condition b holds, and the second set those pairs in which the condition does not hold. There is no evaluation of these sets in some order. They simply contain or fail to contain certain pairs.

The meaning of a WHILE statement with Boolean condition b and statement d is defined recursively:

$$\boxed{\text{WHILE b DO d}} = \boxed{\text{IF b THEN BEGIN d; WHILE b DO d END}}$$

The right side of this definition can be rewritten as the composition of two functions:

$$\boxed{\text{WHILE b DO d}} = \boxed{\text{IF b THEN d}} \; o \; \boxed{\text{WHILE b DO d}}$$

Although this definition does not permit us to derive the meaning of a WHILE statement, it is a recurrence equation whose solutions (the meaning of the WHILE statement) can be checked by substitution. A function f is the meaning of a WHILE statement if it satisfies three conditions:

1. domain(f) = domain($\boxed{\text{WHILE b DO d}}$)

2. ($\boxed{\text{NOT (b)}} \rightarrow f$) = ($\boxed{\text{NOT (b)}} \rightarrow I$)

3. f = | IF b THEN d | *o* f

2.5. Determining the Meaning of Program Parts

A *concurrent assignment* summarizes the effects of several statements, mapping one state to another. A list of variables is written on the left side of the assignment operator, and a list of expressions on the right side, these two lists being of equal length. The expressions, computed all at the same time, are the values taken by the corresponding variables.

Conditional assignments can be defined recursively by the following rules:

(1) A concurrent assignment is a conditional assignment.

(2) If b is a Boolean condition and c is a conditional assignment, then $(b \rightarrow c)$ is a conditional assignment.

(3) If b is a Boolean condition and c, d are conditional assignments, then $(b \rightarrow c) \mid d$ is a conditional assignment.

The meaning of a conditional assignment of the form

$$(b_1 \rightarrow c_1) \mid (b_2 \rightarrow c_2) \mid \ldots \mid (b_n \rightarrow c_n)$$

for any number of Boolean conditions (b_i) and conditional assignments (c_i) is the meaning of first conditional assignment, say c_i, such that

(1) all Boolean conditions before b_i have value false in state s, and

(2) Boolean condition b_i has value true.

The meaning is undefined for state s if any of the following occur:

(1) none of the Boolean conditions evaluates to true in s;

(2) the first Boolean expression that does not evaluate to false is undefined for s;

(3) the conditional assignment selected by the Boolean expression is undefined for s.

For example, the meaning of the statement

```
BEGIN
  V1 := V2;
  V2 := V3;
  IF V1 < V2 THEN V3 := V1
  ELSE V3 := V2
END
```

can be expressed as the conditional assignment:

$$(V2 < V3 \rightarrow V1, V2, V3 := V2, V3, V2) \mid (V2 \geq V3 \rightarrow V1, V2 := V2, V3)$$

Symbolic execution is a method of tracing the values of variables through execution using only their names, not particular values. A *trace table* is a systematic method for carrying out symbolic execution. Like an execution table, a trace table has a row for each statement that is executed, and a column for each variable that might acquire a new value during execution. However, the "values" in a trace table are expressions, and the rows keep track of current expressions in terms of the original, starting expressions. A *conditional trace table* is a trace table with an additional column of conditions, namely those required for the assignments in the table to take place. For example, the BEGIN statement above will use one of two sequences of assignments, namely

V1 := V2; V2 := V3; V3 := V1 or V1 := V2; V2 := V3; V3 := V2

depending on whether the THEN or ELSE part of the IF statement is selected during execution. Each sequence can be handled by a separate conditional trace table. The table for the case when the THEN part is executed is shown below.

Statement	Condition	V1	V2	V3
V1 := V2		V2		
V2 := V3			V3	
IF V1 < V2	V2 < V3			
THEN V3 := V1				V2

Each row of the table shows values in terms of the original variables. The condition V2<V3 in the third row is the value of V1<V2, because at that point V1 has the original value of V2, and V2 has the original value of V3 (obtained from the row above). The net result for this conditional trace table is a conditional assignment

$$(V2 < V3 \rightarrow V1, V2, V3 := V2, V3, V2)$$

2.6. Program Correctness

Given a program specification relation r and a program P, we say that P is correct with respect to r if, for every member x of the domain of r (an instance of input data), P produces some member of the range of r which corresponds to x. That is, for each input x, P produces result y such that $<x,y> \in r$. What P does to input data not in the domain of r is not important since r should define all behavior important to the problem solver. A simplifying condition for demonstrating that a program satisfies its specification is given in the following theorem, called the Correctness Theorem.

Correctness Theorem. Program P is correct with respect to specification relation r if and only if

$$\text{domain}(r \cap \boxed{P}) = \text{domain}(r).$$

Note, if r is a function, f, then the following Corollary holds.

Correctness Corollary. Program P is correct with respect to specification function f if and only if

$$f \cap P = f.$$

2.7. Data Abstraction Correctness

The essence of data abstraction is captured by a diagram showing the relationship between the *concrete* world objects manipulated by Pascal procedures (e.g., P), and the *abstract* world objects the programmer manipulates with abstract operations (e.g., m) to achieve a solution. A mapping must be defined between the values of concrete objects and the values of the corresponding abstract objects. We call this the *representation mapping,* and for any type denote it A_{type}. By convention, for objects common to the concrete and abstract worlds, the representation mapping is identity. Then for any concrete state, the representation mapping can be extended to map the state to an abstract state.

$$\begin{array}{ccc} \{\text{abstract states}\} & \xrightarrow{\quad m \quad} & \{\text{abstract states}\} \\ \uparrow A_{type} & & \uparrow A_{type} \\ \{\text{concrete states}\} & \xrightarrow{\quad \boxed{P} \quad} & \{\text{concrete states}\} \end{array}$$

Intuitively, an implementation is correct if its data objects are manipulated in such a way that the abstract objects to which they correspond, appear to be transformed according to the abstract operations. That is, correct implementation uses the concrete procedures and data, but in a way that mirrors the abstraction. To decide if this property holds, we show that the diagram commutes.

$$A_{type} \circ m \subseteq \boxed{P} \circ A_{type}$$

Of course abstract operations like m do not really exist except in users' minds. Pascal procedures implementing abstract operations are written with two sets of comments labelled "abs:" and "con:." The "abs:" comments are added to modules so that users, those in the abstract world, need not examine the code (or even the "con:" comments that document it). The "abs" comments replace the abstract operations in demonstrations that diagrams commute. If the implementation has been done properly, the abstract comment can be believed, and used in proofs at the abstract level.

3. A Partial Example

In this section, we carry out a partial example that illustrates both stepwise refinement and data abstraction. The example, to print a list of prime numbers, is large enough to require the judicious use of formal proofs, embedded in a broader activity of informal reasoning and design. In particular, the example illustrates that stepwise refinement permits the control of details, step by step, in both data and operations. For example, a subspecification need only treat variables that are used in the design it supports and not the variables that are introduced for its implementation. This property of deferring details while maintaining absolute control of the design is essential in scaling up methods of "programming in the small" to "programming in the large." Both stepwise refinement and data abstraction are vital in this scaling up exercise. Stepwise refinement permits the deferring of details directly as a program is elaborated a program part at a time. Data abstraction permits the deferring of details indirectly, but with even more power, by increasing the capability of the underlying design primitives from Pascal to whatever data abstractions (written in Pascal) are needed.

3.1. Developing and Proving the Solution

In this section, we illustrate a typical design step in a small problem. Given a number $N \geq 2$, we want to print the list of prime numbers P such that $2 \leq P \leq N$. One solution is printing the only even prime number and constructing a list containing the remaining prime numbers which are all odd. By dividing the next odd number by each of the list elements, we can determine if the number is prime. (In this example, the list is denoted by angle brackets and list concatenation by ampersand (&).)

```
Design Part 1
{print the list of prime numbers P such that 2≤P≤ N}

WRITELN(2);
EmptyList(Primes);
NextP := 3;
{Primes := Primes & ND(NextP,NextP,N,Primes)};
{print Primes}
```

EmptyList is an operation on abstract objects of type "list of integers" that initializes a list object that contains no elements,

```
PROCEDURE EmptyList(VAR L: List);
  { abs: L := < > }
```

ND(L,C,U,Primes) is a list of numbers between C and U that are not divisible by any of the numbers in Primes nor any of the numbers between L and C-2. It is defined as follows:

$$ND(L,C,U,Primes) = \begin{cases} \langle C{:}\forall P \in (Primes\&ND(L,L,C-2,Primes)),\ (C \bmod P) \neq 0 \rangle \\ \qquad \&\ ND(L,C+2,U,Primes) \text{ if } L \leq C \leq U \\ \langle\rangle \text{ if } L \geq C > U \end{cases}$$

We can use a trace table to calculate the value of Primes that is printed at the end of Design Part 1.

Condition	Primes	NextP
	<>	
		3
	<> & ND(3,3,N,<>)	

Assuming $N \geq 3$ and expanding ND's definition, we obtain

```
ND(3,3,N,<>)   = (<3:∀ P∈(<>&ND(3,3,1,<>)), (3 mod P)≠ 0>
                  & ND(3,5,N,<>))
               = <3> & (<5:∀ P∈(<>&ND(3,3,3,<>)), (5 mod P)≠ 0>
                  & ND(3,7,N,<>))
               = <3> & (<5:∀ P∈(<>&<3>)), (5 mod P)≠ 0>
                  & ND(3,7,N,<>))
```

When an odd number i is considered for membership in ND, it is divided by the odd numbers between 3 and $i-2$ that are already members of ND.

The fourth step of Design Part 1 can be refined into the following design part.

```
Design Part 1.1
{Primes := Primes & ND(NextP,NextP,N,Primes)}

WHILE NextP <= N
DO
  BEGIN
    {IsPrime := (for all members P of Primes, (NextP mod P) ≠ 0)};
    IF IsPrime THEN Append(Primes,NextP);
    NextP := NextP + 2
  END
```

Append is another operation on list objects that concatenates a singleton list to the end of an existing list.

```
PROCEDURE Append(VAR L: List; Elt: EltType);
  { abs: ( Length(L) < MaxSize → L := L & <Elt> ) |
       ( Length(L) ≥ MaxSize → I ) }
```

If the design is under intellectual control at this point, we need to demonstrate that the WHILE statement above (which we call W) meets its function specification. In order to do this, we first determine f, the meaning of W, and show that it has the three properties listed at the end of Section 2.4.

```
f =   (NextP≤N → Primes := Primes & ND(NextP,NextP,N,Primes) ) |
      (NextP>N → I )
```

f is identical to the comment in Design Part 1.1 because ND(NextP,NextP,N,Primes)=< > when NextP>N. In order to make the verification process easier, we eliminate details introduced by purely local variables (like NextP whose value is not needed after W terminates), and size constraints on objects (like the length of Primes).

The three steps of the proof are:

1. domain(f) = domain([W])

$$\text{domain}(f) = (\text{NextP} \leq \text{N and ND(NextP,NextP,N,Primes) is defined})) \text{ or } (\text{NextP} > \text{N})$$

ND(NextP,NextP,N,Primes) is defined whenever the mod function within it is defined, i.e. if either $0 \notin$ Primes or $0 \notin$ ND(NextP,NextP,N-2,Primes). The second condition could be false only if Primes=$< >$, NextP=0, and NextP$<$(N-2). W terminates immediately if NextP$>$N. If NextP$\leq$N, the body of W is executed, and normal termination occurs if NextP is incremented on each execution of the body of W and if the result of the mod function is defined for all members of Primes on each iteration. The mod function is defined if $0 \notin$ Primes and if 0 is not one of the values of NextP appended to Primes (i.e., Primes=$< >$, NextP=0, and NextP$<$(N-2)).

2. $(\text{NextP} > \text{N} \rightarrow f) = (\text{NextP} > \text{N} \rightarrow \text{I})$

When f's domain is restricted to those states for which the WHILE condition evaluates to false, f is an identity function.

$$\begin{aligned}
&(\text{NextP} > \text{N} \rightarrow f) = \\
&\quad (\text{NextP}>\text{N and NextP}\leq\text{N} \rightarrow \text{Primes} := \text{Primes \& ND(NextP,NextP,N,Primes)}\ ) \mid \\
&\quad (\text{NextP}>\text{N and NextP}>\text{N} \rightarrow \text{I}\ )
\end{aligned}$$

which reduces to

$$((\text{false} \rightarrow \ldots) \mid (\text{NextP}>\text{N} \rightarrow \text{I}\ )) = (\text{NextP}>\text{N} \rightarrow \text{I}\ ),$$

an identity function.

3. Let IF be

```
IF NextP <= N
THEN
  BEGIN
    {IsPrime := (for all members P of Primes, (NextP mod P) ≠ 0)};
    IF IsPrime THEN Append(Primes,NextP);
    NextP := NextP + 2
  END
```

then $\boxed{\text{IF}}$ is

$$\begin{aligned}
&(\text{NextP}\leq\text{N and } (\forall \text{P} \in \text{Primes, (NextP mod P)} \neq 0) \rightarrow \\
&\qquad \text{Primes, NextP} := \text{Primes \& } \langle\text{NextP}\rangle\text{, NextP+2}) \mid \\
&(\text{NextP}\leq\text{N and } \exists \text{P} \in \text{Primes, (NextP mod P)} = 0 \rightarrow \\
&\qquad \text{NextP} := \text{NextP+2}) \mid \\
&(\text{NextP}>\text{N} \rightarrow \text{I}\ )
\end{aligned}$$

We must demonstrate $f = \boxed{\text{IF}} \circ f$. Trace tables provide a convenient way to study the composition, showing the effect of each part of $\boxed{\text{IF}}$ composed with f.

Condition	Primes	NextP
NextP≤N and (∀P∈Primes, (NextP mod P) ≠ 0)	Primes & <NextP>	NextP+2
(NextP+2)≤N	Primes & <NextP> & ND(NextP+2,NextP+2,N, Primes&<NextP>)	

This trace table computes the part function:

$$\text{(NextP+2)} \leq \text{N and } (\forall P \in \text{ Primes, (NextP mod P)} \neq 0) \rightarrow \\ \text{Primes} := \text{Primes } \& <\text{NextP}> \& \text{ ND(NextP+2,NextP+2,N,Primes } \& <\text{NextP}>)$$

We need to show

$$(<\text{NextP}> \& \text{ ND(NextP+2,NextP+2,N,Primes}\&<\text{NextP}>)) = \text{ND(NextP,NextP,N)}$$

in the domain of this part function. Since ND(NextP,NextP,NextP-2,Primes) is < >, when ND(NextP,NextP,N,Primes) is expanded, we obtain

$$\text{ND(NextP,NextP,N,Primes)} = \begin{cases} <\text{NextP}:\forall P\in\text{Primes, (NextP mod P)}\neq 0> \\ \quad \& \text{ ND(NextP,NextP+2,N,Primes) if NextP}\leq\text{NextP}\leq\text{N} \\ <> \text{ if NextP}\geq\text{NextP}>\text{N} \end{cases}$$

Expanding ND(NextP,NextP+2,N,Primes) next, we get

$$\text{ND(NextP,NextP+2,N,Primes)} =$$

$$\begin{cases} <\text{NextP+2}:\forall P\in\text{(Primes\&ND(NextP,NextP,NextP,Primes)), ((NextP+2) mod P)}\neq 0> \\ \quad \& \text{ ND(NextP,NextP+4,N,Primes) if NextP+2}\leq\text{NextP+2}\leq\text{N} \\ <> \text{ if NextP+2}\geq\text{NextP+2}>\text{N} \end{cases}$$

$\text{ND(NextP,NextP,NextP,Primes)} = <\text{NextP}: \forall P\in\text{Primes, (NextP mod P)}\neq 0>$. Thus, where the domain guard of the part function is true, ND(NextP,NextP,N,Primes) is

$$<\text{NextP}> \& <\text{NextP+2}:\forall P\in\text{(Primes\&}<\text{NextP}>\text{), ((NextP+2) mod P)}\neq 0> \\ \& \text{ ND(NextP,NextP+4,N,Primes)}$$

When <NextP> & ND(NextP+2,NextP+2,N,Primes&<NextP>) is expanded in the part of its domain in which NextP+2≤N, we get

$$<\text{NextP}> \& <\text{NextP+2}:\forall P\in\text{(Primes } \& <\text{NextP}>\text{), ((NextP+2) mod P)}\neq 0> \\ \& \text{ ND(NextP+2,NextP+4,N,Primes\&}<\text{NextP}>)$$

These two sequences are identical if

$$\text{ND(NextP,NextP+4,N,Primes)} = \text{ND(NextP+2,NextP+4,N,Primes\&}<\text{NextP}>)$$

Both these terms represent sequences of numbers between NextP+4 and N that are tested to determine if they are divisible by any number in another sequence of numbers. The first term checks candidate numbers against those in Primes, NextP, and NextP+2. The second term uses numbers from Primes&<NextP> and NextP+2. Thus the terms must be identical, and the part function can be rewritten as

$$\text{(NextP+2)} \leq \text{N and } (\forall \text{P} \in \text{Primes, (NextP mod P)} \neq 0) \rightarrow$$
$$\quad \text{Primes := Primes \& ND(NextP,NextP,N,Primes)}$$

The next case resulting from this composition is

Condition	Primes	NextP
NextP≤N and (∀P∈ Primes, (NextP mod P) ≠ 0)	Primes&<NextP>	NextP+2
(NextP+2)>N	Primes & <NextP> & ND(NextP+2,NextP+2,N, Primes&<NextP>)	

This trace table computes the part function:

$$\text{(N-2)} < \text{NextP} \leq \text{N and } (\forall \text{P} \in \text{Primes, (NextP mod P)} \neq 0) \rightarrow$$
$$\quad \text{Primes := Primes \& } \langle \text{NextP} \rangle \text{ \& } \langle\ \rangle$$

In the domain (N-2)<NextP≤N where no member of Primes divides NextP evenly

$$\text{ND(NextP,NextP,N,Primes)} = (\langle \text{NextP} \rangle \text{ \& } \langle\ \rangle)$$

so this part function could be combined with the previous part function to obtain

$$\text{NextP} \leq \text{N and } (\forall \text{P} \in \text{Primes, (NextP mod P)} \neq 0) \rightarrow$$
$$\quad \text{Primes := Primes \& ND(NextP,NextP,N,Primes)}$$

We need to perform four more function compositions to obtain the rest of the function:

$$\text{(NextP} \leq \text{N and } (\exists \text{P} \in \text{Primes, (NextP mod P)} = 0) \rightarrow$$
$$\quad \text{Primes := Primes \& ND(NextP,NextP,N,Primes))} \mid$$
$$\text{(NextP} > \text{N} \rightarrow \text{I)}$$

which, combined with the already computed parts yields a function that is identical to f.

3.2. Verifying the Data Abstraction

In refining the remainder of the loop body, additional operations must be added to the abstract data type so that the values of the elements in the list can be obtained sequentially in the manner in which characters are read from a TEXT file. The abstract type used to represent Primes is "list of integers with a reading pointer." The operations of this type are EmptyList, Append, Head, and Next. EmptyList produces List values. Head and Next are operations that applied repeatedly both carry List objects back to their integer components in the concrete world, and map Lists to Lists in the abstract world. Like RESET, Head(Primes,Trial) assigns Trial the value of the first element in Primes (if Primes is not empty) and the value EndList otherwise. In addition, Primes is prepared for reading, which we indicate by writing the elements in Prime as

<already-read values of Primes> & <to-be-read values of Primes>.

The other operation, Next(Primes,Trial), performs a function like that of the READ statement, assigning the next value to be read in Primes to Trial and advancing the reading pointer. If no more values remain to be read from Primes, Next assigns Trial the value EndList.

A representation for list objects and its representation function must be chosen.

```
TYPE
  EltType = EndList..MAXINT;
  List = RECORD
         Values: ARRAY [1..MaxSize] OF EltType;
         Size, Current: 0..MaxSize
        END;
```

The representation function for List, A_{List} is:

```
{(s,t): t is the same state as s except List(t) =
    <L.Values[1],...,L.Values[L.Current]> & <L.Values[L.Current+1],...,L.Values[L.Size]>
    if 0≤L.Current≤L.Size≤MaxSize, and t contains no members whose first elements are
    L.Values, L.Current, or L.Size}
```

Finally implementations are written for each operation. In the interest of space, only the implementation of Head is given. Each implemented operation comes with two comments describing their function. The users' expectations can be captured by writing comments about the procedure part functions in the abstract state. These comments are labeled "abs:" in the code. Of course, the concrete procedure themselves are concrete-state mappings, and have part functions in that world as usual; these are labeled "con:".

```
PROCEDURE Head(VAR L: List; VAR Result: EltType);
  { abs: (L = <> → Result := EndList) |
       (L = <L1,...,Li-1> & <Li,...,Ln> →
            L, Result := <L1> & <L2,...,Ln>, L1)
    con: (L.Size > 0 → L.Current, Result := 1, L.Values[1]) |
       (L.Size ≤ 0 → L.Current, Result := 1, EndList) }
  BEGIN {Head}
    IF L.Size > 0
    THEN BEGIN L.Current := 1; Result := L.Values[1] END
    ELSE Result := EndList
  END; {Head}
```

The correspondence between the body of Head and its concrete comments is apparent from the meaning of the IF statement. We need to demonstrate

$$A_{List} \circ Head_{abs} \subseteq Head_{con} \circ A_{List}$$

Again, trace tables prove to be a useful tool for computing function compositions.

A_{List} o $Head_{abs}$		
condition	L	Result
0≤L.C≤ L.S≤MaxSize	<L.V[1],...,L.V[L.C]> & <L.V[L.C+1],...,L.V[L.S]>	
<L.V[1],...,L.V[L.C]> & <L.V[L.C+1],...,L.V[L.S]> = <>		EndList

The condition evaluates to true when

<L.V[1],...,L.V[L.C]> = <> and <L.V[L.C+1],...,L.V[L.S]> = <>

Picking L.S and L.C to be 0 achieves this result. Thus the function is

MaxSize ≥ 0 and L.S = 0 and L.C = 0 → L, Result := <>, EndList

A_{List} o $Head_{abs}$		
condition	L	Result
0≤L.C≤ L.S≤MaxSize	<L.V[1],...,L.V[L.C]> & <L.V[L.C+1],...,L.V[L.S]>	
<L.V[1],...,L.V[L.C]> & <L.V[L.C+1],...,L.V[L.S]> = <L1,...,Li-1> & <Li,...,Ln>	<L1> & <L2,...,Ln>	L1

This condition is true when i≥1 (i.e, L.S≥L.C≥1) and L.V[1]=L1, ..., L.V[L.S]=Ln. Thus the function is

(MaxSize≥L.S≥L.C≥1 → L, Result := <L1> & <L2,...,Ln>, L1

The composition A_{List} o $Head_{abs}$ yields

(MaxSize ≥ 0 and L.S = 0 and L.C = 0 → L, Result := <>, EndList) |
(MaxSize≥L.S≥L.C≥1 → L, Result := <L1> & <L2,...,Ln>, L1)

$Head_{con}$ o A_{List}			
condition	L	L.C	Result
L.S>0		1	L.V[1]
0≤1≤ L.S≤MaxSize	.<L.V[1],...,L.V[L.C]> & <L.V[L.C+1],...,L.V[L.S]>		

Thus the function is

MaxSize≥L.S≥1 → L, Result := <L.V[1]> & <L.V[2],...,L.V[L.S]>, L.V[1]

$Head_{con}$ *o* A_{List}			
condition	L	L.C	Result
L.S≤0			EndList
0≤L.C≤ L.S≤MaxSize	<L.V[1],...,L.V[L.C]> & <L.V[L.C+1],...,L.V[L.S]>		

Since the condition requires both L.S≤0 and L.S≥0, it must be the case that L.S=0, L.C=0, and the list

<L.V[1],...,L.V[L.C]> & <L.V[L.C+1],...,L.V[L.S]>

must be empty. Thus the function is

MaxSize ≥ 0 and L.S = 0 and L.C = 0 → L, Result := <>, EndList

The composition $Head_{con}$ *o* A_{List} yields

(MaxSize≥L.S≥1 → L, Result := <L.V[1]> & <L.V[2],...,L.V[L.S]>, L.V[1]) |
(MaxSize ≥ 0 and L.S = 0 and L.C = 0 → L, Result := <>, EndList)

This composition yields the same results as the previous composition, but on a slightly larger domain since it places no restriction on the initial value of L.C.

3.3. Testing The Result

Once the design phase is complete, we switch to the development process. In this stage, abstract data types are tested independently, and design parts are incrementally assembled into execution form and tested. For example, Design Parts 1 and 1.1 in Section 3.1 would be assembled, and later design parts that refine

IsPrime := (for all members P of Primes, (NextP mod P) ≠ 0);

would be replaced by

IsPrime := true;

which permits a development program to be tested (although in this case all odd numbers would be added to Primes). This development program would be tested with various values of N (including at least odd and even values).

To test the data abstraction functionally, we should consider the possible logical sequences of the operations: EmptyList, Append, Head, and Next. For example, to check valid combinations of operations we might:

(1) build a list,

(2) sequence through a list,

(3) go back to the head of the list after partially sequencing through the list (after a Head or a Next),

(4) append an element to the list while sequencing through it (after a Head or a Next),

(5) empty the list after sequencing through or building it.

These operations should be considered with at least three different kinds of list values: an empty list, a partially full list, and a full list (since we have chosen an array implementation). Some other combinations of operations are not legal and are not tested. For example, applying the Next operation to a list without executing the Head operation first will cause an error.

To check that we have covered all cases, we should consider all combinations of operations, noting whether they are legal or illegal combinations and whether the combination appears in the finished program.

Case	Operations	Legality	Used
1	EmptyList;EmptyList	legal	no
2	EmptyList;Append	legal	yes
3	EmptyList;Head	legal	no
4	EmptyList;Next	illegal	no
5	Append;EmptyList	legal	no
6	Append;Append	legal	no
7	Append;Head	legal	yes
8	Append;Next	illegal	no
9	Head;EmptyList	legal	no
10	Head;Append	legal	no
11	Head;Head	legal	no
12	Head;Next	legal	yes
13	Next;EmptyList	legal	no
14	Next;Append	legal	no
15	Next;Head	legal	yes
16	Next;Next	legal	yes

To test the data abstraction properly so that it can be used again, we should at least check the possible combinations of operations listed above on three representative list values: an empty list, a partially full list, and a full list.

Design, analysis and testing provide a three-pronged approach to assuring confidence in the correctness and quality of the developing program. The design formalism assures that the program developed from the functional specification is a correct elaboration of that specification. The ability to perform a formal or informal analysis based upon that design formalism offers the programmer and the reviewer the ability to check for consistency and correctness in a systematic way. Incremental testing of the program permits us to check details normally suppressed in proofs (e.g., range errors), as well as the environmental aspects of executing a "correct" program (e.g., does the Pascal implementation correspond to its formal definition which was used during analysis).

4. Experience With The Course

The course requires new ways of thinking even for experienced computer science educators. The material is deep and quite different from the traditional "first course" in programming. However, the material is no harder for students than traditional introductory courses in other scientific disciplines such as calculus or physics. We have a strong sense of satisfaction teaching this course because it formalizes basic ideas of computer science and provides the student with a solid foundation in the principles of programming.

Because many students learn about computers before they come to the university, they enter with very different computer backgrounds. Those who know a lot about programming, even in Pascal, will not be able to skip this course. It is *not* a course in Pascal programming. The mix of backgrounds in programming and in mathematics causes student expectations and reactions to vary widely. Some are disappointed that they are not writing big, realistic programs. They may think the material is too simple until they are surprised by the real depth in the course. Others are initially overwhelmed because of their lack of background or intimidated by the programming knowledge of classmates. There will always be a few good students who have trouble simply because the course does not live up to their expectations. It is more important than usual to make it clear early what the course is about and what is expected. This motivation should be reinforced at regular intervals.

We find it useful to distinguish between useful *tasks* and useful *skills*. Programming based on the program calculus and mathematical correctness is an unnatural activity that also takes faith and practice to master. In learning to type, it is natural to look at the keys while typing. We know that we should learn to type in a systematic way (that is, without looking at the keys) because it is a better way to type in the long run, even though it is a terrible way to try to type on the first day. We learn not to do something that looks useful initially, but to begin to learn useful skills instead. The improvement of mathematical approaches to programming over what comes naturally can be as dramatic as that of touch typing over hunt-and-peck.

Once they have mastered these ideas, programmers can use the Cleanroom software development method [Currit 86]. The key components to the method are a mathematically-based design method, implementation without unit testing by developers, and a statistically-based testing strategy performed by a third party. This method changes testing and debugging from program development strategies to quality assurance measures. A study of the development of an electronic message system by 15 three-person teams helped demonstrate the feasibility of this approach [Selby 85]. All development teams were allowed 3 to 5 test submissions. Cleanroom developers tended to make all their scheduled deliveries, while the control group members (who used a more standard method) did not. Cleanroom-developed products more completely meet the requirements and had a higher percent of test cases succeed.

5. References

[Currit 86]

P.A. Currit, M. Dyer, and H.D. Mills. Certifying the reliability of software. *IEEE Trans. Soft. Eng* 12, 1, (January 1986), 3-11.

[Dijkstra 72]
E.W. Dijkstra. Notes on structured programming. In *Structured Programming*, Academic Press, New York, (1972), 1-82.

[Dijkstra 76]
E.W. Dijkstra. *A Discipline of Programming*. Prentice-Hall, Englewood Cliffs, N.J., (1976).

[Floyd 66]
R.W. Floyd. Assigning meanings to programs. In Proceedings of the Symposium in Applied Mathematics 19, (J.T. Schwartz ed.), (1967), 19-32.

[Hoare 69]
C.A.R. Hoare. An axiomatic approach to computer programming. *Communications of the ACM* 12, 10, (October 1969), 576-580, 583.

[Hoare 71]
C.A.R. Hoare. Proof of correctness of data abstraction. *Acta Informatica* 1, (1972), 271-281.

[Hoare 72]
C.A.R. Hoare. Notes on data structuring. In *Structured Programming*, Academic Press, New York, (1972), 83-174.

[Mills 72]
H.D. Mills. Mathematical foundations for structured programming. In *Software Productivity*, Little, Brown and Company, Boston, Massachusetts, (1982), 115-178.

[Mills 86]
H.D. Mills, V.R. Basili, J.D. Gannon, and R.G. Hamlet. *Principles of Computer Programming: A Mathematical Approach*. Allyn and Bacon, Boston, (1986).

[Naur 66]
P. Naur. Proof of algorithms by general snapshots. *BIT* 6, (1966), 310-316.

[Parnas 72]
D.L. Parnas. A technique for software module specification with examples. *Communications of the ACM* 15, 5, (May 1972), 330-336.

[Selby 85]
R.W. Selby, V.R. Basili, and F.T. Baker. Cleanroom software development: An empirical evaluation. University of Maryland, Department of Computer Science, Technical Report TR-1415, (February 1985).

[Wirth 71]
N. Wirth. Program development by stepwise refinement. *Communications of the ACM* 14, 4, (April 1971), 221-227.

A SUPPORT TOOL FOR TEACHING COMPUTER PROGRAMMING

Marvin V. Zelkowitz, Bonnie Kowalchack, David Itkin and Laurence Herman

Department of Computer Science
University of Maryland
College Park, Maryland 20742

Abstract

At the University of Maryland, freshmen Computer Science majors are introduced to the process of computer programming through a new course that emphasizes methodology with mathematical formalism and program correctness as fundamental issues. An IBM PC-based environment, called SUPPORT, is being used for this class to enhance the concepts taught as well as to aid program development. This paper briefly describes the course, describes the SUPPORT system, and gives some early data on the use of this tool in the course.

Keywords: Computer programming; Education; Microprocessor; Pascal; Programming environment; Workstation

1. Introduction

The ability to write good programs for a computer is a fundamental concept taught to Computer Science majors. However this is usually accomplished more as an *art* than as a *science*. An instructor gives the student a series of sample programs, and the student soon learns (we hope) to emulate the instructor when new programs need to be written. The instructor supplements this process with a series of heuristics, concepts like structured programming, modular design, information hiding, and test plan development. By the end of the course the good students have learned, in a somewhat informal manner, most of the characteristics of good software design and development.

More formal concepts like program verification and correctness issues have been deemed *graduate school* concepts, and are only talked about in a fuzzy manner at the introductory level. However, correctness is not an add-on feature - a poorly designed program cannot be made "reliable" by adding "verification ideas" later. Reliability must be an early goal, and the student needs to incorporate such ideas *ab initio*, much like programs must be designed top down *ab initio;* one cannot effectively remove "spaghetti code" **gotos** and still expect to have an understandable program.

A further need for such formalisms early is to demonstrate to the student (and to the professional world for that matter) that programming is not easy. While the syntax of a given language is easy to understand (e.g., we are talking about FORTRAN, Pascal and BASIC here, not Ada), the ability to construct a correct program is hard. This leads to the view held by many that almost anybody can learn computer programming, yet these same people often complain about the low quality of the resulting programs. As stated by McCracken, computer science education is much more than teaching programming [McCracken].

This problem had been apparent at the University of Maryland in our pre-1981 set of graduation requirements for Computer Science majors. Previously students needed to pass a calculus sequence as a graduation requirement. We found that many students did adequately in our old freshman programming course, only to flounder during their senior year in both the freshman level calculus course and our own senior level Computer Science courses. It was clear that they were not up to the standards we wished to impose on our graduates.

We have changed this process by now requiring both calculus and the freshman programming courses to be corequisites, and are finding that students having trouble with one usually have trouble with the other. This has been an effective way to warn the student early in his or her college career about potential problems.

Of more importance, we have redesigned the freshman course to more adequately reflect our views of introducing the programming process. This course emphasizes the formalism necessary to build correct reliable programs. By the end of the two semester sequence, not only is the student well versed in programming in Pascal, understands the operational aspects of top down design, information hiding, modular design and structured programming, but also has a good introduction to the concept of program correctness, and program verification and data abstraction.

Section 2 of this paper will briefly describe this course, and will emphasize its programming aspects. In section 3, the SUPPORT Environment for the IBM PC is described as a companion tool for use in this course. Section 4 will provide some data on the use of this tool in the course.

2. Computer Science I

The freshman computer science course emphasizes functional correctness as the means to design computer programs. A program is viewed as a function which transforms an input data space into an output data space. Each statement is added to a program with a view of how it transforms that data space. For example, if a **while** statement is added, the student is required to consider the invariant of the loop and the exit conditions from the loop. While it is not necessary to formally verify every line of code, the idea that each executable statement will transform one data space into another is pervasive. Students need this structure in order to properly think about program design. A text has been written to support this concept [Mills 87a] and another paper in this proceedings describes this course in more detail [Mills 87b].

For pedagogical reasons, Pascal is divided into three subsets: CF Pascal, D Pascal and Pascal. By the end of the two semester sequence students are well versed in the entire language.

The goal for the first semester is to teach the students to design programs formally and algorithmically. A small subset of Pascal, called CF Pascal, is used to enforce simplicity. This is a highly restricted subset that avoids all "frills" in the language. Since there are a limited number of ways to express any idea, the major task of the student is the development of an algorithm without the need of considering the myriad of ways of converting a concrete design into executable Pascal code. CF Pascal is also limited to ideas that can be formally defined and verified as a means of expressing the formalisms of the course.

CF Pascal stands for *Character File Pascal* which represent the only data types available. All information must be expressed in these types. Concepts like arrays, integers and boolean variables are not included. (See the Appendix for the Syntax of CF Pascal.) In addition, the control structures are generally limited to one way of expressing an idea. Thus CF Pascal has a **while** statement, but no **repeat** and **for** constructs. Similarly, there are **if** and **procedure** statements, but no **case** and **function** statements. All procedure parameters are call-by-reference.

In addition to simplifying the language and providing a subset of Pascal that lends itself to program verification, CF Pascal forces the student to think about modularization and data abstraction early. For example, when numbers are needed, the student needs to abstract the ideas from the basic character and file data types. For example, a single digit can be represented as a character variable. An arbitrary integer can be represented as a file of characters. Students write procedures to increment such numbers, add numbers, compare numbers, etc.

However, most of the programs in this course stay away from such concepts. It is most informative for the student to use CF Pascal to program non-numerical problems early, rather than viewing the major purpose of programs as simply implementing square root routines and other numerical approximation algorithms.

In the second semester, D Pascal, or Design Pascal, is taught. This is a more complete subset that adds additional primitive data types and control structures. It is closer to a more traditional subset used at other institutions. Finally, by the end of the second semester, the student is programming in full Pascal, with records, pointers, and all other features of the language.

3. The SUPPORT Environment

When the freshman course was redesigned according to the above goals, computing facilities consisted of several large mainframe computers accessed via remote terminals. Students were taught the various subsets of Pascal and then had to program their solutions using standard text editors and compilers. This solution had two major deficiencies: (1) Students needed to learn a great deal about the operating system, logon procedures, standard text editing and the Pascal compiler before they could even start their programming activities. This was a great intellectual hurdle to overcome before they entered their first line of text; and (2) Since they were using a standard Pascal compiler, they could accidentally or intentionally access features of Pascal that were supposedly beyond their knowledge at that point. A system organized around CF Pascal seemed like a worthwhile addition.

In 1984, the University of Maryland began acquiring a large number of IBM PCs as part of an IBM Advanced Educational Program grant to the University. One of the tasks supported by the grant was the development of the SUPPORT Environment as the companion software to use in this first computer science course. The following is a brief description of SUPPORT, (cf. [Zelkowitz 85]). The system has been in use since early 1986 and the next section will describe our experiences to date.

SUPPORT is an integrated Pascal development environment for PC-DOS systems. Its major components consist of a syntax directed editor for building Pascal programs, a Pascal interpreter for executing these programs and a consistent user interface that communicates to the programmer via a series of windows - horizontal bands of text that divide the PC's CRT screen. A major goal was the self-sufficiency of the system; all computing needs are to be handled internally to SUPPORT. Knowledge of the underlying PC-DOS operating system had to be kept minimal. The system is implemented in Pascal, and will run on any PC with 256K of memory. In 256K it can be used to develop programs of approximately 500 statements. Since the system uses whatever memory is available, in a full 640K system, programs of over 3,000 lines can be written.

While SUPPORT was designed as a closed integrated environment, without the necessity of using any other tools for Pascal program development, it was designed with an open interface. Thus, commands are available for moving program and data between the SUPPORT environment and the DOS file system, and hence to other Pascal processors, PCs, or even other computers.

Using SUPPORT

A student enters the SUPPORT Environment by placing the SUPPORT system disk in the floppy disk drive, and then typing "SUPPORT". When SUPPORT is initially invoked, the students are communicating with the Program Text window and the syntax directed editor. This editor only knows about the CF Pascal subset mentioned previously, thus it is impossible to enter Pascal text outside of the scope of this first course. In this window, text is entered via a series of function keys (button responses) to menus (replacing nonterminals on the screen by the right hand side of productions) or by text which is parsed via an internal LALR parser.

For example, if the cursor (reverse video text) surrounds the statement nonterminal, as in:

<.statement.>

and the student wants to insert a **while** statement, the student can either enter the corresponding button from the displayed menu or can type in the text:

while <.condition.> do <.statement.>

In either case, the screen will now contain the text:

while <.condition.> do

<.statement.>

The contents of the program window *always* represent a syntactically valid program (which is stored as a correct parse tree). It is impossible to enter invalid text via this method. In general, the menu buttons are used to enter the larger constructs like statements or procedure declarations, and the internal LALR parser is used for smaller constructs like expressions; however there is no inherent limitation of when each can be used [Zelkowitz 84].

For the beginning student, this eliminates the frustration of trying to build a syntactically valid program the first time before receiving any positive reinforcement via some execution output. Most beginners have trouble with the explicit syntax needed by most compilers. Since people have good error correction strategies in their heads and can usually understand a program containing a few minor syntax errors, it is often hard for students to understand the need for absolutely correct input.

If the text that the student entered is syntactically incorrect, it is placed in a small window which can be accessed via the internal Character Oriented EDitor (COED). The student can either retype the invalid line of text or can enter COED to modify it, have it parsed by the internal parser and then inserted into the program tree. COED consists of a series of simple cursor commands for adding and deleting characters and lines of text. It is limited to one screenful of text (about 22 lines), and is not meant to be a general text editor.

COED is the major tool for modifying program text. The student wraps the cursor around the section of code to be modified, pulls this code into the COED window, modifies it, and exits COED whereupon the parser is invoked.

The use of COED solves one of the problems inherent with syntax directed editing. Since the program must always be represented as a valid syntax tree, it is usually impossible to make modifications that temporarily upset that correctness. For example, inserting the **begin** keyword destroys this balance until the corresponding **end** keyword is entered. Via COED, this syntactic balance can be temporarily modified, but the program text from the COED window will be inserted into the Program Text window only if it passes correctly through the parser.

Students need to be able to create data files, but in keeping with the goal of making SUPPORT a total environment, we did not want to teach them an alternative text editor to use. COED can also be used to construct arbitrary files (up to the

22 line window size) and save them in the PC-DOS file system. While this is sufficient for student programs, it is not for a production environment. However, professional programmers would have no problem going outside of the environment to utilize another text editor for data preparation.

The use of COED also solves one additional problem with syntax directed editing. With a more strict formalism in creating program text via a series of menus, the student does not get a thorough knowledge of the Pascal syntax. While a desirable trait initially, the student will need the ability to create correct programs without the use of SUPPORT later. With COED the student learns that syntax.

SUPPORT can save any part of the Program Text window to the file system. This allows for programs to be printed, or to be exported to another system (e.g., compile on the PC-DOS Pascal compiler). In addition, the internal parser can process any PC-DOS file and insert it into the program tree. If the parsed text matches the nonterminal at the cursor (e.g., <.program.> or <.procedure.>) then it will be added to the Program Text window. This feature can be used to import any externally generated program fragment into the SUPPORT environment. While not important in the student environment, it is important for effective use of the system in other applications.

Small sections of code can be moved using the COED window. The code is put in the window. the cursor is moved in the Program Text window, and then COED is exited via the internal parser. Larger sections of code can be moved by saving that section into the file system and rereading it through the parser.

Program execution is controlled by a Pascal interpreter. While execution speed is not crucial, the system has to be perceived as fast enough. Cursor motion is essentially instantaneous, and the interpreter executes about 90 statements per second on a PC. Since SUPPORT resides totally in memory, the lack of hard disks on a PC is no handicap. The few accesses to the floppy disks to read or write programs or data take the few seconds that people "expect" them to take.

Since CF Pascal makes heavy use of files, we made sure that file processing is efficient - especially on a floppy disk system. If a program does not explicitly link an internally declared **text** file to a PC-DOS file name via the **assign** statement, as in:

assign(InternalFileName, 'MYDATA.XYZ') {MYDATA.XYZ is on disk}

then SUPPORT makes the file internal, and implements it as a linked list of records. Only external program data actually needs to be on disks, and most files execute at CPU speeds. Typically a student would need only one or two external files for final output and several internal files.

In one test, a 300 line program that makes heavy use of files was executed with SUPPORT and with Microsoft's Pascal compiler using an IBM PC/AT with hard disk. Although Microsoft Pascal typically generates code that is well over 100 times faster than SUPPORT's execution time, the heavy external file use resulted in a 18.67 second execution time for the Microsoft Pascal version, but only a 6.48 second execution time with SUPPORT.

In order to simplify the generation of program output which is normally displayed on the CRT screen, SUPPORT provides a logging function. All lines written via **write** or **writeln** statements are automatically written to the file

SUPPORT.OUT. It is then a simple matter when the student exits from SUPPORT to rename that file, copy it to another floppy disk or to print it.

Monitoring Execution

SUPPORT also contains a large number of features for interfacing between the Program Text window and program execution. The Pascal interpreter can be stopped via a keyboard interrupt. Variable values can be displayed in a Debug window. Program execution can also be monitored via the Program Trace window. By watching the program execute a token at a time, the beginner gets a better relationship between the syntax of the program, the infix notation used in Pascal, and the underlying postfix of the executing program tree.

At any point when execution halts, the student can interrogate the run time activation records and view all data in an easily readable format, or can type in any executable Pascal statement and have it executed within the environment of the halted program. This provides a dynamic debugging system oriented towards the CF Pascal language. By halting executing and meandering through the activation records, the student gets a clearer picture of the activation record concept of procedure invocation, the effects on local and non-local data declarations, and the effects of recursive procedures on data storage. All of these are possible with the integrated environment in SUPPORT, and would be difficult to provide in a more traditional edit-compile-execute-debug cycle.

Besides providing a total closed environment, SUPPORT also provides features for allowing students to understand the nature of a Pascal compilation and of the stack-model of Pascal program execution. This is provided via three windows: the Debug, Trace and Run-time Display windows. The Trace window monitors program execution while the other two access the program's runtime data structures. Unlike in the PMS system [Tomek] which has a fixed tiled format for window displays, in SUPPORT users can open or close windows as needed.

Consider the program in Figure 1(a) (taken from [Mills 87a]). Note that *eliding* is used to hide sections of program text to permit larger segments of a program to be contained on a single CRT window display. Each line beginning <.proc ...> represents the text of a separate procedure. If needed, these *panned* nonterminals can be opened up to reveal the details of the source code hidden by this placeholder. The user can also insert comments above each panned nonterminal so that once debugged, only the specifications to the procedure appear on the screen and not the details (e.g., code) of how the procedure was implemented.

In Figure 1(b), the program of Figure 1(a) is executed with both the Trace and Debug windows active. The user can move the cursor on to any variable and turn the monitoring of that variable on. Its name as well as its scope are listed in this window. Whenever the value of the variable is changed, its new value will be updated in this window.

The Trace window is used to monitor program execution. As execution proceeds this window is updated in real time at a rate of about 3 statements per second. Users can monitor execution flow and halt execution at any time.

Execution monitoring is displayed on a token by token basis instead of line tracing as in other systems. Rather than simply stating that an assignment statement like "A := B + C" is being traced, the Trace window will successively indicate by moving the cursor that the following constructs execute in order:

A:=B+C

B+C

B

C

A

This corresponds to the execution sequence:

Execute assignment statement (A:=B+C)

Compute the right hand side expression (B+C)

Evaluate operand B

Evaluate operand C

Evaluate assignment to A

Also note in Figure 1(b) that the banner of the Trace window gives a history of currently active procedures. This gives the user a dynamic picture of how his statically specified program behaves with respect to procedure invocation and exit, as explained below.

Languages like Pascal all use the activation record model for data storage. Associated with each active procedure is a block of memory to contain the values for all the variables declared in that block. As each new procedure is invoked (e.g., called), a

new activation record is allocated; when the procedure finishes, the activation record is freed. In this manner, storage is used more effectively than in most FORTRAN or BASIC implementations where data storage for each subroutine remains allocated for the lifetime of the program's execution. In Pascal, storage freed by one activation record can be used by the next. In general, a stack is used to contain all of these activation records and is a simple implementation strategy for this data.

The use of activation records allows for recursive procedures with no increase in complexity since each invocation of a procedure is simply a new activation record added to the stack. It does not matter if that same procedure already exists as an earlier (recursive) invocation on the stack.

When execution is halted, the user can actively interrogate these run time activation records of the halted program via the Run-time Display window (Figure 1(c)). In this case, the currently active activation record names are displayed on the window banner line. Using the → and ← keys, the user can move the cursor on top of any one of these, and cause the contents of that activation record to be displayed in the window. If there are more variables than will fit in the window, the ↑ and ↓ keys can be used to scroll up and down through the activation record. Recursive procedures pose no additional problems for this display.

If the data item is a simple scalar variable, its value is displayed in the window; however, if it is a more complex type (such as an array), then only its type is given. The user can move the cursor on top of this variable and then *zoom* into it to open up its contents. Using the arrow keys, zooming and panning (the inverse of zooming), the user can nagivate through the run-time display to acquire an intuitive feel of how

data is organized and stored during program execution.

Since the activation record structure is available to the debugging system, it is also possible to execute statements in the halted environment (Figure 1(d)). Any legal Pascal statement, often a **writeln** statement for debugging, can be typed and then executed. This allows for a powerful debugging tool without the need to learn anything other than Pascal.

SUPPORT is initialized by reading in an external grammar description of the language it processes. This paper described the CF Pascal variant. We also have a larger subset that includes integer, real, boolean and array type. We haven't done so, but it would be an easy operation to increase the number of subsets greatly. For example, you could have a subset with only **read** and **write** statements for allowing students to write their first trivial programs. CF-Pascal could be a second subset, adding integers a third, adding additional control structures a fourth, etc. The basic SUPPORT package would not change but the underlying language that was processed would expand with each new subset. One could have Pascal.ch1, Pascal.ch2,... where each subset reflected the next chapter in the course text book. This would allow an instructor to introduce new language features in a controlled manner.

4. Experiences with SUPPORT

SUPPORT was first used in a Computer Science course during the Spring 1986 semester; approximately 240 students were registered for the course. About 300 students used SUPPORT during the fall of 1986. Two surveys were taken during each semester: one in the third week and the other at the end. Performance in the course was evaluated. During the first semester, the class was divided into SUPPORT users and mainframe users; during the second semester all students used both systems. Beginning with the Spring, 1987 semester, only SUPPORT was used.

For the SUPPORT group, 16 PCs with only floppy disk drives were available, as well as 50 or more other PC's across the campus. Any computer center user could use these machines, but demand for them was low and with the small number of SUPPORT users, access was generally good. Every student was given a copy of the SUPPORT system disk.

The mainframe users could access the large mainframe from about 200 terminals scattered across campus as well as through dialup lines. Since the computer center has several large machines from assorted manufacturers available to a large computing population, access to these terminals is usually difficult. In both cases, students could use their own PCs or terminals if they had them. About 20% of the students had their own machines.

As a new product undergoing "beta test" we did have a few problems. In general, whenever a serious problem surfaced, we had a new generation of SUPPORT diskettes ready for distribution within a few days. We did go through 4 distributions during the first semester, but only 1 mid-semester distribution in the second semester. While we do not believe that any of these problems were serious, redistributions adversely influenced some of the data collected since they caused the students frustration.

Student Profiles

Our initial survey was used to determine the backgrounds and goals for each section. The population that we measured is detailed in Figure 2. In general, the course experiences about a 50% drop in enrollment during the semester, with drop rates of 50% and 43% for these semesters being comparable to previous classes. (In many cases, some students give up and do not even withdraw from classes, so, we consider only those with passing grades, not total grades issued.)

We also asked each student what his or her future career goals would be. Their responses are given by the chart in Figure 3. The low percentages for both Ph.D. and careers in teaching certainly are indicative of the current problems that colleges are having in recruiting adequate faculty.

Figure 4 shows that the background of the students in both semesters were quite similar. For both semesters, between 73% and 82% of the students were taking their first university Computer Science course. The percentage repeating the course was about 10% in all sections. Over half the students had programming courses previously in high school while a comparable one quarter in each section had never programmed before. As expected, since we allowed students to switch sections during semester 1, more than half of the SUPPORT section preferred to use a PC for their programming while a majority of the mainframe section preferred to use the larger computer. We assume that the other 40% in each section either had schedule conflicts which prevented them from switching to the time period of the other section or else didn't care which computer system they used. Finally, and not unexpectedly, over half of the SUPPORT section already had their own computer while less than half of the mainframe section had one. While only 14% of the first semester and 18%

of the second semester class had IBM PCs or PC-compatibles, the fact that half the students had experience with some machine and the general ability to edit and compile programs did affect the later ratings.

Student Evaluations

Most of our evaluation data was collected by the final subjective survey form. While not objective, it does indicate trends which we intend to study more fully during the coming semester.

Students were asked to estimate the number of hours spent on all class activities each week. While these numbers varied from 0 hours (probably) to 40 hours (unlikely), both sections of semester 1 had similar averages of around 16 hours per week; meanwhile, the average was approximately 9 hours per week in semester 2 (Figure 5). Figure 5 also presents the percentage of time devoted to different computer tasks and are remarkably similar across all groups in both semesters. The differences between the 16 and 9 hours per week of effort between semesters is probably due to different instructors teaching the course. A single person taught all sections of each course in a given semester.

In evaluating the SUPPORT section of semester 1, we observed a significant difference among the students who have their own computers (hence having greater programming experience) and those that did not. In the figures that follow. we divide the SUPPORT data according to the 15 respondents that owned computers and the 13 that did not.

During semester 1, the average time spent on course activities for all students was 16.4 hours, and 16.1 hours for the mainframe group, and it varied between 14.3 hours for the non-computer-owner SUPPORT group and 19.2 for the computer-owner SUPPORT group. Since both groups spent about the same percentage of time on computer activities (68% and 69%) this translates into 12.9 hours for the PC owners and 9.7 hours for the non-PC group. It is our guess that since the PC owners "liked" having machines, they used them more. The mainframe group spent 61% of time on the computer, or 9.8 hours, similar to the non-PC owner SUPPORT group.

In looking at the percentage of time devoted to different computer activities, all groups seemed comparable. Each spent about 25% of time thinking about their programs, rather than editing or designing their solutions. However, the SUPPORT group spent a greater time at the terminal (about 10%) than the mainframe group (about 6%). One hypothesis for this is that PC access was easy while mainframe terminal access - since the terminals could be used by any campus computer user - was difficult. Students staring at a listing were frowned upon by the queue behind them. Some of the data on terminal access, which is presented later, seem to support this view.

We asked all students to rate the computer system they used according to a series of criteria, and the results are presented in Figure 6. Each item was rated from 1 (very poor) to 5 (very good). In general the mainframe usage came out better than the SUPPORT usage, although when the microcomputer owners are filtered out from this group, SUPPORT fared almost as well as the mainframe group.

Students rated the mainframe higher with respect to response time of the system, text editing capabilities, complexity of the system, and ease of use. SUPPORT was rated higher for debugging capabilities and availability of terminals to use. Both were comparable, with the mainframe group slightly higher, on program execution time.

One clear effect of these ratings can be called technological inertia. The microcomputer owners had a definite idea of how computers should operate, and the seeming restrictions source on code generation via a syntax directed editor upset them more than students without such a background.

This has been observed before. In the early 1970's, the attitude was: Why use structured programming when **gotos** are good enough? Today, the view is: Why learn Pascal when FORTRAN is good enough? In each case, the underlying technology must be greatly superior or it will not be adopted even if marginally better than its predecessor. This resistance has been reported by others who presented syntax editing to professional programmers.

The final rating in Figure 6 was a general satisfaction of the system they used. In this case the mainframe was preferred over the PC, although less so for the group that did not own a computer. One interesting anecdote: during semester 2, while students seemed to prefer the mainframe system, those that used SUPPORT first during the semester had higher grades on the mid-term examination [Chin].

On the final survey, we asked the students for comments on how to improve the system that they used. For the mainframe group, there was probably an equal number that commented on either the complexity or ease of use of the mainframe text editor; you cannot please everyone. Since people tend to comment on the feature that is their chief problem, about half of the students in the mainframe group complained about the lack of terminal access or the large number of inoperative terminals.

For the SUPPORT group, while a few had comments about the restrictions imposed on editing programs, most were concerned about the unreliability of the system early in the first semester. This is obviously of concern to us, and is an issue that we believe has been rectified. Meanwhile, during the second semester, there were more comments about the restrictions of syntax directed editing. Several did comment that the diagnostic tools were extremely useful in program development.

The results provide useful information and insight on how to proceed next. For one thing, the SUPPORT ratings were hurt by two events:

(1) The few bugs in the system lowered overall confidence in SUPPORT. Although they were repaired quickly, the lack of absolute reliability removed the trust necessary in a computer system.

(2) In semester 1, the final program overloaded the capacity of the machine for many students. SUPPORT can handle about 500 statements in 256K, and this program grew to over 700 statements in some cases. This was fixed by increasing memory for each machine to at least 512K.

While these problems hurt the SUPPORT ratings, it is also important to note that SUPPORT fared poorer among those students with significant programming experience. Syntax editing has received a mixed reception among professional programmers, and most likely, technological inertia is causing this resistence. We believe that by extending the editing capabilities of a syntax directed editor in order to handle code modification better, the system will be viewed as more productive to existing programmers.

As an overall evaluation, we believe that for the first year we have been fairly successful in using a syntax directed editor in our Computer Science I course. Although the mainframe was the preferred system, among users with less of a computer background SUPPORT fared almost as well. Based upon this experience, we believe that we have a much more reliable product and have added some necessary features to enhance the usefulness of the tool.

Students seemed pleased with the interactive debugging capabilities of a system like SUPPORT over traditional software development paradigms. It is our expectation that with a reliable product, SUPPORT will be rated at least as high as the mainframe system. We believe that we have achieved a good mix between traditional screen-oriented text editing and the newer syntax-directed paradigm in an integrated environment. A more complex question is the acceptance of syntax directed editing among those with previous computer experience. The answer to this is not yet clear.

5. Acknowledgements

This work was partially supported by Air Force Office of Scientific Research grant F49620-85-K-008 to the University of Maryland. Computer resources were provided by the IBM AEP grant to the University of Maryland. In addition we would like to acknowledge the contributions of others who have contributed to this project:

Jennifer Drapkin, Gordon Lyon, and Michael Maggio. We also would like to thank the students in CMSC 112 at the University of Maryland during the Spring and Fall 1986 semesters for their help in testing this system.

6. References

[McCracken] McCracken, D., Viewpoint, *Communications of the ACM* 30, 1, January, 1987, pp. 3-5.

[Chin] Chin J., Private communication (paper in progress).

[Mills 87a] Mills H., et al. *Principles of Computer Programming: A Mathematical Approach,* Allyn Bacon, 1987.

[Mills 87b] Mills H., et al., A first course in computer science: mathematical principles for software engineering, (this proceedings).

[Tomek] Tomek I. and T. Muldner, Learning Pascal with the aid of a compiler, *Perspectives in Computing* 6, No. 1 (Spring, 1986) pp. 22-37.

[Zelkowitz84] Zelkowitz M. V., A small contribution to editing with a syntax directed editor, ACM SIGSOFT Symposium on Practical Software Development Environments, Pittsburgh PA, April, 1984, pp. 1-6.

[Zelkowitz85] Zelkowitz M. V., et. al., The engineering of an environment on small machines, IEEE International Conference on Computer Workstations, San Jose, CA, November, 1985.

7. Appendix - CF Pascal Syntax

```
<program>         ::= program id ( input , output ) ; <pgmblock> .
<pgmblock>        ::= <decs> <procblock> | <procblock>
<decs>            ::= var <declst>
<declst>          ::= <decl> <declst> | <declst>
<decl>            ::= <iddecllist> : <type> ;
<proc>            ::= procedure id <plst> ;
<plst>            ::= <paramlist> ; <pgmblock> | ; <pgmblock>
<procs>           ::= <proc> <procs> | <proc>
<paramlist>       ::= ( <parmlist> )
<varparam>        ::= var <iddecllist> : <type>
<iddecllist>      ::= id , <iddecllist> | id
<parmlist>        ::= <varparam> ; <parmlist> | <varparam>
<procblock>       ::= <procs> <block> | <block>
<block>           ::= begin <more stmts> end
<more stmts>      ::= <stmt> ; <more stmts> | <stmt>
<stmt>            ::= <block> | <if> | <while> | <call> | <:=>
                      | <I/O stmts> | <null>
<if>              ::= if <condition> then <thenprt>
<thenprt>         ::= <stmt> else <stmt> | <stmt>
<while>           ::= while <condition> do <stmt>
<call>            ::= id ( <more exprs> ) | <id>
<more exprs>      ::= <expr> , <more exprs> | <expr>
<I/O exprs>       ::= <expr> , <I/O exprs> | <expr>
<:=>              ::= <id> := <expr>
<null>            ::=
<iduselist>       ::= id , <iduselist> | id
<expr>            ::= <id> | <string>
<condition>       ::= <and/or/not> | <equal> | <grthn> | <lsthn>
                      | <greq> | <lseq> | <noteq> | <eof> | <eoln> | ( <condition> )
<and/or/not>      ::= <not> | <or> | <not>
<and>             ::= ( <condition> ) and <and>
<or>              ::= ( <condition> ) or <or>
<not>             ::= not <condition>
<equal>           ::= ( <expr> = <expr> )
<grthn>           ::= ( <expr> > <expr> )
<lsthn>           ::= ( <expr> < <expr> )
<greq>            ::= ( <expr> >= <expr> )
<lseq>            ::= ( <expr> <= <expr> )
<noteq>           ::= ( <expr> <> <expr> )
<char>            ::= char
```

<type>	::= <char> | <text>
<string>	::= string
<text>	::= text
<id>	::= id
<I/O stmts>	::= <read> | <readln> | <write> | <writeln> | <assign> | <reset> | <rewrite>
<read>	::= read (<iduselist>)
<readln>	::= readln (<iduselist>) | readln
<write>	::= write (<I/O exprs>)
<writeln>	::= writeln (<I/O exprs>) | writeln
<assign>	::= assign (<more exprs>)
<reset>	::= reset (<id>)
<rewrite>	::= rewrite (<id>)
<eof>	::= eof (<id>) | eof
<eoln>	::= eoln (<id>) | eoln

Figure 1a. Sample Program to Execute

```
PROGRAM TEXT:-----------------------------------------------------------
program TestRem (input,output); { TestRemove }<.decs. ...>
   <.proc. CopyToEol...>
   <.proc. EmptyQ...>
   <.proc. AddQ...>
   <.proc. DelQ...>
   <.proc. HeadQ...>
   <.proc. WriteQ...>
   { TestRemove }<.proc. RemBlanks...>
begin
   EmptyQ;
   write('The input is :');
   while not(eof) do
      begin
         while not(eoln) do
            begin
               read(Ch);
               write(Ch);
               AddQ(Ch)
            end;
         read(Ch);
```

Figure 1b. Use of Variable and Statement Trace Windows

```
input>a b#
VARIABLE DISPLAY:-------------------------------------------------------
EXECUTING:
 [CopyToEol]-Ch=                              [RemoveExtr]-LineEnd=
 [TestRemove]-Switch=      1


TRACING: [TestRemove]---------------------------------------------------
               AddQ(Ch)
            end;
         read(Ch);
         if not(eof) then begin
            write(Ch);
            AddQ(Ch)
PROGRAM EXECUTION:------------------------------------------------------
***** 1: Start Execution
```

Figure 2. Population surveyed

	Semester 1			Semester 2
	SUPPORT Section	Mainframe Section	All	All
Registered	85	151	236	307
Survey 1	59	117	176	226
Survey 2	28	61	89	145
Received Grades	57	110	167	248
Non-failing Grades	40	78	118	174
% Drop	53	48	50	43

Figure 3. Career Goals for Students

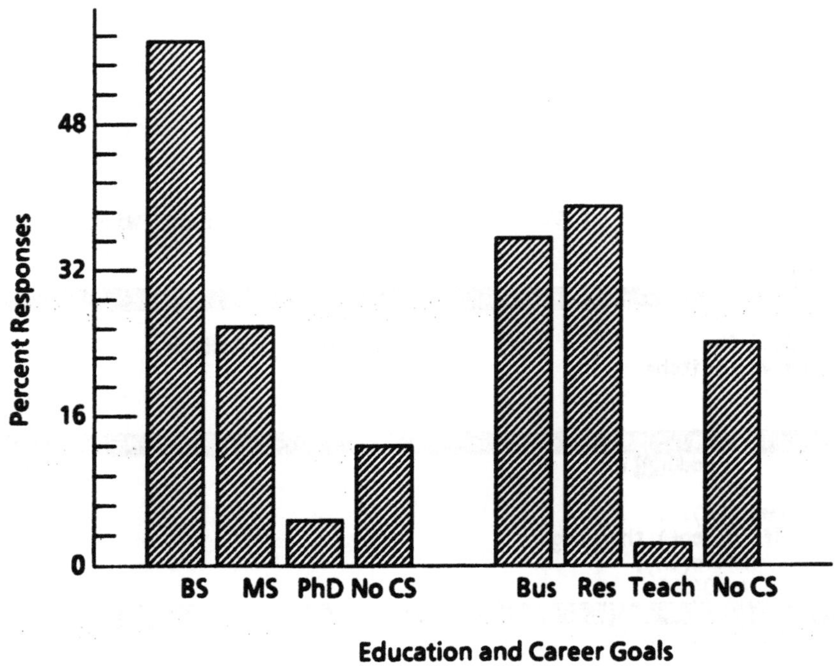

Figure 4. Background of students

	Semester 1			Semester 2
	SUPPORT	Mainframe	All	All
First university computer course (%)	73	74	73	82
Took course previously (%)	10	13	12	9
High school programming (%)	53	63	59	55
Never used computer (%)	24	27	26	24
Prefer current system (%)	60	58	59	*
Own microcomputer(%)	56	45	49	51

*Not applicable to Semester 2

Figure 5. Effort involved in programming

	Semester 1				Semester 2
	SUPPORT own PC	SUPPORT no PC	Mainframe	All	All
Population	15	13	61	89	145
Hours/week	19.2	14.3	16.1	16.4	9.0
% Programming	68	69	61	63	52
% Design	38	32	35	35	36
% Editing	18	12	18	17	15
% Execution	20	32	23	24	24
% Thinking at terminal	9	11	6	7	8
% Thinking Not logged in	13	15	18	16	15

Figure 6. Evaluation of systems (1=poor, 5=good)

	Semester 1			Semester 2	
	SUPPORT own PC	SUPPORT no PC	Mainframe	SUPPORT	Mainframe
Response time	3.2	3.5	4.1	3.3	3.5
Text editing	3.7	3.3	3.8	2.7	3.7
Debugging tools	3.0	3.8	3.1	3.0	2.9
Execution time	3.4	3.5	3.7	3.5	3.7
Complexity	3.0	3.2	3.6	3.0	3.5
Ease of use	2.9	3.1	3.7	2.8	3.4
Availability	3.3	3.9	2.8	3.0	2.9
Overall satisfaction	2.8	3.2	4.0	2.6	3.4

Stalking the Typical Undergraduate Software Engineering Course: Results from a Survey

Laura Marie Leventhal and Barbee T. Mynatt
Computer Science Department
Bowling Green State University

ABSTRACT

A survey of undergraduate software engineering courses was conducted. The survey covered the issues of course level, course content, course organization, project characteristics and department demographics. The descriptive statistics show that the typical course focuses on the software development life cycle and includes a project intended for actual use. The project is carried out by teams of students, with student leaders. A factor analysis disclosed that three different sorts of courses are currently being offered. The most predominant course is the Later-Life-Cycle course, which focuses on the later stages of the software life cycle. Detailed design, coding, testing and maintenance receive in-depth coverage in this style of course, and the students' grades are heavily dependent upon the project. The Early-Life-Cycle course emphasizes requirements analysis, specification and system design. Written reports are an important component of this course, and the project is again a large portion of the students' grades. The third style of course is the Theoretical-Issues course. Software metrics, project management and legal and ethical issues are covered. The students are upper level, and use journal articles as a source of materials. The issues of suitable textbooks and sources of materials and training for teaching user-interface design surfaced as problem areas.

I. INTRODUCTION

XYZU has a well-established computer science program; the department has an excellent academic reputation as well as an outstanding placement record. Several recent computer science graduates from XYZU have suggested that the program would be strengthened by the inclusion of undergraduate courses in software engineering. Industrial recruiters have echoed the idea. Dr. Q. has a strong background in operating systems software and has enthusiastically volunteered to develop the new software engineering curriculum. Like many computer science faculty members, Dr. Q. is a relative novice in the area of software engineering. Dr. Q. begins to address the questions of course staffing, course content, computer facilities, and student characteristics.

In a traditional computer science course such as introductory programming, a review of popular textbooks and accredidation guidelines quickly reveals common trends in course content and logistics. Unfortunately for Dr. Q., the development of a software engineering curriculum is more problematic. Great variety exists in textbook content and organization. Dr. Q. is uncertain of her choices; she is even more unsure of which parameters are relevant. In short, Dr. Q. is having a hard time finding a description of a "typical" course in software engineering, let alone developing a course tailored for the computer science students at XYZU.

Although several reports of undergraduate software engineering curricula have appeared in the educational literature of computer science, the majority of these reports described one particular software engineering course. They do not provide guidelines for a generalized curriculum in software engineering ([1] and [2] are possible exceptions). However, there are several issues that are common among these reports of specific courses:

1. Placement of software engineering courses in an undergraduate computer science program
2. Topics included in software engineering course(s)
3. Organization of software engineering course(s)
4. Role of and characteristics of a project component

Software Engineering in the Computer Science Program

When and how should computer science students be exposed to software engineering materials? Shooman [3] suggested at least three alternatives: a dedicated course, incorporation of software engineering techniques into other courses, and reliance on on-the-job experience in cooperative education settings. Within the dedicated course option, he described several alternatives. Software engineering techniques could appear in freshman level courses before the students learn "bad habits", or the material could appear in junior and senior level courses when the students are mature enough to appreciate the benefits of software engineering. An issue implicit in the question of course level is that of appropriate prerequisites. Should the students be beyond a significant program milestone (e.g, completion of a data structures course)?

Carver [4] described a course specifically designed for junior and senior computer science students and listed data structures as a prerequisite. Other courses targeted for juniors or seniors were reported in Mazlack [5] and Shooman [3]. In contrast, Lapalme and Lamy [6] proposed a course for freshmen.

Course Content

Collofello and Woodfield [7] have suggested that one of the difficulties in teaching software engineering is the vastness of the subject area, particularly for a one-semester course. Shooman [3] listed eight design topics and seven management topics as potential course items. The list included such diverse items as design topics, programming style, reliability estimates, and software quality control. Typically, textbooks highlight stages of the software lifecycle (e.g., [8] and [9]). However, Jensen and Tonies [10] included legal issues as a chapter in their software engineering text.

Course Organization

Course organization refers to issues of course materials, student course requirements, faculty requirements, and computer facilities. Shooman [3] cited staffing and facilities as primary difficulties in the construction of a software engineering course. Bickerstaff [11] described an ongoing lack of an adequate textbook to meet the particular needs of his curriculum. Henry [12] listed the reading materials for her course. She had primarily selected journal articles rather than a single software engineering textbook.

Materials and resources may include more than textbooks and journals. For example, Shooman [3] and Waguespack and Haas [13] described extensive and cost-effective programmers' workbenches. Both of these facilities were specifically designed to support software engineering education.

Project

By far the most common issue that is addressed in the software engineering education literature involves course projects. Among the existing articles there is little disagreement on the benefits of a project component. There is, however, variety in the characteristics of the project element. For example, Carver [4] described two courses; one included a single project, completed by all of the students, and one included multiple projects. In the multiple-project model, groups of different students worked on different projects. In her subjective comparison of the two approaches, she found that the time component for the end user was most problematic in the single project case, while selecting equivalent projects was the most difficult aspect in the multiple-project approach.

Several other articles have also noted the difficulty in project selection ([11], [14], [4] and [15]). Woodfield, Collofello and Collofello [15] suggested that a project which is too large to finish has a negative effect on student motivation, while a project which is too small allows the students to use ad hoc techniques rather than software engineering methods. An additional issue in project selection is the type of project. Is the project a "toy" or will it really be used? In Henry's course [12], the students selected their own game to implement. This is in sharp contrast to Bickerstaff's [11] use of real projects. In the course he described, the students not only implemented systems for use, but also interacted directly with the end users.

A third major theme which arises from the descriptions of projects concerns team organization, management, and evaluation of team members ([7], [19], [15] and [12]). Typical problems which have been reported include workable team sizes, team formation and team evaluation.

II. METHODOLOGY

The case studies suggest both trends and recurrent problems in software engineering education. However, the resourceful Dr. Q., and others in similar positions, are in search of a description of a model or "typical" course. It is not clear that the case study literature is a representative picture.

In order to provide a more reliable and complete description of software engineering courses currently offered, we recently conducted a survey of undergraduate programs in computer science. Two-hundred-forty programs which mininally grant a bachelor's degree in computer science were randomly selected to participate in the survey. The programs were selected from the approximately 820 programs in the United States and Canada listed in the ACM 1984 Administrative Directory [16]. The surveys were sent by mail and a self-addressed return envelope was included in the package.

The survey was divided into five parts. (Appendix A contains a facsimile of the questionnaire.) The first part consisted of open-ended demographic questions, including questions on the numbers of undergraduate majors and minors, the numbers of full-time and part-time graduate students, the school calendar, and the name of a contact person in the program. Four additional sections addressed the the themes which emerge from the case study literature reveiwed above: course level, course content, course organization and project components. For each question in these sections the respondent was asked to provide a rating. The rating was on a four point scale, from "not at all true" to "very characteristic".

II. RESULTS

Twenty-five percent of the surveys were returned in time to be included in the analyses. While the use of surveys in software engineering practice is not unknown, it has not been widely used in the educational arena (e.g., [17]). In fact, a common criticism of mailed surveys in the more general area of citizen feedback is that they are biased because only the most highly-motivated participants respond. The response rate is generally low, occasionally falling below ten percent [18].

Our relatively high response suggests that the population from which we drew our sample is generally highly-motivated and interested in software engineering education. Consequently, we believe that there was less likelihood of bias in our results than in the typical situation.

Demographics

The first part of the survey included a series of items to elicit a description of the respondent's department and program. The respondent was asked to identify his or her department and school. Although eleven different department titles were specified, these were collapsed into the four different catagories shown in Table 1. The largest category was Computer Science, which was indicated by 57 percent of the respondents. Twenty-one percent were from Mathematics departments or combined Mathematics and Computer Science. Thirteen percent were from departments that included the word "Information" in their titles (e.g., Computer Information Science or Information and Computer Science) and the remaining eight percent were from Electrical Engineering and Computer Science departments.

Thirteen uniques responses were given for school affiliation. These were collapsed into the five categories indicated in Table 2. Thirty percent of the respondents' departments were in Liberal Arts or Arts and Sciences colleges. Thirty percent were from the College of Science or a college with Science as the primary word (e.g., Science, Technology and Health or Applied Science). Fourteen percent were from Engineering colleges, and eight percent were from Business colleges. Seventeen percent did not respond, or indicated in some way that the question was not applicable in their case.

The distribution of faculty size per department is given in Table 3. As the table shows, the majority of respondents were from smaller departments - 50 percent were from departments of ten or fewer faculty. The mean number of faculty is 15.8 with range of 2 to 84.

The number of majors and minors per department is shown in Figure 1. The mean number of majors is 288 with range of 0 to 1200. Forty-five percent of the schools surveyed do not have minors, and 45 percent have less than 100 minors. Of the schools that do have minors, the mean number of students is 96. Clearly, a computer science minor is not widely offered among the schools responding, nor is a minor widely taken when it is offered.

Fifty-nine percent of the responding schools offer Master's degrees and 37 percent have doctoral programs. The number of full-time and part-time graduate students per department is shown in Figure 2. The mean is 76 full-time graduate students, and 115 part-time. Nationally, 54 percent of all schools offering at least a bachelor's degree in computer science offer a master's degree as well, and 29 percent offer doctoral degrees in computer science. Thus our sample seems quite representative of the population.

Finally, Table 4 shows the number of software engineering courses offered. Currently, 33 percent of the schools do not offer a course in software engineering. Of those offering a software engineering course, the majority (63 percent) offer only one course.

In summary, it appears that the typical or modal respondent to the questionnaire is from a Computer Science department in an Arts and Sciences or a Sciences college. Their department has fewer than ten faculty members, has 288 majors, has fewer than 100 minors, and offers a Master's degree. Furthermore, they offer one course in software engineering to their undergraduates.

The next four sections present the findings concerning course descriptions, course content, course organization and project characteristics. The course description section includes course title, level, prerequisites and effectiveness responses. The section on course content examines the subject matter of the courses currently being offered. Issues concerning demands on students, sources of materials, and staffing are described in the course organization section. Characteristics of the project portion of the courses are reported in the last section.

Course Description

A total of 59 software engineering courses were described in the questionnaires returned. There were 31 different titles using a wide variety of terms given for these courses. The most frequently used title was Software Engineering (37 percent) and 19 percent of the titles referred to different stages in the software lifecycle or to subject areas in software engineering. The complete list of titles is given in Appendix B. The variability in the titles and the fact that some of the titles give no indication that traditional software engineering techniques are being covered, indicates the newness of the courses in the computer science curriculum and the lack of concensus concerning both the courses' place in the curriculum and the courses' content.

A breakdown of the reported courses by student level showed seven percent are intended for freshmen, ten percent for sophomores, 47 percent for juniors and 37 percent for seniors. Sixty-eight percent of the courses are for three hours of credit. Twenty-five percent of the courses are for four hours of credit. There is one case (1.7 percent) for each of the other categories: one, two, five and six hours of credit. The split between three and four hours of credit may be an indication of the different academic calendars in use. Seventy-four percent of the schools responding are on semesters or trimesters. The remainder are on the quarter system.

Figure 3 shows the percent of software engineering courses requiring different numbers of prerequisite courses. There is large variability in the number of prerequisites, although, not surprisingly, every course has at least one prerequisite. Although some of the variability can probably be attributed to the calendar differences, much of it is no doubt due to where the course is put in the curriculum. While some departments may feel the concepts are important introductory material, others may feel that students need a wide variety of computer science experience before they can understand the role of software engineering and apply its precepts. Eighty percent require a data structures course as one of the prerequisites.

Overall, 61 percent rated their courses as highly effective in educating students. Thirty-six percent felt the courses were moderately effective, and three percent felt the courses were low in effectiveness.

Course Content

In the Course Content section of the questionnaire, respondents were asked to rate the importance of 10 different topics to their software engineering courses. The topics included: Requirements Analysis and Specification, System (Preliminary) Design, Detailed Design, Coding and Programming Practice, Testing, Software Metrics, Project Management, User Interface Design,

System Maintenance and Modifications, and Legal and Ethical Issues. Figure 4 shows the percent of courses which included the queried topics, along with a rating of the amount of coverage the topic received in the course. Each bar in Figure 4 represents the total percent of courses which include the associated topic. The bar is subdivided into three segments. The darkest segment represents the proportion of respondents who rated the topic as receiving in-depth coverage. The middle, moderately-shaded segment represents the proportion who rate the topic as receiving moderate coverage, and the rightmost, lightly-shaded segment represents limited coverage.

It is clear from Figure 4 that, as a whole, the five topics related to the software development life cycle (Requirements, System Design, Detailed Design, Coding and Testing) are covered most frequently and receive much more in-depth and moderate coverage than the other topics listed. Of the remaining topics, User Interface Design receives the most frequent coverage. In fact, 25.5 percent of the courses contain in-depth coverage of this topic. This finding is surprising, because the majority of available software engineering texts do not include chapters on user interface design. The least frequently covered topic of those listed was Legal and Ethical Issues.

Course Organization

In the Course Organization part of the questionnaire, respondents indicated how well each of a series of statements described their courses. The statements dealt with course materials, organization and staffing. The exact statements were:

Textbooks are the primary source of materials

Journal articles are the primary source of materials

Students complete written reports

Students give oral reports

Students take exams

The reading load for the course is heavy

Staffing the course is a problem

Obtaining suitable hardware is a problem

Obtaining suitable software is a problem

Each statement was rated as being not at all true (never occurs), somewhat characteristic (rarely occurs), moderately characteristic (frequently occurs), or very characteristic (occurs very often).

Figure 5 shows the results from the Course Organization portion of the questionnaire. The different course aspects, corresponding to the statements presented, are listed on the y-axis. Each bar represents the total proportion of courses which were characterized by the corresponding aspect. The bar is divided into segments. The leftmost, dark segment represents the percent of respondents who felt the aspect occurred often. The middle, moderately-shaded segment represents the percent who felt the aspect occurred frequently, and the rightmost, lightly-shaded segment represents the rarely occuring responses.

In examining the results for the written materials used in the courses, it is clear that the majority of the courses do not rely heavily on published materials. Thirty-two percent state that textbooks are very often their primary source of materials, while 10 percent rate usage of journal articles highly. On the other hand, 29 percent use textbooks rarely or not at all as a source of materials, and 71 use journal articles rarely or not at all. This result is probably due to two primary factors - the project-oriented nature of many of the courses (see below), and the lack of textbooks suitable for the course as it is taught.

Four different aspects listed in Figure 5 represent demands on the students. These are: requiring written reports, requiring oral reports, exams and heavy reading loads. In contrast to typical computer science courses, written reports were most frequent cited as characteristic of the courses, and were cited by 67 percent as being very characteristic. Again, this outcome is probably related to the project-oriented nature of the course. Exams are cited as very characteristic by 64 percent. Oral reports are also quite common (60 percent cited them as occuring very often or frequently). Heavy reading loads were least emphasized (18 cited a heavy reading load as very often). Nonetheless, a large proportion, 54 percent, frequently have a heavy reading load.

It is also evident from Figure 5 that staffing software engineering courses is a problem. Fifteen percent of the respondents indicated that staffing is very often a problem, while 31 percent replied that staffing is frequently a problem. Obtaining suitable software is also a problem in many cases, with 21 percent finding it a problem very often, and 21 percent frequently finding it a problem. Hardware is less of a problem. Only 25 percent have a problem obtaining suitable hardware very often or frequently. Seventy-five percent rarely or never have a problem obtaining hardware.

Project Component

Ninety-five percent of the schools that offered software engineering courses include a project component in at least one of their courses. (Note that 62 percent of the schools offering software engineering courses offer only one course.) Figure 6 presents a profile of some of the characteristics of these projects. For 40 percent of the respondents, the project is very often or frequently a toy project. By implication, in 60 percent of the cases the project is intended for actual use. However, that does not mean the project involves users from outside. In 72 percent of the cases, the user is very often or frequently the instructor. Classes typically tackle several projects, as 62 percent rarely or never have the entire class work on the same project.

The most dominant trend among the project characteristics is the use of teams. Ninety-eight percent use teams at least some of the time and 90 percent use them very often or frequently. The second most dominant trend - the use of student leaders - completes the picture of teams composed of and lead by students. Eighty-five percent use student leaders very often or frequently.

The suggestion that the project is a major focus of the typical software engineering course is highlighted by the large proportion (58 percent) who said that the project counts for 40 percent or more of the student's course grade. An additional 14 percent say the project frequently accounts for at least 40 percent of the grade. Finally, in most cases the instructor is entirely responsible for grading the projects, as only 39 percent report that the students help determine the project grades.

IV. EXTRACTION OF COURSE PROFILES USING FACTOR ANALYSIS MODELING

The descriptive statistics which have been presented tell a great deal about the undergraduate courses reported in the current survey. However, the analysis of these data is potentially incomplete without consideration of what, if any, underlying regularities exist in the data. Can the relatively large number of responses for each course be reduced into some small number of recurring patterns?

Factor analysis refers to a family of statistical techniques which are widely used in behavioral research to extract underlying categories or dimensions out of a large data set. In general, factor analysis consists of three steps: generation of an interrelation matrix, extraction of initial factors, and rotation to a final factor structure. In the first step, the interrelationships among variables or individuals, expressed typically as correlations or covariances, are generated pairwise. From the resulting matrix of interrelationships, a set of initial factors is extracted. The initial factors may incorporate *a priori* assumptions about underlying regularities. Each initial factor describes a linear combination of the original variables or individuals. The initial factors are then rotated to a final solution. The final solution forms an n-dimensional structure. Each dimension typically contains one or more of the original variables or individuals. Category membership is determined by loadings of the original variables or individuals and the factors. The variables with strong loadings are considered to be category members; the final rotation highlights high factor loadings. The original variables or individuals which are grouped in the same dimension are presumed to be thematically similar ([19] and [20]).

In the current analysis, each of the 59 reported courses was considered as a separate data point. A matrix of correlations between all pairwise combinations of course description items (Requirements Analysis and Specification, System Design, Detailed Design, Coding Practice, Testing, Software Metrics, User Interface, System Maintenance and Modification, Legal and Ethical Issues) was generated. The initial factors were extracted using a principal components factor analysis. No *a priori* assumptions about underlying structure were required for this technique. A varimax rotation was performed on the initial factors. This rotation technique produces a set of orthogonal, or uncorrelated, factors.

Course Dimensions

Three course topic dimensions emerged from the factor analysis of the course content variables. Appendix C contains graphical descriptions of the factor structure.

Later-Life -Cycle Course : The course content issues of Detailed Design, Coding Practice, Testing, User Interface, and System Maintenance and Modification, combined, formed the first emergent dimension of the final factor structure. The variables of Coding Practice, Testing and System Maintenance and Modification, combined, were loaded the most heavily on this dimension. The structure of this factor indicates that in many of the courses, these topics, together, receive heavier coverage than the other topics queried in the survey. We have labeled this dimension the Later-Life-Cycle Course.

Early-Life-Cycle Course: The course content topics of Requirements Analysis/Specification and System (Preliminary) Design were strongly loaded on the second dimension of the final factor solution, suggesting that another typical software engineering course might be labeled the Early-Life-Cycle course.

Theoretical-Issues Course: The course content topics of Software Metrics, Project Management, and Legal and Ethical Issues form the third emergent dimension. We have labeled this type of course the Theoretical-Issues approach.

Course Dimensions and Other Variables: Emergence of Course Profiles

Each of the extracted dimensions describes a potentially different style of software engineering course in terms of course emphasis. Clearly it would be useful to develop more detailed course profiles. We developed such profiles based on the interactions of the course dimensions and the other course variables of level, organization, and project features.

The extracted factor loadings were multiplied by the original course content variables for each reported course. In this way, factor scores for each of the three dimensions were calculated for each individual course. Pearson product-moment correlations between the factor scores and other course variables were calculated. Several correlations were significantly different than zero, at or below the .05 significance level.

Later-Life -Cycle Course : A significant positive correlation emerged between the Later-Life-Cycle Course and the number of prerequisite courses, as well as the proportion of the final grade related to the project (r=.33 and r=.33, p<.02 and p<.02). These two results suggest that this type of course is product-oriented and is taken by experienced students. The course is product-oriented because it focuses on those stages of the software life cycle which produce the end-product, such as tested code, and because of the large proportion of the final grade related to the project. The evidence that the course is taken by experienced students is supported by the correlation with number of prerequisites.

The Later-Life-Cycle Course also has a significant positive correlation with the perceived effectiveness of the course (r=.41, p<.005). This strong correlation suggests that instructors who emphasize the pragmatic elements of software development and produce a working software product see the course as more effective than courses which focus on other aspects of software engineering and/or produce non-software products. The perceived effectiveness of the course may also be the result of feedback from students. Computer science students are practiced at producing software, and may find the contents of the Later-Life-Cycle-Stages courses more familiar and comfortable than courses with alternate approaches.

Early-Life-Cycle Course: The Early-Life-Cycle course factor has a strong positive correlation with the use of written reports and a large percentage of course grade from the project (r=.42 and r=.35, p<.003 and p<.02). These correlations suggest that a course which emphasizes the early stages of the life cycle includes projects which produce written reports. This is not unexpected, as many of the tangible products of early life cycle tasks are written documents.

Surprisingly, the typical Early-Life-Cycle course factor has a significant positive correlation with the instructor acting as the end user (r=.30, p<.04). One can infer that an instructor who emphasizes these stages of the life cycle would like the students to practice their skills in a "controlled" setting. In the controlled situation the students would be able to focus on the techniques of requirements analysis, specification, and preliminary design without dealing with the idiosyncracies of real users.

Theoretical-Issues Course : The Theoretical-Issues approach showed significant positive correlation with course level and the use of journal articles ($r=.40$ and $r=.32$, $p<.01$ and $p<.03$). These results suggest that a course which emphasizes these topics is an upper-level course. The students in this type of course are required to deal with more theoretical material than the students in the other types of courses. Since much of this theoretical material is not included in textbooks, the students are forced to read primary sources such as journals. This dimension also is positively correlated with partial student determination of project grades ($r=.41, p<.005$). One can infer that in the small number of courses which emphasize these theoretical issues, the students have reached a status advanced enough to evaluate themselves fairly and effectively.

Course Profiles and Project Characteristics

In general, the project characteristics showed little correlation with the three types of courses described above. On the surface, this result seems to be a surprising one. Intuitively, one might expect that the project features, such as use of teams, toy projects, and multiple projects per class would be positively correlated with the two life cycle courses, the Late-Life-Cycle Courses and the Early-Life-Cycle Courses. Similarly, one might expect negative correlations between the Theoretical-Issues courses and any of the project variables. However, the lack of relationship between the content dimensions and the project variables actually is consistent with the results of the descriptive statistics. The descriptive statistics clearly show that projects are a key component in nearly all software engineering courses.

Course Profiles and Department Demographics

None of the three course dimensions are significantly correlated with any of the departmental demographics results. This suggests that the topics which appear in software engineering courses are relatively independent of department or program size. Patterns of course content appears to be stable across a variety of departmental settings.

V. SUMMARY AND CONCLUSIONS

The question which motivated this survey was "What is a typical undergraduate software engineering course?" The descriptive statistics show that the typical course focuses on the software development life cycle and involves a significant project worked on by teams of students, with student leaders. The course appears at the junior or senior level, and requires the students to produce written reports and oral reports, as well as to take examinations. The project is often a real project, intended for actual use. In most cases, the instructor acts as the user, and the class works on more than one project.

A more fine-grained analysis of the results, however, shows that there are in fact three sorts of courses currently being offered. The first and most predominant style of course is the Later-Life-Cycle course. The Later-Life-Cycle course focuses on the phases of the software life cycle that produce functioning code, including detailed design, coding, testing and maintenance. This course is offered to experienced students, and the grade is heavily based on the project. The second sort of course is the Early-Life-Cycle course. It emphasizes requirements analysis and specification and system design. Written reports are a significant component of the course, and the students' grades are heavily based on the project. Theoretical-Issues form the basis of the third sort of course. Software metrics, project management and legal and ethical issues are typically covered in a Theoretical-Issues course. The course is aimed at higher level students, and journal articles are commonly used as a source of materials. Students are also involved in grading the projects in this course.

In reviewing the results, the lack of an adequate textbook - a concern raised in the case-study literature - is echoed by the survey respondents. The Theoretical-Issues course, in particular, uses journal articles as a source of material instead of textbooks. Undergraduate courses in any subject typically use textbooks - not journal articles. Although there may be many reasons for using textbooks, readability is certainly an important factor. Lemos [21] studied the readability of the ten most popular computer science journals and found that they have a mean difficulty level of 33.7 on the Flesch Reading Ease scale. Scores of 0 to 30 are considered to indicate very difficult reading (scientific journals) and scores of 30 to 50 indicate difficult reading (academic journals). Furthermore, these ten journals had an average reading grade level of 15.32. This indicates that the reader needs to read at least at the level of a college junior. Lemos states that "it is questionable whether such a high degree of difficulty is appropriate [in journal articles], especially if unfamiliar material is being read" (p. 157). We believe this statement applies to the materials chosen for use in an undergraduate software engineering course as well. Journal articles are probably not appropriate at this level. What is needed, then, are textbooks written at the reading level of undergraduates, and oriented towards the three sorts of courses we have described. In particular, the textbooks need to be project oriented, and ought to include sufficient detail on the various techniques to guide the development of projects.

A second problematic area is the course-content topic of user interfaces. This topic is given in-depth or moderate coverage in nearly 60 percent of the courses. However, very few software engineering textbooks contain even a single chapter on this topic. Few books are available which provide a survey or introduction to the topic. Furthermore, most computer science curricula do not include courses in cognitive psychology or human factors - the two disciplines most closely allied with user interface design. Given these facts, one wonders where instructors are obtaining their materials and their own training to teach this facet of software design.

Overall, however, the convergence of the reported software engineering courses into three main streams is heartening. It suggests that the domain may be gaining some degree of maturity and a sense of direction. The on-going problems of support materials and content-specific qualifications are reminders that challenges still lie ahead for software engineering educators.

REFERENCES

[1] R. H. Austing, B. H. Barnes, D. T. Bonnette, G. L. Engel, and G. Stokes, "Curriculum '78, Recommendations for the Undergraduate Program in Computer Science," *Commun. ACM*, vol. 22, no. 3, pp. 147-166, March1979

[2] E. Kant, "A Semester Course in Software Engineering," *Software Engineering Notes,* vol. 6, no. 4, pp. 52-76, August 1981.

[3] M. L. Shooman, "The Teaching of Software Engineering," in *ACM SIGCSE Bulletin,* February 1983, pp. 66-69.

[4] D. L. Carver, "Comparison of Techniques in Project-Based Courses," in *ACM SIGCSE Bulletin*, March 1985, pp. 9-12.

[5] L. J. Mazlack, "Using a Sales Incentive Technique in a First Course in Software Engineering," in *ACM SIGCSE Bulletin*, February 1981, pp. 37-40.

[6] G. Lapalme and J. Lamy, "An Experiment in the Use of ADA in a Course in Software Engineering," in *ACM SIGCSE Bulletin*, February 1986, pp. 124-126.

[7] J. S. Collofello and S. N. Woodfield, "A Project-Unified Software Engineering Course Sequence," in *ACM SIGCSE Bulletin*, February 1982, pp. 13-19.

[8] R. S. Pressman, *Software Engineering: A Practitioner's Approach.* New York: McGraw-Hill Book Company, 1982.

[9] R. E. Fairley, *Software Engineering Concepts.* New York: McGraw-Hill Book Company, 1985.

[10] R. W. Jensen and C. C. Tonies, *Software Engineering*. Englewood Cliffs, NJ: Prentice-Hall, 1979.

[11] D. D. Bickerstaff, "The Evolution of a Project Oriented Course in Software Development," in *ACM SIGCSE Bulletin*, March 1985, pp. 13-22.

[12] S. Henry, "A Project-Oriented Course on Software Engineering," in *ACM SIGCSE Bulletin*,

February 1983, pp. 57-61.

[13] L. J. Waguespack and D. F. Haas, "A Workbench for Project Oriented Software Engineering Courses," in *ACM SIGCSE Bulletin*, February 1984, pp. 137-145.

[14] J. S. Collofello, "Monitoring and Evaluating Individual Team Members in a Software Engineering Course," in *ACM SIGCSE Bulletin*, March 1985, pp. 6-8.

[15] S. N. Woodfield, J. S. Collofello, and P. M. Collofello, "Some Insights and Experiences in Teaching Team Project Courses," in *ACM SIGCSE Bulletin*, February 1983, pp. 62-65.

[16] Publications Dept. of the ACM, *ACM 1984 Administrative Directory*. New York: ACM, 1984.

[17] L. L. Beck and T. E. Perkins, "A Survey of Software Engineering Practice: Tools, Methods, and Results," *IEEE Trans. on Soft. Eng.*, vol. SE-9, no. 5, pp. 541-561, Sept. 1983.

[18] K. Webb and H. P. Hatry, *Obtaining Citizen Feedback: The Application of Citizen Surveys to Local Governments*. Washington, D.C.: The Urban Institute, 1973.

[19] H. H. Harman, *Modern Factor Analysis, 3rd ed.* Chicago: University of Chicago Press, 1976.

[20] D. Child, *The Essentials of Factor Analysis*. New York: Holt, Rinehart and Winston, 1973.

[21] R. S. Lemos, "Rating the Major Computing Periodicals on Readability," *Commun. ACM*, vol. 28, no. 2, pp. 152-157, February 1985.

Table 1

DEPARTMENT AFFILIATION OF RESPONDENTS

DEPARTMENT	PERCENT
Computer Science	57
Mathematics	21
Information Science	13
Electrical Eng. and CS	8

Table 2

COLLEGE AFFILIATION OF RESPONDENTS

COLLEGE	PERCENT
Liberal Arts, A and S	30
Science	30
Engineering	14
Business	8
No Answer or N/A	17

Table 3

NUMBER OF FACULTY PER DEPARTMENT

SIZE RANGE	PERCENT
1 - 10	50
11- 20	26
21- 30	18
> 30	6

Table 4

NUMBER OF SOFTWARE ENGINEERING COURSES OFFERED PER SCHOOL

NUMBER OF SE COURSES OFFERED	PERCENT
0	33
1	41
2	12
3	3
> 3*	1

*Note: The questionnaire only allowed feedback on three courses. However, one respondent included information on 7 courses.

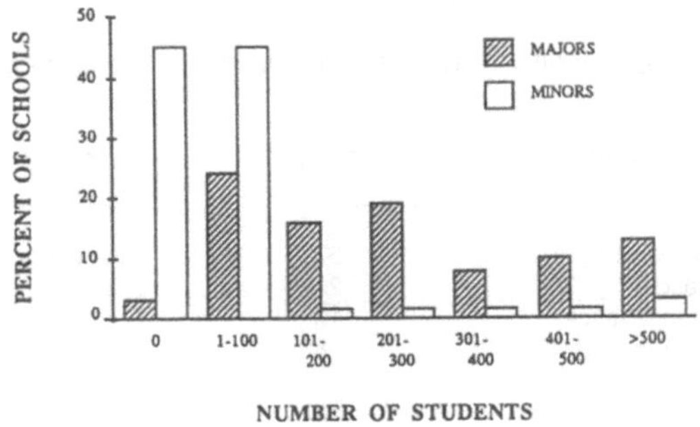

Figure 1: The distribution of number of majors and number of minors at the schools responding to the survey.

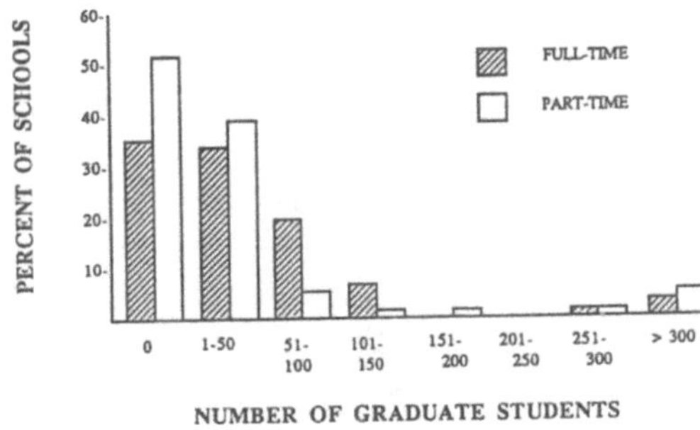

Figure 2: The distribution of number of full-time and number of part-time graduate students at the schools responding to the survey.

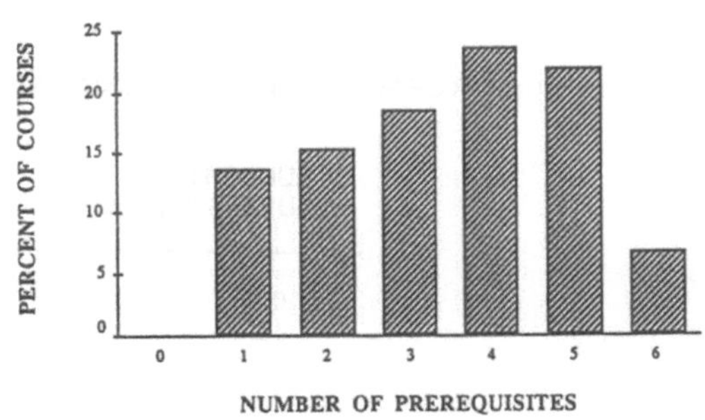

Figure 3: The percent of courses described in the survey requiring different numbers of prerequisites.

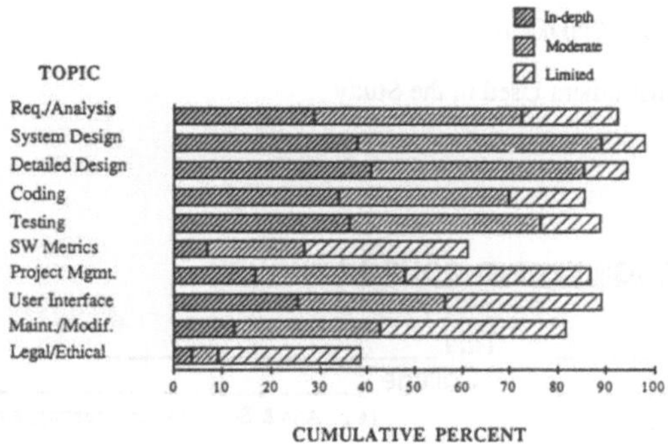

Figure 4: The cumulative percent of courses including In-depth, Moderate or Limited coverage of ten different course content topics.

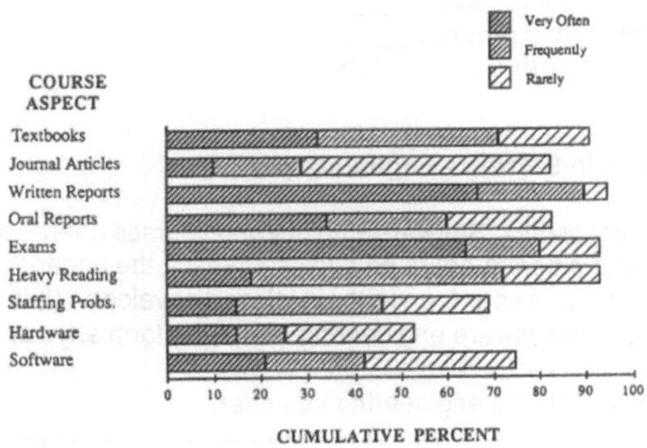

Figure 5: The cumulative percent of courses rated as Very Often, Frequently or Rarely being characterized by nine different course aspects.

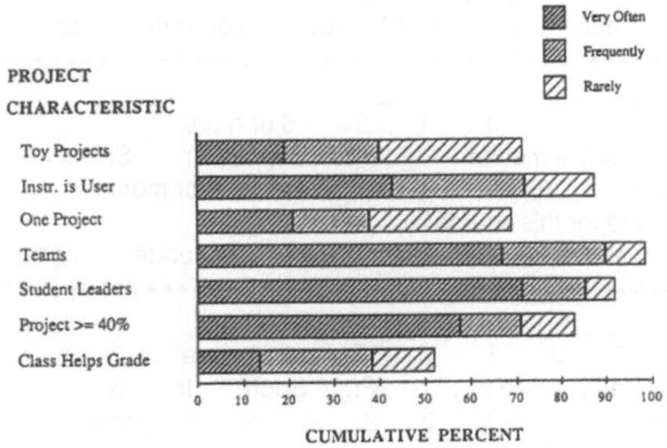

Figure 6: The cumulative percent of project-components rated as Very Often, Frequently or Rarely being characterized by seven different project characteristics.

APPENDIX A

The Survey Instrument Used in the Study

SOFTWARE ENGINEERING COURSE SURVEY

Your name ______________________________ Title ______________________________
Department ______________________________ College ______________________________
Institution ______________________________ (e.g., Arts & Sciences, Engineering, etc.)

Number of full-time faculty members in your department ____
Number of undergraduate majors in your program ____
Number of undergraduate minors in your program ____
Graduate degrees offered: M.S. __ Ph.D. __
Number of full-time graduate students in your program ____
Number of part-time graduate students in your program ____
Calendar System: semesters __ trimesters __ quarters __

SECTION 1 - Undergraduate Courses in Software Engineering

Section 1 contains general questions concerning Software Engineering courses offered to undergraduates in your program. If your program offers no such courses at the undergraduate level, **check here** ____ , and return your form in the enclosed envelope. (It is important that programs with no courses in software engineering return the form anyway.)

Fill in one box below for each course in software engineering you offer.

+++
1 Course #1: Title ______________________________ +
1 Number of credit hours : 1 2 3 4 5 6 or more +
1 Level of student course is primarily aimed at : Fr. Soph. Jr. Sr. +
1 Number of prerequisite courses : 0 1 2 3 4 5 6 or more +
1 Is Data Structures a prerequisite for this course? yes no +
1 How effective is this course in educating students? low moderate high +
+++
2 Course #2: Title ______________________________ +
2 Number of credit hours : 1 2 3 4 5 6 or more +
2 Level of student course is primarily aimed at : Fr. Soph. Jr. Sr. +
2 Number of prerequisite courses : 0 1 2 3 4 5 6 or more +
2 Is Data Structures a prerequisite for this course? yes no +
2 How effective is this course in educating students? low moderate high +
+++
3 Course #3: Title ______________________________ +
3 Number of credit hours : 1 2 3 4 5 6 or more +
3 Level of student course is primarily aimed at : Fr. Soph. Jr. Sr. +
3 Number of prerequisite courses : 0 1 2 3 4 5 6 or more +
3 Is Data Structures a prerequisite for this course? yes no +
3 How effective is this course in educating students? low moderate high +
+++

SECTION 2 - Course Content

For each of the following content areas, rate the importance of the topic to your software engineering course(s). For each content area, circle a 0 if that area is Not Covered in the course. Circle a 1 if the area has Limited Coverage, a 2 if the area recieves Moderate Coverage or a 3 if the are is covered In-depth. Fill in one column for each of the corresponding courses you listed on page 1.

Remember, **0** = Not Covered **1** = Limited Coverage **2** = Moderate Coverage **3** = In-depth Coverage

	Course 1	Course 2	Course 3
Requirements analysis and specification	0 1 2 3	0 1 2 3	0 1 2 3
System (preliminary) design	0 1 2 3	0 1 2 3	0 1 2 3
Detailed design	0 1 2 3	0 1 2 3	0 1 2 3
Coding and programming practice	0 1 2 3	0 1 2 3	0 1 2 3
Testing	0 1 2 3	0 1 2 3	0 1 2 3
Software metrics	0 1 2 3	0 1 2 3	0 1 2 3
Project management	0 1 2 3	0 1 2 3	0 1 2 3
User interface design	0 1 2 3	0 1 2 3	0 1 2 3
System maintenance and modifications	0 1 2 3	0 1 2 3	0 1 2 3
Legal and ethical issues	0 1 2 3	0 1 2 3	0 1 2 3

SECTION 3 - Course Organization

For each statement below concerning course organization, indicate how well it describes each of the courses in software engineering you listed on page 1. Fill in one column for each course. Use the following scale in rating the statements below:

0 = not at all true, never occurs
1 = somewhat characteristic of the course, occurs rarely
2 = moderately characteristic of the course, occurs frequently
3 = very characteristic of the course, occurs very often

	Course 1	Course 2	Course 3
Textbooks are the primary source of materials	0 1 2 3	0 1 2 3	0 1 2 3
Journal articles are primary source of materials	0 1 2 3	0 1 2 3	0 1 2 3
Students complete written reports	0 1 2 3	0 1 2 3	0 1 2 3

Students give oral reports	0 1 2 3	0 1 2 3	0 1 2 3
Students take exams	0 1 2 3	0 1 2 3	0 1 2 3
The reading load for the course is heavy	0 1 2 3	0 1 2 3	0 1 2 3
Staffing the course is a problem	0 1 2 3	0 1 2 3	0 1 2 3
Obtaining suitable hardware is a problem	0 1 2 3	0 1 2 3	0 1 2 3
Obtaining suitable software is a problem	0 1 2 3	0 1 2 3	0 1 2 3

SECTION 4 - Project Component

Fill in this section if any of your software engineering courses include a project component. If none of your courses include such a component, **check here** ___, and return your form in the enclosed envelope.

For each statement below, indicate how well it describes the project component of your software engineering courses. Fill in one column for each of the courses you listed on page 1. Use the following scale in rating the statements:

0 = not at all true, never occurs
1 = somewhat characteristic of the course project, occurs rarely
2 = moderately characteristic of the course project, occurs frequently
3 = very characteristic of the course project, occurs very often

	Course 1	Course 2	Course 3
Projects are "toy" projects, not intended for actual use	0 1 2 3	0 1 2 3	0 1 2 3
The instructor serves as the "user" or system requestor	0 1 2 3	0 1 2 3	0 1 2 3
Teams of students work on the project(s)	0 1 2 3	0 1 2 3	0 1 2 3
All teams (or the entire class) work on the same project	0 1 2 3	0 1 2 3	0 1 2 3
Students serve as team or project leaders	0 1 2 3	0 1 2 3	0 1 2 3
Class members help determine the grade the project(s) receive(s)	0 1 2 3	0 1 2 3	0 1 2 3
The project grade is a large part (40% or more) of the student's course grade	0 1 2 3	0 1 2 3	0 1 2 3

-ALL DONE. THANK YOU! -

APPENDIX B

Titles and Frequencies of the Undergraduate Software Engineering Courses Described in the Results

Those titled "Software Engineering" or including the word "Engineering":

Software Engineering (12)

Software Engineering Project (2)

Introduction to Software Engineering (3)

Software Design and Engineering (1)

Computer Systems Engineering (1)

Those whose titles reflect stages in the software life cycle, or topics in SE:

Systems Analysis (2)

Systems Analysis and Design (1)

Software Design (2)

Software Design Methods (1)

System Design (1)

Project in System Design (1)

Software Project Management (1)

User/System Interface (1)

Titles related to the development of software systems:

Software Development Lab (3)

Software Construction (1)

Program Development Methods (1)

Computer Projects (1)

Software Lab on Large Computers (1)

Design and Construction of Large Software Systems (1)

Miscellaneous:

Algorithm and Structured Methods (1)

Programming Techniques (1)

Information Systems (3)

Database Management Systems (2)

System Programming (1)

Application Programming (1)

Program and Data Structures (1)

Advanced Programming (1)

Programming II (1)

Introduction to Structured Programming (1)

Topics in Computer Applications (1)

Introduction to Programming in HOL (1)

APPENDIX C

Factor Plots

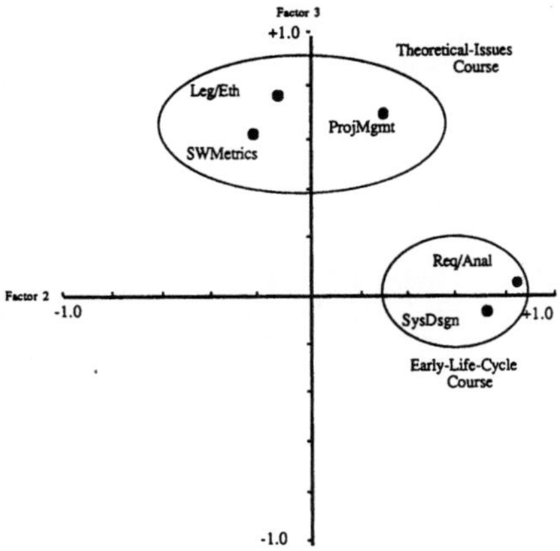

Figure 8: The factor structure for Factor 2 and Factor 3

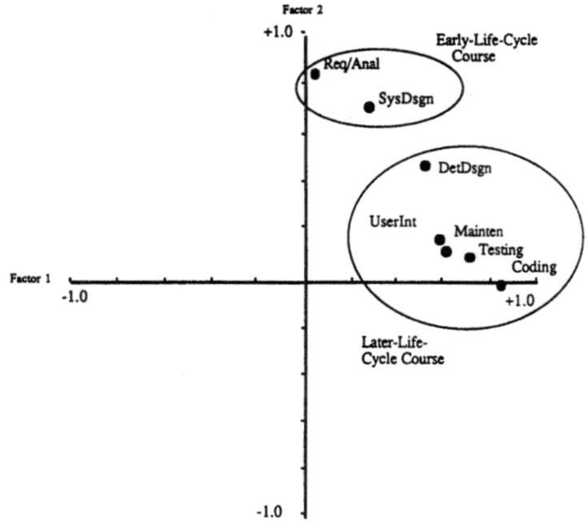

Figure 7: The factor structure for Factor 1 and Factor 2

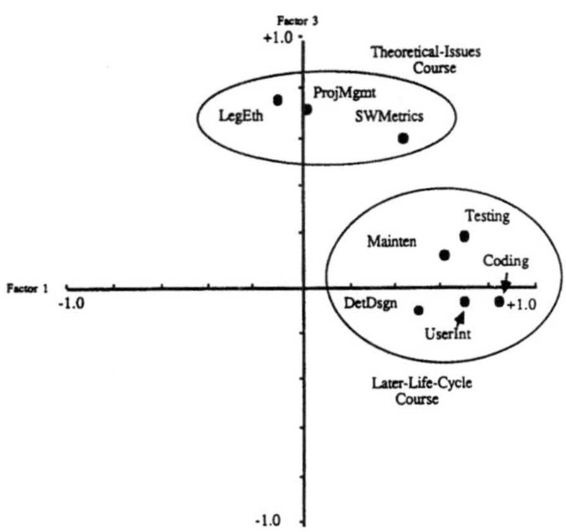

Figure 9: The factor structure for Factor 1 and Factor 3

SECTION II

PART 2

TEACHING PROJECT COURSES

Most software engineering educators agree that project courses are essential components of software engineering education. This section presents six papers on various considerations related to teaching these courses. Topics presented here include some observations on teaching project courses; two complementary sequences on design and implementation of software products; the system factory approach to software engineering education; performing requirements analysis project courses for external customers; an academic environment for software engineering projects; and the myth of the real world in project courses.

Four papers from Part 2 were presented at the Conference. A synopsis of each presentation and a question/answer session are included at the beginning of Part 2.

Synopsis of Presentation

Dr. Tom Nute

Dr. Nute presented the main points in his paper, tied them into some of the other presentations at the workshop, and provided some of the background and rationale for the ideas presented in his paper. Among the points he made in his presentation were the following:

- The purpose of a software development course, is to teach students how to develop, implement, and manage a large software project; learning comes through experience.
- The best objective for an instructor is to exert a lot of supervision, but with a minimal amount of guidance and suggestion. Thus, be unobtrusive, but always present.
- From the point of view of the instructor, it is difficult to select a project.
- The problem with going out and getting projects from real customers, is that they tend to intimidate the students and faculty since it is usually a multimillion dollar project.
- He advocates having a clean, precise project that allows students enough time to finish, without feeling frustrated.
- A one semester project is barely large enough to use some of the important tools.
- Projects that involve Artificial Intelligence concepts do not tend to divide up well. Dr. Nute prefers to pick a project that lends itself to partitioning among a team of anywhere from three to six students.

- He advocates using a project that includes a lot of realism. Otherwise, students may develop the feeling that it has been contrived to illustrate some point, and they don't bother to believe it.
- Unit level testing is very important; students should devote at least one of those two semesters to testing their system.
- There are a number of drawbacks to using part–time faculty from industry. They are not always available; they often do not have an office on campus. Moreover, after they teach a class, they immediately turn around and leave again.

Synopsis of Presentation

Dr. Ed Robertson

Dr. Robertson presented the main points in his paper, which were tied into some of the other presentations at the workshop. In his paper, he provided some of the background and rationale for the ideas which were presented. Among the points he made in his presentation were the following:

- During the senior year as well as the first year of the Graduate program, students are exposed to concepts in terms of depth rather than breadth.

- There is a two–semester sequence which combines two related courses: Information Systems and Software Engineering Management.

- Abstraction is a major tool in designing, and mathematics is an appropriate vehicle for practicing that type of abstraction.

- Having firm milestones is a major step in a successful project. Among these milestones, with the exception of coding and testing, are large written documents and oral presentations.

- Participation of all the group members in the oral presentations is stressed.

- Having a two semester course allows the opportunity during the semester–break, to stop, realign the teams, and redefine the project scope if necessary.

- The students from the management course supervise the teams in the undergraduate course. This takes some of the burden off the professor, who may have up to 10 teams to supervise at a time.

- The biggest advantage of having this extra help in the course, is that it opens the channel of communication. Students are sometimes very hesitant to talk to their professor about certain things, whereas the supervisors, often viewed as other students, tend to be a little less intimidating.
- Because of the affiliation with real clients, students and professors are often caught between the pressures of delivering a real product to a real client, and the constraints of the educational environment.

Synopsis of Presentation

Dr. Walt Scacchi

Dr. Scacchi presented the main points in his paper, which were tied into some of the other presentations at the workshop. In his paper, he provided some of the background and rationale for the ideas which were presented. Among the points he made in his presentation were the following:

- It is important to understand how large systems come to be the way they are, no matter what kind of setting they are in.
- In working with software technology transfer, it is possible to combine software engineering, research development, and education together.
- Software engineering is difficult because it has to be done in a real world environment; the laboratory setting limits the kind of resources that are available.
- However, there are enough similarities, that you can use a laboratory to a certain degree, to understand how the real world works.
- When building bigger systems, organizational problems start to dominate engineering problems. It is the organizational problems that are the more critical ones to solve.
- With regard to quality assurance reviews, someone is usually assigned to be responsible for the quality of somebody else's project. Consequently, reciprocal relationships are formed.
- For intraorganizational technology transfers, each group is assigned to be a user of some other group's tools.

- In an academic environment, he doesn't see a need to build production quality systems — there's no reward for it. However, there are rewards for building research prototypes; they can be published and supported by industry and government.

Synopsis of Presentation

John Brackett

Dr. Brackett presented the main points in his paper, tied them into some of the other presentations at the Workshop, and provided some of the background and rationale for the ideas presented in his paper. Among the points he made in his presentation were the following:

- Students who study requirements analysis typically learn some of the techniques for doing requirements analysis, but they do not gain experience in obtaining raw information from a variety of sources, synthesizing the requirements, and getting user review and approval.

- Most students have very little experience in verbal or written communication with people who are not sophisticated in the use of computers; most of them have never met a customer.

- The project course (which has been offered three times) has the following characteristics: The projects only produce requirements specifications, and do not go through the entire lifecycle process of design, development, etc.; projects are done by teams of three to five students; all projects are done for external customers; the projects produce industrial quality results; the customers are nonprofit organizations.

- There were three objectives for the requirements analysis project course: (1) the projects (which are done for external customers) provide professional quality documents and presentations for the customers; (2) the students gain real experience with some of the methods they learned in the Software Engineering course and understand what the work products really are; and (3) they gain experience in working with noncomputer knowledgeable people, to understand different points of view, to get that on paper, and to get some degree of agreement among different people.

- There must be at least one customer representative who has reasonable expectations of what computers can do; the customer must also recognize the benefits of what the students are doing and be open to analysis and recommendations by an external body.
- Projects produce three deliverables: The requirements specification for the recommended system; a report to the senior executive in the organization; and a one hour presentation to the Board of Directors.
- The instructor must work with the students to guide them in effective use of their time, and sort out intermediate milestones for the project. The instructor must also estimate the scope of the project accurately.

Questions and Answers on The Project Course Panel

Jim Tomayko: There are two general curriculum questions I'd like the panel to discuss. The first one is, where do you put the project? Do you mix it in with existing course work, so that they can be mutually re-inforcing, or do you wait until they've learned something, and then unleash them on it at the end, which is what you'd be doing if it was a Master's Thesis Project?

Tom Nute: At TCU, at the undergraduate level, we have a one semester course that all of the students are required to take. They have to take it as a senior. It's called Senior Design Project. However, we strongly encourage them to take it in the Fall semester of their senior year, because, while we strongly discourage incompletes, if they screw it up, that leaves them a 15-week fall-back position, which has been used on more than one occasion. At the graduate level, we generally have the two semester project run concurrently with at least one other course that's taught in their last two semesters that they are in the program. On occasion, students will, for personal reasons, elect only to take one course a semester, in which case they're limited to just taking that project course as the last course in their sequence. But as a rule, we try to overlap some of the course work, with the project course, more because of administrative constraints than any pedagogical reason.

Walt Scacchi: At USC, in our Master's Program, which is a Master's in CS, the project course represents roughly 30 percent. It's eight units out of 26, required for the degree. We have no thesis for the Master's. We run fall through spring. We don't give incompletes, although we do encourage people, who are part-time or who can stay on, to do directed research, during the summer. Since our graduate student population is split between one–year students, the full–time people do our project in conjunction with typically two or three other semester courses. For the industry people, who take two years, they have the choice of doing it the first year or the second. Most take it the first year since this is the kind of course that they really wanted to have.

Ed Robertson: In our context, since we have two full–year sequences, which are taken by Master's students, I think the question is, is the first year team project course necessary, in order to be a good supervisor in the Software Engineering Management Course? I think it definitely is. I have, once or twice, let people who've had other team experience, be project supervisors, without going through the information systems class. But otherwise, they just don't have the sensitivity, to the various issues, that they need to have, to actually manage a team.

John Brackett: I think that Dick Fairley's talk and Mark Ardis' talk answer the question. We require at least five out of the six required courses, before we can do the first of the projects, because the projects are regarded as integrating what you learned in the course curriculum.

Jim Tomayko: For my second question, should they have to write an evaluation of what they have done, in some form?

Walt Scacchi: Well, as part of our documentation regime, we do require that all deliverables, and there were eight, provide a narrative description, according to a scheme that we've given them, as to basically the kinds of problems that they're running into, what they're learning, what they would do if they could do it again or do it differently. So, we do require them to provide that, as part of the deliverable, because we think that's one of the things that is traditionally left out of systems and often tells you a lot more about what's going on in the system, than the specifications do.

Ed Robertson: We have attempted, in previous years, to get students to keep a project log book, that has been almost consistently observed in the breach. We do have them, however, do a post–mortem at the end. It's not a very large one, but it's something that they approach with a great deal of trepidation and after it's done, they're very grateful for. I think it's definitely a good idea and I wish we had more time to do that.

Tom Nute: One of the requirements that I impose on my students, is that they provide a critique at the end of the course, and I make that generally anywhere from five to 10 percent of their grade. Usually the team, as a whole, is required to put in a critique of what they found successful and what they felt was either unsuccessful or not all that productive. Then, I have each individual turn in a critique of their own, about what they think of working in a team and in particular, what they think of the other team members. I try to stress to them that this is not an attempt to fink out on their co-workers, but, on the other hand, they should be honest, since I'm not aware of all of the work that went in. A lot of times, things go on behind my back and there may be an individual who just likes to work, two to six in the morning. Since I never see him, I assume that he doesn't contribute as much as the others, and often times, his critiques give me some insight.

I might also add that I do, on occasion, give different grades to members of the same team and, on one occasion, I had to take even more extreme measures.

John Brackett: I guess mine is about closest to Ed's. As part of the project notebook, besides all the deliverables to the customer, there is a student post-mortem, which is also presented in the public presentation of both the project results and the evaluation. Also, what is delivered to the customer has to have a very precise description of what didn't get done and what the recommended steps are that ought to be performed.

Ed Robertson: I've decided, after this meeting, that it behooves me to put my money where my mouth is and I'm going to go back and give a post-mortem of myself, in the presentation of the class.

Jim Tomayko: I'd also like to add that at Wichita State, we can have them do a practicum, under their existing supervisor at work. The supervisor and two of our professors form a committee. The student writes a technical report and gives an oral presentation on the report and is then given an oral exam, which is fairly similar to the MS-type situation. Are there any questions from the audience?

Bob Lechner: I have a question for Walt Scacchi about his long-term research project tools. It's a very good idea and I'm surprised that no one else is apparently doing that, although we've been doing it at Lowell, on a much smaller scale. It's a similar tool development project and it does involve static analysis, using Ingress and GKS interface for graphics. Our intent is to ultimately be able to browse through text and graphics, using this system, automatically extracting data from program libraries.

My question is, do you have any experience with using the tools you developed? Are these software development analysis tools useful to you, in further project development or is it too early for that? If you have such experience or even if you don't, do you know any way that you can quantify the way in which the productivity of your teams might increase, during any life cycle phase, by using some of the tools that you're developing or can make available to others?

Walt Scacchi: The first question on the experiences, yes, we do use the tools in the projects, as well as in some of the contract works. We do have practical experience and some of these tools are out there in industry.

On productivity measurement work, as I mentioned, we initially looked at the cost estimation work of Kokomo's cost estimation. You can twiddle it to do productivity measurement, because in a forthcoming paper which is cited in my paper, we basically found that that's unreliable technology. There is no such thing as productivity measurement technology, in our view.

Chuck Pfleeger: I can infer from the comments made on the panel that all of you are very dedicated teachers who are very concerned about this course, and that you're very willing to contribute to the course and project to make them succeed. It's clear from the reactions of people sitting in this room that anyone who has ever run such a course has to invest an enormous amount of time in it. After doing this for a few times around you may reach a burnout point. Does anyone on the panel have some good suggestions for reducing the high instructor involvement for the course, while still maintaining the quality?

Ed Robertson: The one thing that we have done is to take the sections of the course and divide them horizontally, rather than vertically: I did the "book learning" part of both sections and Jim Burns did the project part of both sections. That worked much better, from several points of view. Next year, I hope to have three people signed up: one person will do the book learning part of the project course or the information systems course, one person will do the project part of both courses, and one person will do the software engineering lecture part of the second course sequence.

Tom Nute: I might add that there's also something of an administrative problem here. You have to have a chairman who will convince your dean that even though you're not standing in front of the class three hours a week, you deserve consideration for that many contact hours, if not more. This hasn't been a bad problem, fortunately, but it's been one that's required a certain amount of salesmanship.

Walt Scacchi: The way that I've addressed this is basically I trained myself to do it. I may be more of a marathon runner than a sprinter, but I didn't try to go out in the first year and run a marathon. I went out and ran a 1K. Over the years, I have trained myself to endure an outrageous amount of work. On the other hand, you start to find out the value of project management skills!

Ed Robertson: The other issue you addressed was a major motivation for me to start the supervisor's course, which has been successful, all the way around. It has been better, educationally, for the students. They have produced better products. The supervisors have gotten a lot out of it and it has been much easier on the instructors.

John Brackett: The reward structure that Dick Fairley mentioned earlier is an important component of having this level of project courses at the Wang Institute. A project course, even though there's only five or six students, is regarded from a teaching credit point of view as being equivalent to a course that has 30 or 40 people in it.

Jim Tomayko: I would like to reinforce what Walt said: You can bring yourself to delegate properly, over a period of time. Experience always helps. Also, I keep a bottle of Aspirin in my briefcase and I recommend early retirement!

Daniel Hoffman: I'd like to direct my comment and question to Walt Scacchi. You talked about developing a 30,000 line prototyping Pascal and you said that your programmers' productivity, in lines of code per unit time, is about 10 times greater than the industrial average. I'd just like to point out that this average corresponds very closely to Brooks' prediction for productivity, working on prototypes versus production quality code. So actually, it's not a 10 times increase in what's currently being done, it's a different product that's being produced.

Walt Scacchi: My comment on that would be that the numbers I cited were for the same kind of system in the industry; that is, for building a prototype in industry and not for building production. I got these numbers from Barry Boehm.

Daniel Hoffman: My question is, you said that your students wrote specifications for all of the code and I'd like to know in what specification language did they write the specifications?

Walt Scacchi: Over the years, the choice of specification languages has evolved. We started, early on, with more informal ones. In 1981 and

1982, we were working with RSL for early specifications, MIL 75 for architecture and PDL. We are currently working with Gist, in doing functional specifications. In addition, we have a language of our own, called New Mil, which is what we use for specifying architecture, configurations, and versions. Then, we implement in C, C++, or Common Lisp.

Harvey Hallman: Ed, I have a couple of questions I'd like you to answer. I understand your program is optimal, a student elective. What motivates the student to take such a project course? What do you do when the class size is either too small or too large? What happens when a student drops the course, because he got in over his head?

Ed Robertson: Well, we've never had a class where the class size has been too small. It is a very popular course. Of all of the sequences that I mentioned, it is, by far and away, the most popular one, not only by students, but we just completed a poll of our alumni and that feeling seems to prevade, that of all the courses they had, that was the most important one, for their later professional development. Moreover, the students recognize this.

As far as dropping the course, it has been necessary to reconfigure teams, as we go along.

Harvey Hallman: What happens when you have too many students enrolling for it? Some colleges restrict the number of students.

Ed Robertson: Well, we have kept caps on, but a cap of 50 students is totally unreasonable. We're down to about 30 students in a section.

Jim Tomayko: Walt, what was your smallest group?

Walt Scacchi: We've had as many as 87 and as few as 22 students, but those numbers change over a year. For example, we actually had 87 last Fall and now, we only have 48. So, having a 30 to 40 percent drop–out rate, at the semester point, is not at all unusual, because some people graduate midyear or maybe they just weren't prepared for the work.

On the other hand, we decided to try and experiment with turning Brooks' law upside down. In the project, we actually staff heavy early on and find out who's really interested in the project. So, if you have a one–year option or a two–semester option, you should be prepared for shrinking numbers, look at that as an opportunity of getting the dedicated people.

Jim Kiper: The problem we face in an undergraduate course, is that we have a projects course and it doesn't have a software engineering course as a prerequisite. This is a first introduction to software engineering, so you have these concepts you want them to understand. You want to talk about them, before they do it, but on the other hand, you have this large project you want them to get into, as early as they can. How do you solve that problem?

Ed Robertson: There is a very, very standard comment I get at the end of the course: "Gee, I really wish we'd followed the advice you gave us early on in the year." My feeling is kind of a velcro theory of education, that these ideas aren't going to do any good, unless there's something to stick to anyway. So, I generally found that I can lecture myself blue in the face about some of these ideas and they're just not applied. Now, it's partly the fact that the project is simply not massive enough in scope. But I think there has to be this, if not failure, you're skirting along the edge of disaster, before they really appreciate the value of some of these things.

Jim Tomayko: I'd like to reinforce that. I think getting them involved, as soon as possible, even though they're maybe one week experienced, is still better than trying to lecture it all out and then going into it.

Jim Kiper: Would you advise kind of a spiral view then? I mean, maybe covering everything really quickly, give them a flavor, and then go back and hit it again?

Walt Scacchi: Well, the approach that we've taken, is somewhere close, but not your last alternative—do it and then do it again. The first time through, we focus more on the reading and assimilation of concepts and ideas and ability to reason through those. The practice in the project gives people a very different understanding of some of the concepts.

We have another strategy, which is regularly reconstructing people's understanding of what's going on. We use the class meetings during the project stage to talk about problems that people are having, to go back and go over the appropriate concepts again.

Jim Tucker: In many areas we have projects courses that deal with some aspect of full-sized projects. In this sense, couldn't we increase the magnitude of the projects from tens of thousands to hundreds of thousands of lines, realizing that once we design the specifications of a program that we're convinced we could write, we don't have to write it? What do you think?

Tom Nute: My feeling is that it's probably not how large projects get designed in practice. Usually, whether you want to admit it or not, there's a prototype system developed. It's either developed at the end of the original schedule, or you face up to it immediately. But if I were to have them design a system of 100,000 lines initially, without ever getting in there and getting their hands dirty, then turn it over to somebody else and say "implement it," I think it would be a little artificial. I'd rather see them carry it a little further through and maybe scale the project down, so that they can see the transition, from the design, to the implementation, and then realize that they have to go back and iterate on the design again. If you cut off that feedback path, I think that you sacrifice a lot of the realism of the project.

Walt Scacchi: I'll look at things a little differently, which is to say that I think the kind of challenge that was posed, is one whose time has come. It may be possible to do for large scale software what our electronics friends did for large-scale integration.

Some Observations on Teaching a Software Project Course

by

James R. Comer
Tom Nute
David J. Rodjak

Computer Science Department
Texas Christian University
Fort Worth, TX 76129

Abstract:

The main purpose of a software project course is to give students experience in developing large software systems. The authors offer some observations and suggestions based on their experience teaching such courses. In particular, they make recommendations about selecting suitable projects, organizing student groups, use of development schedules, difficulties in finding qualified instructors, and the need for extra administrative support when teaching such a course.

Introduction:

Most of the software engineering programs described in the literature include a one or two semester project course.[1] The objective of this course is to prepare students to implement and manage large software projects.[2] The authors make some observations based on their experiences teaching such a course. In particular, some of the problems associated with selecting suitable assignments, use of student teams, development schedules, finding qualified instructors, etc. for a project course are discussed. The authors do not cover the mechanics of teaching a project course which is discussed in the references [Tha86], [Wor86], [McK86], and [Bus79]. A greater value than the suggestions offered is that the reader is made aware of some of the potential difficulties that may be encountered in a project course so that they can be better prepared to handle the problems when they arise.

---

1. This includes the Software Implementation Projects I and II courses offered at Texas Christian University, the Software Engineering Project Course offered at the Wang Institute of Graduate Studies [McK86], the Software Engineering Laboratory offered at Seattle University [Lee83], the Software Engineering Methods course offered at Carnegie-Mellon University [Kan81], the Computer Program Engineering course offered at the University of Toronto [Wor86], the Clinic course offered at Harvey Mudd College [Bus79], and the software engineering project laboratory offered at the California State University at Sacamento [Tha86].

2. Thayer [Tha86] gives a more detailed set of objectives for a project course.

Shortcomings of Traditional Course Projects:

The primary objective of the project course is to give students experience in the development of a large software system. Generally, students have worked alone on relatively short programming assignments whose purpose has been to illustrate some algorithm, language feature, data structure, or methodology. These projects have a narrow scope, are will defined, and are small enough that they can be attempted with little preliminary planning or organization. In particular, there is little need to develop the support materials, such as requirement specifications, detailed designs, design reviews, code walkthroughs, test plans, user manuals, etc., usually associated with a large software system.

A drawback to these small programming assignments is that the support materials identified above, which are essential for large software development and maintenance efforts, are inappropriate for a small programming assignment. Indeed, most student assignments can be completed in a few days or weeks; do not require extensive interaction with other designers, programmers, and users during the implementation; are not required to be maintained; and the detailed information necessary to debug and test the program can be readily determined by reading the code. Thus, when a student is required to develop these support items as part of their assignments, they are left with the impression that the items are an unnecessary extra burden. It is difficult for a student not to carry this same attitude over to the larger projects that they will encounter in practice. Consequently, while small programming assignments can be an effective means of teaching a specific point, such assignments may actually encourage the student to avoid the very methods that should be used in a more realistic setting. Hence, students need to learn that when "scaling up" from a small system to a large system, the level of effort increases in an exponential, not a linear, fashion.[3]

Selecting a Suitable Project:

As stated above, the primary purpose of a project course should be to expose students to the types of problems that are encountered when developing and maintaining large software systems. It is necessary to select projects that are realistic, large enough that the support items identified above are of value, and at the same time remain feasible with the resources and time available to the student. This presents a major challenge to the instructor of such a course. Some of the problems that an instructor must face are described in the following paragraphs.

If a project is too artificial, then it begins to look contrived. This is likely to leave the student with the impression that the project was "staged" to promote the use of the support materials, but that these items may not be necessary for the more typical large system. This impression only serves to further confirm the

---

3. Thayer [Tha86] describes several of the characteristics that distinguish a large system from a small system.

incorrect ideas that a student may have formed when developing small programming assignments. One means of avoiding this danger is to select projects from actual "customers" who intend to make use of the resulting system. This not only lends creditability to the project, but can lead to a sense of accomplishment as well as provide an additional incentive to do a complete and professional job. Busenberg [Bus79] and Thayer [Tha86] discuss potential sources for customers. They include the instructor, others within the department or academic environment, and sources in business, industry, and government.

If the project is too small then the student is once again faced with the problem of having to develop extensive support materials which are not actually required to implement a successful small system. Furthermore, if more than one student is working on the project, then there may not be a natural way of dividing the problem into reasonable subproblems that can be developed more or less independently by different members of the team. This is just a repeat of the problem described above when the student is given short, specific, programming assignments.

Conversely, if the project is too large, the student is unable to complete it. This often leads to frustration even though the objectives of the assignment (i.e. the development of the necessary support materials) may have been met. This frustration can mask from the student the benefits that the support materials contributed towards the partial development of the project. Indeed, the student may be left with the impression that had they not been required to devote so much effort to the apparently extraneous support materials then a successful project might have been completed. Again, the end result may be just the opposite of the intended objective of the project.

The prior two paragraphs imply that a balance must be struck between selecting a project which is too small and a project which is too large. Unfortunately for the instructor, there is no general method for selecting a project which satisfies these two requirements. A great deal depends on the prior experience and training of the members of the class. What appears to be a large programming task to a novice might be viewed as a small exercise to an experienced individual. Even individuals with similar backgrounds may approach the same assignment in different but equally effective ways -- one student may be successful by approaching a problem as if it were small and immediately begin coding while another student, equally qualified, may find it more advantageous to view the same problem as large and begin by developing written requirement specifications and detailed designs. Hence, the instructor must take the background and talents of the students into account when selecting projects. Kant [Kan86] offers several suggestions for possible projects.

Use of Student Teams:

Most large software systems are implemented by teams rather than single individuals. Thus, students should be expected to work in groups to give them experience at working in teams. A group consisting of two individuals is too small to adequately illustrate many of the advantages and problems associated with groups. However, as the size of a group increases there is a corresponding risk that one or more members will not perform their share of the assignment. The authors' experience suggests that five is about as large a group that should be allowed. Therefore, groups should be limited from three to five students with three or four being the ideal.

The particular organization of group members is not as important as ensuring that all members gain some experience in various capacities. Thus, everyone should be expected to perform certain clerical tasks, such as being group secretary or librarian, as well as serving in a role requiring leadership and management skills, such as the chief programmer or project leader. Since too frequent a change in the roles of individuals is likely to lead to confusion, the number of role changes should be minimal consistent with the need to have all members serve in various capacities. A logical time to perform these changes is between stages in the life cycle of the development effort, such as after the design effort and prior to programming. Alternatively, the change can be made at a logical breaking point in the course such as between semesters. It is probably best to have the stronger, more experienced individuals serve in the leadership roles at the beginning of the project when the greatest organizational skills are required. Thayer [Tha86] and McKeeman [McK86] offer additional suggestions on how to organize students and the assignment of responsibilities in a software project course.

One side benefit to the instructor from using groups is that the differences in talent between individuals tends to be evened out. Group efforts work at a level which is common to the majority of the members, assuming everyone is making a sincere effort to participate. The weaker members are pushed to exert more effort than they might otherwise put forth while the stronger members must take more time to make their thoughts clear to the other group members. The net effect is to reduce the variation in effective performance between members of a group. Assuming that the talent is spread more-or-less uniformly across all the groups, this has the effect of having all groups have nearly the same capability. Since the problem of selecting an appropriate sized project is compounded by differing levels of capability, the use of groups tends to simplify the task of choosing the correct size project.

Development Schedules:

Another area that deserves special attention in a project class is schedules. Students should be required to develop a realistic schedule initially and then be expected to adhere to this schedule. The schedule should include dates for concrete milestones, such as the customer giving written approval of the requirements, design walkthroughs being completed, a given module successfully compiled and linked with the other modules, unit level test completed for a given module, etc. It is important that milestones have some tangible evidence that they have been accomplished to avoid the problem of relying on percent completed estimates made by the students.

Any variances from the initial schedule should be justified in advance and in writing. The instructor should extract a grade penalty for any schedule slip unless it is completely beyond the student's control or ability to anticipate. This hard-nosed approach has the advantage of discouraging incompletes at the conclusion of the semester and introduces the student to the realities of schedule constraints in the "real-world."

Potential Problems with Customers:

A word of caution is in order when dealing with customers who expect a usable piece of software at the conclusion of the project course. As has already been noted, such customers are useful sources of realistic projects with the added benefit that the resulting system may prove to be beneficial to someone. However, such customers are generally not as interested in the educational value of the project as they are in its potential value to them. In particular, customers have little understanding of the types, sizes, or schedules for projects that can serve as good pedagogical devices.

Furthermore, customers must understand that student developed projects may not be completed or of the same quality as professionally developed software (though student projects are often of extremely high quality). Also, after the project is completed, the students will no longer be available to maintain the system.

A number of steps may to be taken to help reduce the potential problems with software developed by students for a customer. The most important step is to establish firm requirements as early as possible. Once established, these requirements should not be allowed to change except in the most dire of circumstances and even then not without a thorough review of the potential impact on the remainder of the schedule. It is important that the instructor be included in any discussions about requirement changes and have final say in any decisions. The problem with letting the students and customer try to negotiate a change on their own is that neither party may fully appreciate the potential impact on the rest of the project from even an apparently minor change. Furthermore, without the stabilizing influence of the instructor, the customer may exert undue pressure on the students to accept nonessential changes. As has been often noted, frequent requirement changes may account for more schedule slips than any other factor in the development of a system.

While it is important to protect the students from changes in requirements, students must also understand their obligation to satisfy customers. One method that is gaining acceptance is to use rapid prototyping to debug the requirements and initial design. Rapid prototyping involves developing a preliminary and partial system which exhibits many of the external properties of the system under development. This allows the customer and developers to identify and correct flaws in the requirements and proposed design approach early in the implementation process. Customers and students must understand that a prototype system, even a rapidly developed one, requires time in the schedule. However, rapid prototyping is not just an academic exercise, this investment should ultimately result in a better system being developed in less time. Rapid prototyping is simply a formal recognition that successful large software systems are not developed correctly on their first attempt -- the first attempt merely serves to identify what does and does not work so that a successful system can be developed on a subsequent attempt.

Selecting Instructors & Administrative Support:

The final area that deserves attention deals with the administration of a project course rather than with how it should be taught. Finding qualified faculty is a particularly difficult problem. Ideally, the instructor should be an effective teacher, well versed in computer science and management principles, and have extensive experience in the development of a wide variety of large software projects. In practice, it may be difficult to even find someone willing to teach the course, much less obtain someone who is anywhere near ideal. Part of the problem is that regular faculty may not consider such a course legitimate computer science or management science. Furthermore, those individuals who have the desired experience are more likely to be found in business, industry, or government than in an academic environment. Indeed, the bulk of the large software systems are developed outside of academia so it is not surprising that most of the experienced practitioners are not part of the regular teaching faculty.

Often the answer to finding a project course instructor is to rely on part-time help recruited from the business world. However, there are often problems with relying too heavily on part-time instructors. Real or apparent problems associated with part-time instructors include:

- Not being available to answer student questions except during class (part-time instructors may not even have access to an office on campus).

- Part-time instructors are often viewed as second class citizens by administrators, regular faculty, accreditation boards, and even the students.

- Because they may not be readily available and because of their perceived lesser status, part-time instructors are frequently not consulted about ways of improving curriculum, facilities, etc.

- Part-time instructor teaching methods may not be as well developed as those of a regular faculty members.

- The demands of their regular jobs may take precedence over their part-time teaching obligations (i.e. part-time instructors may lack the commitment expected of a teacher).

- Part-time instructors may show an excessively strong bias towards teaching the methods used in their regular job (i.e. there may be a loss of objectivity).

Another administrative concern is the relatively high cost of a project course. The demand for computer resources is usually high, there may be a need for special software development tools and hardware facilities, and the class size is frequently small. Since software engineering is not a mature discipline, there is a lack of good texts and an instructor may require extra time for preparations, reviewing proposals from potential customers, grading large student assignments, and generally ensuring that the somewhat unconventional course runs smoothly.

In addition to its high cost, the project course may have to compete with the expanding needs of more traditional computer science courses. Such conventional courses may appear to offer more return for the educational investment dollar due to their large enrollment, their relatively low resource demand per student, and the availability of qualified instructors, teaching materials, etc. However, the apparently high cost of teaching a project course should be viewed in terms of the benefits gained by the students. It is the authors' belief that many of the most important lessons concerning the development of software systems are learned as a result of the students taking a project course.

Summary:

The purpose of a software projects course is to expose students to the unique problems associated with large systems development and to allow students to apply the principles, tools, and methodologies taught in other courses. Since this experience is an important part of a student's education, a project course is an essential component of any software engineering program. However, there are a number of problems associated with offering such a course. Some of these problems include identifying suitable projects for students to work on, developing and adhering to realistic schedules, finding qualified instructors, and obtaining the support for the administration to offer the course in the face of its apparent high cost. The authors have offered some ideas for addressing these problems, but there are no general solutions that cover all cases. However, being aware of the problems in advance may allow administrators, faculty, and students to cope with them better as the difficulties arise.

Bibliography:

[Bus79] Busenberg, Stavros N., and Tam, Wing, C. "An Academic Program Providing Realistic Training in Software Engineering," *Communications of the ACM, 22*, 6, June 79, 341-345.

[Kan81] Kant, Elaine. "A Semester Course in Software Engineering," *ACM Sigsoft Software Engineering Notes, 6*, 4, Aug. 81, 52-76.

[Lee83] Lee, Kyu Y., and Frankel, Eric C. "Real-Life Software Projects as Software Engineering Exercises," *ACM Sigsoft Software Engineering Notes, 8*, 3, July 83, 39-43.

[McK86] McKeeman, W.M. "Experience with a Software Engineering Project Course," *Technical Report TR-86-01*, Wang Institute of Graduate Studies, Tyngsboro, MA, Jan. 16, 86 (reprinted in *Proceedings of the SEI Education Workshop*, Feb. 27, 86, Carnegie-Mellon University, Pittsburgh, PA).

[Tha86] Thayer, Richard H., and Endres, Leo A. "Software Engineering Project Laboratory: The Bridge Between University and Industry," *Proceedings of the SEI Education Workshop*, Feb. 27, 86, Carnegie-Mellon University, Pittsburgh, PA.

[Wor86] Wortman, David B. "Software Projects in an Academic Environment," *Proceedings of the SEI Education Workshop*, Feb. 27, 86, Carnegie-Mellon University, Pittsburgh, PA.

Two Complementary Course Sequences on the Design and Implementation of Software Products

JAMES E. BURNS AND EDWARD L. ROBERTSON

Abstract—For many students, the first chance to produce software as part of a team comes with the first work experience outside a university. The difficulties of working with others are compounded by the problems of working in a new environment and for a client with ambiguous and changing goals. Although it is difficult to approximate the "real-world" accurately in an academic course, we have implemented two full-year course sequences which apparently give our students some insight into the problems they will face when they leave the university. One course requires the development and implementation of a software product by a team of undergraduates, and the other requires experienced graduate students to act as supervisors for the undergraduate projects. We describe the content and structure of these two sequences, emphasizing how they support and enhance each other. We believe other curricula would benefit from similar courses.

Index Terms—Computer Science education, software engineering, team projects.

I. INTRODUCTION

As pointed out cogently by Fairley [4], the needs and desires of industry are not being consistently satisfied by bachelor level computer science graduates. In particular, industry wants software engineers, while most undergraduate programs produce entry-level computer scientists. One reason that software engineering is not part of the core of more undergraduate programs is that it is difficult to teach. Students without professional programming experience seem unable to appreciate the importance of accurate and complete specifications, planning and scheduling, test plans, good documentation, *etc.* We

James E. Burns is now with the School of Information and Computer Science, Georgia Institute of Technology, Atlanta, GA 30332.

Edward L. Robertson is with the Department of Computer Science, Indiana University, Bloomington, Indiana 47405.

encourage our students to obtain professional experience through internships, but these opportunities are not available to all. Experience with a realistic group software development project in an academic environment can be a valuable part of an undergraduate education in computer science. Unfortunately, it is difficult to find suitable projects and to administer a course with many such projects. We have developed a pair of courses at Indiana University which largely overcomes these difficulties. Although we make no claim of producing full-fledged software engineers with these courses, we do feel that we convey many of the skills deemed important by Mills [9].

Our key innovation is to use students in a graduate level software engineering course (the *supervisors course*) as supervisors for teams of students producing a software product as part of an undergraduate course (the *project course*). Our supervisors are analogous to teaching assistants in a course at Carnegie-Mellon University described by Kant [6]. However, our supervisors are also students who gain valuable experience pertinent to the graduate course from their supervisory duties.

Project courses have been discussed as tools for teaching software engineering at least since Horning and Wortman [5]. However, our projects are almost always drawn from the business community, local government agencies, and University departments. This presents some difficulties in administration of the course, but we feel that the problems are more than outweighed by the benefits of dealing with real clients, who often have ambiguous and changing needs. This inherently avoids some of the problems in teaching software engineering to undergraduates which were pointed out by Shaw [13]. For other experiences with courses using projects from real users, see Bolz and Jones[3], Lee and Frankel [7], Oman [10], Perkins and Beck [11], and Sanders [12].

The final distinction between our project course and most others with which we are familiar is that our course is taught as a two semester sequence. This allows the time to go through the full development cycle, including installation and evaluation, but omitting maintenance. It would be difficult to compress the course into a single semester while continuing to use real projects, given the lack of experience that the students in the project course have with software development by teams. A single semester course is feasible if the students have extensive professional experience (see McKeeman [8]).

The next sections describe our experiences with the graduate course (Section II) and project course (Section III) over the last four years. The final section gives our conclusions.

II. The Graduate Course Sequence

The Software Engineering Management course sequence has recently been added to the graduate curriculum after being taught as a special topic for several years. Our course, similar in objective to the Software Project Management course taught at the Wang Institute [1], is a graduate level seminar with a limited enrollment (maximum fifteen, typically twelve). Students are required to have taken the Information Systems sequence at Indiana or to have comparable (usually professional) project experience. Although we have had occasional disappointments, most of the students admitted to the course are highly motivated and do a good job.

A. Typical Seminar Content

The two semesters of the Software Engineering Management sequence are different in structure and format. The first semester (three credit hours) includes, in addition to supervisory duties, a traditional seminar with students taking turns leading the discussion. The second semester (one credit hour) usually consists solely of supervising the completion of projects.

Course materials for the first semester seminar are drawn from classical works and current papers pertinent to the course. The specific materials covered vary from semester to semester, but a typical reading list is given in Figure 1.

Bab	*Software Configuration Management.* Wayne A. Babich. Addison-Wesley, 1986.
Bau	*Software Engineering: An Advanced Course.* F.L. Bauer, Ed. Springer-Verlag, 1975.
Bro	*The Mythical Man-Month.* F.P. Brooks. Addison-Wesley, 1975.
Boe	*Software Engineering Economics.* B. Boehm. Prentice-Hall, 1981.
Dav	*Tools and Techniques for Structured Systems Analysis and Design.* W.S. Davis. Addison-Wesley, Reading, MA, 1983.
DeM	*Concise Notes on Software Engineering.* Tom DeMarco. Yourdon Press, 1979.
Fai	*Software Engineering Concepts.* Richard Fairley. McGraw-Hill, 1985.
Kin	*Current Practices in Software Development.* D. King. Yourdon Press, New York, 1984.
Kop	*Software Reliability.* H. Kopetz. Macmillan Press, 1979.
Met	*Managing a Programming Project.* P.W. Metzger. Prentice-Hall, Englewood Cliffs, NJ, 1973.
PW	*In Search of Excellence.* Peters and Waterman. Warner, 1982.
Shn	*Software Psychology.* B. Shneiderman. Winthrop, 1981.
Sho	*Software Engineering: Design/Reliability/Management.* M.L. Shooman. McGraw-Hill, 1983.
Som	*Software Engineering. Second Edition.* I. Sommerville. Addison-Wesley, Reading, MA, 1985.
Wei	*The Psychology of Computer Programming.* G.M. Weinberg. Van Nostrand Reinhold, 1971.

Fig. 1. Typical Reading List for Software Engineering Management.

A syllabus similar to Figure 2 is distributed and students are assigned to lead specific class discussions. A substantial portion of a student's grade depends on the quality of the seminars they lead and their degree of participation in the seminar. The ordering of the material in the seminar is designed to complement the companion project course. *E.g.*, management issues are discussed before the software life cycle because the supervisors earliest responsibilities are concerned with selecting teams and projects. Note that some classes are devoted explicitly to discussion of project status, but every class meeting devotes at least a few minutes to the projects.

Week	Reading	Topics
1	Som 1. Fai 1.	Introduction to Software Engineering.
2	Som 10,11. Fai 2. Wei 4,5. Bro 3,4. Shn.	Managing people and projects.
3	Dav B,C,Q. Kin 5,6.	System Life Cycle. Interviewing techniques. Feasibility studies.
4	Som 2. Fai 4.	Requirements definition. *Outside speaker.*
5	Dav G. Fai 3. Sho 6.4. Boe.	Cost/benefit analysis.
6	Dav D,E,L. Som 4.1.1. Sho 2.5,6.5.	Data flow diagrams and data dictionaries. Scheduling
7	Som 3. Fai 5. Dav H,I,K.	Software design. Specification techniques: HIPO, pseudocode, Warnier-Orr.
8	Dav N. Som 9.	Interface design. *Outside speaker.*
9	Som 8–8.5. Sho 6.6.2. Bau 4.B.	Documentation. *Outside speaker.*
10		Discussion of Requirement Definition Documents. *Outside speaker.*
11	Som 2.6.1. Current papers.	Prototyping. Project review.
12	Som 3,4. Dav F,M.	Physical design, systems flowcharts, file design, modularizing.
13	Som 5,7. Sho 2,4.	Programming design; implementation issues. Testing, debugging and validation.
14	PW	Final discussion of projects.

Fig. 2. Typical Syllabus for Software Engineering Management

B. Outside Speakers

Several notations of *outside speaker* appear in the syllabus. We have been fortunate to have had four or more visitors from industry in each offering of the seminar. The visitors are usually from firms that hire our graduates and feel that such contact is mutually beneficial. Often, the visitors are former students, some of whom have taken one or both of the courses described here. Talking with working practitioners enlivens the seminar and emphasizes the importance of the material. The students have been very positive about this feature of the course, and we strongly encourage its use.

C. Supervision Responsibilities

In addition to the seminar, the students have substantial responsibilities as supervisors for the student teams in the project course. The supervisors act as advisors to the teams; since they have been through a similar experience, their advice is usually valuable and often (but not always) heeded. Another responsibility of the supervisors is to monitor and report team activities. They provide early warning before milestones are missed so that remedial action can be taken.

To invest the supervisors with the appropriate level of authority, it is imperative that their position be made clear to the students in the project course. In a professional situation, a supervisor achieves authority with the power to hire or fire, promote or demote, *etc.* Since the only ultimate authority in an academic class rests with the final grade, the project course students might ignore the advice and demands of supervisors if there is no grade relevance. We emphasize the importance of the supervisors by making it clear that the supervisors have a significant input into final project grades and by requiring that all deliverables be turned in to the supervisors rather than the instructors. We have found that it is valuable to stress the authority of the supervisors and have devised mechanism (described below) to enhance this authority.

D. Evaluation of Supervisors

Because the graduate course enrollment is small, our grading policy has been informal. We evaluate the students both on their participation in the seminar portion of the course and on their performance as supervisors. (There are no formal examinations.) They are judged somewhat on the basis of the success of the project, but the variability in projects makes their behavior relative to their particular circumstances more important. We seek comments from students and clients in judging a supervisor's ability, and the supervisors are aware of this.

III. THE PROJECT COURSE SEQUENCE

The Information Systems course sequence has two major components, one based on traditional class work (lectures, exams, homework, *etc.*) and the other on a major team project. The lecture component covers file media (corresponding to CS 5 of Curriculum 78 [2]) during the first semester and database systems (corresponding to CS 11) during the second. The team project component, which is the focus of this paper, serves the goals of CS 14 of Curriculum 78, although it is not taught as a separate course. Both semesters in the sequence carry four hours of credit (recently raised from three).

Information Systems is nominally a senior level course sequence, but a number of juniors and graduate students are usual. (A mixture of backgrounds and maturities is educationally beneficial.) Normally, two sections are offered with a maximum enrollment of 50 students each. We expect the students to have had exposure to several high level languages with substantial experience and skill in at least one. Although programming assignments based on the lecture material are often given, our concerned here is with the course project, which spans both semesters.

Projects from real users are not commonly assigned as part of an academic course because of difficulties in finding suitable projects, problems with organizing teams, difficulties in monitoring, and inadequacies of the academic reward mechanisms. Although we cannot claim to have a foolproof method for handling team projects, our techniques do provide decent feedback and monitoring with a tolerable administrative load.

A. Finding Projects

Although it is possible to use internally generated projects, there are many difficulties.

If all teams are given the same project the adminstrative burden is reduced, but it is nearly impossible to assure that all teams work independently. If distinct projects are assigned to the teams, then much time will be spent in clarifying the design of each project. We recommend instead that projects be solicited from interested users in the community. We have had no difficulty in soliciting projects from large and small businesses, government agencies, charitable organizations, as well as university departments.

On the first day of class, the students are assigned to find and report on a possible project. (We usually have a number of leads which can be made available to students who request help.) We encourage students to look for projects which will be appropriate in scope and content. (Because the project is part of the Information Systems course, we require that projects include development of a system for maintaining and accessing a data base.) Students are given two weeks to find a project and write a two page description. Those who are unable to find a project are asked to report on the current status of projects from previous years or to write a short report on an article selected from a software engineering journal.

We have generally had good luck in finding enough suitable projects. In the 1985–1986 school year, over fifty projects were suggested by the ninety students in the two sections. Of these, ten were rejected immediately because they did not satisfy our requirement relative to Information Systems or because the client was not located in the vicinity of the University. (From past experience, we have found that the chances for a successful project are severely reduced if the entire team does not have ready access to the client.) For 90 students, 13 to 18 projects are desired, so having 40 allowed selection of the most appropriate projects.

Maintaining good relations with the clients is important. The client must be aware of the time and other resources that will be required for the project and of the possibility that the project will fail. It is important to emphasize that maintenance will not be provided.

(If a client does have a problem after the end of the course, we try to find students who are willing and able, perhaps for a fee, to make changes or fix errors. However, we cannot guarantee this service.) We depend on the supervisors to make sure that clients are aware of the responsibilities and liabilities entailed.

B. Assigning Teams

A professional manager usually knows something about the strengths and weaknesses of his staff and how well individuals work together. Because of the time constraints of an academic course, team assignments must be made before the instructor has much information about the students as individuals. (Teams are usually assigned in the fourth week.) We evaluate programming skill from a pre-test given on the first day of class (the pre-test has no affect on grading) and writing skill from the project proposals and alternative writing assignments. This helps us to balance skills across the different teams, but it doesn't help with personality incompatibility problems.

Classes are divided into groups of approximately fifteen students, with approximately the same number of skilled programmers and writers in each, as determined by the pre-test and writing samples. Supervisors are to become familiar with all the individuals in one of the groups. They then assist in choosing teams of four to seven students on the basis of personalities as well as skills. A team with three students is minimal if the students are to learn the appropriate lessons about working in groups, but larger teams are preferred because of attrition. Seven is the maximum size since a larger group would probably need some internal management structure. If a very large project is undertaken, it would be best to partition it into smaller subprojects and use the supervisors to coordinate the efforts of the teams.

C. Monitoring Progress

Because it is easy for a project to get into major trouble before the instructor is aware

that anything is wrong, we depend on the supervisors to keep in close contact with their teams. The supervisors are expected to help the teams overcome their problems and to keep the instructors informed of project status.

D. Milestones

As a standard against which to measure progress, we use a set of milestones with fixed due dates. Of course, individual projects can vary somewhat from the ideal schedule, so the supervisors are allowed some variance.

The milestones shown in Figure 3 correspond to our own version of the software life cycle, tailored to the needs of the course. An extensive handout describes what is required for each milestone. Here, we give only a brief description of the milestones and explain how they interact with the administration of the course.

Milestone	Semester	Week Due	Description
0	First	2	Project Proposal.
1	First	4	Feasibility Study.
2	First	8	Requirements Definition and Preliminary Project Plan.
3	First	14	Logical Design and Test Plan.
4	Second	3	Physical Design.
5	Second	7	Implementation.
6	Second	10	Testing Completed.
7	Second	13	Installation.
8	Second	14	Post Mortem.

Fig. 3. Project Milestones.

The Project Proposal is a very brief document used to make a preliminary judgement on the appropriateness of a suggested project. The Feasibility Study gives a more in-depth look at the need for the project and the resources required. One purpose of the Feasibility Study is to assess the commitment of the client toward the project, since experience has shown that this is a strong indicator of project success. After considering the Feasibility

Studies carefully, the supervisors in consultation with the instructors decide which projects should continue. Then teams are selected and assigned to projects.

The Requirements Definition is the first substantial piece of documentation produced by the teams. It must be approved by the client before the project can continue. We also require a Preliminary Project Plan, which include a schedule for meeting the future milestones. Although the students are unlikely to produce an accurate schedule, we feel they benefit from their errors in planning.

The final milestone of the first semester is the Logical Design, which is supposed to specify precisely what the product will do to satisfy the Requirements Definition, but not say how the product will be built. We encourage supervisors to require early drafts of designs and to give substantial criticism. Having a predefined point during the project when the Logical Design must be completed has presented minimal difficulties. The Logical Design document and an in-class presentation of the design are the primary basis for the project grade in the first semester.

The deadline for the Physical Design milestone comes early in the second semester. (Preliminary work is done on the Physical Design in the first semester.) This detailed design should give all the design decisions necessary for project implementation.

The Implementation is deemed complete when 100% of the coding has been compiled without syntax errors. The Testing milestone is met when the error-free software has been demonstrated to the supervisor. Of all the milestones, these are the most fluid. Supervisors have great discretion in adjusting these due dates for the individual projects. The objective is to deliver the final product on time; the individual milestones merely assist in this process.

Installation is complete when the final software and all its documentation (user's guide, training manual, programmer's guide, *etc.*) has been delivered to the client and the client has received appropriate training. Verification of installation is the responsibility of the supervisors, but the instructors try to attend an on-site demonstration of the final product. The instructors also try to contact the client during the final two weeks between Installation and the end of the course to determine client satisfaction directly.

The final milestone, Post Mortem, consists of an in-class presentation and a brief document describing the team's experiences during the project. Its purpose is to contemplate what happened during the project, what went wrong, and how problems were overcome. We encourage the students to suggest ways that problems could be avoided in the future. The in-class presentations are important so that the class as a whole can benefit from the experiences of all the teams.

There is an inevitable and unfortunate conflict between the success of the team project and the value of the learning experience. A team is likely to do better if members can specialize in what they do best. However, this would deprive some students of participating in coding and debugging, while others would never do documentation. The milestone approach helps mitigate this problem, since it forces the entire team to focus on one aspect or another at different times.

E. Grading

It is always difficult to assign individual credit for a group project. Our solution is to grade the projects first, then to decide on grades for team members. Projects grades are based primarily on the written documentation provided with the delivered product, class presentations, product demonstrations, client feedback, and supervisor recommendations. Since the project grade is typically 40% of the course grade, the students are highly motivated to do well.

Students are advised early that they will be evaluated by their fellow team members. Each team member provides a written report explaining what was done (or not done) by each member and a numeric evaluation in which a fixed number of points are distributed among the team. This information and supervisor evaluations are carefully considered in assigning grades for individuals. The most common occurrence is that all students in a team receive the same grade, but it is not unusual for one student to receive an 'A' or a 'C' while the other members receive 'B's.

Occasionally, one or two students in a class seem to be unable or unwilling to work on a team project. In the past, we have used the threat of a poor grade as a means to encourage participation. Unfortunately, it has still been necessary to assign a grade of 'F' occasionally. Although this might punish the offending student sufficiently, it does not compensate for the additional difficulties encountered by the rest of the team. A more successful strategy has been used in recent years. We give the supervisor the option of *firing* the student from the team. The fired student could appeal to another team for admittance; if this plea fails, the student would be assigned an individual project with a maximum grade of 'B.' We have not yet needed to use the firing mechanism and have had no grades of 'F' on projects since it was in place. We are not sure whether the threat of firing or luck was responsible for the improved situation.

F. Results from the 1985–1986 Offering

After evaluation of the feasibility studies by the instructors and supervisors, we selected twenty projects (out of forty) to go forward. In retrospect, we should have selected fewer projects, for the average team size soon dropped below five when several students dropped late in the course.

Two of the twenty projects were cancelled at the end of the first semester. One client was unable to provide the necessary access to a time-shared computer because of security concerns at the corporate (non-local) level. In the other case, access to the client's microcomputer system was inadequate for development, and no alternate system was available.

Of the remaining eighteen projects, all but four appear to be completely successful. Two of the unsuccessful projects were not completed on time; grades were withheld until completion. The other two unsuccessful projects were inadequate for the intended purposes. In both cases, the projects suffered because of unavailability of the client.

Most of the projects were well received by the clients. The typical project was developed on a microcomputer using commercially available database tools. While these types of projects are not good models for large scale product development, they do provide valid experience in working with a team to develop software and in interacting with a real client.

IV. Conclusions

Our confidence in the validity of our approach is high because of the positive feedback we have had from the employers who have hired veterans of both the project course and the graduate course. There is keen competition for admittance to the project course, at least partly because student perceive that it is an asset when looking for a job.

While the instructors certainly benefit from the supervision performed by the students in the graduate course, the students can benefit even more. We have had many unsolicited comments indicating that the Software Engineering Management sequence has been very valuable to our graduates. The supervisory part of the course is essential in conveying the relevance of the material discussed in the seminar.

The use of students from the graduate course as supervisors in the project course augments and enrichs both courses and makes it feasible to offer real project experience in a large, undergraduate course. We would be interested in hearing from others who have had experiences with similar courses or who are contemplating offering such courses.

Acknowledgment

We wish to thank all of the students who have participated in the Information Systems and Software Engineering Management course sequences at Indiana University over the last four years. Their criticism and participation helped to develop a much better pair of courses. We also want to thank the individuals from outside Indiana University for participating in our graduate seminar and their employers for allowing them to come. A special thanks goes to Sid Kitchel, who greatly assisted with the administration of both course sequence in the 1985–1986 school year. Finally, we wish to thank the editor and the referees for their comments.

References

[1] M. Ardis, J. Bouhana, R. Fairley, S. Gerhart, N. Martin, and W. McKeeman, "Core course documentation: Master's degree program in software engineering," Technical Report TR-85-17, School of Information Technology, Wang Institute of Graduate Studies, Sep. 1985, 39 pp.

[2] R.H. Austing, B.H. Barnes, D.T. Bonnette, G.L. Engel, and G. Stokes, (eds.), "Curriculum 78: Recommendations for the undergraduate program in computer science—A report of the ACM Curriculum Committee on Computer Science," *Comm. ACM*, vol. 22, no. 3, pp. 147–165, Mar. 1979.

[3] R.E. Bolz and L.G. Jones, "A realistic, two-course sequence in large scale software engineering," *SIGCSE Bulletin*, vol. 15, no. 1, pp. 21–24, Feb. 1983.

[4] R. Fairley, "The role of academe in software engineering education," in *Proc. 1986 ACM Fourteenth Annual Computer Science Conference*, Cincinnati, Ohio, pp. 39–52, Feb. 1986. (Also available as Technical Report TR-85-19, School of Information Technology, Wang Institute of Graduate Studies, Oct. 1985.)

[5] J.J. Horning and D.B. Wortman, "Software hut: A computer program engineering project in the form of a game," *IEEE Trans. Software Eng.*, vol. SE-3, no. 4, pp. 325–330, July 1977.

[6] E. Kant, "A semester course in software engineering," *ACM Software Engineering Notes*, vol. 6, no. 4, pp. 52–76, Aug. 1981.

[7] K.Y. Lee and E.C. Frankel, "Real-life software projects as software engineering laboratory exercises," *ACM Software Engineering Notes*, vol. 8, no. 3, pp. 39–43, July 1983.

[8] W.M. McKeeman, "Experience with a software engineering project course," Technical Report TR-86-01, School of Information Technology, Wang Institute of Graduate Studies, Jan. 1986, 17 pp.

[9] H.D. Mills, "Software engineering education," in H.D. Mills (ed.), *Software Productivity*, Boston, MA: Little, Brown and Company, 1983, pp. 251–264.

[10] P.W. Oman, Jr., "Software engineering practicums: A case study of a senior capstone sequence," *SIGCSE Bulletin*, vol. 18, no. 2, pp. 53–57, June 1986.

[11] T.E. Perkins and L.L. Beck, "A project-oriented undergraduate course sequence in software engineering," *SIGCSE Bulletin*, vol. 12, no. 1, pp. 32–39, Feb. 1980.

[12] D. Sanders, "Managing and evaluating students in a directed project course," *SIGCSE Bulletin*, vol. 16, no. 1, pp. 15–25, Feb. 1984.

[13] M. Shaw, "Making software engineering issues real to undergraduates," in Wasserman, A.I., and Freeman, P. (eds.), *Software Engineering Education: Needs and Objectives*. New York: Springer-Verlag, 1976, pp. 104–107.

The System Factory Approach to Software Engineering Education[1]

Walt Scacchi
Computer Science Dept.
University of Southern California
Los Angeles, CA 90089-0782

Abstract

The System Factory project seeks to investigate the problems of large-scale software engineering through a combine effort in research, development and education. This report describes the System Factory approach to software engineering education as developed and practiced at USC. It describes the genesis and history of the System Factory project, the SF approach to software engineering, our experiences in softwre technology transfer, and concludes with some observations and potentials for large-scale software engineering projects in academic settings. Central to the SF approach is a joint focus on three key determinants of the outcomes of large-scale software development: the products developed, the process through the products are developed, and the production setting where the process of creating products occurs. Accordingly, we outline the software tools we employ, the techniques we developed for engineering software systems throughout their life cycle, and the strategies for managing large software engineering projects we employ.

1. Introduction

How does large-scale software development (LSSD) occur? What can we learn from conducting experimental studies in LSSD? Can we teach and practice LSSD in an academic computing environment and institutional setting? Can we develop substantial

---

[1]The System Factory project has been supported over the years through contracts, grants, or gifts from the USC Faculty Research Innovation Fund, AT&T Information Systems, Carnegie Group Inc., Hughes Radar Systems Group, IBM through the Socrates Project at USC, System Development Foundation, and TRW Systems Engineering and Development Division. Additional research support was provided by DARPA contract MDA 903-81-C-0331 to the Information Sciences Institute at USC. Finally, more than 300 graduate students in computer science at USC have elected to participate in the System Factory project since 1981. Without their participation and commitment to success, this project would not occur. We are truly grateful for all of their support.

and interesting LSS systems in an academic setting? Can we follow both an evolutionary and revolutionary approach to LSSD [3]? What sort of tools, techniques, and project management strategies should we implement to support LSSD? Can we develop LSS systems with tools, techniques, and strategies that can be reused or distributed to other academic/industrial research settings? Can we practice software technology transfer and transition? These are fundamental questions in the development of large-scale software systems with a large staff in an academic setting. Therefore, our purpose is to describe our approach to investigating these questions and concerns through a long-term research, development, and education project at USC we call the System Factory.

Through six years of work in the System Factory project, we have produced and documented a variety of results and products. These outcomes include both technological and organizational artifacts, and numerous research contributions. We have produced an inventory of *reusable software components* that we can configure into different application systems or environments [50, 30, 52, 44, 17, 55, 56]. Each of these components has a record of formal specifications and narrative descriptions that characterize their development life cycle. We have produced a set of *techniques for engineering the life cycle* of software applications and environments [57, 45]. These techniques primarily address how to articulate and transform software system specifications into concrete source code realizations, whether employing existing software components, or prototyping entirely new application systems. We have produced a set of *strategies for managing LSSE projects* that can be specialized to specific organizational and technological arrangements [36, 61, 53, 54, 59, 7]. These strategies employ policies for managing LSSD projects that we have observed realize substantial improvement in software productivity and quality. We are also continuing our investigation to develop a *paradigm for flexible manufacture of large software systems* [20], and articulating a *knowledge base of software technology transfer know-how* [49, 58] based upon our research of effective transfer and transition practices.

Our simultaneous focus on system engineering activities, and organizational patterns and processes in which they occur, is the unique aspect of our approach. It also represents, in our view, the best opportunity for realizing substantial improvements in software productivity, quality, and long-term cost reduction. We believe that our research results and products increasingly substantiate this.

Overall, this report is about the System Factory (SF) project and its approach to interrelating software engineering research, development, and education. This interrelationship is a recurring theme in the organization of this report. In the next section, we present an overview of other efforts that investigate research topics in software engineering through project courses. This serves as a point of departure into the SF itself. We begin our discussion of the SF in terms of its intellectual roots and project history. This is followed by a description of the products, process, and production setting that characterize the SF approach to software engineering research and education. This section describes the computer-aided software engineering environment of the SF, the software life cycle engineering techniques employed as part of the SF software production process, and the strategies we use for managing a large, long-term software engineering project in our institutional setting. We then turn to examine our experiences with SF technology transfer. Finally, we close with some observations about the SF approach to software engineering, as well as the potential for replicating the SF approach in other academic or industrial settings.

2. Related Efforts

The SF follows from a long standing approach to experimental investigations in the practice of software engineering education. The basis of this approach is to mobilize software engineering students in an academic setting to perform software development projects under the control and guidance of a faculty member [69, 25]. This is software engineering education via hands-on experimentation with selected development tools or techniques. What distinguishes this approach from traditional classroom training is the faculty researcher's commitment to conduct an experimental research evaluation of a new software technology through some sort of comparative study. In simple terms, an interesting software concept or technology is selected, and students are grouped into clusters and directed to develop some software product(s) with this technology. The technology thus serves as the dependent variable, while the student clusters or (attributes of) the products produced as the independent, comparison variable.

Among the classic investigations, Wasserman and Freeman [69] were among the first to identify collective motivation and descriptions of software development projects in academic or industrial training settings. Horning and Wortman [28] at UToronto introduced one of the early innovations in software education by their explicit structuring of groups of students into "software huts" that were motivated to produce a quality software system by economic incentives. This project-as-game approach was an attempt to replicate certain features of the real-world of competitive, commercial software development houses. Basili and colleagues at UMaryland [6] began conducting controlled experiments that sought to statistically compare the effectiveness of different software development techniques as employed by student groups. Barry Boehm, a central figure in the emergence of software engineering, also began conducting small-scale experiments in software engineering in the late 1970's first at USC, and then at UCLA [10, 12]. These studies sought to evaluate the effectiveness of certain software development techniques (e.g., structured programming, specification versus prototyping) with 4-8 teams of students developing the same system. While his studies produced frequently cited results, Boehm readily acknowledges they do not empirically prove the efficacy of selected techniques over one another.

Perhaps motivated by the precedent of these studies, or by the perponderance of faculty researchers assigned to teach the growing student enrollments of software engineering courses, we witnessed a notable growth in software researchers' intermix of their teaching and research interests. Selby, Basili, and Baker [63] at UMaryland report the results of Selby's dissertation study of a carefully designed experiment to evaluate the effectiveness of their CLEANROOM approach to software development and off-line, statistically based software testing. In another quantitative experiment, Avizienis and Kelly [1] at UCLA, and Knight and Leveson [37] at UVirginia and UCIrvine report their findings on the relability of N-version programs developed from a single specification by programmers (students) with comparable skill levels. As these studies are very similar though independently conducted, their results are comparable, and the differences in interpreting the experimental results notable. McKeeman and colleagues [42] report on their experiences at the Wang Institute in conducting a number of software engineering projects between 1982-1985 where their objective was to simulate industrial software development organization, methods, and products. Berzins, Gray, and Naumann [9] at UMinnesota report on their project-oriented case studies from 1981-1985 on the use of process and data abstractions in developing software systems. They characterize their effort as successful and replicable in other universities, though successful replication may require access to the kind of software tools they employed. Interest in research-oriented courses is prevalent in other areas of computer science including data structures and algorithms [15], networks and distributed systems [64], and CAI courseware [5]. Finally, the Software Engineering Institute [26, 25] at CMU has recently taken responsibility for developing graduate curriculum materials, researching new software technologies, and facilitating the transfer of the products of these endeavors between universities and industrial firms.

In summary, a number of observations can be drawn from the research efforts cited above:

* case studies and controlled experiments that evaluate software engineering tools and techniques are possible, publishable, and popular in university settings.

* educational projects can replicate many (not all) features of software development practices found in industry in a classroom laboratory.

* nearly all university-based project courses focus on the development of small-scale software systems (typically 500-5,000 lines of source code) constructed by teams of 2-7 students utilizing modest but increasingly sophisticated software technologies.

However, other challenges of software engineering are yet to be addressed by research project courses.

Many universities are implementing complex campus-wide computing arrangements built from networks of personal computers, workstations, and special-purpose processors (e.g., supercomputers) [68]. This means that students are being exposed to new computing environments, multi-vendor systems, and computing support staffs that are frequently changing. A challenge here for software engineering faculty researchers is how to organize a software development project that utilizes complex computing arrangements in order to develop software systems that operate in such a setting. This suggests that a large team of students (15-60) must be organized to engineer a LSS system (10,000 to >100,000 lines of code), but within the usual constraints of an academic setting. Typical constraints include little or no discretionary budget, project schedules delimited by academic terms, shared and congested computing resources, annual staff turnover, grading voluminous project deliverables, little or no dedicated project support staff, etc. Such opportunities and constraints mean that new project forms must be investigated, and new software development technologies used (and reused). This is the challange we faced and chose to investigate through the development, use, and evolution of a software engineering environment in a software factory [14, 29, 41, 40, 66, 55].

3. Genesis and History of the System Factory Project

The SF is an investigation into LSSD with large staff in an academic setting begun in 1981. At that time, few studies of software engineering project courses or LSSD projects had been published. But a growing number of studies of the evolution of new computing technologies and large computing systems in complex organizational settings were available [33, 34, 35, 49, 36]. These studies indicated that the development and use of large systems was plagued by a background of recurring dilemmas that diminished the potential benefits, decreased productivity, and raised the cost of system development and use. These studies found that the structure and function of computing systems was inextricably bound (or "webbed") to the organizational settings where they were produced and consumed, and to the jobs, careers, and circumstantial interests of the people who animated them. This meant that if we were to engage in a LSSD project, we needed to investigate not only the role of new software tools and techniques, but also how the project's setting would interact with the system products being developed, how they would be developed, and who would be doing the development work. As such, if the interaction was benign, then the new software technology might be most effective. On the other hand, if the interaction was substantial, then we could expect to encounter problematic situations that could decrease development staff productivity, reduce product quality, or otherwise raise the cost of LSSD.

The ideal candidate for such a study would therefore be a multi-year, LSSD project that would require a complex organization of people and computing resources situated within some larger institutional context. A long-term project would assure a dynamic project organization in terms of staff turnover and innovations in local computing facilities. A LSSD project would inherently require a large staff, extensive use of available computing resources, schedules, production plans, administrative controls, and software engineering tools and techniques. The larger institutional context would create a marketplace of occupational and career contingencies for project staff, of external administrative units to manage base computing facilities and provide support staff, of extramural research and development funds, and of computing system vendors to provide upgrades to local computing facilities. Finally, the LSS system to be developed should be unfamiliar to allow us to experience the uncertainty in the final shape of things to come, so that we could try, fail, learn, and manage as we go. The SF would therefore be an experiment that represents a complex, real-world LSSD project based in an academic setting.

3.1. Initial Conditions of the SF

Our objective was to mobilize available staff and computing resources to develop a language-independent software engineering environment (LISEE) [50] within schedule, budget, and computing resource constraints. The LISEE would initially be the LSS software we would develop in the SF.[2] If successful, we could in principle then employ the LISEE tool ensemble in other LSSD projects.

In January 1981, we started with a development staff of 57 graduate software engineering students who elected to take a 15-week semester course in LSSD. These students were competent small-scale Pascal programmers possessing an undergraduate degree in computer science or the equivalent, but generally assumed to lack prior skills in

---

[2] This LISEE eventually evolved into the SF's current software engineering environment described in a latter section.

LSSD. Students were expected to commit 10-12 hours per week to this course. Since this was a course televised from USC to local industrial settings, this meant there was a partial geographic distribution of students in 5 different remote TV centers in addition to the majority of in-house students. There was a visible ethnic diversity of students represented by at least 10 different cultural or national backgrounds. At least one-third of the students spoke English as a second language. All software development was to be performed on a centralized, time-shared DECsystem-10 mainframe system with minimal programming support environment. There was a firm schedule for software delivery (end of the semester deadline is absolute) and budget (no discretionary funds available) in place. We then started with a modestly articulated model of software engineering technology (as of 1981) as found through a comprehensive literature review and reading list 12 pages long, with about 200 citations, prepared by the author.

Following a number of introductory lectures, we provided the staff with the software technology reading list partitioned into general reference materials and potential LISEE components. This initiated the beginning of the project. Next, we randomly assigned small number of students to review selected reference materials and become knowledgeable about one domain of software tools pertinent to the LISEE. Example domains included structure-oriented editors, testing systems, database management systems, user interfaces, etc. [50]. We then provided the staff with initial development requirements in the form of a conceptual LISEE architecture. This architecture served as the basis for dividing project staff into project teams of 2-7 cooperating students. Ten teams were established, five in-house and one at each remote site. Each team was then responsible for developing one component tool of the LISEE. We followed by providing the staff with techniques for developing the LISEE. These techniques addressed the the conventional stages of the system life cycle: requirements analysis, functional specification, architectural design, detailed design, implementation and integration, testing, user documentation, and maintenance. Basic background in these techniques was derived from examples available in the literature at that time (cf. [53]). Last, we provided the staff with background lectures on the organizational problems and strategies of LSSD as derived and transformed from the previously cited studies of the consumption of computing systems in complex settings.

Actual LISEE development was scheduled for eight weeks, following seven weeks of introductory lectures and background preparation (readings, class discussions, homework assignments, exams, and informal out-of-class discussions). The project's development was scheduled to reiterate the techniques, problems, and strategies for performing one system development life cycle stage each week, while staff performed that life cycle activity [53]. Thus we could use class time to discuss problems that different teams encountered as examples during that system development life cycle stage. Of course, we did not know if this was reasonable or if it would work overall. But we were there to learn through success or failure. After the project's eight week development, all ten components of the LISEE were prototyped, demonstrated, documented, and delivered by the staff of then 53 graduate students.

3.2. Outcomes and Implications of the Initial SF Experience

Version 1 of the LISEE represented 30K+ lines of Pascal code operating on a TOPS-10 based DECsystem-10 mainframe. The tools developed ranged in size from roughly 1500 to 4000 lines of code. All LISEE components were demonstrated to be operational, although there was variation in the quality and amount of system development work completed by the different SF teams. Each LISEE tool provided an operational interface or stub for interconnecting to at least one other component in the LISEE architecture. This LISEE was clearly not production-quality, but our objective in the SF experiment was to demonstrate that a LSS system of the complexity of a LISEE could be prototyped by a large staff in an academic setting in a relatively short time.

Each team submitted project team documentation that recorded their work completed in each system life cycle stage. There were eight chapters to each team's documentation, one chapter per life cycle stage. On average, each team delivered 50-100 pages of system life cycle documentation per person. That is not to suggest that every person produced that volume of documentation, but rather that a two-person team might produce 150 page project document, while a five person team might produce a 300 page project document. In total, about 3000 pages of LISEE development life cycle documentation were delivered.

Overall, the general feeling among all project participants was that the project was a success, and that most students valued the software tools and project documentation they developed. For a number of students, this was the most substantial and best engineered piece of software they had yet developed, and the largest group project in which they had ever participated.

3.3. SF Iterations: 1982-1986+

Although the initial SF project was successful, maybe we were just lucky or misleading ourselves. That is, could the experiment be replicated with an entirely different staff and produce comparable results? In order to answer this question, we decided to repeat the experiment with the same objectives but with entirely new staff and same computing environment. However, this time a smaller staff of 30 undergraduate students was employed using same computing facilities as before, and same development techniques and project management stretegies followed. Roughly comparable results were produced in terms of a smaller, less ambitious LISEE and related documentation.[3] This repetition of the SF experiment indicated to us that the SF concept was sufficiently viable for further experimentation, refinement, and development. Since then, we have repeated the SF experiment in an iterative manner, incorporating new refinements, insights, and technological enhancements. Some highlights follow.

In the next iteration, we chose to utilize the first generation SF documentation and software as prototype available for reuse if desired by team members. We revised the basic LISEE architecture, the functional capabilities of its tools, the software life cycle development techniques, and the project management strategies to better accomodate defiencies observed in the initial iteration. Each subsequent iteration would also give rise to a revised set of tools and architecture, techniques, and strategies.[4] Also, the computing environment was upgraded to TOPS-20 operating system on the same computer system. This was not our decision, but it happened in our work setting, thus we had to transition to it in order to continue.

Next iteration, we were given another opportunity to migrate to a new computing environment, this time to a VAX-VMS system. We also decided to migrate the LISEE from Pascal to C, and to expand the scope of the LISEE to support experiments in VLSI circuit design [51, 30, 52]. However, as our experience, teaching materials, and software tools expanded, we came to find the seven week introduction, and eight week development schedule too confining. The choice we opted to implement was to expand the one semester course into a two semester, academic year length course. This would allow us to take more time and explore at greater levels of detail, the tools, techniques, and strategies we were putting into practice. This also would be a good time to again migrate, revise, and redevelop the LISEE (now called simply a SEE) in C to a VAX-750 running Unix 4.2bsd [55]. This migration then represented the next iteration. Finally, for the current iteration, the SF was expanded to utilize a loosely coupled network of heterogeneous computers. The SEE was continued in C++ on two VAX-Unix 4.3bsd

---

[3] Of course this is not a true replication of the original experiment. But we felt this case study experiment was a close approximation of the first, and therefore comparable.

[4] For example, the original LISEE required a relational data base management system to be used as a central archive of project related information. Development of a RDBMS was then started and continued until the SF migrated to a Unix 4.2bsd environment, where we were able to use the existing Ingres RDBMS, a system more capable than ours. Continuing development our the original SF RDBMS was then halted, and another new software tool was added to the SEE for ongoing development.

systems and two SUN-3 workstations all on a common LAN, as well as migrated to operate on a separate network of AT&T 3B2 and 3B20 computers all running Unix System V. A TI Explorer Lisp Machine was made available, as were a number of IBM-PCs running MS-DOS. These latter machines were used for prototyping next generation knowledge-based SF tools, document preparation, development of small program modules, and remote file transfer.

In sum, we refined and redeveloped the SF's tools, techniques, and strategies through six iterations. In the course, we provided hands-on training with the development, use, and evolution of the SF's technologies for more than 300 graduate students in total over the six year period. We now turn to describe the SF approach as it now stands in terms of the SEE, software life cycle development techniques, and project management strategies we employ.

4. The System Factory Approach: Product, Process, and Setting

Central to the SF approach to software engineering is a joint focus on three key determinants of the outcomes of LSSD: the *products* developed, the *process* through which the products are developed, and the *production setting* where the process creating the products occurs. The SF's products embody a technological structure and function.[5] The software production process, whether organized according to a "waterfall model" or prototyping-incremental development system life cycle must be planned, staffed, directed, scheduled, budgeted, and controlled to accomodate smooth production of the intended technological products by available staff. Formal software development techniques may be used to further structure this process. The production process therefore serves to structure the flow and transformation of organizational resources into technological products and work arrangements.[6] Finally, the production setting provides the staff and resources that are mobilized according to organizational policies, procedures, histories, incentives, and pressures in its marketplace to animate the process of product manufacture. In particular, we find the organizational and technological arrangements that support software production often have a profound affect in shaping how software development occurs. For example, the base computing environment used

---

[5]The SF's products include programs, documentation, software development techniques and analyses, application-domain knowledge, routines for SF use and evolution, strategies for managing LSSD, and people trained and skilled in LSSD. In addition, a number of research publications have been produced, presented, and disseminated.

[6]Elsewhere we refer this transformation of organizational resources into technology-based work arrangements as "packaging", and the ensemble of products a "computing package" [35, 49, 36].

in the SF was changed five times (once each project cycle) primarily due to actions of the university's computing facility through their attempt to provide modern computing services that are easier to sustain and operate. However, we find that many researchers seem to ignore the importance of how idiosyncratic features of each setting uniquely influence how computing resources are consumed, how software systems are produced, and what products are produced.

Clearly there has been increasing attention directed in the software community as to whether LSSD depends more upon the nature of the product or the process. However, little attention is directed at the organizational setting where a particular group of people must work together using available resources to develop software system products according to some formal or ad hoc development process. Academic computer science departments, computer system manufacturers, aerospace contractors, banks and insurance companies, and national scientific laboratories represent some of the places where LSSD occurs. Clearly there are differences across and within such settings in terms of the kinds of software applications developed, development tools employed, computers and operating systems utilized, programming languages primarily used, professional background and skill level of the software developers, budget and development schedule constraints, and so forth. As such, we find the influence of the organizational setting on the products produced, the process through which they are produced, and the joint influence of each on the other is fundamental [36, 53]. In our view, overlooking these patterns of influence is thus a fundamental mistake in attempting to understand how LSSD occurs.

This section therefore describes selected products, production process techniques, and project management strategies used in the SF. After this, we then describe our experiences in transferring these SF technologies to other organizational settings.

4.1. SF Product: A Large-Scale Software Engineering Environment

The SF's software engineering environment (SEE) is designed to support the computer-aided engineering of software systems or VLSI systems throughout their life cycle [30, 51, 52, 55]. Our focus in this report is limited to large software systems. The SEE is designed to support the family of languages that describe each life cycle activity by using an appropriate set of language-directed tools that process them. For instance, one way this is realized is by generating and configuring a set of language-directed tools that can evaluate language-based system descriptions for consistency and completeness. Another way is to generate and configure a set of tool components to serve as the base for specifying, rapidly prototyping, and validating particular application systems. With these objectives in mind, we built these SEE component tools on top of, and integrated with, the Unix operating system environment. The SEE tools constitute the SF's production infrastructure of software machinery used for fabricating, analyzing, transforming, and evolving software system descriptions. The following components are incorporated into the SF SEE:

* *Language-directed editor generator*: utilizes formal language specifications to produce a language-specific editing environment that detects syntax errors and inconsistencies in type declarations and construct usage at keystroke entry time. Lanugage-directed editors for software specification, design, coding, and animation languages have been generated and put into to use in the SF. It also constructs an abstract syntax tree and symbol table that can be used as inputs to the testing system and Gist specification processor. We have used this tool to rapidly construct a facility for generating formal system specifications from table-structured input of narrative system requirements. This was done by restructuring LDEG to accept object-oriented (semantic network) specifications, thus becoming a kind of knowledge-directed editing environment [70].

* *Flow analyzer and testing system*: performs static control flow and dynamic data flow analysis of source code descriptions, produces augmented source programs with probes for execution monitoring and debugging, and provides a rule-based mechanism for generating test cases for software modules interfaced to a debugger. This tool supports validation of a software application's performance requirements. We intend to integrate this testing system with the CMS to support a knowledge-based tester of multi-version system configurations.

* *Configuration management system*: (CMS) provides automated mechanisms for controlling multi-version system descriptions (e.g., specifications and source code implementations), through use of a module interface and interconnection definition language (NuMIL) and compiler [44, 43]. The NuMIL language and processing environment are used to specify the architectural configuration of new applications, or used to generate such a specification for existing applications. These specifications coupled to their source code implementations provide an appropriate medium for maintaining large evolving software applications [44, 43]. This system is currently being extended to support the design and configuration management of distributed, real-time multi-processor systems. We also intend to further extend this system to incorporate mechanisms for reasoning about alterations made to the structure and function of software system configurations.

* *Window-based user interface and command processor*: provides a window-based command/shell processor, mail handler, and display manager that other tools or application systems can use as their "front end." We are currently incorporating an additional mechanism for creating active display devices (real-time gauges and digimeters).

* *Gist specification analyzer and simulator*: provides a basic facility for constructing, analyzing, querying, and functionally simulating system specifications written in the Gist specification language [2, 17, 57]. We intend to extend this facility to support mechanisms for explaining the behavior of operational system specifications. These mechanisms are being developed in conjunction with the FSD environment at USC/ISI [4].

* *Document integration facility*: (DIF) provides a facility for creating and maintaining a multi-version electronic encyclopedia of system documentation hypertext [71, 38]. This enables us to interrelate and trace textual/graphic system documentation across all system life cycle activities that can be uniformaly queried, browsed, revised, and archived. Life cycle product descriptions for all SF SEE tools are currently included in the DIF database archive. A new facility has been designed to help coordinate and communicate to staff the modification of configured system components for large development projects [31, 65]. We intend to extend DIF by integrating it with the CMS to document multi-version system configurations, with SAG and PPSS to support electronic project management documents, and VIZ to create animated documents that visualize system features in-the-large and in-the-small.

* *Spreadsheet application generator*: (SAG) provides a special-purpose environment for specifying and rapidly generating interactive spreadsheet-like application programs. SAG has been used, for example, to develop a modest decision support system (PEST) for developing software cost estimation models and calculating computer system acquistion costs. SAG is interfaced to a relational data base management system so that it can utilize data bases created by other tools (e.g., PPSS). We are currently experimenting with techniques for generating rule-based spreadsheet applications [18], as well as non-rectangular, n-dimensional, distributed, and dynamically reconfigurable spreadsheet applications. Potential applications of this kind include simulation of dynamic systems, cellular automata, distributed intelligent system shells, and emulation of reconfigurable supercomputer system architectures [27, 62].

* *Project planning and scheduling system*: (PPSS) provides a rule-driven data base system for planning project schedules, work breakdown structures, task precedence networks and diagrams, and their interdependence (cf. [22]). These mechanisms can be employed to establish and assess the impact of changing requirements on a development project's budget, schedule, and production plan. We are currently integrating the services of this system into those provided by the PMSS.

* *Knowledge-based project management support system*: (PMSS) a knowledge-based software process support system (cf. [48]) that incorporates an operational model of the software life cycle processes embodied in KBSF development techniques and project management strategies [60]. PMSS is a kind of intelligent system that represents, simulates, and reasons about

software development processes and production settings. The initial demonstration version of PMSS was implemented by manually transforming Gist specifications of selected software development subprocesses into an OPS5 rule-based system. However, the current version of PMSS is being redeveloped using the Knowledge Craft[7] environment operating on a TI Explorer. This system will then be interfaced to the other SEE components via a hetereogeneous remote procedure calls over the LAN.

* *System prototyping and dynamic visualization system*: (VIZ) a visual programming, system prototyping, and diagram building facility [21] that supports the visual specification and script-based animation of 2D/3D software system descriptions [47, 39]. We are currently extending this system by integrating it with the CMS to produce multi-dimensional (2D/3D color graphics) layouts of static and dynamic configurations of multi-version systems, and system components. (These layouts resemble the complex circuit diagrams used to design, animate, debug, and document VLSI circuits.)

* *Unix* (lex, yacc, ingres, rcs, mm, troff, curses, more, OPS5, prolog,...): many of the language development, relational data base management, revision control, and related tools available in the Unix operating system serve as a foundation for most of the SEE tools listed above.

Figure 4-1 provides a simple functional arrangement of the these tools, together with the objects they process. Other SEE configurations and data flow articulations are accomodated as well. However, each of these components (and others systems not listed) were developed and evolved as part of the SF project and coursework. Subsequently, a number of these tools have then become the subject of further development and use by doctoral students as part of their dissertation research plans.

4.2. SF Production Techniques for Software Life Cycle Engineering

Many tools in the System Factory SEE are language-directed. This means we can configure and generate a software tool set that can process alternative language-based descriptions for a particular system engineering application.[8] It is possible to specialize a family of tools supporting system descriptions occurring at each software life cycle stage. Using this approach, system life cycle product descriptions such as software requirements, functional specifications, architectural configuration specifications, detailed module specifications, user-system dialogues, executable source codes, test case

---

[7]Knowledge Craft is a trademark of Carnegie Group Inc.

[8]For example, this suggests that it is possible to generate a tool set that can check/enforce local software quality assurance standards or design/coding style rules when encoded in the (attributed) language specification used for tool initialization.

Figure 4-1: The System Factory SEE

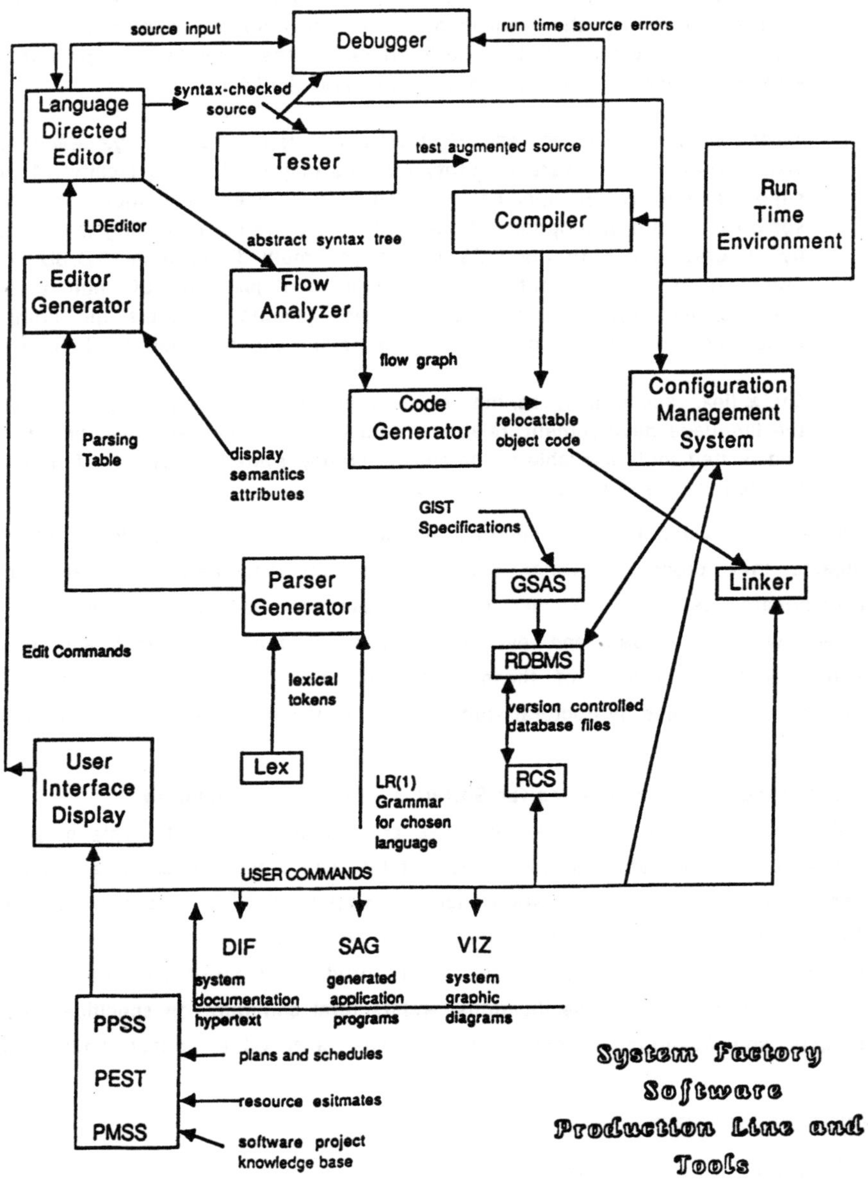

specifications, maintenance procedures, and structured diagrams can be processed as long as they can be described via the LR(1) or attributed-object language specification formalisms we use. Subsequently, these kinds of language-based descriptions are also amenable to automated manipulation supporting system evolution [44, 43].

Thus, a central facet of the SF techniques for engineering software systems throughout their life cycle is to specify each stage of development in a formal, processable language. Processing tools can then be configured in ways that check the consistency and completeness of a given specification, and thereby reinforce the specification technique appropriate to each stage of system development. In addition, such SF techniques must incorporate strategies for incrementally developing software descriptions in ways that utilize available processing tools. In the following subsection, we consider the intermediate stage of system development where a software system's architectural configuration must be specified.

4.2.1. Production Technique for Architectural Configuration Specification

A technique for specifying the architectural configuration (or structure) of a LSS system requires identifying a network of operational modules that progressively transform required objects into provided data resources. The portals through which these imports and exports move are the module interfaces. But structural specification first requires partitioning the system's functional specifications into realizable functional components. Accordingly, we must choose between alternative partitions of software components, depending on whether such components are readily available (reusable) or must be built. The selected partition then circumscribes decisions for allocating computing resources and staff to module development. As such, the structural system specification defines the boundaries for distributing concurrent computation across the system, as well as dividing the detailed design and coding work among available development staff. Thus, if the division of work changes (due to staff turnover for example), then the system's configuration may evolve, and vice versa.

Since LSS configurations inevitably evolve over time, then there is need to describe the evolving system architecture in a form whose consistency and completeness can be checked and maintained. Further, in LSSE projects, dispersed groups of developers may specify, code, test, and modify different modules asynchronously. This means that a given module might exist in a number of different but related versions at any time. It also indicates that insuring configuration integrity is a major problem in LSSE project coordination. Similarly, the upward-compatibility of a modified module or subsystem with respect to the rest of the system (and related component families) must be checked for consistency [45]. Subsequently, LSSE projects can benefit from a *system architecture specification processor, module interconnection and interface definition language,* and *configuration diagram visualizer* for managing families of multi-version modules. A module interconnection language is the medium for specifing system architectural design and configuration [46]. However, we require a MIL that can represent families of multi-version modules and subsystems. In our case, we developed and employ NuMIL, a MIL designed with these requirements in mind [43]. Various NuMIL processors then check and maintain the consistency and completeness of multi-version software specifications and source code implementations. An example in the following figure shows a NuMIL specification of a family of subsystems with different processor versions, each composed of different versions of two common modules.

```
subsystem S is
   provide a,b;
   require c,d;
   configurations
   /*** Subsystem S has two configurations IBM-PC and VAX ***/
      IBM-PC = { M_1 : version_1, M_2 : version_2 ;}
      VAX = { M_2 : version_1, M_1 : version_2 :}
end
```

```
module M_1 is
   provide a, foo;
   require d, b;
   implementations {
   /* M_1 has two versions */
      version version_1 {
         realization x.c;
            provide
            int a;
            short foo;
            require b(), d;}
      version version_2 {
         realization y.c;
            provide
            float a;
            int foo;
            require b(), d;}}
end
```

```
module M_2 is
   provide b;
   require c, foo;
   implementations {
   /* M_2 has two versions */
      version version_1 {
         realization m.c;
            provide
            int b(s,t) char *s, *t;
            require c, foo;}
      version version_2 {
         realization n.c;
            provide
            int b(m,n) char *m, *n;
            require c, foo; }}
end
```

Figure 4-2: Example NuMIL Specification

Overall, these processing requirements represent what the SF SEE *configuration management system* provides [44, 45, 43], as portrayed in the last figure. Clearly, such a CMS benefits by incorporating UNIX utilities such as make, sccs/rcs. A *relational database management system* (e.g., Ingres, Unify, or Oracle) allows system developers to store, browse, and query information about families of configured system components, and to control concurrent access to these components. However, such RDBMs require a separate object-oriented interface to properly map the descriptions of configured system components into a relational format [43].

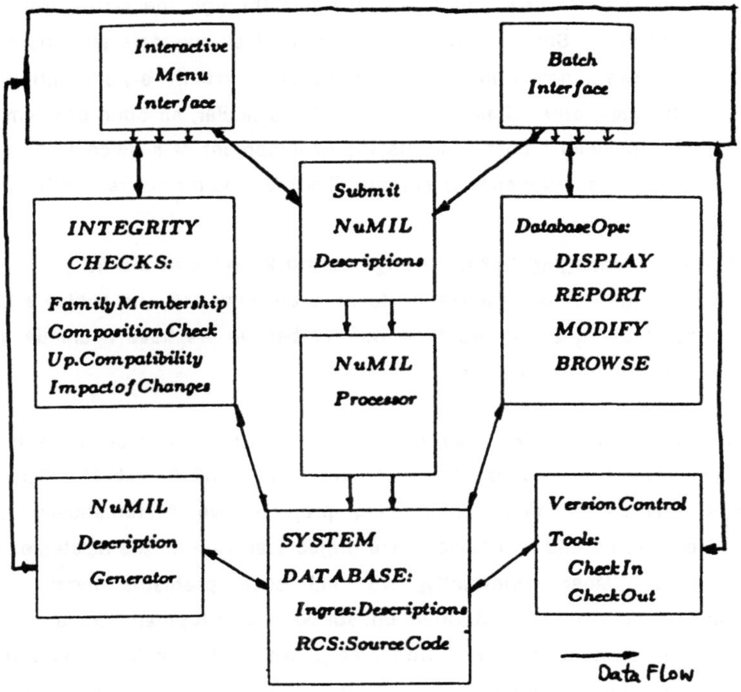

Figure 4-3: The SF Configuration Management System

4.2.2. Other Production Techniques

The SEE tools described earlier support a diversity of possible software development techniques. For example, the Gist specification language, analyzer, and simulator supports the development of new application systems through the construction and refinement of a series of ever more accurate system prototypes [2]. The complete ensemble of SEE tools can be used in different configurations to support each system life cycle activity [50, 30, 52, 55]. Alternatively, new software production techniques might use tools such as the software documentation hypertext system (DIF) and diagram animation system (VIZ) operating on a network of coupled processors to support experimental techniques for prototyping animated multi-media descriptions of application systems under development. Also, the development of new application systems through the reuse, (re)configuration, and enhancement of the SEE tool components themselves suggests still another approach to application software development. While we are currently experimenting with these (and other) techniques, other challenges remain. In particular, an open problem is deciding which production technique best supports the development of a given kind of application for a particular target environment or setting. This requires further research.

4.3. Strategies for Managing Software Engineering Projects in the SF

How do we manage a large engineering team to develop, use, and evolve a LSS system? That of course is the question we face. But we believe we have a unique approach to investigating this important question.

Over the past six years, we have conducted in-depth field studies of large system development projects in various real-world settings [49, 36, 61, 54, 7]. Through careful comparative analysis of many engineering projects, we systematically identify the problems of organizing and managing these projects as well as the strategies to mitigate these problems. Most importantly, we find such problems most often reflect organizational circumstances that drive up software development costs or drive down productivity and product quality. Conversely, we find effective solution strategies represent organizational strategies for reducing costs while increasing productivity and quality. Rather than describe the analysis and the problems,[9] we instead outline four strategies we find useful for managing large software engineering projects, whether in industrial or academic settings. These follow.

---

[9] See [35, 49, 36, 13, 61, 54, 7] for detailed studies and analytical frameworks. Also consider [32] for a popular introduction to the problems.

4.3.1. Focus on the coordination of development work and workers

One set of concepts we find useful emphasize the importance of establishing a *socially proactive, democratic workplace* intended to facilitate computer-aided system development work [8, 16, 23, 24, 60, 7]. The particular concepts to follow include:

* provide for both system developers and eventual users to participate in the decisions determining the system's features, purpose, and modes of use;
* openly share strategic information regarding the purpose, intended uses, and expected outcomes with participants developing and using the system;
* provide a fair sharing of the benefits between participants arising from both the development and use of a new system;
* guarantee participants will not be penalized for speaking out or criticizing proposed directions for local system development efforts;
* provide an organizational mechanism for a fair settling of disputes between (or among) system developers, managers, and users;
* encourage a participatory, democratic awareness among system developers, managers, and users so that they will be committed to cooperate to do the best job possible with available resources, and to work through (or around) the problems that arise in developing or evolving software systems [7];
* continually seek to provide new tools and techniques that facilitate the conceptualization and collaboration of system development activities by a large staff working in a complex organizational setting.

These concepts thus provide a basis for the other strategies for organizing system development work that follow.

4.3.2. Design project organization to facilitate staff commitment

Everyone will be responsible for managing some portion of overall system development work activities. However, project managers in particular will be responsible for coordinating work and resources within the local computing infrastructure, they need to know about production bottlenecks and other troublesome conditions. Maintaining a high rate of software production requires the commitment of staff and resources to achieve it. Continuity of staff commitment to project and colleagial objectives is more important than mangerial control over these staff [49, 36]. Management control in large projects is distributed and more subject to contention. Project staff who must be coerced into performing undesired tasks cannot be expected to perform those tasks with high productivity and care. Maintaining staff commitment requires regularly assessing the conditions that bind their commitment to work: desired resource availability, local (dis)incentives, and career opportunities. Such an assessment emerges when staff participate in deciding (rather than being told) how to realize project objectives. The regularity of assessment depends on the perceived stability or uncertainty of local project management conditions. Unexpected circumstances will always emerge and give rise to destabilizing conditions. However, strong commitment will often provide staff members idiosyncratic motivation to accommodate local contingencies until the prevailing order is reestablished, unless their commitment is sufficiently weakened.[10] But if their commitment to project objectives is strong, so that their perceived investment (or stake) in project activities is clear, then they can build on their investment by discovering new ways to perform their work activities.

4.3.3. Identify the incentives that motivate project participants

Why are software developers as productive as they are? This may seem to be an odd question, since many people are fond of asking how do we make software developers more productive. But we find that to answer the latter, you must first be able to answer the former. In particular, we find that what motivates software developers to be as productive as they can be is often idiosyncratic and circumstantial [49, 36]. What motivates developers today, may not motivate them equally well tomorrow. For example, in working with a student staff in the SF, one might assume that they seek to be very productive to insure earning a high grade. This seems true for some staff, but not all. Some students seek to gain first-hand experience and research skill in the development and use of state-of-the-art software tools. Other students hope for advancement or promotion in their job, based on their acquisition of certain new technical skills, such as LSSD. Still other students have an entreprenuerial spirit, and hope to identify new software or services through their participation that they could eventually develop and profit from in the private sector. Finally, many students are motivated by more than one of these situations. In sum, near-term rewards such as a high grade may provide an incentive for certain staff, while other staff are primarily concerned with long-term professional, occupational, or financial opportunities. Therefore, in the SF, we seek to regularly assess and cultivate the incentives that might provide intrinsic motives for each staff participant to be highly productive and quality conscious.

[10] The cyclic building of strong commitment for some ("signing up"), and the weakening of commitment for others ("burning out") is a key element in what gives a new system its soul [32].

4.3.4. Develop new software technology as a package

LSS systems are more than a simple collection of many programs and source code files. Every large software system assumes some configuration of hardware, telecommunications facilities, software base, documentation, time, money, skills, organizational units, management attention, and other resources for its productive development or use [34]. This "package" of computing resources outlines a set of requirements that must be met by participants working within the local computing infrastructure. Each package must fit transferred, inserted, and transitioned into an idiosyncratic local setting. As such, users need to know what resource requirements are built into a new technology in order to assess both the costs and ease with which it can be transferred into existing computing arrangements. However, as a new technology is transferred and assimilated into ongoing organizational routines, the local computing infrastructure will be altered to reflect its repackaging. Historical trends in software engineering indicate that this repackaging is done to make the work activities more productive and routine. However, these trends also indicate a finer division and specialization of labor among participants as well as increase the number of resources to be coordinated. Accordingly, an important cost of using new software technologies intended to make the work activities more productive is increased demands for attention to detail, coordination, and routine. This is a form of work management that individual participants must increasingly perform. Thus, in developing a new software systems, tools, or engineering methodology, a strategy for managing its life cycle in its target setting must explicitly be built into its package to facilitate its transfer, insertion and transition [49].

4.3.5. Project Management Strategy Summary

What the preceding four strategies describe are inherently organizational approaches to more effectively deal with the problems of managing LSSD projects. These strategies are quite different than those derived from a traditional rational planning and control approach to engineering project management [19, 67, 11, 31]. Elsewhere, we identify many additional strategies for handling other problems in organizing and managing system engineering projects [36, 61, 53, 54, 7]. However, we have limited experience with these strategies outside the SF laboratory setting, thus we cannot yet prove their universal effectiveness in all kinds of settings. However, as we continue to investigate, apply and evaluate these strategies, they will be further refined and specialized to different settings, but kept practical. This is one of the goals of this line of long-term experimental research in the SF.

5. Experiences in SF Technology Transfer

Some people hold that the primary purpose of a school of science, engineering, or information technology is technology transfer. Such transfer nominally occurs via educated students who take their newly acquired academic scholarship to their workplace, and then apply this knowledge to practical problems. We consider this the baseline for software technology transfer. But the successful practice of the software technology transfer (STT) on a larger scale requires understanding much more than this [58]. Subsequently, we use this section to describe some of our experiences in STT.

We observe two different modes of STT through the SF project: *intraorganizational* and *interorganizational*. Within the SF project, the value of internal STT is taught and practiced. This happens in three ways. First, project teams are given access to the prior year team project deliverables. Students are encouraged to reuse and incorporate the prior project life cycle products (e.g., subsystem functional specifications and source implementation) into their own, with shared products duly acknowledged. Many project teams choose to do this and therefore are able to deliver more substantial and more capable products. Second, since project teams are focussed primarily on their respective tools or subsystems to engineer, all team members are required to conduct project specification and design reviews for some other project component. This gives the student staff an opportunity to evaluate and compare their deliverables, and provide orchestrated quality assurance reviews. This also gives the students a chance to learn more about other parts of SF products and processes. Third, students are directed to use different SEE components to support the development of their deliverables. Thus, students become users of advanced prototype software engineering tools, and can evaluate the tools' strengths and weaknesses when applied to in a large project setting.

Moving SF products, production techniques, or project management strategies into other organizational settings takes the preceding STT efforts further. Interorganizational STT occurs in a number of ways. First, all students who complete their project deliverables are encouraged to share them with other team members and to take to their workplace.[11] Thus, students can take parts of the SF away with them to their workplace.

Second, some entreprenuerial students have elected to use their project deliverables as the basis for developing commercial software products. They seem confident in their own

[11] Such exchanges require an agreement not to further disseminate, license, or market other people's work or university resources without prior written agreement. Thus, the agreement is intended to have the form of an extended loan of borrowed property, but not an entitled claim to ownership or exclusivity.

technical ability and in the capabilities of the prototypes products they have delivered as part of their coursework. The personal computer software arena seems to be a favorite area these budding entreprenuers seek to find a niche for their eventual product. However, the emerging computer-aided software engineering (CASE) marketplace is gaining more attention. Many of the student start-up firms remain relatively small and last less than two years. On the other hand, others seem to survive and grow. But such experiences are part of process of real-world continuing education in STT for these students.

Third, as witnessed through this report, researchers participating in the SF project (such as the author) regularly produce research publications, conference presentations, and academic/industrial research colloquia for peer group consumption. A growing number of research publications are co-authored by students writing about the products of their completed coursework in the SF. Students can thus pursue the option of diffusing their knowledge and technological concepts through research publications, thereby adding value to both the educational experiences and professional status.

Next, as the SF project continues to push both the state of the practice and the state of the art in LSSD, various industrial organizations actively seek access to SF products, production processes, and project management strategies. These technologies are diffused through consulting contracts, contract research, and licensing arrangements. As might be expected, consulting arrangements facilitate the transfer of expertise through on-site short courses, project or proposal reviews, and product/process designs via research reports or technical memoranda. Contract research represents a greater level of commitment from an industrial firm, usually in the form of an IR+D subcontract. We restrict our involvement to undertakings directed at basic software engineering research problems rather than commercial products. Accordingly, we deliver our research results in the forms of technical reports or prototype systems. For example, for one contractor, we delivered a prototype system specification generator that accepts structured English requirements and paraphrases them into an operational specification language. In another case, we are actively exploring advanced techniques for specifying and documenting distributed, real-time multi-processing systems. Since we use the SF project to produce these technologies, we also then incorporate these products into subsequent SF configurations. Last, technology licensing agreements represent the direct acquisition of SF deliverables through the university for commercial purposes. Here we find interest not only in acquiring prototype software implementations, but also (or sometimes only) interest in acquiring rights to software specifications or designs, since these are viewed as being technologies reusable in many potential applications.

Clearly, all of the the preceding channels for diffusing SF technologies into other organizational settings do not complete the STT process [58]. The successful transition and prolonged use of the concepts, artifacts, and packages we produce may take years. However, we do note that most of our industrial sponsors seek sustained relations that get reiterated, and we continue to be approached by more firms interested in gaining access to SF technology and student staff.

6. Conclusions: Observations and Potentials

The SF project provides a hands-on learning and research experience in LSSD for all project participants. We have demonstrated the large-scale software engineering project coursework can prototype complex full-scale systems in a relatively short time. Our early experiments in developing a computer-aided software engineering environment demonstrate this. Similarly, we were able to integrate and operationalize a diverse collection of reusable software tools and life cycle engineering techniques. A LSSD effort such as the SF project immediately gives project participants insights into the importance identifying and practicing many different project management strategies. This happens as soon as participants find that the most difficult LSSD problems to solve are primarily organizational, rather than technical. Last, although seemingly ignored in most software engineering coursework, we find that software technology transfer can be taught and practiced by all LSS project participants. As such, we believe that other software engineering researchers and educators should consider adopting reiterated and sustained project courses such as the SF project.

Developing LSSD projects is possible but by no means limited to the types of tools, packages, or software engineering environments developed in the SF. For example, domains amenable to LSSD include graphic programming environments, production of "feature-length" computer animated movies, reconfigurable user interface management systems, group design of application-specific VLSI processors, interactive CD ROM-based undergraduate CS curriculum courseware, system factories for computer integrated manufacturing, environments and simulators for developing integrated multi-sensory intelligent systems, and so forth.

Many universities are becoming equipped to conduct LSSD projects due to extensive institutional commitments to create computerized campuses [68]. Most of these universities will seek a heterogeneous, open system network of computing resources distributed across many institutional locations. This increasing diversity of computing environments will lead to a greater spanning of multiple organizational units in order to successful complete LSSD projects. In our view, the trailblazers best positioned to capitalize on such opportunities will be faculty and researchers in the area of large-scale software engineering.

7. References

1. A. Avizienis and J. Kelly. "Fault Tolerance by Design Diversity: Concepts and Diversity". *Computer 17*, 8 (1984), 67-80.

2. R. Balzer, N. Goldman, and D. Wile. "Operational Specifications as the Basis for Rapid Prototyping". *ACM Software Engineering Notes 7*, 5 (1982), 3-16.

3. R. Balzer, T. Cheatham, and C. Green. "Software Technology in the 1990's: Using a New Paradigm". *Computer 16*, 11 (1983), 39-46.

4. R. Balzer. "A 15 Year Perspective on Automatic Programming". *IEEE Trans. Software Engineering SE-11*, 11 (1985), 1257-1267.

5. M.G. Barnes, et. al. "A Computer Science Courseware Factory". *SIGCSE Bulletin 18*, 1 (1986), 318-323.

6. V.R. Basili and R.W. Reiter. "A Controlled Experiment Quantitatively Comparing Software Development Approaches". *IEEE Trans. Soft. Engr. SE-7*, 3 (1981), 299-320.

7. S. Bendifallah and W. Scacchi. "Understanding Software Maintenance Work". *IEEE Trans. Software Engineering 13*, 3 (1987), 311-323.

8. P. Bernstein. *Workplace Democraticization: Its Internal Dynamics*. Kent State University Press, 1976.

9. V. Berzins, M. Gray, and D. Naumann. "Abstraction-Based Software Development". *CACM 29*, 5 (May 1986), 402-415.

10. B.V. Boehm. "An Experiment in Small-Scale Software Engineering". *IEEE Trans. Soft. Engr. SE-7*, 5 (1981), 482-493.

11. B. Boehm. "Seven Principles for Software Engineering". *J. Software and Systems 3*, 1 (1983), 3-24.

12. B.W. Boehm, T. Gray, and T. Seewaldt. Prototyping vs. Specifying: A Multi-project Experiment. Proc. 7th. Intern. Conf. Soft. Engr., 1984, pp. 473-484.

13. F. van den Bosch, J. Ellis, P. Freeman, L. Johnson, C, McClure, D. Robinson, W. Scacchi, B. Scheft, A. van Staa, and L. Tripp. "Evaluating the Implementation of Software Development Life Cycle Methodologies". *Software Engineering Notes 7*, 1 (1982), 45-61.

14. Harvey Bratman and Terry Court. "The Software Factory". *Computer 8* (May 1975), 28-37.

15. M. Brown, N. Meyrowitz, and A. van Dam. "Personal Computer Networks and Graphical Animation: Rationale and Practice". *ACM SIGCSE Bulletin 15*, 1 (February 1983), 296-307.

16. J.S. Brown and S. Newman. "Issues in Cognitive and Social Ergonomics: From Our House to Bauhaus". *J. Human-Computer Interaction 1*, 4 (1986).

17. A. Castillo, S. Corcoran, and W. Scacchi. A Unix-based Gist Specification Processor: The System Factory Experience. Proc. 2nd. Intern. Conf. Data Engineering, 1986, pp. 582-589.

18. R. Cronk and D. Zelinski. ES/AG: A System Generation Environment for Intelligent Application Software. Proc. SOFTFAIR II, IEEE Computer Society, 1985, pp. 96-100.

19. J. Distaso. "Software Management - A Survey of Practice in 1980". *Proceedings IEEE 68*, 9 (1980), 1103-1119.

20. L. Eliot and W. Scacchi. "Toward a Knowledge-Based System Factory: Issues and Implementations". *IEEE Expert 1*, 4 (1986), 51-58.

21. S. Feiner, D. Salesin, and T. Banchoff. "Dial: A Diagrammatic Animation Language". *IEEE Computer Graphics and Applications 2*, 7 (1982), 43-56.

22. M.S. Fox and S.F. Smith. "ISIS: A Knowledge-based System for Factory Scheduling". *Expert Systems 1*, 1 (1984), 25-49.

23. L. Gasser. "The Integration of Computing and Routine Work". *ACM Trans. Office Info. Sys. 4*, 3 (1986), 205-225.

24. E.M. Gerson and S.L. Star. "Analyzing Due Process in the Workplace". *ACM Trans. Office Info. Sys. 4*, 3 (1986), 257-270.

25. N. Gibbs and R. Fairley (Ed.). *Software Engineering Education.* Springer-Verlag, New York, 1987.

26. M. Barbacci, A.N. Habermann, and M. Shaw. "The Software Engineering Institute: Bridging Practice and Potential". *IEEE Software 2*, 6 (November 1985), 4-21.

27. B. Hannaford. The Electronic Spreadsheet: A Workstation Front-End for Parallel Processors. Proc. COMPCON 1986, 1986, pp. 316-321.

28. J.J. Horning and D.B. Wortman. "Software Hut: A Computer Program Engineering Project in the Form of a Game". *IEEE Trans. Soft. Engr. SE-3*, 4 (July 1977), 325-330.

29. H. Hunke (ed.). *Software Engineering Environments.* North-Holland, 1981.

30. R. Katz, W. Scacchi, and P. Subrahmanyam. "Development Environments for VLSI and Software Engineering". *J. Sys. Soft. 4*, 2 (1984), 14-27.

31. B.I. Kedzierski. Knowledge-Based Project Management and Communication Support in a System Development Environment. Proc. 4th. Jerusalem Conf. Info. Techology, 1984, pp. 444-451.

32. T. Kidder. *The Soul of a New Machine.* Avon Books, New York, 1982.

33. R. Kling and W. Scacchi. "The DoD Common Higher Order Programming Language Effort (Ada): What Will The Impacts Be?". *SIGPLAN Notices 14*, 2 (1979), 29-41.

34. R. Kling and W. Scacchi. Recurrent Dilemmas of Computer Use in Complex Organizations. Proc. 1979 National Computer Conference, 1979, pp. 1067-116. Vol. 48.

35. R. Kling and W. Scacchi. "Computing as Social Action: The Social Dynamics of Computing in Complex Organizations". *Advances in Computers 19* (1980), 249-327. Academic Press, New York.

36. R. Kling and W. Scacchi. "The Web of Computing: Computer Technology as Social Organization". *Advances in Computers 21* (1982), 1-90. Academic Press, New York.

37. J.C. Knight and N. Leveson. "An Experimental Evaluation of the Assumption of Independence of Multiversion Programming". *IEEE Trans. Soft. Engr. SE-12*, 1 (January 1986), 96-109.

38. D. Lenat, A. Borning, D. McDonald, C. Taylor, and S. Weyer. Knoesphere: Building Expert Systems with Encyclopedic Knowledge. Proc. IJCAI-83, 1983, pp. 167-169.

39. N. Magnenat-Thalmann, D. Thalmann, and M. Fortin. "Miramin: An Extensible Director-Oriented System for the Animation of Realistic Images". *IEEE Comptuer Graphics and Applications 5*, 2 (1985), 48-73.

40. J. Manley. Computer-Aided Software Engineering (CASE): Foundation for Software Factories. Proc. COMPCON Fall '84, 1984, pp. 26-37.

41. Y. Matsumato and others. SWB: A Software Factory. In *Software Engineering Environments*, H. Hunke, Ed., North-Holland, 1981.

42. W.M. McKeeman. Experience with a Software Engineering Project Course. In *Software Engineering Education*, Springer-Verlag, New York, 1987, pp. 234-262.

43. K. Narayanaswamy and Walt Scacchi. "A Database Foundation to Support Software System Evolution". *J. Systems and Software 7* (1987), 37-49.

44. K. Narayanaswamy and W. Scacchi. An Environment for the Development and Maintenance of Large Software Systems. Proc. SOFTFAIR II, 1985, pp. 11-25.

45. K. Narayanaswamy and W. Scacchi. "Maintaining Configurations of Evolving Software Systems". *IEEE Trans. Soft. Engr. 13*, 3 (1987), 324-334.

46. R. Prieto-Diaz and J. Neighbors. "Module Interconnection Languages". *J. Sys. and Soft.* 6, 4 (1986), 307-334.

47. C. Reynolds. "Computer Animation with Scripts and Actors". *Computer Graphics 16*, 3 (1982), 289-296.

48. A. Sathi, T. Morton, and S. Roth. "Callisto: An Intelligent Project Management System". *AI Magazine 7*, 5 (1986), 34-52.

49. W. Scacchi. *The Process of Innovation in Computing: A Study of the Social Dynamics of Computing*. Ph.D. Th., Department of Information and Computer Science, University of California, Irvine, 1981.

50. W. Scacchi. A Language-Independent Software Engineering Environment. Workshop Report: VLSI and Software Engineering, IEEE Computer Society, 1982, pp. 99-103. IEEE Catalog No. 82CH1815-0.

51. W. Scacchi. Developing VLSI Systems with a Silicon Engineering Environment. IEEE Intern. Conf. on Computer Design, IEEE, 1983, pp. 472-475.

52. W. Scacchi. The System Factory Approach to VLSI and Software Engineering. Proceedings AFCET Second Soft. Engr. Conf., 1984, pp. 349-359.

53. W. Scacchi. "Managing Software Engineering Projects: A Social Analysis". *IEEE Trans. Soft. Engr. SE-10*, 1 (January 1984), 49-59.

54. W. Scacchi. Applying Social Analysis of Computing to System Development. Proceedings Aarhus Conference on Development and Use of Systems and Tools, August, 1985, pp. 477-500. Aarhus, Denmark.

55. W. Scacchi. The Software Engineering Environment for the System Factory Project. Proc. 19th. Hawaii Intern. Conf. Systems Sciences, 1986, pp. 822-831.

56. W. Scacchi. "Shaping Software Behemoths". *UNIX Review 4*, 10 (1986), 46-55.

57. W. Scacchi. Software Specification Engineering: An Approach to the Construction of Evolving Software Descriptions. USC/Information Sciences Institute, 1987. (in preparation).

58. W. Scacchi and J. Babcock. Understanding Software Technology Transfer. internal report, Software Technology Program, Microelectronics and Computer Technology Corp., Austin, TX.

59. W. Scacchi and C.M.K. Kintala. Understanding Software Productivity. technical memorandum, Advanced Software Concepts Group, ATT Bell Laboratories, Murray Hill, NJ.

60. W. Scacchi, S. Bendifallah, A. Bloch, S. Choi, P. Garg, A. Jazzar, A. Safavi, J. Skeer, and M. Turner. Modeling System Development Work: A Knowledge-Based Approach. Computer Science Dept., USC, 1986. working paper SF-86-05.

61. W. Scacchi, L. Gasser, and E. Gerson. Problems and Strategies for Organizing Computer-Aided Design Work. Proceedings IEEE Intern. Conf. Computer-Aided Design, 1983, pp. 149-152.

62. T. Schwederski and H.J. Siegel. "Adaptable Software for Supercomputers". *Computer 19*, 2 (1986), 40-48.

63. R.W. Selby, V.R. Basili, and F.T. Baker. CLEANROOM Software Development: An Empirical Investigation. TR-1415, Computer Science Dept., Univ. of Maryland.

64. M. Sherman and A. Marks. Using Workstations to Investigate Computer Networks. Proc. IEEE 1985 Intern. Conf. on Computer Workstations, IEEE, 1985, pp. 214-221.

65. S. Sluizer and P. Cashman. XCP: An Experimental Tool for Managing Cooperative Activity. Proc. 1985 ACM Computer Science Conf., 1985, pp. 251-258.

66. D. Tajima and T. Matsubara. "Inside the Japanese Software Factory". *Computer 17*, 3 (1984), 34-43.

67. R. Thayer, A. Pyster, and R. Wood. "Major Issues in Software Engineering Project Management". *IEEE Trans. Software Engineering SE-7*, 4 (1981).

68. D.A. Updegrove. "Computing Intensive Campuses: Strategies, Plans, Implications". *EDUCOM Bulletin 21*, 1 (1986), 11-14.

69. A.I. Wasserman and P. Freeman. *Software Engineering Education: Needs and Objectives*. Springer-Verlag, New York, 1976.

70. R. Waters. "The Programmers Apprentice: A Session with KBEmacs". *IEEE Trans. Software Engineering SE-11*, 11 (1985), 1296-1320.

71. S. Weyer and A. Borning. "A Prototype Electronic Encyclopedia". *ACM Trans. Office Info. Sys. 3*, 1 (1985), 63-88.

Performing Requirements Analysis Project Courses for External Customers

John W. Brackett
Professor of Information Technology
Wang Institute of Graduate Studies

Introduction

The Software Engineering Project is a required course in the Master of Software Engineering Program at the Wang Institute (WI). The objectives of project courses and alternative approaches to organizing them have been described by McKeeman (1). Each student takes two, one semester projects near the end of the program. The projects are team efforts, with teams ranging in size from three to seven members. A project objective, from the viewpoint of the instructor, is to provide a learning experience in thirteen weeks that scales usefully to industrial practice. A project in intended to integrate the knowledge the student has obtained from the courses in the core curriculum (2, 3), with emphasis on team techniques, communication skills, planning, reporting, reviewing and documentation. Projects are judged by both academic and industrial standards, and are closely supervised by a faculty member.

During the summer and fall of 1986, three projects were completed under the author's supervision in which requirements specifications were produced for external customers. The involvement of an external customer, and the concentration on the requirements phase of the software lifecyle, were a major departure from previous projects.

The Challenge of Teaching Requirements Analysis

Requirements analysis is one of the most difficult subjects in a software engineering program to teach since it lacks an adequate underlying body of knowledge and is dominated by market-driven methods. However, requirements analysis must be an integral part of the WI MSE program, given the impact of complete, understandable and testable requirements on the success of any software project. The project course is an excellent vehicle for giving students experience with the analysis methods taught in one of the required courses, while also teaching the oral, written, and interpersonal communication skills essential for performing requirements analysis.

All WI students have industrial software development experience before starting the MSE program, but few have had any experience in specifying requirements. Almost all have worked exclusively in organizations which are very sophisticated in their use of computers. A majority have gained all their experience in development organizations which are totally isolated from customers and users.

Objectives of the Requirements Analysis Project Course

The objectives for the project course are:

1. Project members will understand the work products which must be produced during requirements analysis and the processes used to create them.

2. Each student will gain experience in data gathering, interviewing, and obtaining user review/approval.

3. Each team will produce professional quality presentations and documents which are understandable to an audience that is not sophisticated about the use of computers.

In addition to meeting these objectives, project course members have gained valuable experience in managing the analysis process.

The Need for an External Customer

In order to meet objectives 2 and 3, an external customer is essential. The instructor or other WI staff can not adequately simulate a customer who is unsophisticated about the use of computers.

The capabilities and limitations of methods and computer support tools become much more clear when stressed in a real world project. There is a tendency for the instructor, when designing a simulated project, to ensure it will provide the "right" context for using a given method.

The enthusiasm of the customer for a job well done, and the customer's plans to implement the requirements specification, must substitute in analysis projects for the satisfaction of producing working software. All three student teams became, through their interaction with the customer, highly motivated to deliver professional quality analysis results.

Criteria for Customer Selection

An external customer must meet three criteria in order to be seriously considered:

1. The organization is non profit.

   Since most WI students are company sponsored, and students from multiple companies comprise teams, projects for profit-making organizations are not feasible. The ability to make a contribution to a worthy organization is an important student motivator.

2. The staff and management is supportive of the project and have reasonable expectations for the use of a computer.

   Organizations are rejected if a manager has sought a student team as an alternative to having the project performed by an internal group. WI students are usually unskilled in dealing in a politically charged environment, and such an environment would certainly distract from the educational experience.

3. The instructor estimates the project to be approximately 400-600 hours of work for a trained analysis team.

   A project course team typically is 3-4 students, and each student is expected to invest about 180 hours in the project over a 13 week period. The project course, therefore, has about 540 hours (3 person team) to 720 hours (4 person team) available. Since the students have studied the methods to be used, but are not trained analysts, a project size that allows time for studying methods and tools, plus iteration of the deliverables, is essential.

Preference is given to organizations having at least one senior manager who understands the organization's automation priorities. Progress is much more rapid if one person in the organization is an informed customer!

Preparing for the Project Course

A significant fraction of the instructor's work must be done before the semester starts. Selecting the customer for each team can be time consuming, especially the first time the course is offered. The first step is to obtain candidates, followed by selecting one for each team of 3-4 students. Prior to the start of the course the organization must be counselled on the type of information which the students will initially need so that it will be available without an unreasonable delay. The instructor must learn enough of the organization's operations and needs that he can assess the students' progress during the semester.

In order to generate candidates, WI placed an advertisement in two Sunday newspapers in nearby cities. The ad described the opportunity for a non-profit organization and the work which the students would provide. From 15 organizations that contacted WI, three organizations were evaluated in depth. To do the evaluation the instructor visited each one at least twice in order to understand the organization's needs and to meet the key staff members with whom the students would be working. The evaluation was performed as if the instructor were a senior analyst for a consulting organization who was charged with preparing a quotation for the project. Approximately 6 man days were spent evaluating the three finalists. One organization (the Boys Club in a nearby city) was deemed the best candidate for the first presentation of the project course, since it both met all the criteria and had also recently obtained a donation of a computer system. The other two finalists (a regional visiting nurse/homemaker service and a suburban mental health counseling service) were later selected for the projects to be conducted the following semester.

The first time the project course was given the instructor concentrated on making sure the organization had available the information the students would need to get started, but he did not organize the initial interview process. Due to travel by the Executive Director, vacations, and scheduling conflicts, three weeks passed (out of 13 in the semester) before the students could meet with all the relevant staff members; in estimating the job the instructor assumed the meetings would occur in the first week. For the second project course, which involved two teams, the instructor decided that basic information on the organization's functions, management structure, and operational problems ought to be available at the start of the course. To accomplish this information gathering, while also providing an introduction to key personnel, the instructor conducted on-site interviews which were videotaped by the WI audiovisual staff. As a result the students could review the videotapes and generate relevant questions prior to their first visit to the organizations.

The instructor must also select the computer support tools to be used and ensure they are are ready for productive use at the beginning of the project. The software was selected by the instructor using the same criteria he would have used if the project were being done in a consulting company. Approximately 4 man weeks (by the instructor and other WI personnel), distributed over a 3 month period, were devoted to tool selection, tool setup and tool documentation. Since all of the tools used have a significant learning curve, WI staff had to generate "how to get started" material to enable the students to quickly make use of the tool facilities most needed at the start of the project.

Running the Project Course

Two of the three project teams used Structured Analysis (SA), based upon either DeMarco's text (4) or Ward's text (5), and Excelerator (an IBM PC/XT based tool supporting SA from Index Technology). One group using Structured Requirements Definition (SRD), based upon Orr's text (6), and DesignMachine (an IBM PC/AT based tool supporting SRD from Ken Orr and Associates). All three groups used the Curtice and Jones approach (7) to data modelling, and Lyddia (an IBM PC based tool supporting the data modelling approach from Cascade Software). Two of the three groups performed some prototyping using Cornerstone (a relational data base system for the IBM PC/XT) to demonstrate the implications of their requirements specification.

The first 6 weeks of the projects were devoted to information gathering, model building and assessing areas of potential automation. At the end of the sixth week, a project review was held with the Executive Director. There were two important purposes of the review: for the students to demonstrate their understanding of the organization's functions and needs, and for the customer and students to agree on the areas in which the project work should focus for the remainder of the semester.

The results of the project course are:

1. A report to the Executive Director and the Board of Directors.

   This report must be written for the Board of Directors and non-technical customer staff who are responsible for managing and funding the implementation of the project results. Most WI students have never prepared such a document before, and several iterations were typically required before it was ready for submission.

2. A one hour presentation to the Board of Directors.

   The presentation is a summary of the most important conclusions and recommendations of the report, followed by a question and answer period. The customer presentation is included as part of the WI project presentation, which is attended by the instructor, other faculty and interested students. Students find that the Board of Directors are "lambs" compared to their peers. The WI presentation also includes material on the methods and tools used, and a more technical description of the project results.

3. A requirements specification oriented towards the developers of the system.

   The document is written under the assumption that neither the students nor the instructor will be available when system implementation begins. All SA models, data models and prototype screens/reports developed are included in appendices.

All students on the project normally receive the same grade, unless the instructor has a good reason for a different policy. This grading approach is announced at the beginning of the semester and is designed to emphasize the need for a team effort to satisfy the customer. In three projects there have been only two cases where a student received a different grade than the remainder of the team; in both cases a reduction was made because the student clearly did not contribute equally to the production of the final deliverables.

Role of the Instructor

The first time the project course was given the instructor explicitly played only two, but distinct, roles: Technical Consultant and Customer Interface. He differentiated between the two roles in meetings with the project team. As the technical consultant he was willing to provide information, and give advice, on the the use of the methods and the computer support tools. However, his advice could be freely disregarded. The Customer Interface was the account executive in the sales organization of the simulated consulting organization employing the project team. Whenever issues needed to be resolved with the Executive Director (such as a staff member seeming not to cooperate with the project team), the Customer Interface could be asked to work on the problem. The Customer Interface let the project team know he was particularly interested in customer satisfaction (the potential for additional business!).

The instructor explicitly did not act as the project manager and did not attempt to direct the work of the project team. Project teams do not usually have a project manager in the industrial sense, since the students strongly prefer to function as equals. On a project with a tight schedule and deliverables to an external customer, the conventional WI project organization can become highly stressed. One member of the team, with significant leadership skills, evolved into a project coordinator role. The team established its own schedules for intermediate milestones, which were usually the completion of SA modelling phases. This approach worked reasonably well for the first 11 weeks of the 13 week semester. However, two weeks before the end of the project it became obvious that the preparation of the report for the non technical audience was in serious trouble. The member with the best writing skills did not feel she had the authority to edit the work of the others to the extent necessary. In addition, more material was being invented at the last minute than could be iterated through a review cycle of peers. In the last few days of the project the instructor had to assume the role of Project Manager and make detailed decisions on the format and content of the non-technical document.

Based upon the experience with the first project, the instructor's role evolved in the second project course. In addition to the Technical Consultant and the Customer Interface roles, the instructor acted as Project Manager to the extent of establishing several internal schedule milestones so that the project team did not have the temptation to invest more time than was necessary in early project phases, such as modelling current operations. There is a great temptation for first time users of Structured Analysis to equate the development of the models to the production of a deliverable requirements specification document. The dates for outlines and drafts of the Board of Directors presentation and of the non technical report required the students to begin to prepare the deliverables well before the end of the semester. As a result, the instructor was able to play a much lower key role in the final weeks.

In summary, the instructor must use his experience to keep the students from reaching a situation where their only choices are to produce unprofessional deliverables or to invest far more effort than intended near the end of the semester. Since the students become highly motivated by their involvement with the non profit customers, the instructor must ensure that the project team uses its time wisely and that they do not sacrifice their work in other courses at semester end.

Conclusions

The three requirements analysis projects offered to date have been valuable experiences for the customers, the students and the instructors. In the instructor's opinion the results delivered were comparable to those that would have been produced by major consulting firms, for which they would have charged $25,000 to $35,000. The project course supplied a learning environment for the students very close to industrial practice.

The non profit organizations received results that none of them could have otherwise afforded and all were very appreciative of the students' efforts. Two of the three organizations are making active use of the results, and have secured grant funding to purchase computers.

The project benefits are not without their costs. A project course organized in this manner is time consuming for the instructor; for a course with 2 teams of 4 students each, the time investment is comparable to a classroom course for 30-40 students. The instructor must be technically capable of doing the customer's project and should have previously estimated (accurately!) the resources required to perform such a project. The most devastating mistake the instructor can make when selecting the customer is to seriously underestimate the size of the project. Faculty members with the required experience are the only ones, in the author's opinion, who should undertake student projects with external customers.

In their WI project presentations, the teams include their assessment of the project. In their opinion the most important benefits of the projects were:

- the information gathering skills they learned
- the experience they received in communicating in the language of the

customer

- the opportunity they had to test requirements analysis methods and tools on a project of sufficient complexity that they could apply their experience to a future industrial project.

In the instructor's opinion, these benefits could have only been achieved in projects working with an external customer.

References

1. McKeeman, W., "Experience with a Software Engineering Project Course", in Software Engineering Education (ed. Gibbs and Fairley), Springer Verlag, 1987.

2. Fairley, R., "Software Engineering Education: An Idealized Scenario", in Software Engineering Education.

3. Gerhart, S., "Skills versus Knowledge in Software Engineering Education: A Retrospective on the Wang Institute MSE Program", in Software Engineering Education.

4. DeMarco, T., Structured Analysis and System Specification, Yourdon Press, 1978.

5. Ward, P., System Development without Pain, Yourdon Press, 1984.

6. Orr, K., Structured Requirements Definition, Ken Orr and Associates, 1981.

7. Curtice, R. and Jones, P., Logical Data Base Design, Van Nostrand Reinhold, 1982.

An Academic Environment for Undergraduate Software Engineering Projects

Michael A. Erlinger, member, IEEE

Wing C. Tam, member, IEEE

ABSTRACT

Software projects constitute a crucial component in an undergraduate software engineering education. In this paper we list the requirements for software projects that are essential in providing maximum benefits to the students. We describe the approach taken by Harvey Mudd College, known as the Clinic program, to provide software projects in support of our software engineering education. We follow with discussions of the responsibilities of the principle participants in a clinic project and the advantages of, and our experiences with, the clinic approach.

I. Introduction

The key to a good software engineering education is a combination of computer science core knowledge, software engineering concepts and techniques, and finally a software engineering project. This paper discusses the approach to the software engineering project as developed by Harvey Mudd College (HMC). Of course project oriented software engineering courses are by now common [1] [2] [3]. The objective of such courses is to provide the students with experience in the practice of software engineering concepts in the solution of real-world problems. However, many of these courses fail to meet the objective or cannot maximize the benefits of the project to the students because of the many difficulties in running such a course. Some of these difficulties are:

1) The selection of real-world projects and not artificial pedagogical problems.

2) Inadequate student time to devote to a significant project.

3) The difficulty in finding users who can interact with the students in the project.

In this paper we present our view of the requirements for a good software engineering project and give an overview of the HMC Clinic program, which is our approach for providing real-world projects to our students. We follow with a discussion of each of the participants in a HMC software engineering clinic project and then conclude with the advantages of, and our experiences with, software engineering clinics.

II. Software Engineering Project Requirements

The importance and benefit of software projects in a software engineering education are widely recognized by computer science educators and are stressed in software engineering curriculum recommendations [4]. A software project allows the students to integrate and to practice what they have learned in the classroom. Furthermore, certain skills that are important to software engineers can be more naturally acquired through involvement in a software project than through normal coursework. To reap the maximum benefits from software projects certain requirements must be imposed. We discuss below the requirements that we feel are desirable in producing educationally meaningful software engineering projects.

1) The project should be as realistic as possible. This is probably the most universally-agreed on requirement by software engineering educators. The problems to be tackled in a project should reflect the scale and complexity of the types of problems solved in the real world. Many significant software engineering issues usually are not addressed by simple or artificially created projects. Jensen, Tonies, and Fletcher [4] point out that projects that are simple enough to complete in one quarter are generally too simple to allow the student to gain much experience in the application of the problem-solving techniques learned during his regular classwork. Problems from industry tend to meet the realistic requirement because the problem creator is not constrained by the time limits of a semester or the knowledge of student education levels.

2) The project should provide experiences in all the major stages of a software lifecycle from requirement analysis and specification through design, implementation, verification and validation, and finally to maintenance. A student should not be exposed to just some stages of the lifecycle because the production of reliable and quality software requires the proper interaction of the work done in all the lifecycle stages. Admittedly, owing to time constraints the maintenance phase is usually ignored or slighted.

3) The project should emphasize team effort in contrast to individual work that is invariably stressed in a classroom environment. In fact, experience as a team member in a programmer team should be one of the educational objectives of any software engineering program. To do this properly the project must again be of significant size and complexity so that it is amicable to a team approach.

4) The project should not consist of just routine busy work or involve obsolete ideas, tools, and techniques. Ideally the project should involve the leading edge of software engineering development and should include state-of-art technology. Since we are training future software engineers it is important that the students be exposed to problems that are currently facing the industry. On the other hand, the project should not be a pure research problem because the goals of such projects are difficult to define, predict, and obtain (especially given educational time constraints). We feel the best projects should require the students to do some library research and then develop and implement a solution approach by applying their ingenuity and previous experience. Library research is important because it acquaints the students with the technical literature, published results from similar projects, and the operations of modem research tools, e.g., DIALOG.

5) The project should provide ample opportunity in the training of communication skills, both oral and written. Good communication skills have long been recognized as essential for software engineers. A software project is a natural place to provide such training because of the many types of communication that are needed through out project development: from the preparation of user requirements, to the presentation of a design for review, to the documentation of the final product.

The software project requirements listed above are certainly stringent and are not easily met in a typical undergraduate software engineering program. In the next section we describe the approach taken by Harvey Mudd College in obtaining software projects that meet these requirements.

III. HMC Clinic Program

A detailed description of the organization and operating procedures of the HMC Clinic program has been given by Busenberg and Tam [5]. In this section we provide the background and a brief summary of the Clinic program followed by a description of four sample software engineering projects that were undertaken in the last two years.

A. Background and Summary of the Clinic Program

Harvey Mudd College is a coeducational, undergraduate college of engineering and science with 520 students. The college emphasizes educating students not only in technical subjects, but in the humanities and social sciences as well. One unique feature of Harvey Mudd College is its Clinic programs (Engineering Clinic and Mathematics Clinic), introduced into the curriculum over 20 years ago. Every September about 30 teams, composed of three or four junior and senior students together with a faculty adviser, begin work on professional design and development projects for clients from industry and government. These clients pay a fixed fee (approximately $25K) for work by the student teams on current problems that the company needs solved - one team per problem, although sometimes one company has more than one project. Clients agree to appoint a company liaison who meets with team members and faculty advisers at least once a week to offer clarification and direction. Thus, there are three principle participants in each clinic project: HMC student team, HMC faculty adviser, and company liaison.

The hands-on clinic setup is designed chiefly to expose undergraduates to the realism of engineering practice. The clinic idea brings together the best elements of practice schools, cooperative programs, and the more common closed-end school projects. It also takes a page from the clinic practice setups that teach undergraduates at medical schools.

The students receive regular course credit for their participation in a clinic project (three unit course per semester), and the faculty adviser is provided with some release time for each project that he or she directs. The clinic project is an integral part of the program of all students majoring in either engineering or mathematics with a computer science option (HMC does not have a separate major in computer science). Normally, juniors take one semester of clinic, while seniors take two semesters of clinic. Clients expect 800 to 1,200 manhours per school year per project team.

To insure that clinic projects appropriate for software engineering education are obtained the members of the Computer Science Department work together with the Clinic Directors (engineering and mathematics) in contacting potential clients and in negotiating the individual projects.

B. Some Sample Software Projects

To give an idea of the type of software engineering projects in which our students are involved we describe below four of the projects that have been undertaken in recent years. All these were 9-month projects. As is true for most of the projects, these projects covered the major phases of the software lifecycle from the development of the requirement specifications, through design, implementation, testing, to the final delivery of the product. The maintenance phase is the only phase omitted.

1) The development of a user-friendly interface for a large simulation program [6]. This project involved the design of user-friendly interactive screens on CRT terminals to input large amounts of data for an existing simulation program. A software tool, written in Fortran 77, was developed to allow the user to define and manage data input screens.

2) A survey of the current state of parallel processing and the implementation of a parallel radar tracking algorithm [7]. The parallel processing survey served as the research phase of the project and helped the team choose an appropriate implementation model. and the requirements specification for the parallel radar tracking algorithm. The implementation applied to a specific type of radar tracking problem, decluttering, and was coded using the Ada tasking facility for a shared memory Multiple Instruction, Multiple Data multiprocessor. The parallel implementation was simulated using a VAX 11/750 and succeeded in detecting true targets comparable to an existing sequential algorithm.

3) The development of a user friendly software interface between a commercial database management system and a commercial software graphics package [8]. The project was guided by a list of features specified by the client as necessary in the final software package. The team followed a software development cycle that was standard to the client company. The final software package was written in a combination of C, Pascal, and languages internal to the commercial packages.

4) The development of an Ada implementation of the CAIS (Common APSE Interface Set) for the iAPX432 [9]. Two parallel tasks were accomplished by the team: analysis and implementation of the CAIS node model in standard Ada and acting as a beta test site for the iAPX432 Cross Development System.

IV. Participants in a Software Engineering Clinic Project

As mentioned above there are three principle participants in a clinic project: the client company and liaison, the project team, and the faculty adviser. Each of these groups has particular responsibilities and gains particular advantages from a chosen clinic project.

A. Client Company and Liaison

Each client company sponsoring a clinic project must give careful thought to choosing both the clinic project and the clinic liaison. Over the years we have developed a few do's and don'ts that we encourage a client company to consider when choosing a project.

- Don't give the clinic an *impossible dream*. Students need to be motivated by both excitement and by achievability. The *holy grail* type of project maybe exciting, but is probably not achievable by a student team in nine months.
- Don't choose a project with a long learning curve. If it takes years of experience before the problem can even be understood, then the clinic team will probably spend all nine months just learning background material.
- Don't choose a project that is in the company's critical path. The clinic team should not be put into a position where if they fail to complete the project the client company has serious problems.
- Do's - the clinic project should be something that the company really wants and cares about. Something that the clinic team can either finish or that can provide a solid foundation from which the company can continue at a later date.
- Do's - the most important point in considering a project is to choose a project in which the company has a continued interest and to which the company is willing to assign an active liaison.

The liaison plays an important continuing role in the conduct of a clinic project. The liaison is in the critical position of advising, directing, and evaluating the ongoing work of a clinic team. His position is one of *customer* to the clinic team, but not just a demanding customer such as might be found in industry. Rather, the liaison must recognize the inexperience of the team in developing software, and together with the faculty adviser, the liaison must continually provide technical assistance to the team. Regular communication (ideally, once a week) between the liaison and the team is necessary to keep the project on course (weekly meetings with the liaison, team, and faculty adviser are encouraged).

The liaison represents the client company's needs, but must also serve as a source of technical information. One of the worse things that can happen to a clinic project is to have a liaison who has neither the time nor aptitude to assist the clinic team. Teams with inactive liaisons tend to flounder in a sea of technical and administrative problems. An active liaison who acts as both customer and technical adviser provides students with the experience of meeting deadlines and responding to changing customer needs.

B. The Project Team

Obviously, it is the performance of the team that eventually determines whether a clinic project achieves its objectives. Students indicate a preference for particular clinic projects, but it is not unusual to have students inexperienced in the particulars of their clinic project. During the first few weeks of the fall semester the students organize as a team and in discussion with the faculty adviser, a team leader is chosen. The team then prepares a written proposal in response to the client's problem statement. This proposal is usually developed in close communication with the liaison. After numerous iterations the proposal becomes the contract between the client and the team. Normally, the team establishes two to three weekly meeting times: one meeting with the adviser, liaison, and the team; one meeting between the adviser and team leader, and working sessions for the team. It is imperative to the success of the project that meetings be held and that the appropriate parties be present. Students must view the scheduled meetings as course times with required attendance.

Teams proceed on their own schedule (part of the proposal) towards completion of the project. Team members immerse themselves in all the professional activities that enable the spontaneous practice of management, interpersonal relationships, ethics, and job performance. The team reports orally at three scheduled technical sessions during the year: fall, spring, and end-of-the year. These presentations are given to an audience composed of faculty, students, and members of client companies. Besides the proposal, there are two written reports, mid-year and final. The mid-year report is a status report generated before the end of the fall semester. The content of this report depends on the team's progress, but usually includes the team's written proposal and the project requirement specifications. The final report summarizes the team's effort for the entire year and includes the requirement specifications, design specifications, user manuals, implementation documentation, and code. It is the team's responsibility to execute the work; to interact among themselves, vendors, liaison, and faculty adviser; and to manage the project such that successful completion is assured.

C. The Faculty Adviser

The faculty adviser plays numerous roles in the clinic project: senior project management, contract management, technical supervision, but never team member. As senior project manager the faculty adviser insures that the team maintains its technical direction and schedule. He monitors each team member's activities and progress, insuring that team members are actively pursing the project goals. Most advisers hold a weekly meeting with the team leader. During these meetings the adviser and the team leader review the team's progress during the previous week and discuss (not set) goals for the current week. The word **discuss** was used because it is imperative that the adviser not dictate the team's activities, but only provide inputs to the team leader. it is the team's project, not the faculty adviser's.

The other important weekly meeting that the adviser attends is the team meeting with the liaison. It is at this meeting that the adviser acts as a contract manager smoothing out the rough points between the team's project proposal (contract) and the interpretation and changes requested by the liaison. The adviser has the experience to evaluate what are realistic goals for a particular project.

Finally, the third hat the adviser wears is that of technical superviser. Whenever any member of the team encounters technical obstacles that he cannot handle, the faculty adviser steps in and trys to assist the student. Occasionally, faculty advisers give short seminars on some technical material that the students have not encountered in their course work.

V. Advantages of the HMC Software Engineering Clinic

Basically, the Clinic program is the reverse of the traditional industry cooperative programs or intership programs in which students are sent to a sponsoring company for a certain period of time. Instead, our program brings industrial problems and experience onto campus. There are several advantages to this approach for the students and for the college:

1) A much larger number of students can participate in the program. The experience not only benefits the students, but also the faculty members involved.

2) Since students participate in the program as part of their regular course load, their academic education is not interrupted.

3) The faculty has much better control of the types of training and education that the students receive.

4) The college benefits financially from the fees paid by the client companies for the projects. This allows the college to increase its equipment and thus to attract additional clients.

The client also gains numerous benefits by having his project done at HMC.

1) Establishes ties with the academic community. A clinic project may provide a way for the client and HMC to share in other academic research efforts.

2) Provides the potential for the client to influence HMC towards the client's approach to software development. For instance, a previous clinic client required that DeMarco's structured analysis and structured design techniques [10] be used during the project. This allowed, HMC students to reviewed actual implementation of techniques they had studied and allowed the client to have an unbiased reviewed of the client's implementation of DeMarco's techniques.

3) Provides a solution to a problem that the client may have neither the resources nor the time to complete. The project may also be restricted to a prototype or feasibility study leading to future internal client efforts.

4) Provides an opportunity for the client to evaluate all students and to recognize and recruit top students more effectively. This is especially effective for students that do not have a high grade point average, but who may excel in the work place. Also, all clinic presentations are open to all clients. Thus it is possible for client representatives to review other clinic projects and to approach the students involved in those projects. About 70% of HMC students seeking employment upon graduation are hired by companies sponsoring clinic projects.

VI. Conclusion

The Clinic program has shown itself to be an ideal environment for supporting the software project that is needed in software engineering education. It provides an environment in which students can obtain truly valuable experience in the practice of software engineering concepts for the solution of real-world problems. We have discovered that overall there are two key facets to a successful clinic project: good liaison and good project. As mentioned above, one of the most severe problems for a clinic project to overcome is an inactive liaison. The only real contact the students have with the sponsoring company and in particular the company's attitude towards the project is the liaison. Almost all projects have some liaison problems because liaisons have many tasks within their company. One of the most common causes of liaison demise is assignment to a proposal team or change of job function. It is up to the faculty advisor to insure that adequate liaison activities continue during such periods. Realistic software engineering projects were initially a problem. But through active participation by the faculty, we have been able to communicate with industry about appropriate project content. It has never been a problem getting projects from industry (probably due to the shortage of software engineers), only getting projects that can be completed in the nine months. In the Clinic program it becomes the joint responsibility of faculty and the Clinic Director to communicate with industry about the appropriate content for a Clinic project. Overall the HMC clinic approach allows the requirements for software engineering projects to be satisfied: realistic projects provided by client companies; projects encompassing the entire software lifecycle; and team oriented projects requiring development of communication skills.

References

[1] S. Henry, "A project oriented course on software engineering," **SIGCSE Bulletin,** vol. 15, no. 1, pp. 57-61, Feb. 1983.

[2] B. Barbara, "Integration of methodology and tools: an approach to teaching system development," **SIGCSE Bulletin,** vol. 16, no. 1, pp. 10-14, Feb. 1984.

[3] D. L. Carver, "Software engineering for undergraduates," **SIGCSE Bulletin,** vol. 16, no. 3, pp. 23-25, Sept. 1984.

[4] R. W. Jensen, C. C. Tonies, and W. I. Fletcher, "A proposed 4-year software engineering curriculum," **SIGCSE Bulletin,** vol. 10, no. 3, pp. 84-92, Aug. 1978.

[5] S. N. Busenberg and W. C. Tam, "An academic program providing realistic training in software engineering," **CACM,** vol. 22, No. 6, pp. 341-345, June 1979.

[6] L. Moyal, et. al., **User-friendly Interface Program,** Engineering Clinic Final Report, Harvey Mudd College, Claremont, CA, June 1986.

[7] W. Wenjen, et. al., **Algorithms For Parallel Encoding,** Engineering Clinic Final Report, Harvey Mudd College, Claremont, CA, June 1986.

[8] D. Brown, et. al., **Integrated Graphics Information Processing,** Engineering Clinic Final Report, Harvey Mudd College, Claremont, CA, June 1985.

[9] K. Fluechiger, et. al., **Ada Implementation of CAIS on the iAPX432 Cross Development System,** Engineering Clinic Final Report, Harvey Mudd College, Claremont, CA, June 1985.

[10] T. DeMarco, **Structured Analysis and System Specification,** Prentice-Hall,Inc, Englewood Cliffs, New Jersey, 1979.

A Project-Based Software Course: The Myth of the "Real-World"

Dr. Pierre-N. Robillard,
Dept. of Electrical Engineering
Ecole Polytechnique de Montreal

Abstract

We discuss an approach to project-based software engineering courses. Considerations based on experience illustrate the myth of the real-world environment to project-based course in university. Characteristics of real projects are outlined and conditions that make them applicable are stressed. The experience with a real project-based course is briefly described.

Index Terms Project-based course
Software Engineering
Cooperative team approach
Software tool
Project environment
High-level documentation
Software engineering education

1. Introduction

There is a strong need in the software industry for students with training extending beyond programming ability. The responsibilities and challenge of teaching software engineering lie with the universities [1]. Students must understand why the programming of a system is not the real problem and must have enough background to deal with projects involving software engineering.

Few textbooks are available on the topic and they rarely present well-defined solutions to the problem of teaching software engineering [2-10]. There are currently no known methods of solving the problem of teaching Software Engineering other than a list of recommendations and suggestions for improving the process of software development. We believe that students should be made aware of the problems associated with software development projects and that they should realize for themselves what it means to apply software engineering practices [11].

Principles of software engineering can be learned from conventional lectures based on textbook material or can be learned by experience. Because the field of software engineering is a broad one and the techniques are fluid, many instructors feel that software engineering should be taught through project-based courses [12]. It is often the goal in software engineering courses to give the students not only a broad background in software engineering issues but also real-world, hands-on experience in the design and integration of large systems.

One of the difficulties associated with teaching software engineering in the university is how to choose an appropriate software project. It is generally believed that the projects chosen have to be representative, but without being so long as to extend beyond one or two semesters. On the other hand, software engineering principles are most needed when the size and complexity of the software project are so great as to be beyond the comprehension of any single person (including the instructor!) [13].

Students, in any case, must gain experience in developing a system using the team approach. Many approaches to project-oriented courses have been described in the literature, and they tend to fall into two categories [14]. One is based on multiple groups working on the same project while the other approach involves each group working on a different project. A later section of this paper outlines the advantages of having the entire class work on a project cooperatively.

Students should be made aware of the fact that there is something beyond structured programming, that they could be involved in a software project that goes beyond their understanding and that methodologies must be applied in order to manage the project.

They do not actually manage the project but they are kept continuously informed about how it is being managed. A software engineering course should not be geared toward turning out project managers, but toward developing an understanding of software principles [15].

This paper is a report of four years' experience with project-based software engineering courses at Ecole Polytechnique de Montreal, courses designed in an attempt to deal with this problem.

2. The "Real-World" Myth

Very often project-based software courses aim at giving participants real-world experience. The real-world approach can be misleading when applied to the project-based software course. The following considerations illustrate this point.

A. Real teams

In the real-world you rarely find teams of JUNIORS only. Ideally, you would have a mixture of senior and junior members. The juniors learn from the others, have less responsibilities and their abilities can be tested without jeopardy to the project. The seniors receive the recognition due to them, are more confident, and are willing to assume some leadership. They know how to do the job themselves and are willing to teach the juniors how to do it. There is no classroom anywhere, however, with this team structure. In the classroom there is one boss, the instructor, and a bunch of juniors. Moreover the "boss" is not a real boss, since he will keep his job even if the project never comes to fruition.

B. Real time

The real-world is a full-time job. It is everyday interactions with other fellow workers. It is special meetings in the middle of the day to solve a technical or specification problem. It is social gatherings to ease tensions among team members, who will be working together full-time for months and sometimes years. A typical classroom team meets once a week for a few hours. Timewise, a classroom team adds up to only 25% of time spent in a full-time real-world team, based on a 15-week (3 hr) semester course, and assuming that every student spend 2 hrs of personal work for each hour in the classrooms.

C. Real motivation

The project is a major concern for real-world team members. It is a job preoccupation that is part of the work function and part of the individual's career track. Most students view a course project as just one course among others. Their main concern is the mark they will get for it. This mark is only a portion of the total grade for the semester and sometimes is not very significant as far as earning the degree is concerned.

D. Real backgrounds

Real-world team members are selected on the basis of background and skills. One of the harsh realities of a project course if that the backgrounds and abilities of the students in any one semester are quite variable, and subject to the vagaries of the annual registration process. These considerations suggested to us that we should not attempt to simulate real world conditions in classroom software project. If we want the students to have real-world experience we should explore other avenues like letting them go out for a full-time one-semester practium in a software shop. The university is not the appropriate forum for teaching real-world environmental issues to software engineers: its role should lie in other directions.

3. The real project

Our contention in the previous section is that simulating the real-world environment surrounding software engineering projects in the university is utopic. A real-world project, however, is appropriate [16, 17].

A. What is a "real-world" project?

It could be described as a project with real-world users! Although that is true, it is also a project that requires expertise going beyond any one-semester course. Without pretending to define the new software life cycle, we could nevertheless identify the following steps as being typical of real world projects:

Problem Definition (including interviews with the user)
Analysis
Data Base definition
Architecture Design
Detailed Design
Programming
Module Testing
Module Integration
System Testing
Documentation
Maintenance

A project where all the students can do all the steps in one semester can not be too big so that the questions may legitimately arise as to whether it is meaningful at all. Splitting up the steps among team members, however, is no solution. Most of the steps are sequential and cannot be performed simultaneously, and only one team could be working while other teams are twiddling their thumbs waiting for data and reports that might not be satisfactory anyhow.

In a university environment only part of a real project can be attempted. It is up to the instructor then to decide which part of the project will meet the course requirements.

For a project to be real, however, it must be completed. A course limited to problem analysis or data base definition is merely an academic exercise unless the project is actually completed. The nicest architecture designs we have ever seen are the ones that have never been implemented. It is very easy to design something that will never be tested.

The students should know whether they will be evaluated on the quality of their design or the quality of the product they design. Therein lies the whole difference between a course in software design and a project-based course in software engineering.

B. Do we need a real project?

The question could be asked whether we need real projects at all in software engineering courses. A real project is not needed when the objectives of the courses relate to some technical aspect of software engineering, (ex. new language, design techniques, use of tools, etc.). It is actually better to let the students on their ability to use the techniques taught rather than to let them believe that a real-life real project is that simple.

A real project is needed, however, when we want the students to understand the mechanisms involved in software engineering and to address the problems related to the software processes which should be oriented: managing, planning, organizing, tooling, scheduling, controlling, documenting, testing, etc. [10].

Real projects require a substantial amount of effort by the instructors and a lot of resources. We believe that project courses based on real projects should be kept for mature students in their final year or for graduate students.

4. The cooperative team approach

The point we address in this section is how to manage a real project in the university setting. The project should be organized in such a way that the students can do the job without being in the best environment for doing so. The method that follows is the fruit of four years' experience with such courses. All the students are at the same level: detailed design, programming and testing. The course is restricted to a maximum of 20 students. A small test at the beginning of the course allows us to separate out students with gaps in their background. We find that a sound mechanism for selecting students is crucial to the success of the course. We ask the students to apir off with a teammate. We found it unnecessary to try to match up strong students with weaker ones, although we had all the information needed to do so. Motivation has proven to be a much stronger impetus for success than good grades.

Each pair of students is assigned a task which constitutes a part of the whole project. We call this the cooperative team approach. Each team works on its own project, which is part of the greater whole. Each team must interact with the other teams in order to get information as the project proceeds.

One of the teams is called the supervisor group. They are the ones responsible for integrating all the modules. A senior analyst is also assigned to the project. He is a professional with experience in similar projects, and is available for consultation 3 hours a week.

We believe that students working on a cooperative team project will learn the meaning of the following words, despite not working in a real-world environment:

project leader
software quality control
milestones
documentation
software integration and testing
schedules
data base integrity

The understanding should be among the objectives of a software engineering course.

5. Project description

This section is a report on a project used in a graduate course at ECOLE POLYTECHNIQUE DE MONTREAL. The project was to design a management system for swim team competitions. Officials from the Quebec Swimming Federation, the organization responsible for swimming events in Quebec, defined the project for us. They also supplied a booklet containing the rules governing swim team competitions.

The data base was wholly designed by the professors involved in the course. All files and records were done in dBASE III™[1]. The software package was to be written in dBASE III™ and executable on an IBM-PC with standard options (256K, 2 disk drives, Epson FX-80 printer).

The software would have to do all the steps required in planning, preparation, record-keeping and wrapping up a swimming competition. Special care would have to be given to screen design [19, 20]. It had to be user-friendly because the users were not expected to know anything about computers. The package also had to be reliable and efficient.

Project analysis was done by the Ecole Polytechnique professors and the project was divided into small modules. Integration of the modules was done by a course assistant who did not write any modules except for the main supervisor, which was menu-driven.

The students had to do the module analysis, its detailed design, programming testing and integration work. The system analysis, data base definition, and architecture design were done by the instructors. The database was designed with the dBASE III language. The architecture design was done by means of the EXCELERATOR™[2] [21] tool and the students used the SCHEMACODE™[3] tool to design and document their programs [21]. The project was big enough so that any one group of students would not be able to solve the whole project by itself.

Final integration

One week after the end of the course, the students were invited to the presentation of

---

[1]DBASE III™ is a trademark of ASHTON-TATE

[2]EXCELERATOR™ is a trademark of INDEX TECHNOLOGY

[3]SCHEMACODE™ is a trademark of SCHEMACODE INTERNATIONAL

their collective product. Integration of the individual modules therefore had to be done first, and all modules were integrated into the complete system. This undertaking also served as a means of evaluating the students work [22, 23]. No hand-written code was accepted. Students were required to hand in only high-level documentation which was stored on diskettes. All source code was automatically regenerated by SCHEMACODE™ from the high-level documentation. Modules were then tested and integrated. Integration tests were conducted.

Almost all the students attended the integration presentation. The product was presented on a large screen in front of the audience. Special guests are usually invited, officials or typical users. This final public presentation of the product has proven to be a very strong incentive for good work, and contributes to maintaining a high level of motivation. We find that this final presentation is a must, to make students believe in the reality of the project. Finally the software was successfully used for managing the Canadian Pan Pacific trials swim meet set the Olympic Pool of Montreal.

6. Concluding remarks

Software developed within a project-based course is not ready for commercial use. To make the software commercial, it would need a few more modules, more testing and validation, a professional user manual, consistent screen design, a consistent file management system, etc.

The purpose of the course was not to get a software package ready for the commercial market but to incorporate software development as part of a real project. The main reason why it is not ready for commercial use is that we are not in a real-world environment. Project management is not geared toward the Production of commercial software. Project staff numbers are fixed and likely to decline during the semester (students dropping out), meeting hours are set and limited to 3 hours a week, the deadline is irrevocable and the budget is simulated.

The purpose of the project was for students to learn to produce real software, not commercial software. They need to work in teams so that they share their knowledge, skills and the like, in other words so that they learn from others. Team projects help students to learn faster (ideally), and not to do bigger software projects. This suggests that the software project should be quite independent of course enrollments. Students should understand their own assigned modules clearly and they do not have to and preferably ought not be able to understand the details of the whole project. The students are likely to develop an understanding of and feel for the need for methodology and general principles.

Sometimes, the availability of human and physical resources put severe constraints on the choice of a project. It is our belief that it is more motivating and informative for the students to live with strong resource constraints while developing a real software product than to limit themselves to producing an artificial sub-product.

Acknowledgments

We thank anonymous referees for their helpful comments. We are grateful to the members of the Federation de Natation du Quebec for their collaboration at the arly stage of this project.

References

1. Robillard, P.N., Dupras, M. and Mili, A., "Software Engineering Education in Academia and Industry Synthesis of Some Practical Experience", *Proceedings 4th World Conference on Computers in Education WCEE/87*, North Holland, July 1985, pp. 753-756.

2. Yourdon, E., Techniques of Program Structure and Design, Prentice-Hall, Inc., 1975.

3. Tauseworthe, R.C., Standardized Development of Computer Software, Prentice-Hall, Inc., 1977.

4. Jensen, R.W. and Tonies, C.C., Software Engineering, Prentice-Hall, Inc., 1979.

5. Peters, L.J.,Software Design: Methods and Techniques, Yourdon Press, 1981.

6. Fox, J.M., Software and its Development, Prentice-Hall, Inc., 1982.

7. Turner, R., Software Engineering Methodology, Reston Publishing Co., 1984.

8. Lustman, F., Managing Computer Projects, Reston Publishing Co., 1985.

9. Robillard, P.N., Le logiciel de sa conception a sa maintenance, Gaetan Morin Ed., Quebec, 1985.

10. Thayer, R.H., Pyster, A.B. and Wood, R.C., "Major Issues in Software Engineering Project Management", *IEEE Transaction on Software Engineering*, Vol.SE-7, No.4, July 1981, pp. 333-342.

11. Shooman, M.L., "The Teaching of Software Engineering", *ACM, SIGCSE Bulletin*, Vol.15, No.1, February 1983, pp. 66-69.

12. Henry, S., "A Project Oriented Course on Software Engineering", *ACM, SIGCSE Bulletin*, Vol.15, No.1, February 1983, pp. 57-61.

13. Carver, D.L., "Comparison of Techniques in Project-Based Courses", *ACM, SIGCSE Bulletin*, Vol.17, No.1, March 1985, pp. 9-12.

14. Sanders, D., "Managing and Evaluating Students in a Directed Project Course", *ACM, SIGCSE Bulletin*, Vol.16, No.1, February 1984, pp. 15-25.

15. Woodward, M.R. and Mander, K.C., "On Software Engineering Education, Experience with Software Hut Game", *IEEE Transaction on Education*, Vol.E-25, No.1, February 1982, pp. 10-14.

16. Ballew, D., "A Senior Design Course for Computer Science", *ACM, SIGCSE Bulletin*, Vol.18, No.1, February 1986, pp. 131-133.

17. Riley, M.W., "Phases Encountered by a Project Team", *IEEE Transactions on Education*, Vol.E-23, No.4, November 1980, pp. 212-213.

18. Galitz, W.O., Handbook of Screen Format Design, QED Information Sciences, Inc., 1985.

19. Morland, D.V., "Human Factors Guidelines for Terminal Interface Design", *Communications of the ACM*, Vol.26, No.7, July 1983, pp. 484-494.

20. Robillard, P.N., "Schematic Pseudocode for Program Constructs and the Computer Automation by SCHEMACODE" *Communication of the ACM, Computing Practices*, Vol.29, No.11, November 1986., pp. 1072-1089.

21. Collofello, J.S., "Monitoring and Evaluating Individual Team Members in a Software Engineering Course", *ACM, SIGCSE Bulletin*, Vol.17, No.1, March 1985, pp. 6-8.

22. Woodfield, S.N., Collofello, J.S. and Collofello, P.M., "Some Insights and Experiences in Teaching Team Project Courses" *ACM SIGCSE Bulletin*, Vol.15, No.1, February 1983, pp. 62-65.

SECTION II

PART 3

GRADUATE LEVEL SOFTWARE ENGINEERING EDUCATION

At the present time, the primary emphasis in the software engineering education community is on graduate level education and industrial training. Part 3 is concerned with graduate level education. Topics presented in the five papers in this Part include education for research in software engineering; accommodating the evolution in software engineering education; the evolution of Wang Institute's software engineering education program; teaching a software design methodology; and software engineering at Monmouth College.

The paper, "Education for Research in Software Engineering," was written and presented by Professor Caroline Eastman of the University of South Carolina. A synopsis of her presentation and a question/answer session are included at the beginning of Part 3.

Synopsis of Presentation

Caroline M. Eastman

Caroline Eastman presented the main points in her paper, tied them into some of the other presentations at the workshop, and provided some of the background and rationale for the ideas presented in her paper. Among the points she made in her presentation were the following:

- Software engineering can be described as a science of the artificial. It involves the design and study of artificial designs.
- Software engineering, in terms of the structure of the community, could be classified as a professional adhocracy. This is a term used by sociologists of science to refer to one form of a loosely structured scientific community.
- One of the things that a scientific community does is exercise control over research activities.
- Mechanisms of control include textbook development and selection, employer directions, funding agency priorities, and peer review of papers and proposals.
- Her approach advocates an emphasis on design, which is practical because it tends to insure a steady flow of new designs. Moreover, it encourages the skills and attitudes needed in design.
- Rather than dealing with an unending stream of design languages, we want to be able to compare them.
- Performance evaluations can be used to compare alternative designs.
- Theoretical analysis can be used to study the efficiency of algorithms.

- Two problems that exist with the use of information resources are that people are sometimes not familiar with previous work in an area and that frequently, people are unfamiliar with related work in another area. Occasionally, people in academic environments attack problems which have already been resolved.

- It is important to take a broad view of information resources.

- Information resources include not only research literature, but also information about products, information about patents, and professional information about companies, standards, activities, and professional societies.

- A problem with information resources is that education in science and engineering relies almost exclusively on the use of textbooks. This can encourage the overuse of textbooks.

- Standard textbooks should be used as an initial source of information, not as the last word.

- Methods for the study of human factors include controlled experimentation, surveys, protocol analysis, case studies, participant observation, and introspection.

- In terms of research, she feels that the right approach is to have more interdisciplinary teams of people doing software engineering research, rather than trying to make programmers out of psychologists or psychologists out of programmers, for example.

Questions for Caroline M. Eastman

Bob Glushko: You basically were emphasizing how you would take computer science people and teach them to do research in software engineering. You alluded to some of the problems of needing to know a lot about statistics and experimental design and so on. I've noticed the opposite problem, where a lot of research in this area is being done by people who are social scientists, who don't have a lot of knowledge about computer science. This suggests that the right approach in many areas is to have more interdisciplinary teams of people doing this SE research.

Caroline Eastman: I would agree that in many areas interdisciplinary collaboration is needed at this point. Yes, my emphasis was on people with a computing background carrying out research, as opposed to people who have come from other disciplinary traditions.

Bob Glushko: I've seen methodologically impeccable work by a psychologist that is naive about software engineering, and I've seen good work by computer scientists,that is attacking the right problems, but which is statistically and empirically naive.

Caroline Eastman: That's one reason why I was trying to make a distinction between the quality of the work and the significance of the work.

Education for Research in Software Engineering

Caroline M. Eastman
University of South Carolina

Abstract. *Graduate education serves as preparation for research as well as practice. However, this aspect of education in software engineering has often been given little emphasis. Several curricular issues involved in education as preparation for research are considered here. They include mathematical foundations, statistics and experimental design, use of information resources, and research methods for the study of human factors.*

1. Introduction

Much of the emphasis in curricular development for software engineering programs has appropriately been on education for professional practice. However, this aspect should not be allowed to completely overshadow the traditional role of graduate programs, especially at the doctoral level, of education for research as well as practice. Some of the curricular requirements to support this role are discussed here.

2. What is Software Engineering?

The computer-related disciplines, including software engineering, computer science, computer engineering, and information science, are all sciences of the artificial [32]. Research in these areas involves the creation and study of designs for computer-based systems. The objects of design include algorithms, languages, hardware architectures, systems software, software tools, and application systems. It is not always possible or even desirable to draw clean lines separating these disciplines. However, the focus of software engineering is on software systems which are technologically and economically feasible at the present time.

The relationship between software engineering and computer science is often compared to that between electrical engineering and physics or chemical engineering and chemistry, e.g. [10, 22]. These analogies are weak since both physics and chemistry are natural sciences and computer science is not. The difference is more subtle, involving different emphases within the design space and a different mixture of research approaches. In addition, the field of computer science has been more willing to accept any knowledge about the design space as a legitimate goal, even if it involves designs which are currently impractical. (The nature of the field of computer science is discussed by Traub [34].)

3. Research in Software Engineering

Research in software engineering seeks to add to the body of knowledge about software. This contrasts with development, which seeks to produce useful products. There can be a close interaction, but they are separate activities with separate goals. As Denning [5] points out, merely building systems is not experimental science. Software engineering is concerned with practical aims, and graduate programs, especially at the masters level, are appropriately aimed at professional practice. However, an emphasis on design and development to the exclusion of other concerns can easily give the impression that research in software engineering consists primarily in the construction of bigger and newer systems.

Research involves not only the creation of designs but also their understanding. Because software engineering draws upon foundations from several disciplines (e.g. [10, 22]), a variety of research methodologies are appropriate. The study of designs can be approached from several directions: mathematical theorems of properties or performance bounds, experimental observations of their performance, and focused comparisons among design alternatives. Ferrari [14] presents a strong argument for the inclusion of performance evaluation considerations throughout the curriculum; Graham [19] discusses the inclusion of performance evaluation in the software engineering curriculum. Gilb [17, 18] emphasizes the importance of measurement.

Fairley [10] discusses appropriate research topics and methodologies in software engineering and mentions four approaches in particular: "original contributions to knowledge, development of outstanding software artifacts, experimental studies involving human subjects, and significant case studies of technological and/or managerial issues." It is not clear what kinds of activities are included in "original contributions to knowledge," since the purpose of experimental studies, case studies, and even many design activities is also to contribute to the body of knowledge about a specific subject.

At least four aspects of research projects can be considered in judging their suitability as doctoral projects: topic, methodology, quality, and significance.

Topic. What area is investigated? What questions are asked?

Methodology. How are answers to the research questions sought? What approaches are used?

Quality. How well is the investigation carried out? Are results clearly presented? Is relevant literature cited? Is the methodology appropriately applied.

Significance. Are the results new? Are they important?

In a scientific community there is generally broad agreement about what topics and methodologies are appropriate in the area and about what standards of quality and significance are to be applied.

Fairley [10] points out that topics and approaches appropriate for software engineering may not be regarded as appropriate by researchers in traditional computer science programs. However, it is important to distinguish between topic and methodology. In addition, reservations about significance and quality should not be confused with reservations about topic and approach. For example, a design project may be objected to, not simply because it is a design, but because it does not differ significantly from similar designs. A project involving case studies may be objected to, not because it involves case studies, but because the research question addressed is unclear.

4. Education for Research in Software Engineering

Research in software engineering clearly requires a background in software engineering with some appropriate balance of breadth and depth. However, it also requires an understanding of the range of research methods appropriate in this area. The question addressed here is the educational structure appropriate to support adequate understanding of research methods. These problems are in large part independent of the choice of specific subject topics chosen for required and elective courses; this latter issue is not discussed here.

In a few cases examples have been chosen from the literature to illustrate the need for increased emphasis on research methodologies. Of course, such anecdotal and isolated examples do not provide conclusive evidence of the extent of such problems. There have been few comparative studies of research methodology in the computer sciences; one such study involves approaches to the study of multiattribute file structures [7]. It is evidence from such studies that would be required, but such methodological research is outside the scope of this paper.

Examples have been selected from recent issues of *Communications of the ACM* and *IEEE Transactions on Software Engineering*. This approach to selecting examples can be compared to the setting of traps for agricultural pests. The discovery of such insect pests in a trap can be regarded as indicative of a problem, even though further investigation is required to determine the extent of the problem. It is all too easy to find examples of poor methodology in the unreferred literature. And I observed many similar problems in research proposals submitted to the National Science Foundation when I was Program Director for the Information Science Program. However, papers published in top journals are scrutinized by reviewers and editors as well as authors and are generally held to fairly high standards.

Four general areas are discussed here:

1. mathematical foundations
2. statistics and experimental design
3. information resources
4. methods for the study of human factors

The creation of designs is also an important aspect of research as well as practice in software engineering. However, this topic has been extensively examined in the context of software engineering curricula and will not be further considered here [10, 11, 12, 13, 20, 22, 33, 35]. Simon [32] contains an extended discussion of material appropriate for a science of design.

4.1. Mathematical Foundations

This is an area in which current curricula provide reasonable support; this is especially true for programs based upon a computer science foundation. A background in discrete and continuous mathematics at the undergraduate level is generally expected. Frequently at least some theoretical courses are offered at the graduate level. This coursework provides both a background in specific useful models and exposure to approaches involved in the use of such models in research.

4.2. Statistics and Experimental Design

Mathematical proofs and software development can be done without a knowledge of statistics, but understanding and performing research across a broad spectrum of software engineering topics does require such knowledge. Ralston and Shaw [31], who address the needs of practitioners rather than researchers, claim that "A basic knowledge of statistics is essential to almost all aspects of work in computer science." Practitioners need to be able to assess the claims made in the research literature. Researchers need to be able to choose appropriate statistical methods. Although it is possible to build interesting and novel systems without statistical tools, it is not possible to do good experimental work without statistics. Denning [5] issues a strong call for more attention to experimental methodology.

The statistical approaches used in the software engineering literature are often unsophisticated, poorly chosen, or simply nonexistent. Examples of misapplication include:

1. Misuse of measurement scales. For example, Fleming and Wallace [15] point out an improper use of measurement scales in performance evaluation.
2. Comparing multiple alternatives using a series of pairwise tests. For example, Konstaam and Wood [24] examine the impact of different counting rules for operands and operators on software science metrics. Four different approaches are compared by using t-tests for a series of pairwise comparisons; this is an approach warned against in introductory statistics texts.
3. Brute force correlations. If the purpose of data collection is largely exploratory, a common practice is to run correlations on everything in sight. Kearney *et al.* [23] discuss the problems associated with this practice in the context of published experiments involving software complexity measures.

The misuse of statistics can be a problem, but perhaps the failure to use experimental approaches at all when they are appropriate is an even greater problem. For example, of the 57 published papers on multiattribute file organization surveyed by Eastman [7], only 2 used statistical tests for hypothesis testing, even though many involved implementation and collection of performance data. Both Denning [5] and Ferrari [14] discuss the need for greater attention to experimental approaches.

Courses in statistics are often recommended as requirements or electives in curricula in the computer-based disciplines [2, 16, 29, 30]. The recommendations for masters programs in computer science in Magel *et al.* [28] suggest one course in statistics as appropriate background for graduate study. Fairley [12] suggests that the undergraduate background in mathematics should include probability and statistics. Of course, "probability and statistics" is often implemented as probability. Despite the widespread recognition of the importance of statistics in curricular recommendations, actual statistics requirements are far from universal. I am not aware of any collected data on statistics requirements in computer-related programs. However, in informal questioning I have found a few programs with statistics requirements at the graduate or undergraduate levels. However, there appear to be many more (across a broad range of quality) that do not have any specific requirements in this area.

4.3. Information Resources

Research builds upon the results of previous research. It is necessary to be familiar with previous work related to current projects and to be able to use information resources to locate such work. Resources devoted to problems which have already been solved are not available for new problems.

In general it is not possible or even desirable to completely survey all published literature that might possibly have some bearing on the problem under investigation. The expectations of the research community largely determine what is regarded as an "appropriate" literature search. Neither computer science nor software engineering have a strong tradition of scholarship. The scope of literature searches is often quite narrow; it rarely extends beyond the discipline and is often limited to a specialized subarea. (I have heard rumors of research labs where a literature search is expected to include only previous work in the lab.) This practice allows concentrated effort but often leads to limited vision and needless reinvention.

It is generally expected that at least the major journals in the research area should be examined. An example of failure to adequately investigate even the relevant core literature is presented by the papers referenced by Luccio [27], who discusses methods for representing data items of unlimited length. He builds upon earlier work by Baber [3], whose method largely duplicates that presented by Even and Rodeh [9]. (Luccio cites both papers, as well as later correspondence discussing the similarities.)

In addition, connections to relevant work in other disciplines are often disregarded. An example is presented by work involving the estimation of block accesses; this is an important problem in the implementation of database management systems. A survey of this work appears in [8]. Many of the models used for this problem are occupancy models, which have been extensively investigated and described in the probability and statistics literature. However, almost all of the work described in [8] on estimating block accesses has been performed independently of the work on occupancy models; it has thus involved substantial reinvention.

Undergraduate curricula in software engineering and computer science rarely provide opportunities for undergraduates to become familiar with the research literature. Kuhn [26] observes that scientific education in general relies almost exclusively upon the use of textbooks, and that use of research literature is often deferred until a graduate student actually begins research. Thus it is especially important that such opportunities are provided in graduate curricula at both the masters and doctoral level. The ability to effectively utilize the current literature is specifically cited as a goal in recommendations for masters programs in computer science by Magel *et al.* [28]. Fairley [11] identifies the "ability to use state-of-the-art tools and techniques" as a goal of masters programs in software engineering.

4.4. Methods for the Study of Human Factors

Many research areas within software engineering involve studies of individuals and groups. Examples in Volume 11 of *Transactions on Software Engineering* include Adelson and Soloway [1], Jarke *et al.* [21], and Draper and Norman [6]. Jarke and his colleagues examine differences in subject use of a structured database query language and a restricted natural language interface. Adelson and Soloway investigate individual programmer behavior during design tasks. Draper and Norman discuss some of the issues involved in designing user interfaces. There are a number of other system and language designs proposed in Volume 11 for which such evaluation might well be appropriate.

Such studies often draw upon methods widely used within the social sciences, including surveys, controlled experimentation, protocol analysis, and participant observation. The methods, problems, and limitations involved with such research approaches have been thoroughly investigated within the context of the social sciences. It is worth noting that all three of the papers mentioned have coauthors with training in the social sciences in addition to coauthors with training in the computer sciences.

5. Curricular Considerations

Education in research methods in the computer-related disciplines has been largely relegated to on-the-job training during the writing of a thesis or dissertation. Additional perspective is assumed to be a by-product of graduate coursework. This approach has been more appropriate for mathematically oriented computer science programs than it is likely to be for software engineering.

There are several ways in which additional emphasis on research methods could be incorporated into a graduate program in software engineering. At least some statistics should be expected at either the undergraduate or graduate level. Additional background in research methods can be incorporated in both formal and informal settings.

Formal coursework traditionally covers a specific body of knowledge. At the graduate level, it should also provide some perspective on how that level of knowledge was achieved and how it can be extended. Thus textbooks should be used that connect the information presented to the supporting literature. This is true of many, but not all books, used in graduate level courses in computer-related disciplines. For example, Comer *et al.* [4] suggest Kroenke [25] as a text in a graduate course in database design. This book presents a very good introduction to database concepts. However, it includes few references and is not structured in a way which allows it to be used as an entry point to the current literature. Ferrari [14] points out the advantages to be gained by including material on performance measurement and evaluation throughout the curriculum rather than isolating it in separate courses. In addition, research papers and experimental designs can be assigned in addition to the more traditional proofs (in theory courses) and projects (in everything else).

One problem with relying solely upon an informal approach is that the range of research approaches used within software engineering is fairly broad. It is reasonable to expect faculty members to have expertise in the methods most frequently used in their specializations. But it is unlikely that faculty will achieve the same level of expertise across the entire range of methods appropriate in software engineering. And although the ability to use research literature is important in all areas, but it is all too easy to find faculty members who are not familiar with many important bibliographic tools, such as *Current Contents* or on-line databases.

An alternative or complement to an increased informal emphasis on research methods within the current structures is to provide more formal training in at least some aspects. Seminars or short courses in such areas as information resources, research methods, or professional practice can fill some of the gaps. When I was a graduate student in Computer Science at the University of North Carolina, the department had seminars in both teaching and professional practice. However, such courses do not appear to be common.

6. Conclusions

The recommendations discussed above include the following specific suggestions:

1. Require at least some coursework in statistics and experimental design for all graduate students at either the undergraduate or graduate level

2. Choose textbooks for graduate courses that provide good connections to the research literature

3. Incorporate appropriate discussions of performance measurement and evaluation in courses

4. Require a mixture of research papers and development projects appropriate to the goals of the program

5. Consider supplementing course work with formal instruction related to research methods

Bibliography

[1] B. Adelson and E. Soloway, "The role of domain experience in software design," *IEEE Transactions on Software Engineering,* Vol. SE-11(11), pp. 1351-1360, November 1985.

[2] R. H. Austing, B. H. Barnes, D. T. Bonnette, G. L. Engle, and G. Stokes, eds., "Curriculum '78: recommendations for the undergraduate program in computer science: a report of the ACM curriculum committee on computer science," *Communications of the ACM,* Vol. 22(3), pp. 147-166, March 1979.

[3] R. L. Baber, "A method for representing data items of unlimited length in a computer memory," *IEEE Transactions on Software Engineering,* Vol. SE-7(11), pp. 590-593, November 1981.

[4] J. R. Comer, H. C. Conn, and K. A. Schember, "Software design and development: a graduate curriculum in software engineering," *Proceedings of the Sixteenth SIGCSE Technical Symposium on Computer Science Education,* Vol. 17(1), pp. 335-341, March 14-15, 1985.

[5] P. J. Denning, "What is experimental computer science?," *Communications of The ACM,* Vol. 23(10), pp. 543-544, October 1980.

[6] S. W. Draper and D. A. Norman, "Software engineering for user interfaces," *IEEE Transactions on Software Engineering,* Vol. SE-11(3), pp. 252-258, March 1985.

[7] C. M. Eastman, "Current practice in the evaluation of multikey search algorithms," *Proceedings of the Sixth Annual International ACM SIGIR Conference,* pp. 197-204, Washington, DC, June 1983.

[8] C. M. Eastman, "Estimating block accesses as an occupancy problem," Technical Report 87001, Department of Computer Science, University of South Carolina, August 1986

[9] S. Even and M. Rodeh, "Economical encoding of commas between strings," *Communications of the ACM,* Vol. 21(4), pp. 315-317, April 1978.

[10] R. E. Fairley, "The role of academe in software engineering education," *Proceedings of the 1986 Computer Science Conference,* pp. 39-51, Cincinnati, Ohio, February 4-6, 1986.

[11] R. E. Fairley, "Educational issues in software engineering," *Proceedings of the 1978 ACM National Conference,* pp. 58-62, Washington, DC, December 1978.

[12] R. E. Fairley,, "MSE79: second draft of a master's curriculum in software engineering," *Software Engineering Notes,* Vol. 4(2), pp. 13-16, April 1979.

[13] R. E. Fairley, "MSE79: first draft of a masters curriculum in software engineering," *Software Engineering Notes,* Vol. 4(1), pp. 12-17, January 1979.

[14] D. Ferrari, "Considerations on the insularity of performance evaluation," *IEEE Transactions on Software Engineering,* Vol. SE-12(6), pp. 678-683, June 1986.

[15] P. J. Fleming and J. J. Wallace, "How not to lie with statistics: the correct way to summarize benchmark results," *Communications of the ACM,* Vol. 29(3). pp. 218-221, March 1986.

[16] N. E. Gibbs and A. B. Tucker, "A model curriculum for a liberal arts degree in computer science," *Communications of the ACM,* Vol. 29(3), pp. 202-210, March 1986.

[17] T. Gilb, *Software Metrics,* Studentlitteratur, Sweden, 1977.

[18] T. Gilb, "Response to "Stimulating software engineering progress":SEN April 1983," *ACM Sigsoft Software Engineering Notes,* Vol. 3(3), pp. 72-73, July 1983.

[19] R. M. Graham, "Performance analysis as a fundamental objective in software engineering education," *Software Engineering Education: Needs and Objectives,* Anthony I. Wasserman and Peter Freeman, eds., Springer-Verlag, New York, NY, pp. 120-122, 1976.

[20] A. A. J. Hoffman, "A proposed masters degree in software engineering," *Proceedings of the 1978 ACM National Conference,* pp. 54-57, Washington, DC, December 1978.

[21] M. Jarke, J. A. Turner, E. A. Stohr, Y. Vassiliou, N. H. White and K. Michielsen, "A field evaluation of natural language for data retrieval," *IEEE Transactions on Software Engineering,* Vol. SE-11(1), pp. 97-114, January 1985.

[22] R. W. Jensen and C. C. Tonies, *Software Engineering,* Prentice Hall, Inc., Englewood Cliffs, New Jersey, 1979.

[23] J. K. Kearney, R. L. Sedlmeyer, W. B. Thompson, M. A. Gray, and M. A. Adler, "Software complexity measurement," *Communications of the ACM,* Vol. 29(11), pp. 1044-1050, November 1966.

[24] A. H. Konstaam and D. E. Wood, "Software science applied to APL," *IEEE Transactions on Software Engineering,* Vol. SE-11(10), pp. 994-1000, October 1985.

[25] D. Kroenke, *Database Processing,* 2nd edition, Science Research Associates, Palo Alto, California, 1983.

[26] T. S. Kuhn, *The Structure of Scientific Revolutions,* 2nd edition, University of Chicago Press, Chicago, Illinois, 1970.

[27] F. Luccio, "Variations on a method for representing data items of unlimited length," *IEEE Transactions on Software Engineering,* Vol. SE-11(4), pp. 439-441, April 1985.

[28] K. I. Magel, R. H. Austing, A. Berztiss, G. L. Engel, J. W. Hamblen, A. A. J. Hoffmann and R. Mathis, eds., "Recommendations for master's level programs in computer science: a report of the ACM curriculum committee on computer science," *Communications of the ACM,* Vol. 24(3), pp. 115-123, March 1981.

[29] M. C. Mulder and J. Dalphin, "Computer science program requirements and accreditation," *Communications of the ACM,* Vol. 24(4), pp. 330-335, April 1984.

[30] J. F. Nunamaker, Jr., ed., "Educational programs in information systems: a report of the ACM curriculum committee on information systems," *Communications of the ACM,* Vol. 24(3), pp. 124-133, March 1981.

[31] A. Ralston and M. Shaw, "Curriculum '78 -- is computer science really that unmathematical?," *Communications of the ACM,* Vol. 23(2), pp. 67-70, February 1980.

[32] H. A. Simon, *The Sciences of the Artificial,* 2nd edition, The MIT Press, Cambridge, Massachusetts, 1981.

[33] L. J. Stucki and L. J. Peter, "A software engineering graduate curriculum," *Proceedings of the 1978 ACM National Conference,* pp. 63-67, Washington, DC, December 1978.

[34] J. F. Traub, ed., "Quo vadimus: computer science in a decade," *Communications of the ACM,* Vol. 24(6), pp. 351-369, June 1981.

[35] A. I. Wasserman and P. Freeman, eds., *Software Engineering Education: Needs and Objectives,* Springer-Verlag, New York, New York, 1976.

ACCOMMODATING THE SOFTWARE ENGINEERING EVOLUTION IN EDUCATION

William Lively and Sallie Sheppard

ABSTRACT

Teaching software engineering (SE) in our universities and colleges is crucial as a means to help offset the software crisis. This paper describes an evolutionary approach used at one university to address the problems of teaching software engineering. Issues of difficulty in teaching software engineering, the evolution of software engineering techniques and our specific evolutionary approaches to teaching software engineering are presented. The nature of our courses, projects and laboratories in the curriculum is examined. Suggestions are presented on enhancements to existing approaches to software engineering education techniques, with an emphasis on guidelines for projects.

INTRODUCTION

As software engineering with its techniques, tools, and methodologies has evolved over the years, a major question in academic environments has been how to teach the new discipline in our universities and colleges. At Texas A&M University we are particularly concerned with this question since the university is a land grant school with a charge to serve the people and industry of Texas. The software industry is big business in Texas with such companies as Texas Instruments, IBM, Exxon, Shell, Texaco, General Dynamics, Johnson Spacecraft Center – NASA, and others located in the state. Consequently, software engineering education in Texas is important and we at Texas A&M University feel we have a responsibility to include appropriate coverage in our curricula.

The authors are with the Department of Computer Science, Texas A&M University, College Station, Texas 77843

Our purpose in this paper is to summarize some of the approaches to software engineering education which we have explored in the last fifteen years. Like software engineering, our approaches in teaching the tools and techniques have evolved. We begin by exploring some of the difficulties in teaching software engineering, some of the milestones which have influenced and affected our evolution of teaching these subjects and a discussion of our graduate and undergraduate curricula in software engineering. Finally, we present the role of our Laboratory for Software Research and discuss the effectiveness of our approaches and note remaining trouble spots. It is our hope that this paper can serve to stimulate discussion on the teaching of software engineering and that some of our lessons learned can benefit others involved in software engineering education.

GOALS OF OUR SOFTWARE ENGINEERING EDUCATION EFFORTS

The goal of our endeavors in software engineering education is to produce quality software engineers who understand the software crisis and have acquired a knowledge of the basics of the software development process; that is, they understand the interactions of people, machines, software, tools and methodology in developing software. Specific areas of emphasis include the development of skills dealing with communication, problem solving, planning, and the definition of system requirements.

We have included basic coverage of software engineering in our core curricula at both the graduate and undergraduate levels. By taking one elective course at the bachelor's level and one or more at the graduate level the student has an opportunity to develop more expertise in software engineering. In these courses they acquire at least a limited experience in working on complex systems through projects. Hopefully, we start them on a long term activity of acquiring software development skills which will aid them in keeping up with software engineering approaches as they evolve over the coming years.

DIFFICULTIES IN TEACHING SOFTWARE ENGINEERING

We have found several major impediments in software engineering education. Rapidly evolving technology makes it difficult to stay abreast of current concepts in computer science with almost daily advances in hardware greatly influencing software approaches and technology. Added to this is the fact that many evolving technologies have no basis on a theoretical or empirical level that allow them to be justified for widespread use. On an intuitive level many techniques can be justified, but scientific proofs cannot be generated to support their usage. As has been noted by other researchers [1], our inabilities to quantify improvements in productivity for evolving techniques continues to cause a major problem with technology transfer on a broad scale. In SE education, this causes questions such as the following to arise:

* What are the right concepts to teach?
* How can we demonstrate that they are the right concepts?
* How can we most effectively teach these techniques?

Software engineering deals with concepts relating to large projects where many people are involved producing possibly hundred of thousands of lines of code over a period of several years. Teaching the concepts designed to deal with such large systems in the limited academic environment is complicated, especially since many students (particularly at the undergraduate level) have never worked on large software systems. Often it is difficult for them to even understand the motivation for the approaches. When teaching the concepts within the confines of the classroom setting, it is difficult for the students to derive a real appreciation of them. For example, students need to realize that there are phases and activities associated with the development of software. Other activities, such as documentation and management, occur throughout the development life cycle and are not limited to particular phases.

For many years there were no good software engineering textbooks. Appropriate teaching materials have been difficult to develop because of the diversity of the field and magnitude of the problems, our lack of understanding of the software development process in general and particularly the evolving tools and techniques, and our inability to quantify the productivity of the new techniques. In recent years an increased awareness of the need for software engineering textbooks has been brought about by such major efforts as the DoD STARS initiative; the Ada* language, environment and methodology activities; the formation of the Software Engineering Institute (SEI); and our evolving understanding of software engineering. As a result, good textbooks are now beginning to appear [2-7].

Another problem in teaching software engineering is the difficulty in obtaining state of the art tools for use in the academic setting. Although a proliferation of tools and techniques have been developed over the years, industry has been reluctant to make these available to academia because of proprietary concerns. Industry may sometimes appear to make the products available to academia, but our experience in obtaining them has been laden with problems. Long delays in obtaining tools, or complete failure to obtain them after industry has promised them have been experienced. Outright purchase of commercially available tools usually is impossible because of the costs involved.

MILESTONE EVENTS DRIVING THE SE EVOLUTION

In the field of software engineering we have witnessed an evolution that has directed our teaching of the subject. First, individual tools to assist in software development appeared such as assemblers, compilers and operating systems. Since most applications were fairly simple in the early days, these tools sufficed. Education at

* Ada is a registered trademark of the United States Government (Ada Joint Program Office)

this period concentrated on courses devoted to languages (e.g., "FORTRAN Programming"), or classes of languages ("Assembler Languages") and specific tools ("Compiler Construction," "Database Management Systems") and types of software ("Operating Systems"). With increasing sophistication of applications, the realization occurred that simple collections of tools were not sufficient. This conclusion brought about the concept of programming environments with integrated sets of tools such as Unix, Interlisp and Smalltalk. No longer could courses be neatly classified as languages or operating systems but rather we see the emergence of courses integrating the concepts and concentrating specifically on the software development process.

Although these environments assist in the development of programs, as we have moved toward larger and more sophisticated systems we have seen the emergence of the concept of the software development environment (SDE). The SDEs attempt to address software development across the entire life cycle, not just the programming effort. Such systems are collections of tools dealing with the various phases and activities of development, but initially did not provide coherent methodologies for their use. These methodologies are needed to provide an integrated system of technical methods and management procedures covering the entire development life cycle with a uniform interface to the various tools. Such methodologies are now evolving.

The above evolution was brought into sharper focus for our teaching efforts by viewing DoD's efforts toward software development. DoD in the 1970's began to develop the concept of Ada as a means for solving many of the problems associated with software development. The goal of developing a high order language in which to write programs for computers embedded in larger systems was based on the realization that software engineering principles might be more effectively applied through the use of a high order language specifically designed for that purpose. Although software engineering principles are generally language independent, it may be easier to apply them when using higher order languages, especially if the language provides the appropriate facilities. Ada supports features such as structured programming, strong data typing, separate compilation, information hiding, data abstraction, encapsulation, separation of specification from implementation, separation of logical and physical concerns and readability. Additional major thrusts of Ada are portability and reusability. All of these are important concepts to instill in prospective software engineers.

The use of a language alone is not sufficient to support software engineering. This led DoD to the pursuit of environments to embody the concepts of software engineering and provide appropriate support tools. Hence, we saw the appearance of the STONEMAN documents [8] which put forth the concepts of KAPSE, MAPSE and APSE (kernel, minimal, and Ada programming support environments). The need for methodologies to further integrate the language and tools with software engineering concepts led to development of METHODMAN [9]. Tools alone are not enough; a unifying concept of methodologies is an additional aspect needed to create a mature environment to accomplish the end goals of enhanced quality and productivity. Thus, the DoD evolution proceeded from a language, Ada, to environments providing tools, to the development of methodologies to support the entire software development process.

The Ada, STONEMAN and METHODMAN activities were integrated into our approach to teaching software engineering in the 1980's following the same evolutionary lines. First, the language itself was introduced into our graduate course in the design of programming languages. Next, the STONEMAN concepts were incorporated into our graduate programming methodologies course. Finally, a special course was developed integrating the Ada language, the environment issues and the methodological aspects.

Current trends in developing software include influences from artificial intelligence and fifth generation systems. In particular, expert system building tools, such as ART [10], KEE [11], Knowledge Craft [12], and others, provide powerful tools for rapid prototyping within software development. One of the uses of rapid prototyping is in deriving correct system specifications. Since users often do not really know what the requirements for their systems are, they cannot effectively communicate their needs to the developers. Rapid prototyping provides a means for interaction between the developer and user to obtain the requirements that the user really desires.

Fifth generation systems offer the hope of a new paradigm for developing software where requirements definition is done in very high level specification languages that are executable [13]. A means for rapid prototyping is provided and subsequently the very high level language is automatically translated into an efficient code ready for execution. A further advantage of this approach is that maintenance can be performed on the specification. We are exposing our students to these concepts as we feel that this is the direction of software development in the future. A special topics course titled "Artificial Intelligence Approaches to Software Engineering" has been developed to explore current research and work in this area.

Since this evolution of software engineering methodology is continuing, there is an on-going need to consider effective teaching techniques. In the following section we present some of the approaches which we have used.

CURRICULA DEVELOPMENT FOR TEACHING SOFTWARE ENGINEERING

The advent of the formal teaching of concepts of software engineering at Texas A&M University occurred in 1975. The first course taught was a one-semester graduate course called "Programming Methodology" which emphasized techniques dealing with the structure, validation and verification of programs. The prerequisites for this course were knowledge of at least one block-structured language, data structures, computer organization and operating systems.

In two or three years the course evolved into one dealing with the concepts associated with the entire life-cycle of software development including the various phases of development and activity issues such as management and documentation. The course emphasized the use of the evolving body of technical literature on software engineering because of the lack of appropriate textbooks and because these papers provided the most up-to-date information. The literature provides examples of case studies illustrating successes and failures as well as presenting new and innovative techniques.

An approach often used in this course is to take the class on one day field trips. A recent trip to Austin, Texas, is typical of the activities. The class heard a presentation from the project manager of the newly released IBM PC RT, visited a Texas Instruments plant, heard a presentation from representatives of the Microelectronics and Computer Technology (MCC) and concluded the day with a presentation by the Software Technology Center of Lockheed Missiles and Space Company. Trips like this one are valuable in providing outside motivation for the study of software engineering as well as giving students an idea of the environment they will be working in and the types of jobs they might perform in these environments.

As we gained experience in teaching the Programming Methodology course we saw the need to include student projects as part of the learning experiences. These projects were intended to provide students with an opportunity to apply the tools, techniques and software development methodologies which they were studying as well as to experience working together in groups on a common piece of software. Although the projects did meet some of our goals, it became apparent that attempting to cover the basic SE concepts and a project in one semester meant that the project had to be fairly small if it were to be completed by the end of the course. As a result, a second course in software engineering was added to our curriculum in which the students work on a sizable project using the concepts learned from the first course.

The second course in software engineering is always a projects course which attempts to build upon the first course. This provides the student with truly high level experience on fairly large projects. Frequently, this course suggests Master's research projects for the students.

First Experiences in Project Courses

Our first attempt at teaching the second SE course was devoted primarily to projects which provided learning experiences not only for the students but also for the faculty. With the project philosophy determined, the zealous instructors were anxious to select a project which would be both timely and stimulating. The project selected was to design a relational database system as relational systems were very topical at that time and this allowed the class to truly work on a state of the art software system. So that the course could concentrate on the project, we required that the students have as prerequisites both the Programming Methodology course and our Database Systems course.

The class of seven people working as a group adopted a structured analysis approach in the design of the relational database system using dataflow diagrams, data dictionaries, data structure diagrams, and pseudo-code. Periodic structured walk-throughs were held to review the design. It became apparent that only the specification and high level design could be completed during the semester. Therefore, important issues for the class to deal with were documentation, particularly the capture of design rationale. Unfortunately, nothing within the structured analysis technique provides for documenting design rationale. Also, there were no automated tools to facilitate the use of structured analysis beyond word processing capabilities.

Since the class had fallen short of completing the work on the relational database system, a second class one year later was given the task of completing the design. This provided an interesting test of the documentation produced by the first class. It took the eighteen students enrolled approximately half the semester to arrive at the position of understanding where the first class had stopped work, indicating that the flow of information from the first to the second class was not good. The students analyzed this problem and attributed it to three factors: the quality of the first class's documentation, the complexity of the system being worked on, and the failure to adequately capture the design rationale. This was good experience for the class as it allowed the students to see problems that industry deals with frequently.

The instructors learned several things from this experience. A more tractable and less state of the art system should be attempted to allow the student more exposure to all the phases of the software development activity. A successful, already completed project with good historical data might serve as a good selection since pitfalls can be more realistically anticipated and the students could compare their progress and results with the historical project data. Some documentation scheme must be developed to be able to trace design rationale. Although our original goal of designing a relational database system was not met, we did not consider the project to be a failure as both the students and faculty involved agreed that the experience had provided valuable insight into real software engineering problems.

Comparative Projects

In another offering of the project course with 18 enrolled students, a different approach was used. As mentioned earlier, the demonstration of quantifiable measures of productivity with various design techniques is a major issue confronting the software engineering community. As an attempt to experiment with different design approaches, one class undertook the following experiment. The class was divided into three teams with each team being instructed to use a different design approach to the given problem and compare the results. The three design approaches studied were object oriented design [6], SADT [14], and HOS's functional decomposition [15]. Together with the instructor, the group developed the following criteria for comparison of the design approaches:

Ease in learning use of technique

Ease of use

Availability and quality of documentation

Facilitation of communication among developers

Ease of partitioning problem among developers

Ease of capture of design rationale

Ease of facilitating problem solution

Ease of interfacing with requirement specification and implementation techniques

Facilitation of validation and verification

Ease of expressing constraints

Ease of fitting within management schemes

Enhancement of maintainability

Availability of automated aids

Requirements traceability

Facilitation of rapid prototyping

Facilitation of design reviews

Support for production of good documentation

As the students attempted to use these, they found that measures on the above criteria are sometimes difficult to generate. Even factors, such as ease in learning and using the techniques, which at first appeared straightforward to the student were discovered to be quite subjective. Other factors, such as ease of facilitating problem solution are most subjective and evaluated less easily. Clearly, the above criteria provided a framework for evaluation and will be useful in future work environments where they may be responsible for selection of the design approach to follow.

The project for the group was to design a graphics display tool based on Nassi-Schneiderman (N-S) charts [16]. This tool was intended to visually assist beginning programmers in developing programs. As the groups began working on the project, they came to appreciate the complexity of developing complete requirements. All of the students were familiar with Nassi-Schneiderman charts and a number of class members were concurrently teaching the use of the charts to undergraduate students. They were surprised at the difficulty they experienced in developing requirements even where they thought they completely understood the tool to be developed and the environment in which it was to operate. The class also discovered that it is sometimes difficult to differentiate between requirements definition and specification and high level design.

The groups suffered from a lack of automated tools and of sufficient documentation on the techniques resulting in considerable clerical work for the students. Attempts to obtain the tools from industry proved to be very frustrating.

The groups found the various techniques supported decomposition to varying degrees. Some techniques worked better depending on the level of design: some worked better at the higher, more abstract levels, while others worked better at the lower, more detailed levels. One technique appeared to yield a flat design with no hierarchial structure. One group experienced difficulty because the design approach did not interface cleanly with a requirements definition technique.

One group commented that the large amount of time spent on the requirements phase helped produce a better system – a result that many experienced designers endorse. Another group found that, for this particular problem, dataflow diagrams were not effective because of the need to represent control flow. Actigrams which incorporate control [17] were used, thus facilitating design of the system.

A software design problem can vary in a number of ways in regard to hardware. The hardware may already be specified, several choices may exist for the hardware, or the designer may be completely free to choose the hardware. Hardware selection became an important issue in this project because of the graphics capabilities required. The hardware's graphics toolkit could greatly ease the design and implementation of the system.

The machines available for use on the project and the student's familiarity with these machines was important in that learning time for a new machine detracted from the design time. A single group using several different machines experienced increased communication problems.

Current Trends

Ten years elapsed from the inception of a graduate course in software engineering until the introduction of a elective senior level course in software engineering into our curriculum. During the interim, many of the techniques, such as structured programming and problem analysis, were inserted into various courses throughout the undergraduate curriculum. A number of faculty resisted establishing a separate SE course as they felt undergraduate students typically do not have the maturity to deal with the wide spectrum of topics covered in an introductory software engineering course. In September of 1985, when the undergraduate course in software engineering was taught for the first time, fears about student maturity were realized to some extent. Because most of the undergraduates had only worked with small programs developed in an academic environment, they were unable to appreciate the concepts fully. In subsequent semesters we counteracted this problem by providing the students with a better appreciation for the software crisis and system concepts. We presently feel comfortable about the students' perspectives on the development of large software systems.

Besides offering undergraduates an opportunity for a specialized course in software engineering, our new undergraduate course serves as an initial introduction to software engineering concepts for all our students. This early start will allow our first graduate course in software engineering to concentrate on advanced concepts, with a small project on requirements definition and specifications. The added emphasis on requirements and specification will be beneficial in giving more coverage to this critical problem area.

In the fall of 1986, a new graduate course in software engineering, titled "Software Models and Metrics," was added to our curriculum. This course, being taught for the first time in the spring of 1987, examines models of the software development process, looks at attempts to quantify or apply metrics to methods, tools, productivity, software complexity and software reliability. The more success we have developing good models and good metrics, the better we can argue for the use of new techniques and methodologies, thus enhancing technology transfer.

Guidelines for Projects

In order to enhance the benefits of projects and minimize distracting frustrations for students, the instructor needs to do careful planning ahead of time. The selection of the problem for the class project is very important. Depending on the information given to the students, different aspects of the software development process can be emphasized. The availability of a good historical record of a successfully completed project can provide the instructor with valuable insight in guiding the students. In such a case, emphasis could be placed on requirements definition or specification or design. A maintenance project extending the capabilities of the system could also be undertaken. The problem definition, whatever its source, needs to be made available to the students early in the semester.

Students should be provided with automated aids for tools when appropriate and available. Appropriate preplanning and problem selection enhances the possibilities of acquiring automated tools from industry for use in the project. We feel that much of our frustration in getting software donations or loans has been because of inadequate lead-time in seeking industry support for the effort.

The wide disparity in background and experience of students can also cause problems but can be turned to an advantage by careful team assignments by the instructor. The most experienced students should be candidates for project leadership positions as this will not only enhance system development but will also give experienced students opportunities to develop leadership skills. The instructor should attempt to balance ability and experience among various subgroups of the project. This balance allows inexperienced students to learn from more experienced ones and gives everybody the opportunity to work with groups of diverse abilities, experience, and background. Working together in groups teaches the importance of communication and habits of sociability.

Dealing with management concepts of planning, scheduling and allocating resources is critical for the students. In our experience, many students begin to see the need for the software engineering concepts which they have been studying when they are personally involved in a group software development effort. Participating in design reviews helps develop verbal skills and the team spirit in developing software. Each student should be given an opportunity to participate rather than allowing team leaders to repeatedly select the more experienced or able students. In general, we have found students begin to develop an appreciation of the difficulties in developing large complex systems by working on class projects.

THE LABORATORY FOR SOFTWARE RESEARCH

The Laboratory for Software Research (LSR) has proven useful in focusing research attention on software related topics and has become an integral part of our graduate program for those students with special interests in software engineering. The LSR was established within the Computer Science Department in September 1983 with a dynamic structure intended to stimulate and foster the development of research ideas. Any faculty or graduate student with an interest in software research is welcomed to associate with the LSR and share in its resources, discussion groups, and seminar series. The Laboratory has had a very synergistic effect in bringing together those with common interests as well as providing a specific interface for seeking industry support for our research program.

The primary research thrusts of the Laboratory have combined the traditional research areas of software engineering and programming languages, seeking to create software development environments which can improve the productivity of programmers and enhance the maintenance of software systems. Current effort within the Laboratory focuses on the infusion of knowledge-based approaches into software development tools and techniques in order to produce true problem solving environments.

Academic Thrusts

In the research environment, as in the academic arena, the special characteristics of software engineering influence what can be effectively handled. In our experience, the attempt to develop production quality large systems with student labor is not the most successful approach. The primary motivation for most students is not to produce marketable products but rather to use the research exercise as a learning experience. Hence, we have concentrated on involving students in projects which allow them to work on the cutting edge of technology but in narrow enough domains so that they get to experience the joy of following an idea through from its formative stages to its evaluation for inclusion in full-scale environments. Upon graduation, these students are experienced in software design, development, and evaluation as well as knowledgeable in the particular area which they researched. These experiences qualify them to take their place as productive members of the software development industry.

Our approach of encouraging students to define specific aspects of software development and follow the idea through from inception to completion has several additional benefits. Although the research still requires that they practice working together in determining interfaces for their systems with those of others (i.e., group behavior), the approach does reduce the dependence of any student on the work of another one. This regard is different from class experiences described earlier where the emphasis is on team work. We feel, however, when it comes to the thesis or doctoral research each student should have some control over his or her own destiny.

This approach is also seen as beneficial by industry sponsors of our research in that students can provide "in-depth" coverage of ideas which might be deemed "high-risk" by industrial software researchers. Our "prototype" systems do not in any way compete with their own production systems but allow identification and evaluation of ideas which might be ready for inclusion in commercial systems by our industry supporters.

Industry Liaison

One of the most important components of our Laboratory program is our liaison with industry. Although we have traditionally had some industry funding within our department, we have found that the establishment of the Laboratory as a focus for our software research has enhanced our ability to attract sponsors for faculty and graduate student research. At present, we have five funded projects, varying from small grants for student stipends to larger projects involving groups of faculty and students. Within the Computer Science Department, this funding has stimulated interest in software engineering allowing us to attract top students. Within Texas industry, the establishment of the Laboratory has increased the visibility of our efforts.

Although the benefits of industry funding for graduate student research are obvious, we consider these as secondary to the benefits of having students interface with representatives of the software industry. No matter how carefully the ideas and problems of real large-scale software development are presented in an academic setting, nothing can substitute for students getting to see and hear the constraints and problems first hand from those actually involved in the software industry. Interface with industry serves as a primary motivator for the study of software engineering tools and techniques demonstrated in the classroom.

Because of the industry liaison between the Laboratory and the Software Technology Center of Lockheed Missiles and Space Company, we have been able to foster active participation of software engineers from industry in our education program. Specifically in our course, "Artificial Intelligence Approaches to Software Engineering", we used an AI based software development environment being developed by Lockheed as a case study for the class. Lockheed software engineers presented the current status of the SDE and shared with the class the problems and approaches being followed. Within the class we did extensive reading from current technical literature on other environments. Having access to an actual "real world" project and its developers gave the class a context for these readings and class discussions. We received positive feedback from both the students, who appreciated the realism offered by the experience, and from the Lockheed software engineers, who found the class members to be constructive critics.

LSR Activities

When the Laboratory for Software Research was first established, we essentially started from scratch. Initially, three faculty were involved and we simply started meetings to discuss various research ideas. Sometimes these meetings took the form of several sessions on a specific topic utilizing outside speakers, video tapes, or journal articles as focal points for our discussions. Other meetings were devoted to publicizing the research of faculty and of graduate students nearing the end of their work. The popularity of these completely voluntary sessions grew to the point where average attendance had reached over 25. At this point we defined three separate groups which meet at non-conflicting times so that students and faculty are able to attend as many meetings as they would like. Each group meets weekly with monthly schedules of planned activities circulated to all interested faculty and graduate students.

The three research groups within the Laboratory which have been meeting since January 1986 include the software engineering and artificial intelligence group, the parallel languages and algorithms group, and the software tools group. Work in the first group has concentrated on the specification aspects of automated software development environments. This group now has an external funder of some of their work. The parallel languages and algorithms group has devoted considerable effort in surveying and selecting hardware appropriate to support their work and are seeking approval to purchase the equipment. The software tools group has defined and prepared several proposals for tools which they plan to develop and have submitted these to potential funding sources. The activities of each group are largely determined by the group participants, each group having at least one faculty member involved.

Thus, only three and a half years from its creation, we consider the Laboratory to be one of our successes in stimulating interest and in fostering education in software engineering. It provides a focal point for those seeking to develop a speciality in the area and serves as a mechanism for our most advanced efforts in software engineering education.

SUMMARY

Our approach in teaching software engineering has evolved as has the field of software engineering. We feel one of the cornerstone aspects of our curriculum has been our evolving concepts on projects. As one instructor has stated, "No project is a failure!" Although the software results produced by some projects have been less than desirable, the approach allows students to gain valuable knowledge and experience in the safety of the academic environment. We feel that no project is a failure if these objectives have been achieved.

In this paper we have given guidelines and suggestions for selecting appropriate group projects. Based on our experience, we feel that these group experiences give students insight into problems faced in industry. Although somewhat difficult to arrange, active participation by software engineers from industry in student projects is particularly effective in making such experiences meaningful to students.

We feel that our approach to software engineering education helps students build skills that will assist them in keeping up with the software engineering evolution as it continues. Because the technology is dynamic, it is important that students learn how to track and evaluate developments. Such activities as reading and discussing technical papers and selecting and evaluating new software tools prepare them for productive participation in nonacademic environments in the future.

Our success in teaching software engineering is difficult to evaluate. Although real quantitative assessment is difficult, our observations are that students do seem to mature and develop better insights into software systems after the completion of course work and projects. Certainly the feedback from industry on our students has been very positive, with reports of the ability of our students to quickly start contributing in significant ways to major industry software efforts.

The future looks very bright for advances in software engineering education. The SEI's development of a Master's program in software engineering will provide many benefits for software engineering education. Specifically, the developed modules and training for software engineering educators will have a large impact. Continued government initiatives such as STARS will create environments for positive growth and development in software engineering education.

REFERENCES

[1] M. V. Zelkowitz, R. T. Yeh, R. G. Hamlet, J. D. Gannon, and V. R. Basili, "Software Engineering Practices in the US and Japan," *Computer*, Vol. 17, No. 6, pp. 57-66, June 1984.

[2] R. Fairley, *Software Engineering Concepts*, New York: McGraw-Hill, 1985.

[3] B. W. Boehm, *Software Engineering Economics*, Englewood Cliffs: Prentice-Hall, 1981.

[4] I. Sommerville, *Software Engineering*, 2nd Ed., Wokingham: Addison-Wesley, 1985.

[5] M. L. Shooman, *Software Engineering*, New York: McGraw-Hill, 1983.

[6] G. Booch, *Software Engineering with Ada*, Menlo Park: Benjamin/Cummings, 1987.

[7] S. D. Conte, H. E. Dunsmore, and V. Y. Shen, *Software Engineering Metrics and Models*, Menlo Park: Benjamin/Cummings, 1986.

[8] J. N. Buxton and V. Stenning, "Requirements for Ada Programming Support Environments – 'STONEMAN'," Department of Defense Report, February, 1980.

[9] A. I. Wasserman and P. Freeman, "Ada Methodologies: Concepts and Requirements," Department of Defense Report, November, 1982.

[10] ART Reference Manual, Inference Corporation, Los Angeles, 1985.

[11] IntelliCorp KEE Software Development System Reference Manual, 1985.

[12] Knowledge Craft Reference Manual, Carnegie Group, Inc., Pittsburgh, 1985.

[13] R. Balzer, "A 15 Year Perspective on Automatic Programming," *IEEE Transactions on Software Engineering,* Vol. SE-11, No. 11, pp. 1257-1267, November 1985.

[14] M. Thomas, "Functional Decomposition: SADT," Infotech State of the Art Report Structured Analysis and Design, 1978.

[15] M. Hamilton and S. Zeldin, "High Order Software – A Methodology for Defining Software," *IEEE Transactions on Software Engineering*, SE-2. No. 1, pp. 9-32, March 1975.

[16] I. Nassi and B. Schneiderman, "Flowchart Techniques for Structured Programming," *SIGPLAN Notices*, Vol. 8, No. 8, pp. 12-26, August 1973.

[17] P. Freeman and A. I. Wasserman, "Comparing Software Development Methodologies for Ada: A Study Plan," *Software Engineering Notes*, Vol. 9, No. 9, pp. 22-55, July 1984.

The Evolution of Wang Institute's Master of Software Engineering Program

Mark A. Ardis, Member, IEEE

Abstract

Master of Software Engineering (MSE) programs are relatively new. Starting such a program is expensive in terms of human and capital resources. Some of the costs are: preparation of new course materials, acquisition of sophisticated equipment and software, and maintenance of a low student/faculty ratio. In addition, MSE students and faculty have special needs, such as technical background and familiarity with current industrial practices.

Wang Institute's MSE program has evolved rapidly in response to many of these demands. Capital expenditures have been large, and much time and effort have been spent creating and polishing the curriculum. Constant evaluation and refinement have proven invaluable in assuring the success and growth of the program.

Index Terms -- computer science education, Master of Software Engineering, professional-degree programs, programming methods, project management, software tools.

1. Introduction

The Master of Software Engineering (MSE) Program at the Wang Institute of Graduate Studies has evolved rapidly. This paper gives an overview of that evolution, describes some of the problems that appear to be unique to MSE programs, and explains how Wang Institute has responded to these problems.

2. Institutional Evolution

2.1. Origins

Wang Institute of Graduate Studies was founded in 1979 by Dr. An Wang as an independent, non-profit educational institution. It is accredited by the New England Association of Schools and Colleges. The School of Information Technology was established to fulfill a dual mission: to provide the professional graduate education that software engineers require to meet the demands of industrial software development and management, and to help alleviate the acute nationwide shortage of highly skilled software specialists. The School offers one degree: Master of Software Engineering.

The original curriculum was designed by the National Academic Advisory Committee (NAAC), a committee of academic and industrial leaders. An Institute Advisory Committee, mostly local college presidents, was formed to provide guidance in establishing administrative procedures. Corporate donations provided much of the original computing equipment. The Wang family provided an endowment for the purchase of a campus, a former Marist Brothers Juniorate Seminary. Faculty were recruited from academia and industry.

2.2. History

In January of 1981 the first students began classes at the Institute. There were only two full-time faculty at that time. As the Institute grew and matured, courses were changed, but much of the original curriculum's structure remained. Considerable effort was expended on the core courses. For each course-offering a notebook was compiled, containing all of the lecture notes, assignments, solutions, exams, exam solutions, and copies of assigned readings. These notebooks (still compiled each semester) provided the raw material for the work of polishing and integrating the core courses. There have been two comprehensive faculty reviews of the curriculum [1] [2].

The Institute has grown steadily in all dimensions. In five years we ran out of room in the main building, and started construction of a new addition. The new space includes more offices for students and staff, more classrooms, more lecture halls, more library stack space, and more room for computer equipment. In addition, we have cabled the current building with a local area network. Plans for graphics workstations in each of the faculty and student offices are progressing.

The administrative staff has grown to accommodate the growth of the rest of the Institute. In the last two years we have hired a new President, a Director for the Computer Center, and a Director of Special Programs. Additional staff for the computer center and the audio/visual center have been hired as well.

The fifth class of MSE students graduated in August, 1986, bringing the total number of alumni to 81:

Year	Number of Graduates
1982	5
1983	14
1984	15
1985	17
1986	30
Total	81

The successful growth of the MSE program is due to extensive planning and evaluation. Considerable effort was spent in preparing the original plans for conception of the Institute, in preparing the first five-year plan, and in preparing the first computer center plan. The NAAC meets three times each year to evaluate the program. The faculty and student body reviews the curriculum continually. Students and alumni have been surveyed several times to determine the success of the program, both pedagogically and practically [3].

3. Current Status

3.1. Curriculum

Students in the MSE program take six required core courses, three electives and two project courses. The core courses are:

- Formal Methods: Verification, abstraction, specification, formal language theory and analysis of algorithms.

- Programming Methods: Design, coding and testing of modules.

- Software Engineering Methods: Requirements analysis, specification, and system design.

- Computing Systems: Either of two courses:

  - Operating Systems: Synchronization, memory management, process management.

  - Computing Architecture: Interrupt and I/O structure, operand addressing, networking.

- Management Concepts: Survey of business structures, functions, philosophies and methods.

- Software Project Management: Software project planning, monitoring and leadership.

Appendix I contains a more detailed description of each of these courses. The prerequisite structure is shown in Figure 1.

Elective courses cover a wide spectrum of computer science and management topics, including: compiler construction, database management systems, decision support systems, expert system technology, principles of computer networks, programming environments, requirements analysis, software marketing, technical communication, transaction processing systems, user interface design, and validation and verification.

Project courses are designed to allow students to practice skills learned in the core courses. Students work in teams of three to seven on problems of requirements analysis, functional specification, design, implementation, validation and verification, maintenance, or some combination of these. Both the products and the processes of these projects are expected to meet academic and industrial standards. For example, specifications are often written in a formal notation (rather than English prose), and technical reviews are used to ensure adequate progress and product quality.

3.2. Resources

The Institute has a variety of computing equipment for instructional purposes, including a Wang VS 100, a VAX[1] 785, a VAX 750, and several types of personal computers. We have plans for adding several workstations and more mainframe capability.

As would be expected, the Institute has an extensive collection of software tools. In addition to the language processors and utility programs provided with the available operating systems, there are special tools for project planning, requirements analysis and specification, design, coding, testing and configuration management. Appendix II contains a partial list of available tools.

The Institute is particularly rich in human resources. The student/faculty ratio is about 6/1. Audio-visual technicians assist in taping course presentations and software tools workshops. (Most Institute presentations, from faculty colloquia to project reviews, are routinely videotaped and kept in the Institute's audio-visual library.) Secretarial staff routinely assist project courses in clerical duties, such as recording and distributing minutes of meetings, document preparation and program librarian activities. Two full-time software engineers (currently MSE graduates) are employed by the faculty to assist in tool search, evaluation, acquisition, installation and training. Another MSE graduate is employed as a project leader and software developer on a database project.

The library of the Institute has a collection of over 4500 books, conference proceedings, technical reports and audio-visual instruction aids. The topical focus of the library is on software engineering, computer science, business management and mathematics. In addition, the library subscribes to over 300 journals covering all aspects of computer

---

[1]VAX is a trademark of Digital Equipment Corporation

science and technology.

Student tuition, though competitive with other graduate schools, covers only a small fraction of the operating expenses of the Institute. The Wang family has generously endowed the Institute since the very beginning. They are the donors for most of the operating expenses and new capital expenditures.

3.3. Students

The admissions criteria for the MSE program are designed to ensure adequate preparation for technical material and proper motivation for methodological material. Applicants must have knowledge of discrete mathematics, data structures, high-level languages and assembly language. In addition, they must have at least one year of software development experience.

The average student is about 29 years old and has five years of software development experience. Most students live in the greater Boston area, but some relocate from other parts of the U.S. or from other countries. (The Institute has had international students from Australia, Brazil, Canada, China, Colombia, India, Switzerland and Taiwan.)

Each year the Institute admits about 30 new students, about half of whom complete the program in one year as full-time students. The rest of the students take from two to five years to complete the program. Full-time students may be graduate assistants (supported by the Institute in return for assistance in teaching or research), or corporately-sponsored. Of the class that entered in September 1986, about half are corporately-sponsored. Sponsors this year include AT&T Bell Laboratories, Australian Social Security Agency, Canadian Department of Defense, Digital Equipment Corporation, Hewlett-Packard and the U.S. Army.

3.4. Faculty

There are ten full-time faculty in the School of Information Technology. Three adjunct faculty each teach one course per year. This academic year we have one visiting faculty member. There are also positions for visiting scholars, who are not required to teach courses, but contribute their expertise to courses and projects as appropriate.

All of the faculty teach core courses, though no faculty member has taught all of the core courses. Faculty also supervise project courses and teach electives in their areas of interest. Some of the faculty have contracts that allow one day of consulting per week.

4. Problems Unique to MSE Programs

Of course, many of the problems encountered by MSE programs are similar to those encountered by departments of computer science and management science. Some problems are unique to MSE programs, however. In this section I will describe how these special problems were addressed at Wang Institute.

4.1. Student Problems

As mentioned earlier, the average MSE student is older than the average graduate student. Very few undergraduates have sufficient work experience to be admitted immediately after completion of their bachelor's degrees. Most students have established careers in software development. Attending school means disrupting their professional and personal lives. The principal reason that Wang Institute's MSE program is one-year long is to minimize the disruption of the students' careers.

Inadequate technical background is a frequent problem. Often, applicants failed to take appropriate courses in discrete mathematics or data structures as undergraduates. We have tried to address this problem in two ways: by conducting oral admissions exams to determine technical competency, and by offering remedial courses and directed studies in discrete math and data structures. A student with a technical deficiency may be conditionally admitted, and must demonstrate successful completion of coursework before matriculation. Some students appreciate the opportunity to brush up on study skills in remedial courses before starting an intense program. Others would rather focus on specific topics through directed studies.

Part-time students often face conflicting demands from work and school. We insist that applicants discuss work-release time with their supervisors before starting the program. All classes are held weekday afternoons, and most courses require an average of twelve hours homework per week. It is essential that students recognize their commitment to school, and that their employers recognize it also.

4.2. Faculty Problems

Unlike other academic disciplines, it is not enough that faculty members in a MSE program be excellent scholars and teachers, they must have significant industrial experience as well. Wang Institute has tried very hard to recruit faculty with industrial experience, and to keep them up-to-date on industrial methods. Some faculty have recently come from industry. Their experience is usually more managerially-oriented than the average student's experience. Some faculty paid their dues to the industry before attending graduate school. Their industrial experience is similar to the students', though not as recent. Constant attention to software tools, and their developers, provides some awareness of current industrial practice. Consulting is another way to stay in touch with industry. The Corporate Associates Program provides contact between faculty and local industry through seminars, on-site lectures, and joint research projects.

Most educational institutions reward scholarly research (e.g., writing papers) more than experimental research (e.g., building tools). But, it is hard to be an effective teacher of software engineering methods without practicing those methods. Also, the development of appropriate pedagogical material (e.g., course outlines, lecture notes, and homework assignments) is particularly time-consuming in a new area such as software engineering. Faculty at Wang Institute are actively encouraged to devote time to teaching and experimental research. Instead of tenure, we have three and five-year contracts. The resulting model is more like a research laboratory than an academic department, but with an emphasis on excellence in teaching.

4.3. Environmental Problems

A tool-rich environment is essential to a MSE program in order to demonstrate and practice methods effectively. For example, the Institute has several programming environments. Students are able to compare features and examine the interaction of computing capabilities and software development methods. Unfortunately, the need for many tools produces two problems---acquisition and use of the tools.

The Wang Institute Software Environment project [4] was started very early in the history of the Institute to solve these problems. Tool searches and evaluations are performed by technical staff (graduates of the MSE program) at the request of faculty and students. Once appropriate tools are found, they are installed and tested under the direction of the technical staff. Novice users often require additional documentation to that provided by vendors. The technical staff write or supervise the writing of these tutorials.

Entering students are certainly computer literate, but often are ignorant of the specific tools used at the Institute. On average, each course requires that a student learn four new tools. The Institute conducts a series of workshops to demonstrate the use of tools. Additional demonstrations are given during classes. Most demonstrations are videotaped for later review. In addition, expert users are identified for each tool (often the technical staff, but occasionally faculty or students) to handle student and faculty questions.

The use of tools in the curriculum is integrated with the sequence of courses. For example, many project courses use the Unix[2] tools that are taught in Programming Methods and Software Engineering Methods. There is a standard model for project courses [5] [6], that includes a suggested directory structure and templates for documents, specifications, designs, and code. The standard model shortens the learning curve for new students and makes possible the integration of products from different projects. For example, there are projects at the Institute to develop components of

[2]Unix is a trademark of AT&T Bell Laboratories

large systems (e.g., compilers, database systems, project management environments), and projects to integrate those components.

4.4. Pedagogical Problems

Software engineering is more than a collection of topics from computer science and business management. It requires knowledge of a wide spectrum of industrial experience, the application of appropriate methods, and the communication of results to management and other professionals. Reading, homework, lectures and discussion sessions are not adequate to impart all of these skills.

To impart knowledge of industrial experience it is important to have diverse sources of that experience. Wang Institute is fortunate to have a very diverse student body. The twenty corporately-affiliated (i.e., part-time, or full-time but corporately-sponsored) students who entered in September 1986 came from fourteen different institutions, including computer manufacturers, software consulting firms, research laboratories and government agencies. This diversity provides a variety of perspectives on software problems. The faculty, also, have a diversity of experiences and interests. The NAAC provides another source of wisdom. Finally, students participate in off-site visits to local industries and government agencies as part of their study of requirements analysis problems.

Application of methods is a theme of several courses at the Institute. For example, the "Formal Methods" course introduces students to several testing and specification methods, though with inadequate time to practice the methods thoroughly. "Programming Methods" continues the examination of testing methods in the context of programming problems. "Software Engineering Methods" explores the use of specification methods in requirements analysis and design problems. By the time students enroll in project courses, they have sufficient experience with methods for each phase of software development to practice them successfully.

Communication and teamwork are essential to software engineering. They are practiced extensively in our curriculum. Project courses usually have two or three formal technical reviews, including outside reviewers. Some faculty play the role of corporate management, and require board-meeting-style presentations. Project presentations and demonstrations are necessary final components of projects. In addition to the project courses, students typically have two or three project experiences within other courses.

It is clear that the size of classes is a critical factor in making many of these experiences possible. Project teams must be small enough to allow reasonable progress during a semester. Elective course enrollments must be small enough to allow students to share their diverse backgrounds. Even the required core courses must have small enrollments to allow discussion of controversial methods. Instructors must have sufficient time to give to each student to provide accurate evaluation of performance. Finally, an atmosphere of teamwork and cooperation is essential.

5. Summary

The MSE program at Wang Institute has encountered traditional start-up problems, but it has also encountered some problems unique to software engineering programs. Students in MSE programs are typically older and have more heterogeneous backgrounds than graduate students in computer science. Faculty need to stay in touch with current industrial practices. Software engineering education requires a tool-rich environment. Students need to practice methods, especially in small groups.

Wang Institute has responded to these problems by adaptation (e.g., special treatment of students and faculty) and expenditure of resources (financial and human). Growth has been rapid. Careful planning and constant evaluation have been essential ingredients in our success.

I. Core Course Descriptions

Computer Architecture:

The course introduces the underlying principles involved with computer design and the fundamental purposes of the architectural features present in computer systems. The purpose is to provide an understanding of computer systems starting from electronic circuits. Continuing emphasis is placed on cost effectiveness as the decisive factor governing the level at which various functions are supported. Topics studied include interrupt and I/O structure, operand addressing, bus architecture, pipelines, memory hierarchy, multiprocessors, and networks of computers.

Formal Methods:

This course provides a formal foundation for the theory and practice of software engineering. The principal theme of the course is the production of correct, reliable and efficient systems. Underlying this theme is the study of tools for expressing and using abstractions. Formal techniques for specifying abstractions and for defining hierarchies of abstractions, including both operational and definitional specification languages, are presented. Verification techniques for showing that an implementation is consistent with a specification are discussed. State transition and applicative models of computation, regular expressions, and context-free languages are discussed. Fundamental techniques for the analysis of space and time complexity of algorithms are presented. Application of the above to programming languages and to problem-solving are explored.

Management Concepts:

This course provides formal foundations in the management principles that are central to the study and practice of software engineering. It clarifies the role of management studies within the multidisciplinary software engineering field, and provides a conceptual base with which a student can identify, understand, articulate, and synthesize management related issues in software engineering. It also provides skills, contingency frameworks, and strategies for effectively dealing with management dominant issues during the practice of software engineering. Tools and techniques that can support a software engineer manager are identified and studied throughout the course.

Operating Systems:

The course covers the standard operating system topics of process management, process communication, processor scheduling, memory management, file management, segment management, and protection. It also covers the following topics in computer architecture: interrupt structures, hardware memory organization, I/O device and channel architectures, capability based architectures, and reduced instruction set computers. Many example systems are treated both in the lectures and readings.

Programming Methods:

This course covers principles and techniques of programming used by individuals, but within a team context. The quality of programs is discussed in terms of readability, maintainability, correctness and efficiency. Programming principles are illustrated using tools such as profilers, revision control, and static analyzers. Verification and validation are approached via formal reviews, testing and proof technology. Some design methods are introduced to provide a basis for further study in the Software Engineering course and for use in class projects. Appropriate documentation is discussed in conjunction with each topic.

Software Engineering Methods:

The emphasis of the course is on methods for requirements analysis, and specification and architectural design of systems of sufficient size and complexity to require the effort of several people for many months. Fundamental analysis and design concepts are introduced. Analysis and design methods are presented and compared, with examples of their use and discussion of the types of systems for which they are best suited. Two methods, Structured Analysis and Structured Design, are taught at a greater level of detail to allow students to undertake a group project addressing a relatively complex analysis and design problem using these methods.

Software Project Management:

This course introduces the student to many of the concepts, techniques, and tools for planning, staffing, controlling, and monitoring a project from initial inception to completion. The course is intended to provide the student with tools, techniques and interpersonal skills necessary to manage a project of 10-20 staff members. Case studies and a term project (development of a project plan) are used to give the student the opportunity to utilize some of the techniques and tools discussed in class.

II. Partial List of Software Tools

Name	Source	Purpose
AI Tutorials	Smart Systems	Expert Systems
AIDES	Hughes Aircraft	Software Design
Aide-de-Camp	Soft. Main.&Dev.	Configuration Management
APTools	Mitchell Mgmt. Sys.	Application Generation
Arcturus	UC Irvine	Programming Environment
ASLAN	UC Santa Barbara	Specification Language
C++	Bell Laboratories	Object-Oriented Programming
C-Scope	AT&T Bell Laboratories	Static Analysis
Chart	Microsoft	Presentation Graphics
CLU	MIT	Data Abstraction Language
CMS	DEC	Configuration Management
Cocomol	Level 5 Research	Software Cost Estimation
Concurrent Euclid	Univ. of Toronto	Concurrent Programming Language
Cope	Cornell	Programming Environment
Cornerstone	InfoCom	Database System
Costar	Softstar Systems	Software Cost Estimation
CProlog	Edinburgh University	Logic Programming Language
CPS	Cornell	Programming Environment
CSOS	Harvard & Wang Inst.	Operating System Simulation
Demo	Software Garden	Rapid Prototyping Tool
Display	Tom Tullis	User Interface Analysis
Duck	Smart Systems	Logic Programming Language
Excelerator	Index Technology	Requirements Analysis
ExperLisp	Experintelligence	Lisp Environment
Expert Choice	Decision Support Software	Decision Support System
ExperTeach	Intelliware	Expert Systems Instruction
Filevision	Software Products	Visual Database
FirsTime	Spruce Technology	Syntax-Directed Editor
Flavors	Univ. Maryland	Object-Oriented Programming
Fred	Univ. Illinois	Syntax-Directed Editor
Gandalf	Carnegie-Mellon	Programming Environment Generator
GEM	Digital Research	User Interface Tools
Gla	Univ. of Arizona	Lexical Analyzer Generator
Guide	OWL Inter.	Hypertext Document Preparation
INGRES	Relational Technology	Relational Database
Kermit	Columbia Univ.	File Transfer
Lightspeed C	Think Technology	Programming Environment
Lightspeed Pascal	Think Technology	Programming Environment
Lotus 1-2-3	Lotus	Spread Sheet
MacDraw	Apple	Document Preparation

MacExpress	ALSoft	Application Generator
Macintosh Pascal	Think Technology	Programming Environment
MacProject	Apple	Project Management
Methods	Digitalk	Object-Oriented Programming
MicroGANTT	Earth Data	Project Management
MicroPert	Sheppard Software	Project Management
MicroProlog	Logic Programming Assoc.	Logic Programming Language
Microsoft Project	Microsoft	Project Management
Microsoft Windows	Microsoft	Window Environment
Microsoft Word	Microsoft	Document Preparation
MProlog	Logicware	Logic Programming Language
Multiplan	Microsoft	Spreadsheet
Neon	Kriya Systems	Object-Oriented Programming
Objective-C	Productivity Products	Object-Oriented Programming
OPS83	Carnegie-Mellon	Expert Systems
PAWS	Information Research	Performance Analysis
Plantrac	Computerline	Project Management
POE	Cornell	Syntax-Directed Editor
PSL/PSA	ISDOS	Specification/Design
Rapid/USE	UC San Francisco	Interface Prototyping
RCS	Purdue	Configuration Control
Ready	Living Videotext	Document Preparation
Rulemaster	Radian Corp.	Expert System Shell
Safe-C	Catalytix	Static Analysis
SchemaCode	Montreal Poly.	Template Editor
Scribe	Unilogic	Document Preparation
Simpascal	Wang Inst.	Concurrent Programming Language
Smalltalk	Apple	Object-Oriented Programming
SREM	TRW	Specification/Design
SUMACC	Stanford Univ.	Unix/Macintosh Cross Development
Superproject	Computer Associates	Project Management
SUPPORT	Univ. Maryland	Programming Environment
Swsh	Univ. of Maryland	Window Environment
Synth. Gen.	Cornell	Programming Environment Generator
TeX	AMA	Document Preparation
ThinkTank	Living Videotext	Thought Processing
Thor	Fastware	Thought Organizer
TK!Solver	Software Arts	Equation Solution
TML Pascal	TML Systems	Pascal Environment
Total Proj. Mgr.	Harvard Software	Project Management
TurboFlow	Scandura Intell. Sys.	Syntax-directed Editor
TurboPascal	Borland	Pascal Environment
TurboProlog	Borland	Logic Programming Language
UNISEX	UC Santa Barbara	Symbolic Execution

UNIX|STAT	Wang Institute	Statistical Analysis
USE.IT	Higher Order Software	Software Design
VIP	Mainstay	Visual Programming System
Visicalc	Visicorp	Spreadsheet
VisiProg	Univ. Maryland	Programming Environment
Visischedule	Visicorp	Project Management
Wicomo	Wang Institute	Software Cost Estimation

References

1. R. Fairley (ed.), M. Ardis, J. Bouhana, S. Gerhart, N. Martin, W. McKeeman, "Core Course Documentation, Master's Degree Program in Software Engineering", Tech. report TR-85-17, Wang Institute, September 1985.

2. W. McKeeman(ed.), M. Ardis, P. Bernstein, B. Claybrook, R. Fairley, J. Goodenough, D. Lomet, S. Raghavan, G. Perlman, F. Velasco, D. Weiss, "Core Courses, Master of Software Engineering, Wang Institute", Tech. report TR-86-11, Wang Institute, September 1986.

3. W. McKeeman, "Summary and Analysis, Student Retrospective, Master of Software Engineering, Wang Institute", *Wang Institute Software Engineering Review*,Vol. 1No. 2 1986.

4. N. Martin, D. Ligett, J. Kirby, "The Wang Institute Software Environment", Tech. report TR-85-05, Wang Institute, April 1985.

5. T. Gill, "A Simple Environment for Project Development Under Unix", Tech. report TR-85-22, Wang Institute, December 1985.

6. W. McKeeman, "Experience with a Software Engineering Project Course", *Software Engineering Education: The Educational Needs of the Software Community*, Springer-Verlag, 1986.

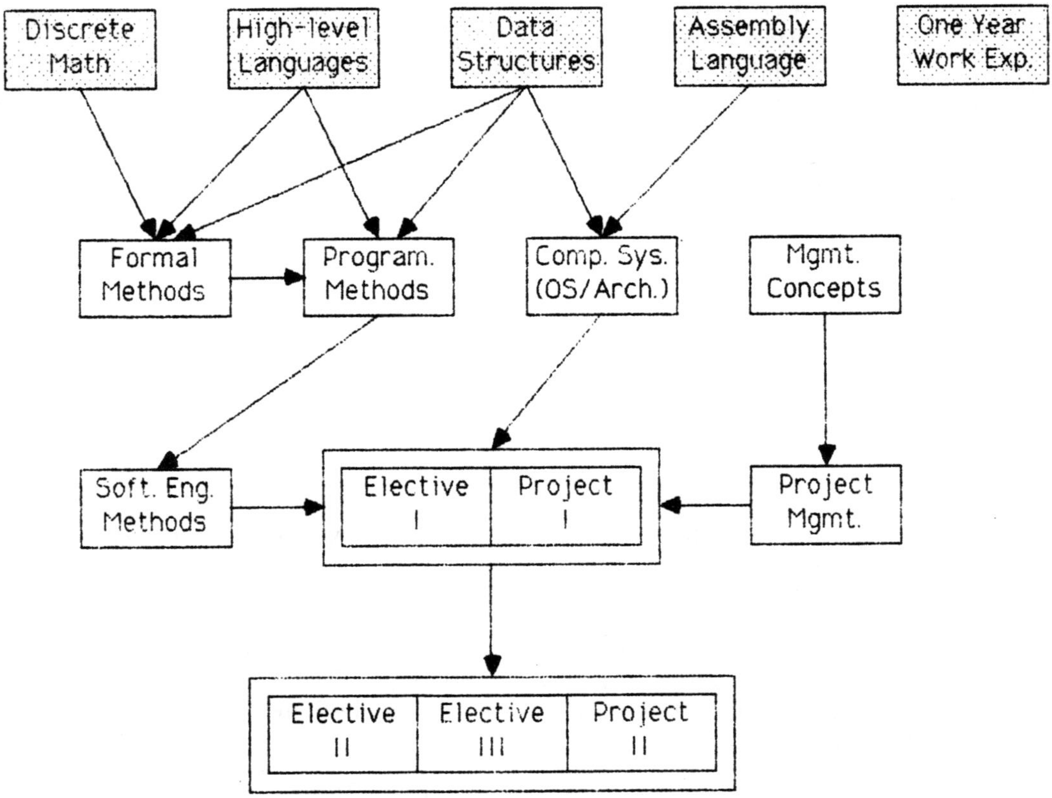

Legend: Vertical arrows denote prerequisites.

Horizontal arrows denote co-requisites.

[shaded box] denotes prerequisite to the program

Fig. 1. Course Prerequisite Structure

Teaching A Software Design Methodology

David M. Weiss[1]

Wang Institute of Graduate Studies

Abstract

This paper describes an approach to teaching a software design methodology used at The Wang Institute of Graduate Studies. The approach is general enough to be used with any of the currently popular design methodologies. Students are first taught the principles underlying the methodology, and the standards used with it. This phase is done in a series of lectures. In the second phase, students are presented with a real design problem, and asked to solve it using the methodology. They are monitored in this process by an expert in the methodology whose job is to assure that the students adhere to the methodology, but who makes no design decisions.

The first phase has been used several times at The Wang Institute both as part of a core course in the regular MSE curriculum and as a one-week summer institute course. The second phase has been implemented once as a project course.

Keywords: Software Engineering Education
Software Design
Teaching Software Design

1. Introduction

This paper describes one of the approaches to teaching a software design methodology used at The Wang Institute of Graduate Studies. The approach is general enough to be used with any of the currently popular design methodologies, such as NRL [Clements and Parnas 86], Jackson System Design [Jackson 83], Structured Design [Yourdon and Constantine 79], or Data Abstraction [Liskov and Guttag 86]. The purpose of this paper is to provide sufficient detail for the reader to be able to use the approach and to

[1] Author's current address: Office of Technology Assessment, Congress of the United States, Washington, DC 20510-8025

know what results to expect.

The approach has two phases: first the students are given an introduction to the principles underlying the methodology and the application of those principles to small well-defined problems. Second, the students are presented with a real design problem, and allowed to solve it on their own, in a simulated working environment, receiving guidance only on methodological issues. The first phase is presented as a series of lectures. The second is supervised by an expert in the methodology.

As a result of the first phase, students gain an understanding of the principles underlying the methodology, see a model application of those principles, and have practice in applying the methodology in academic exercises. They cannot be considered to understand it, but are ready to use it with substantial guidance from an experienced designer (substantial guidance means nearly daily interaction between students and designer). As a result of the second phase, students gain enough experience with the methodology to understand it and to be ready to try it with less guidance, interacting with an experienced designer perhaps once a week.

The first phase has been used several times at The Wang Institute both as part of a core course in the regular Master of Software Engineering (MSE) curriculum and as a one-week tutorial. The second phase has been implemented once as a project course. Because the first phase uses traditional teaching methods, its description here is brief.

2. The First Phase

The first phase of the approach was taught as part of the programming methods course in both the Fall 1985 and Winter 1986 semesters at The Wang Institute. This course was taught jointly by several different instructors, and covered the design, coding, and verification and validation phases of the software life cycle.

As part of the design phase, a series of 5 lectures presenting the principles underlying the Naval Research Laboratory's software development methodology (hereafter known as the NRL methodology) was given, along with homework exercises. Several final exam questions also covered the material. Examples of the application of the methodology were drawn from NRL's Software Cost Reduction project, the model software development project at NRL [Clements and Parnas 86].

The lecturer was one of the developers of the methodology, and had extensive experience in applying it and teaching it. The students were all enrolled in The Wang Institute MSE program.

3. Results of the First Phase

The results of the first phase were often disappointing. Students seemed to grasp one or two major principles. As homework, they were able to produce documentation that conformed to the syntactic standards included in the methodology but that was usually deficient in content. There was little evidence of ability to formulate different design alternatives and to apply the principles presented in class to select among those alternatives.

4. The Second Phase

The second phase was taught as a Wang Institute project course in the Winter 1986 semester. The class size was limited, consisting of 6 students, all of whom had been through the first phase (most in the previous semester). The project followed the organizational model described in [McKeeman 86], with some variations in the roles played and in the environment used. In particular, a quality assurance role was added, and a directory in the environment was established to contain documents and code placed under configuration control. As a result of completing the first phase, the students were aware of the documentation standards integral to the methodology.

Since it was taught as a Wang Institute project class, the second phase did not use a true working environment. The major differences were as follows.

1. The project duration was fixed at 13 weeks.

2. There was no long-term commitment by the students to the project or to a corporate entity.

3. No student had any way of asserting authority over other students.

4. The students' attention was split among the project and several other courses. The normal work load for a Wang Institute course is about 12 hours per week. Full-time students take 4 courses per semester. Students with an assistantship work an additional 12 hours per week. The average project work load, based on records kept by the students during the project, was about 13 hours per week.

5. The roles of customer and high-level management were played by instructors.

6. The penalty for poor performance was a low grade rather than termination of employment or a bad performance review.

7. Outside the project there were no corporate resources that could be made available if needed.

4.1. Application Used

The application chosen was a form manager system that enabled programs to communicate with the operator of a visual display terminal. The form manager was required to provide facilities for handling large volumes of data, for varying the display format, and for interacting with the operator. The requirements could only be satisfied by designing a family of form managers, each member of which operated under somewhat different constraints. The following examples describe family members that result from varying a particular constraint. A complete list is contained in [Kirby and Mayhew 86].

1. Family members that provide means for prompting the operator and family members that don't provide such means.

2. Family members that only display data to the operator and family members that permit the operator to modify displayed data.

3. Family members that support block-mode terminals and family members that support only vt-100 compatible terminals. In each case, the family member should be able to take advantage of the features provided with such terminals.

4.2. Preparation for the Second Phase

At the beginning of the semester, the students were given an incomplete requirements specification, in the style of [Heninger et al. 78], and an incomplete module guide, in the style of [Britton and Parnas 81], that described a possible design. Both documents were produced, before the start of the project, by a student with considerable experience in the application under the direction of a faculty member expert in the methodology. This student then participated in the project as chief architect, and the faculty member participated as an instructor.

At the initial project meeting, students were also given the following (see Appendix I).

1. A list of roles to be played during the project, some of which were preassigned.

2. The expected sequence of major events during the project, as required by the methodology. Included was a list of the documents required to be produced and the order of their production.

3. A short memo describing the configuration control procedures to be used.

4. A short memo describing the responsibilities and composition of the quality control team.

In addition, each student was required to design and document at least one module of the system.

4.3. Student and Instructor Responsibilities

Subject to the preceding rules, the students were responsible for organizing themselves into a team to use the NRL methodology to complete the requirements, to design a (family of) system(s) that satisfied the requirements, and to implement one member of the family. They had to establish a schedule for producing the required documentation, and assign tasks to team members, including the task of monitoring progress, revising the schedule, and organizing project meetings.

Instructors for the project were two Wang Institute faculty members. One played the role of customer and vice-president of software. The other was technical consultant and head of quality assurance (QA).

Conformance to the methodology was enforced through configuration control. For a design document to be accepted for baselining, and therefore releasable for use, it had to pass inspection by a configuration control board (CCB). One board member was the head of QA, a role played by the instructor who was the methodology expert. No design document was baselined without his approval, which was granted solely on the basis of conformance to methodological standards. One result of this policy was that early drafts of all design documents were sent to the head of QA for review. Such reviews were usually done within one day and kept the instructor familiar with the state of the design and with the students' understanding of the methodology.

Other members of the CCB were the customer, the chief architect, and a member of the design team. The latter two were both students.

4.4. Decision Making

Initially, technical decisions were made by the student project team in meetings including all project members. Different technical debates were led by different team members, depending on the issues involved. Where there was difficulty achieving consensus, debates were settled by agreeing to abide by the chief architect's decision. The technical consultant attended more than half of these meetings, and only offered opinions on methodological considerations. In cases where the project seemed to be having difficulty with particular concepts, the technical consultant issued a clarifying electronic memo. Because they were distributed electronically, the memos provided rapid feedback and helped keep the project from floundering. Examples of such memos can be found in Appendix II.

By the midpoint of the semester, the students were able to structure the design task into work assignments suitable for small teams. These teams operated independently and then reported their decisions to the chief architect. The technical consultant attended many, but not all, of the teams' meetings.

In an effort to follow the Moore method of teaching mathematics [Halmos 75], the instructors made no conscious attempts to influence design decisions. Students were freely provided with instruction on the methodology they were using, but were rarely told whether the instructors considered the decisions that were made to be good. On occasions when the instructors gave an evaluation of a design decision, it was always well after the decision had been made, sometimes not until the end of the semester.

When students had trouble arriving at decisions and appealed for help, they were told to adhere to the principles underlying the methodology and make conscious use of those principles in making decisions. The result was that the students nearly always made the same decision that, in the same situation, the instructor would have made, but they often took considerable time to do so.

5. Results of the Second Phase

By the end of the project, the students had produced a complete design and a complete set of design documentation, as required by the methodology. The set included a module guide [Buser et al. 86], reflecting the modular structure of the system as designed, and an abstract interface specification [RedbookWild 84], [Clements et al. 84] for each module. Some inconsistencies in the design remained that would have prevented an implementation from working properly. All such known inconsistencies were noted in lists of remaining design problems that accompanied each design document. A deficiency of the students' design documentation was that design alternatives. although often noted, were not adequately described. One may characterize the product of the second phase as a good first-draft design. The students did not have time to refine the design or to implement any of it.

The result of the second phase was that the students learned the NRL methodology, despite not having completed a product. In the judgement of the instructors they learned a new way of thinking and of documenting their thoughts. The basis for this judgement was observation of project design meetings, discussions with individual students about methodological issues, and review of all the documentation produced.

It was disappointing, more to the students than the instructors, that they did not produce a finished product. Failure to do so was most likely the result of the complexity of the design problem. However, a simpler problem would not have provided sufficient stimulus to force them to learn the thought patterns required by the methodology. The students' views on what they learned were summarized in legacies written by them (a standard practice for Wang Institute project courses); excerpts from these legacies are reproduced in the next section. In general, students felt that they learned the methodology, but were disappointed that they did not produce any code. One remedy for this disappointment would be to offer a continuation project in which the students proceed through one more design iteration and then produce and test an implementation. Such a continuation would likely require one semester.

5.1. Excerpts From Student Legacies

The following are edited excerpts taken from student legacies, and are representative of both the positive and negative comments received. Editing consisted of removing typographical and syntactic errors, leaving meaning unchanged. Excerpts are organized by student.

Student A

My experience with this project was both frustrating and rewarding. I came into the project having already taken a course on the NRL method. I believed that I already understood the method, and that this would be the case with all who would be on the project. My expectation was that this project would yield an opportunity to try the method on a project from design through testing and the completion of a working software product.

I was wrong on all counts. First, I did not truly understand the method, as I believe, may be said of all of us upon entering into the project. This was an important lesson.

...

Despite all my other comments, and the state in which the project ends, I believe the form manager project was a success. Prior to the start of the semester, I commented to another project member with whom I shared another project, that I hoped that learning the method and producing a good design, was not to be compromised for the sake of developing the product of this project. I am pleased that when those decisions were to be made, the product came in dead last. I am also pleased with the real progress on the design which was made.

... I learned a lot about what an interface is, as opposed to how to implement it.

...

Student B

At several points he [the instructor] pushed us toward doing a more complete design as opposed to moving on to coding. At project's end, this leaves one with a slight feeling of dissatisfaction since one of our project goals was to implement a portion of the form manager. However, I think the project was a better one as a result: there was more payoff to the students in concentrating on the design. We do not lack opportunities to produce code;

Student C

The requirements were much too large for a 14 week project.

...

... The purpose of the NRL method is to design for change. Much was learned by designing the system so that these changes could be incorporated at a later date. I believe, though, that the extent of those expected changes was much too great for the amount of time we had and hindered our progress.

...

The module decomposition in the NRL methodology is perhaps it's most significant aspect. It was very difficult to think of breaking down the system design in terms of information hiding instead of planning which modules will call others. This perspective on the world is the most significant lesson I have learned from the project.

...

Student D

...

My understanding of the NRL methodology is reasonable and I think I could design a product using it. However, I'm sure I would still make many mistakes, but I feel I understand the basic concepts.

...

... My feeling is that the NRL methodology is a good approach, but I can't prove this until I carry the process to completion. I would have to implement and maintain the forms manager before I would be able to judge if the upfront work was worth it.

...

The NRL Methodology is difficult to learn. I think the only way to learn this is to participate in a project like we did. I could not have learned the methodology from lectures alone, which will make it difficult for the methodology to catch on.

...

It was difficult to tell how we were doing. Since none of us had done this before, it was difficult to tell if we were accomplishing anything and if we were on the right track.

...

It was fun. I'd do it again.

...

Student E

...

We didn't get a chance to validate the design or to code part of it. As a result, I will always harbor a bit of doubt about the soundness of our design and the methodology itself. Validation or coding would have been a very enlightening experience.

...

To sum it all up, the project was a very worthwhile experience. It met most of my expectations and has provided me with insights that I plan to make great use of in my future work in software.

...

Student F

...

2) The project was much to large for any of us to attempt in one semester, and certainly considering that we were working with a novice system architect.

...

Although we all patted ourselves on the back and claimed that "with another pass the design would be ok", I claim that there was altogether too much mechanism, and that the design would never perform reasonably.

...

6. Factors Contributing To Success

The second phase can be considered a success because it achieved its primary objective: the students learned the NRL methodology. Success was the result of the following factors.

1. An expert in the methodology was available to ensure that the methodology was strictly followed, and a realistic mechanism for ensuring conformance to the methodology was used.

2. A difficult design problem was selected, and the students were forbidden to oversimplify it.

3. The students were forced to make their own design decisions while following the methodology. Neither of the instructors interfered in the decision making process.

4. One student was an expert in the application, was able to answer other students' technical questions, and was able to make technical decisions based on his knowledge of it.

5. The class size was kept small, thereby allowing the instructors to follow progress closely.

7. Recommendations

The method used for teaching the NRL methodology should work for any methodology where the decision-making criteria can be clearly stated. The following recommendations may help others interested in using the same approach.

1. Require as a prerequisite that the students have learned the principles underlying the methodology to be taught. Phase 1 should be used to satisfy this prerequisite. Do not expect them to be able to apply the principles taught in phase 1 without some guidance.

2. The phase 2 instructor(s) must have sufficient expertise to know how to solve the design problem using the methodology and to know how to phrase advice to the students without solving the problem for them.

3. Establish the phase 2 project organization in advance, so that students know what roles are available for them to take. Reserve critical roles, such as head of QA and customer, for the instructor(s).

4. Prepare a set of phase 2 deliverables in advance, without associated milestone dates. Allow the students to manage the phase 2 project by deciding on the dates on which deliverables are due.

5. Use a difficult design problem for phase 2.

6. Keep the phase 2 class size small.

7. Don't expect the students to feel that they have successfully learned the methodology after completing both phases. The instructor must judge success, not the students.

8. Acknowledgements

Without the support of The Wang Institute and its staff, I would not have had the opportunity to try the ideas described in this paper. Without urging from students at The Wang Institute, most notably from E. Hinton and J. Kirby, I would not have had the inclination to teach a project course. J. Kirby worked especially hard to make the form manager project possible. Without critical review from other faculty, especially M. Ardis, P. Bernstein, R. Fairley, and W. McKeeman, I would not have been able to describe the results clearly. My co-instructors in the programming methods course, and R. Fairley, my project co-instructor, were particularly helpful in making me comfortable teaching in The Wang Institute environment. I thank all of them.

References

[Britton and Parnas 81]
Britton, K., and Parnas, D.
A-7E Software Module Guide.
NRL Memo Report 4702, December, 1981.

[Buser et al. 86] Buser, J., Franklin, M., Kirby, J., and Wild, J.
Form Manager Module Guide, Rev. 1.00.
Wang Institute of Graduate Studies, 1986.

[Clements and Parnas 86]
Clements, P. and Parnas, D.
A Rational Design Process: How and Why to Fake It.
IEEE Transactions on Software Engineering SE-12(2), 1986.

[Clements et al. 84]
Clements, P., Parker, R., Parnas, D., Shore, J., and Britton, K.
A Standard Organization for Specifying Abstract Interfaces.
NRL Report 8815, June, 1984.

[Halmos 75] Halmos, P. R.
The Problem of Learning To Teach.
American Mathematical Monthly 82(5), 1975.

[Heninger et al. 78]
Heninger, K., Kallander, J., Shore, J., and Parnas, D.
Software Requirements for the A-7E Aircraft.
NRL Memo Report 3876, November, 1978.

[Jackson 83] Jackson, M.A.
System Design.
Prentice-Hall International, Englewood Cliffs, NJ, 1983.

[Kirby and Mayhew 86]
Kirby, J. and Mayhew, S.
Form Manager Requirements, Rev. 1.00.
Wang Institute of Graduate Studies, 1986.

[Liskov and Guttag 86]
Liskov, B., and Guttag, J.
Abstraction and Specification in Program Design.
MIT Press, Cambridge, MA, 1986.

[McKeeman 86] McKeeman, W. M.
Experience With A Software Engineering Project Course.
Wang Institute Technical Report TR-86-01, January, 1986.

[RedbookWild 84]
Richard Fairley, David Weiss, Jon Buser, Mike Franklin, Ed Hinton, Jim Kirby, Steve Mayhew, Brian Sullivan and Joe Wild.
FORM MANAGER.
Wang Institute of Graduate Studies Project Report.
1984

[Yourdon and Constantine 79]
Yourdon, E. and Constantine, L.
Structured Design: Fundamentals of a Discipline of Computer Program and System Design.
Prentice-Hall, Englewood Cliffs, NJ, 1979.

Appendix I

Memos Used To Initiate The Project Class

To: Form Manager Project Distribution

Subject: Preparations for Form Manager Project

Date: 2 January 1986

In preparation for the form manager project, I have written several brief papers discussing various pertinent topics. The papers include the following, and are attached.

A list of roles to be played, some of which are preset. For the preset roles, the players are identified (atch 1).

The sequence of major events over the life of the project (atch 2).

A discussion of the configuration control procedures to be used (atch 3).

A discussion of the responsibilities and composition of the quality assurance team (atch 4).

An agenda for the first meeting (atch 5).

Project Roles

Customer: Fairley

Vice President for Software: Fairley

Technical Consultant: Weiss

Head of QA: Weiss

Librarian: Sullivan

Chief Architect: Kirby

Designers: All student project members

Coders: All student project members

Unit Testers: All student project members

Integration Test Team:

Scheduler:

Notebook Maintainer:

Legacy Coordinator:

Project Presentation Planner:

Documentation Coordinator:

Toolsmith:

Language Expert:

Meeting Coordinator:

Sequencing of Major Events

1. Choice of roles (first meeting)
2. Familiarization of project team with requirements and module guide (week 2)
3. Establishment of schedule (week 2)
4. Review of requirements and module guide and incorporation of revisions
5. Design of abstract interfaces
6. Review and baselining of abstract interfaces

7. Documentation of uses hierarchy

8. Implementation of abstract interfaces for initial subset, including production of implementation documents

9. Review of implementations

10. Unit testing

11. Integration testing

12. Delivery of initial subset

Configuration Control Procedures

Purpose of Configuration Control

The purpose of configuration control is to manage change in documentation and code. We call any document or piece of code to be placed under configuration control an <u>item</u>. The reasons for managing change in documents and code are as follows.

1. The users of items can rely on the items not to be changed arbitrarily and unilaterally.

2. The users of items can rely on being notified when an item is changed.

3. There is always an unchangeable master copy of each item available to act as a reference. Users can always check that their copies conform to the reference.

In the form manager design project, the following will be placed under configuration control (this is an initial list and may be expanded during the course of the project).

1. The requirements specification.

2. The module guide.

3. Each module interface specification (also known as an abstract interface specification).

4. Each module implementation document.

5. The test plan.

6. The user's manual.

7. The uses hierarchy specification.

Change Control Procedures

Placing an item under configuration control is called baselining it. Following is the procedure for baselining an item the first time (known as initial baselining). Each step assumes successful completion of the preceding steps.

1. The author submits the item to the head of QA for standards review.

2. The author submits the item to the chief architect for technical review.

3. The item is technically reviewed by a review team constituted by the chief architect.

4. The item is submitted to the configuration control board (CCB). Approval is needed from the CCB before continuing to the next step in initial baselining.

5. The CCB assigns an identifier to the item and gives a copy to the project librarian for inclusion in the project library.

6. The project librarian notifies all potential users and the customer that the item has been baselined.

Once an item is initially baselined, it can only be changed by approval of the CCB, with the concurrence of the head of QA. Following is the procedure for changing an item that is already under configuration control.

1. A change request is submitted to the CCB.

2. The CCB either approves or rejects the change. If rejected, the change request is returned to the author with an explanation for the rejection.

3. The job of implementing the change is assigned to a project member by the chief architect.

4. The change implementor submits the changed item to the CCB and the head of QA.

5. The CCB assigns an identifier to the new version of the item (based on the existing identifier). The changed item is given to the project librarian for inclusion in the library.

6. Notification of the change is distributed to all project members who use the item and to the customer.

The preceding describe the formal baselining and change procedures. It is expected. however, that informal reviews and discussions will supplement the formal procedures. In, particular the chief architect should know enough about the state of the design and implementation to know when to expect that a document will be submitted for baselining, and should be conversant with proposed changes before they are submitted to the CCB.

Frequency of Change

For a design document such as an abstract interface specification, initial baselining must take place prior to release of the document to the implementor(s). Changes to the document after initial baselining occur as needed, and are generally suggested by the implementor(s). For a project to be successful, initial baselining must take place early enough so that there is time to implement the design.

Composition of The Configuration Control Board

The configuration control board is composed of the following people. This composition may be varied during the course of the project.

Chief Architect, Head of CCB

Customer

Head of QA

Senior Designer

Responsibilities of The Configuration Control Board

The CCB has the following responsibilities.

1. Maintain a list of all configuration controlled items, including description, identifier, and location. Where several versions of an item exist, the identifier should make obvious the order in which they were baselined. The implementation of this responsibility may be delegated to the project librarian.

2. Approve or reject, on technical and any relevant non-methodological grounds, all changes proposed to a baselined item. (An example of relevant non-technical grounds for rejection of a proposed change is excessive cost.)

The CCB shall operate by consensus. In cases where the CCB cannot reach consensus, the head of the CCB shall have final authority for approval or rejection of a proposed change.

Responsibilities and Composition of QA Team

The purpose of the software quality assurance (QA) team is to ensure that all project products conform to the standards of the methodology and the software development model being used. The QA team examines each product for adherence to standards and must grant approval before a product may be baselined and released. For the form manager design project, the methodological standards adopted are those used by the NRL methodology, as described and modelled in the NRL methodology documentation. The initial procedural standards consist of the procedures for configuration management, as described in reference 1.

The responsibilities of the QA team are summarized in the following.

1. Ensure that documents and code obey methodological standards.

2. Ensure that configuration control process is followed appropriately.

3. Maintain project library.

In addition to the preceding, the head of QA, or his representative, will be a member of the configuration control board.

The software quality assurance (QA) team consists of the head of quality assurance and the project librarian. If the QA workload becomes too great, another QA team member will be added.

Agenda

1. Meeting time

2. Overview (Weiss)

   a. Purpose of project

   b. Application

   c. Available documentation

   d. Prerequisites

   e. Grades

3. **Sequencing of major events (Weiss)**

4. **Controls over the process (Weiss)**

5. **The Application (Kirby)**

6. **Tools and Environment (Kirby)**

7. **Resources Available (Weiss)**

8. **Preset Roles (Weiss)**

9. **Selection of available roles (Project Team)**

Appendix II

Memos From The Technical Consultant to The Project Team

Secrets

A secret is a design decision that is likely to change. Each secret is hidden within a module. Typical examples of secrets are the details of communication with a device, the representation of data, or the implementation of an algorithm. For a more detailed list, see the outline of the modularization lecture given in programming methods last semester.

When identifying secrets, it is important not to confuse the part of a decision that must be revealed to make the software useful with the part that must be concealed to make the software changeable. As an example, in the form manager the decision as to whether or not the operator can modify !variable field value!s[2] should not be hidden. The application program needs to know whether or not it is possible for the operator to do so. This information is likely revealed to the application by the access programs that are available to it. If there is no access program (implemented) that permits the application to obtain a !variable field value! after it has been modified by the operator, then the application knows that it is not possible for the operator to do so. What should be hidden is the mechanism by which the operator can modify the !variable field value!.

Subsets

In the NRL methodology, subsets play a dual role. First, while requirements are being identified, possible subsets of the full system under consideration are specified in terms of differing system capabilities. These subsets may be used to accommodate different customer sites, improved technology, predictable changes to customer needs, and other issues that may be described in terms of differential requirements.

Second, after abstract interfaces have been designed, the uses hierarchy is formed from the access programs defined in the interface specifications. Subsets to be implemented are then specified in terms of the uses hierarchy. These subsets include those requirements subsets to be implemented during the current development effort, and may also include other subsets that allow development in finer increments than those specified in the requirements. (This approach is sometimes characterized as incremental development.)

---

[2] An integral part of the NRL methodology is the use of a notation that helps define and identify different items used in requirements and design specifications, such as input data items and system modes. In particular, items enclosed in exclamation marks, such as !variable field!, are technical terms whose meanings are defined in a dictionary in the requirements specification.

Because the requirements subsets represent one set of expected changes, the flexibility they require strongly influences the modular structure of the system as expressed in the module guide, and the detailed design as specified in the abstract interfaces.

Since the uses hierarchy is composed of access programs drawn from the abstract interfaces, decisions on how to structure the abstract interfaces into access programs strongly influence the subsets that can be implemented.

As an example, the A-7 requirements state that "A subset is required for each HUD symbol..." One would therefore expect to see a module in the module guide whose secret is how to display symbols on the HUD. Furthermore, one would expect to see, in the abstract interface specification for the HUD module, access programs for display of each symbol. Implementing a subset for a particular symbol requires that the access program(s) for that symbol be implemented. Naturally, it is also necessary to implement the processes in which the access programs are invoked to implement the subset.

As a result of the influence of requirements subsets on modularization, and of abstract interface design on incrementally-buildable subsets, there is feedback among the stages of requirements specification, modularization, abstract interface specification, and specification of implementable subsets. One can rarely expect to be such a good oracle that all is predicted correctly at the start. It is important for the subsets describable by the uses hierarchy to be consistent with those specified in the requirements, however.

During the design of the form manager, it should be expected that there will be two chances during the design cycle to identify subsets: during requirements specification and after abstract interface specification. In our experience at NRL, the former is much more difficult than the latter.

Modes and States

Systems can generally be described in terms of states. For software, these states are often characterized by defining a state vector that contains all the variables of interest in the system. A particular state is identified by selecting values for the variables in the state vector. As an example, for a system that describes positions of points, the state vector might simply be a pair (x,y). A possible state in this system is (0,0).

A second approach to identifying states is to give a condition over the variables in the state vector to characterize a state or set of states. As an example, $\{(x,y) | y=x\}$ is a set of states that might be used to characterize certain situations. In particular, if the system is simulating the movement of a point, then when the states of the system are confined to this set the point is moving along the line with equation y=x.

Define a mode to be a set of states. Then a mode can be characterized by a condition. Define a mode class to be a set of modes such that each state belongs to one and only one mode of the mode class. Then the set of states in the system is the union of the modes in a mode class.

As an example, suppose a system has three states, say a, b, c,. We define mode M1 to be {a,b}, and mode M2 to be {c}. Let mode class P be composed of M1 and M2. Now define mode N1 to be {a}, and mode N2 to be {b,c}. Let mode class Q be composed of N1 and N2. Then if the system is in state b, it is simultaneously in modes M1 and N2.

The A-7 requirements have several different mode classes, with a number of different modes in each class. The form manager system currently may be thought of as having one mode class composed of several different modes. (Since there is only one mode class, it has no name and is not explicitly defined.) Introducing a second mode class currently seems unnecessary. It is important to be sure that each mode in the mode class is disjoint from each other mode, and that the modes completely cover the set of system states.

Note that although the word state has a generally accepted definition, the word mode does not. Three common uses are (1) as a synonym for state. (2) as a set of states, and (3) as a data type.

Abstract Types in Requirements Specifications

Abstract types are considered valuable for their usefulness in providing implementation-independent descriptions of objects that are to be implemented in programs, i.e., they are most frequently used in the design of programs. Abstract types may also be used in specifying requirements. Objects with structure may be specified as if they were abstract types by defining their structure in terms of sub-objects. To be consistent with the requirements for requirements, the sub-objects must be specified in an implementation-independent way.

As an example, a !display screen! might be defined as consisting of a !window area!, a !menu area!, a !prompt area!, and a !message area!.

The liberal use of this approach in the current form manager requirements should be continued. It may be extended to include input and output data items as they become better defined.

Software Engineering at Monmouth College

Harris Drucker, Monmouth College, New Jersey
Richard A. Kuntz, Monmouth College, New Jersey
G. Boyd Swartz, Monmouth, College, New Jersey

Abstract

Monmouth College instituted a Master's degree program in Software Engineering in the fall of 1985 as a result of extensive collaboration with high technology industries and encouragement from the state for more interaction between academia and industry. We define software engineering as the technological and managerial discipline concerned with systematic development and maintenance of quality products that are developed, validated, and implemented within a specific time frame and within an estimated cost range. This definition is sufficiently distinct from the objectives of computer science programs to deserve a separate curriculum. Students entering the program are required to have one year of industrial experience, courses or experience in high level and assembly languages, hardware design, discrete mathematics, and probability or statistics. The program is more quantitatively oriented than other software engineering programs we have examined and includes two courses in architecture, database, operating systems, languages, algorithms, two semesters in both computer networks and software engineering and a project course. The program emphasizes group projects and quantitative measurements and predictions.

1. Introduction

In the Fall of 1985, Monmouth College offered its first courses in the new graduate program in Software Engineering, and received approval from the state of New Jersey to grant the Master's degree in June of 1986. Prior to that first offering we went through a self-study including extensive consultation with high technology representatives, the results of which we think should be of interest to students contemplating study in this type of program or colleges interested in starting such a program. We had to answer questions such as: What is software engineering? What qualities does the software industry look for in graduates of a software engineering program? Are computer science graduates different from software engineers? Is software engineering sufficiently distinct from computer science to deserve a special program? Given that a software engineering program is needed, what plan of study gives us the type of graduates we desire?

In the following sections, we try to answer these questions. Some of the responses are unique to Monmouth College but others have universal applicability.

2. Background

Monmouth College is a private, comprehensive institution located on 125 acreas in West Long Branch, New Jersey, one mile from the Atlantic Ocean and ninety miles south of New York City. Baccalaureate and Master of Science degrees are offered in Electronic Engineering and Computer Science, the two department who jointly sponsor the software engineering program. These two graduate programs are offered only at night. Monmouth County has over 200 high technology firms and ranks 17th out of 3100 counties in the nation, in the number of computer programming and data processing firms. The two biggest employers in Monmouth County are AT&T and Ft. Monmouth. We thus have a large base from which to attract students.

The software engineering program was developed in consultation with representatives from our high technology committee: AT&T Bell Laboratories, AT&T Information Systems, Bell Communications Research, Bendix, Concurrent Computers, Syntrex, and Ft. Monmouth. These concerns saw a need for graduates unlike the graduates of typical computer science programs-engineers who would deal with software as part of a commercial product which must be specified, designed, developed, documented, maintained, and upgraded. These representatives considered computer scientists being untrained to attack the large software systems appearing in an industrial setting.

This program was thus developed in response to a need expressed by local high technology industries and government agencies with a push from the state of New Jersey for strong industrial/academic interaction. One of the lessons we learned is that a program such as software engineering requires a strong input from the industry since they are the employers of our future graduates and sponsors of their present employees. They have strong opinions on what a software engineer should be able to do.

3. What is Software Engineering

There is no unique definition of software engineering. Our high technology committee defined software engineering as the technological and managerial discipline concerned with systematic development and maintenance of quality products that are developed, validated, and implemented within a specific time frame and within an estimated cost range. The discipline combines elements of computer science, human factors and engineering. As a result of the growing awareness of the crucial role of software in the performance of critically important or widely used computerized systems, the concepts and practices of this new field have been developing in industrial and academic settings.

Applications of computer communication networks are rapidly proliferating as the number of computer users increases. This creates a need for well-trained professionals to develop and maintain network-based applications. These professionals must be thoroughly familiar with engineering methods, computer science fundamentals, communications network applications, and human factors design. To develop and implement the distributed architectures, operating systems, and database systems of the future, software engineers must be able to integrate their knowledge of computer science and human factors with a quantitative engineering approach to obtain an economical product. It is the integration of software tools, human factors, and hardware considerations directed towards a finished product that distinguishes software engineering from computer science.

The program in software engineering is designed to meet that need. It provides a comprehensive graduate-level survey of the fundamentals of computer science and data communications integrated into a software engineering framework. The emphasis throughout the program is on applying the lessons learned to practical and relevant software development projects.

4. Desired Outcomes

The software engineering program is designed to provide students with the basic skills to: design and evaluate computer networks, database management systems, and operating systems; conduct product evaluation; use the design techniques and tools associated with quality assurance and evaluation techniques, system validation techniques, project management techniques, cost estimation and control.

Many computer science departments offer a two semester sequence in software engineering. Is that not adequate? Our response is that the environment of the other courses in the software engineering program must be different. In all our courses, we use team projects and emphasize the concerns of the software engineer. This is sufficiently distinct from the typical computer science program to deserve a unique program.

Another response to that question also lies in the characteristics of the students at Monmouth College. The typical graduate student in the computer science department has transferred from a non-technical undergraduate curriculum, while our software engineering students typically have an undergraduate degree in computer science or engineering. All of our software engineering students have spent at least a year in the software industry and are thus aware of the problems in working in large teams on large software projects while the typical computer science graduate student has not had extensive industrial experience. This difference in background provides a rationale to the software engineering student to understand the principles of software engineering.

In order to provide the increased faculty-student involvement and the team environment we feel that is so important to software engineering, this graduate program is the only daytime graduate program at Monmouth College. The group projects we envision cannot be done in an evening program. In addition, enrollment is constrained to be smaller than that of the other programs, the program has special facilities, and higher tuition is charged. Students can attend on a full-time or part-time basis.

5. Student Prerequisites

We require all students to have some industrial experience in a software environment so that they can appreciate the value of the techniques and tools learned in the program. We require either courses or experience in high level programming languages, assembly language, data structures, use of some operating system, discrete math, probability or statistics, and logic design. This is usually satisfied by an undergraduate major in computer science of electrical engineering. However, we do have a few students with a non-technical undergraduate degree who returned to school for the prerequisite technical courses and are working in a systems programming environment. All students must get recommendations from their supervisor and a former professor. The letter from the supervisor also informs us that the supervisor is aware that the company must release the student from his job during the day to attend classes. Finally, an interview with the coordinator of the program is necessary.

6. The Program

The program is jointly sponsored by the departments of electronic engineering and computer science and is taught by members of both departments and adjunct faculty. It is administrated by a coordinator, not a department chair. The program consists of ten required courses. When enrollment is sufficiently large, electives will be offered.

We have very quantitatively oriented courses on networks and protocols, database systems, and operating systems. Courses in languages, architecture and algorithms are necessary to round out the education and give the students a fundamental basis necessary for their future growth. A two-course sequence in software engineering methodologies is followed by a project course where students integrate the fundamentals learned in other courses with the tools of software engineering to carry out a complete software cycle on a team-oriented design project.

We describe the courses in the Appendix, but as you read them, it is important to realize the environment in which they are taught-namely as team-oriented projects emphasizing an engineering discipline with quantitative measures of performance and cost. All courses meet the equivalent of forty-five, fifty minute periods. Except for a project course and the operating system course, all courses meet over a regular fourteen week semester. The operating system course is spread over two semesters or may be taken during the summer. The project course is offered summers only (Figure 1).

Full time students would take nine courses during the regular semester and the project course during the summer. A part-time student could finish in two years and two summers by taking two courses per semester and the operating system course and project courses in consecutive summers.

7. Comparisons To Other Schools

We examined the programs at Wang Institute and Texas Christian University although we know of two other schools that offer software engineering programs: Seattle University and Dartmouth. In comparison to our curriculum, theirs is much more management oriented. Our high-technology committee was very insistent that our graduates be able to quantify results. The requires knowledge of advanced queueing theory concepts, optimization algorithms, proofs of correctness, and,. in general a facility in the manipulation of numbers, symbols, and random variables.

8. Special Facilities

In addition to the facilities that are available to the Monmouth College student, special facilities donated by AT&T are available to the software engineering students. The primary computer is an AT&T 3B5 with 3 megabytes of main memory, two 340 megabyte disk drives and 20 hardwired terminals. In addition, all Monmouth College faculty have access to the 3B5 through on-campus and off-campus dial-in ports. At the present time, in addition to the usual UNIX facilities, we use INFORMIX as our database languages. We use DB III as the database for the AT&T 6300 PC's. We are continually adding programming tools, productivity tools, documentors, planning and control, and costing tools.

A local area net is implemented using 3COM network and AT&T 6300 PC's. This network is primarily used as a test bed to examine protocols designed by the students. By setting up a network partitioned from the 3B5 we do not risk crashing the whole system if the network fails.

To support the operating system course we have a mixture of UNIX based machines, MacIntoshes, and MS-DOS machines. We also have a Concurrent Computer XP60 that supports Ada.

To support simulation we use the AT&T Performance Analysis Workstation (PAWS) running on an AT&T 3B2/400 and Network 11.5 running in an MS-DOS environment.

9. Lecture and Seminar Series

To enhance the program and service the surrounding community, we offer a distinguished lecture series, a sequence of single lectures by experts from industry or academia. The series is designed to provide students with a perspective on current problems and trends in software development. Students in the software engineering program are expected to attend and to interact with the lecturers who are available before and after the lecture for small group and individual student interactions. The outside community is also invited to attend. In addition to providing students in the program with exposure to current trends and current issues in software engineering, the distinguished lecture series provides another means to support local high technology industries and publicize Monmouth College and the software engineering curriculum.

Four lectures were given this academic year. Dr. Alfred Aho of AT&T Bell Labs give a talk on "Little Languages", that is, the preparation of special languages for document preparation, information processing and software development. Dr. Derek Morris of Stevens Technical Institute spoke on distributed processing, while Nathan Petschenik of Bellcore spoke to some issues on clarifying expectations between software developers and system testers. Finally, Dr. Alan Garish of AT&T Information Systems gave a presentation on local area networks as perceived from the AT&T viewpoint.

The seminar systems was designed to give a more intense interaction between the students and the lecturers. In this case, the seminar was open only to the Monmouth College community. In one seminar, a software management expert was invited to present his company's software tools for such management. In another seminar, a talk was given on some advanced UNIX tools to control software development.

10. Conclusions

The software engineering program at Monmouth College offered two courses each semester in the academic year 1985086, starting with 18 part-time students. Of those initial students, eleven students dropped out of the program, an attrition rate higher than we anticipated. Some of this the students attributed to the inability to balance school and work. Even though the students nominally had one-half day off from work for each course, supervisors tended to expect the same amount of effort put into their industrial workload. In the future, we plan to sensitize the supervisors to this problem. Another problem was the lack of a quantitative background of some students, in particular the non-CS or non-EE students. These students had the calculus and statistics background that satisfied the prerequisites to get into the program. In practice, their skills were very rusty or they had never developed the facility to manipulate symbols, numbers, and random variables which was so essential to a quantitative understanding of many of our courses.

The remaining students in the program seem very happy with the curriculum, the rigor, and the approach that is so different from a CS curriculum. Our high technology committee also seems happy with our progress and the fact that this program is developing a good reputation locally.

This academic year we are offering a full range of courses. Plans are to add more software tools to our software engineering library and to attract full-time students.

Appendix-Courses

Programming languages: analysis of the underlying structure of high-level languages, including fourth generation languages and applications generators. Existing languages are compared through subjective and objective measures. The principles and techniques of software engineering are used to assess different languages and to highlight the importance of their features. Text: Programming Languages, Design and Implementation, Prentice-Hall, 2nd. Edition, 1984.

Network Design and Protocols I-II: Quantitative analysis and design of the physical, data link, and network layers of the ISO-OSI model; queueing theory, routing, packet switching, and optimization algorithms. Analysis and design of higher layers, simulation techniques, ISDN, advanced queuing concepts in mixed data and voice packets, internetworking, protocol design using finite state machines, and optimization of voice band transmission facilities. Text: Computer Networks, Tanenbaum, Prentice-Hall, 1981.

Algorithm design and analysis: design and analysis of algorithms including computer models, searching and sorting, matrix operations, graph algorithms, pattern matching, proofs, and NP-complete problems. Text: Fundamentals of Computer Algorithms, Horowitz & Sahni, Harper & Row, 1978.

Operating system implementation: Fundamental operating system concepts, multiprocessing, scheduling, deadlock, protection and relocation, virtual memory, security, and file systems. Case studies of UNIX, MacIntosh, MS-DOS, and Ada. Texts: An Introduction to Operating Systems, Deital, Addison-Wesley, 1984; Operating Systems: An Advanced Course, Flynn, et.al., Springer-Verlag, 1979.

Computer architecture: an integrated view of the logical design of a digital computer, including the basic hardware, firmware elements, and operating system software functions. Categorization of computer architectures, trade-off analysis, current trends and issues. Texts: Hardware Organization and Design, Hill & peterson, Wiley, 1978; Computer Systems Architecture, Baer, Computer Science Press, 1980.

Software engineering I-II: A two semester sequence in the design, implementation, debugging, testing, documentation, management, and maintenance of software. The first semester will concentrate on one-person software projects while the second semester will concentrate on team oriented software projects. Texts: Software Engineering: Design, Reliability, and Management, Shooman, McGraw-Hill, 1983; Software Engineering Economics, Boehm, Prentice-Hall, 1981.

Database Management: Theoretical and practical aspects of database management systems and their applications -- hierarchical, network, and relational models for DBMS design, the issues of access, integration, privacy, security, and maintenance for each model in various types of applications. Text: An Introduction to Database Systems, Date, Addison-Wesley, 1986.

System Project Implementation: A team project to conduct a complete software development project from initial requirements to tested, documented final product.

Monmouth College
Master of Science in Software Engineering

Prerequisite Courses

- Statistics
- Discrete Math
- High-Level Languages
- Logic Design
- Assembly Language

SOFTWARE ENGINEERING CURRICULA

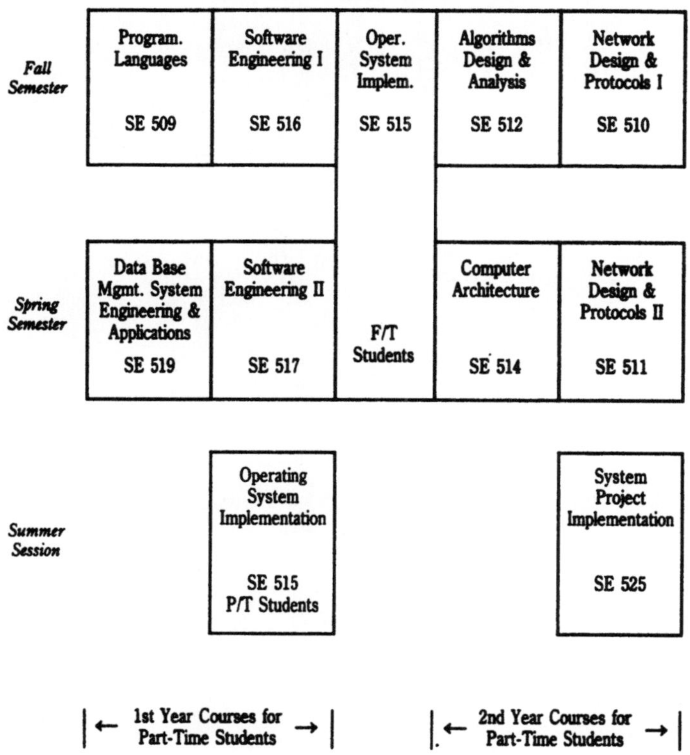

SECTION II

PART 4

INDUSTRIALLY–ORIENTED EDUCATION AND TRAINING

The demand for software engineers has resulted in several different approaches to industrially–oriented education and training programs in software engineering. Part 4 contains six papers that are concerned with this issue. The papers cover synergism of industrial and academic education; the Israel Aircraft Industry programs in software engineering education; a computer science education program within AT&T Bell Labs; formal education in software engineering within IBM; and the challenge of technology transfer.

A SYNERGY OF INDUSTRIAL AND ACADEMIC EDUCATION

D.J. Besemer, K.S. Decker, D.W. Politi, and J.F. Schnoor
General Electric Corporate Research and Development
K1-5C10, P.O. Box 8, Schenectady, NY 12301

Abstract

Both industry and academia educate software engineers, but each has its respective shortcomings. Universities emphasize theory and often ignore meaningful applications, while industry focuses on practical methodologies, failing to sufficiently stress the underlying concepts. Neither of these institutions typically provides the supplementary skills needed by a software engineer. This paper describes these and other problems with software engineering education, and illustrates one industrial training program that is attempting to resolve many of the problems. The training program combines the best features of both academia and industry, resulting in a synergy that successfully eliminates many problems inherent in existing software engineering education.

1 Introduction

Software engineering has evolved as a response to the growing software crisis during the last twenty years. Its failure to mitigate this crisis has directed the focus inward toward the educational methods used to teach software engineering theories and practices. Such an introspective view reveals glaring deficiencies and inherent problems that must be overcome if software engineering is to become pervasive. Some of the most obvious of these are the paucity of curricula, brevity of training, dichotomy of institutional objectives, lack of breadth, and deficiency of technology transfer.

Some industrial training programs are evolving to address these problems. General Electric's Software Technology Program is one of these. While it cannot solve all the problems, this program does solve some of the most important ones. A description of both the problems and their consequences is presented in Section 2; the structure of the Software Technology Program is explained in Section 3; the benefits of this program are highlighted in Section 4; and finally, unsolved problems are outlined in Section 5.

2 Software Engineering Education Problems

2.1 Paucity of Curricula

One of the greatest problems facing computer science is the absence of thorough education in software engineering. Little or no formal training in the area is required at the bachelor's and master's level. Those schools that offer software engineering courses usually do so too late in the curriculum — at the junior, senior, or graduate levels [1] — leaving the student too little time to appreciate the value of and to practice with the available methodologies. Even worse, most computer science curricula stress individualism and competition among peers and ignore *teamwork*, a crucial element in industrial software projects. This lack of general support at the university level produces candidates who are ill-prepared to solve the software crisis and thus places the burden of training on industry [10].

2.2 Brevity of Training

Both university and industrial training courses tend to be short. As a result, hands-on experience is either sacrificed entirely, or the projects on which the students work are insignificant and contrived. "Canned" problems or problems that are new, but are never used on completion, are an inefficient use of resources. The students are not given enough opportunity for creative problem solving and are not forced to deal with major difficulties. Most important, because their solutions will never be used, students are discouraged from producing maintainable code, and the perceived importance of the software engineering

[1] Stanford University, Wang Institute, and the University of Seattle are pleasant exceptions to this rule. Stanford University has recently announced plans to begin the software engineering education at the freshman level and propagate it through the subsequent levels. Both Wang Institute and the University of Seattle offer master's degrees in software engineering [7],[15]. We believe this direction will continue throughout most major computer science universities.

process is diminished. With short problems, the documentation associated with the software engineering life cycle becomes a larger percentage of the total output than in normal practice [7]. This is disheartening to newcomers in the field.

2.3 Dichotomy of Institutional Objectives

Academia and industry attempt to educate the software engineer with methods that lie at opposite ends of a spectrum, neither of which is sufficient alone. University courses try to give a broad view of software engineering, but the brevity of the courses dictates that the student will not attain a firm grasp of the problems and principles. In a one- or two-semester course it is difficult to cover many different methodologies and to give the student in-depth experience in one or more of them. To understand the underlying issues, the student must encounter them through experience; while broad exposure to software engineering is vital, alone it is insufficient.

Industry, in contrast, sacrifices broad and theoretical exposure with its two basic educational formats: training courses and apprenticeships. Training courses are intended to provide the employee with the knowledge needed to understand the specific methods established within the company. Because of the overhead associated with this, most companies want to train their employees quickly so that they can become productive as soon as possible. In an attempt to reduce the total training time, only one methodology is taught. Thus, the employee obtains no experience in other areas of software engineering; practicality is stressed, but the overall educational structure is poor ("toss the theory, you're needed on the front lines").

Apprenticeship, industry's other approach, stresses on-the-job learning. This learning mode shares similar disadvantages with training programs, in that the individual may need time to become productive and may receive little exposure to other methodologies. Constrained by deadlines, the organization to which the individual is apprenticed may sacrifice education for production. "To base one's technology on apprentice training is a risk a technologically oriented company cannot afford to take — especially if it wants to be the industry leader."[4]

2.4 Lack of Breadth

A prevalent problem with software engineering education in both academia and industry is the narrow view that is taught to prospective software engineers [3]. One facet of the problem is the limited role the student is allowed to play during the software engineering life cycle. Most software engineering courses stress only the role of individual producer and fail to give the student proper exposure to the other roles a software engineer must play. These roles include team leader, review participant, technical liaison, and maintainer.

A sharp focus on a single methodology contributes another aspect to the narrow view problem. When the software engineering life cycle is taught, it is natural to apply an accepted methodology to a "well-behaved" application (i.e., one that easily fits within the life cycle model). Using this application, academia teaches the generic methodologies, and industry teaches the methodology applicable to its particular domain. Unfortunately, this practice ignores the many applications that do not fit into the cookbook life cycle and the methodologies that have been developed to deal with them.

Limited access to a wide range of tools is a problem for all areas of engineering education, but because of the large expense involved in acquiring and learning new tools (e.g., editors, operating systems, debuggers, languages, and computers), the problem is more intense in software engineering education. Most universities cannot afford to equip their computer centers with the various types of hardware and software required to give students exposure to a wide range of resources. Corporations educating employees in software engineering see no reason to expose students to equipment that is not used in their environments. The result is that companies employ software engineers who are experts with one or two environments, but who have not been exposed to the multitude of other environments that exist.

Finally, several other skills essential to practicing software engineering are not being sufficiently addressed. Too few educational programs stress technical writing, technical presentation, professional involvement, and technical management skills [6]. Without these skills, a software engineer is ill-equipped to fulfill the unique demands of his profession.

2.5 Deficiency of Technology Transfer

One remaining problem in software engineering education is the absence of instruction that will lead to the effective transfer of software engineering expertise to company components, research centers, and other engineers. This is a longstanding problem that occurs with any new or rapidly developing technology. Generic problems in technology transfer include resistance to change, ignorance, and motivational restraints [12].

The problem of transferring software engineering technology applies particularly to industry. Since a formal education in software engineering was not available to most of the people who manage and practice software production today, there are many people involved that do not have enough training — too many to train effectively as individuals [8]. Thus it becomes important to teach software engineers how to spread their technology to the company components where it is needed.

Another major obstacle to technology transfer is the nature of the "self-contained cultures" of both the researcher and the software developer, which results in two problems. First, there is a gap between software engineering researchers and software developers. Researchers get feedback through their own research community and are not motivated to promote the application of their work, while developers must get the job done and do not wish to take the risks involved in applying a new tool or methodology [9]. Second, software engineering principles are not being applied directly to research programming. Research programmers are faced with the problem of trying to apply software engineering paradigms to the research domain where simple life cycle models do not hold. Clearly, software engineering technology must be transferred to the research and development environment as well as to the production environment.

Finally, software engineers are often isolated from one another, which can inhibit transfer of technologies, including, but not confined to, software engineering. This isolation in the academic environment, where individual performance is stressed, and in the industrial environment, where project-oriented management or job security concerns can isolate a software engineer from his peers, keeps the available expertise from being fully used.

3 The Software Technology Program

The Software Technology Program (STP) was created six years ago to help address the need for thorough software engineering training in General Electric. The three-year training program, located at G.E.'s Research and Development Center, is designed to provide this instruction, through courses and experience, to college graduates in computer science or computer engineering. The program combines the unique environment of a diverse research center with a strong technical university (Rensselaer Polytechnic Institute) to take advantage of the best characteristics of each. Program members gain more from this arrangement than they could from experiencing both institutions independently.

3.1 Initial Training in Software Engineering

The program begins with an intense nine-week course that combines lectures, discussions, and project work, for which graduate credit is granted by Rensselaer Polytechnic Institute (RPI). It is designed to provide each program member with a theoretical background in software engineering, tempered with the experience and pragmatism required by industry. The new program members are assigned to three- or four-member teams, each of which will work on one project for the duration of the nine-week course. Table 1 shows a sample of projects from past courses and the key technologies that were learned from them. As the

Project	Key Technology
Electronic mail interface	Rapid prototyping
Electronic bulletin board	Networking
Factory simulation module	Simulation techniques
Graphics frame editor	Object oriented programming
Robot language translator	Compiler construction
Ethernet monitor	Real-time programming
Feature Extraction and Analysis Tool	Numerical analysis

Table 1: Nine-week course projects

teams work on their projects, they also attend lectures on software engineering techniques that coincide with the current development stages of their projects.

In conjunction with the software engineering course, new members are required to take a business presentation course in which each trainee gives eight oral presentations that are critiqued by both peers and instructors. Members also get instruction through additional forums: introductory seminars on editors, text processing systems, workstation tools, etc.; short courses on programming languages, environments, and methodologies; and weekly seminars on the different projects that are in progress throughout the Center (which provide exposure to the types of projects that are available during the three-year program).

3.2 Practical Software Engineering Experience

Following the nine-week course, each program member works on three one-year projects in a variety of areas, including graphics, networking, communications, VLSI CAD, systems programming, factory simulation, robotics, database systems, artificial intelligence, natural language processing, expert systems, formal language theory, image processing, and control systems. Concurrently, members obtain a master's of science or engineering degree at RPI.

Each year, the program members are grouped into teams based on similarity of projects. A current team is the "Expert Systems Team," comprising projects in distributed expert systems, situation assessment, causal modeling, and reasoning with uncertainty; another team is the "Software Engineering Tools Team," which is composed of projects in incremental parsing, Ada[2] PDL environments, and graphic COCOMO cost modelling. These teams meet regularly to review documentation and to discuss issues, problems, and concerns relating to their projects or to the program itself. Each team is also responsible for organizing a center-wide colloquium by bringing in experts in software engineering or related fields.

STP members also have additional opportunities during their three years in the program. Members attend GE-wide Corporate Entry Leadership Conferences at the beginning and end of their three year tenure, as well as a one-day interview workshop and a multi-day technical leadership workshop. Each member has the opportunity to attend technical conferences and training courses throughout the country, and are encouraged to attend both technical and non-technical Center-wide seminars.

3.3 Graduate-Level Education

The pursuit of a master's degree at Rensselaer Polytechnic Institute is an integral part of the STP. The university lends support for the program, providing program members with a common advisor and expediting the administrative overhead associated with class sign-ups. This support is also evident in the classroom, where professors allow STP members to use Research Center facilities and equipment for projects and assignments. The program attempts to enhance members' technical backgrounds by fostering an environment where work for both institutions can be shared, allowing an individual to devote more time, effort, and care to that work. Because many of the graduate level courses at RPI are taught by Research Center staff, the program members have a better opportunity than the typical student to work closely with their professors. The theoretical approach of the university provides more insight into the reasons underlying the work, while the work experience provides an in-depth feel for the application of the theory.

[2] Ada is a registered trademark of the U.S. Government (Ada Joint Program Office).

During the second year of the program, each member begins work on a master's thesis. This is done in conjunction with a year-long project at the Center, allowing the trainee to devote more time and effort (and use better resources) than the typical RPI graduate student. Because of cooperation between GE and RPI, each program member usually has both an RPI thesis advisor and a sponsor within GE. The latter is normally a scientist involved with the project at the Center who can devote the needed time and effort to the student's needs, questions, and problems. These thesis projects provide the opportunity to try a new and more theoretical approach to the year-long projects. For example, one program member applied concepts learned in his course on fuzzy set theory to his project (the automatic interpretation of data from steam turbine monitors), and developed a unique rule-based approach to the problem. Another member applied a new artificial intelligence approach to his project (the integration of existing computer aided engineering programs), and produced a program that automates the preliminary design of jet aircraft centrifugal stage compressors. The results have been well received within the company, at the university, and in the scientific community.

3.4 Completing the Software Technology Program

As stated earlier, the primary goal of the STP is to provide well-trained software engineers for General Electric. Because of this, many members attempt to choose third-year projects that are highly visible to other GE components. This provides exposure to other company components and facilitates a possible transition upon graduation.

The STP member also gains exposure to other company components by attending conferences (e.g., the annual GE Software Engineering Conference) and panel meetings (e.g., the GE Software Engineering Panel, Ada Panel, and Artificial Intelligence Subcouncil), and by keeping close contact with former STP members who are working for GE components. For instance, each year program graduates attend an STP Panel meeting at the Research Center; this gives the graduates the opportunity to provide information to current members about the jobs that are available throughout the company. The graduates also provide valuable feedback regarding company contacts, interview strategies, etc.

The STP manager directs graduating members' resumes to the hiring managers of the appropriate GE components and sends the members on plant trips and interviews at these locations. The graduating STP member is in high demand throughout the company, and typically receives several job offers.

To give a summary of an STP member's experiences during the program, Figure 1 shows a chronological illustration of one member's activities. The internal STP training can be seen at the top of the chart; the RPI course work is at the center of the chart; various other activities are at the bottom of the chart.

4 Benefits of the Software Technology Program

The problems outlined in Section 2 illustrate weaknesses that exist in both industrial and academic software engineering education programs. The Software Technology Program was

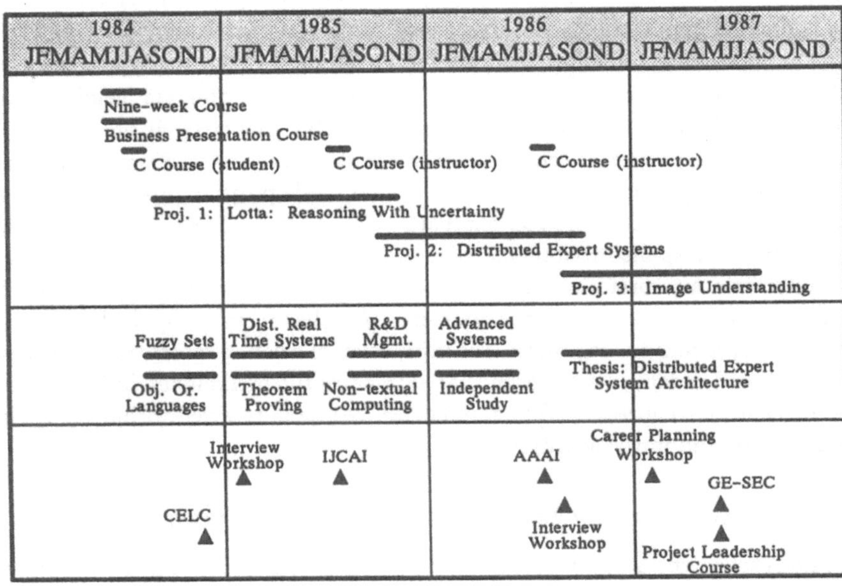

The above chart is logically divided into three sections. At the top of the chart are the internal STP activities that occur at the Research Center. In addition to the usual activities, this program member became an expert in the "C" programming language, and was able to share his expertise with other members by teaching an internal course.

At the center of the chart are the activities that are directly associated with Rensselear Polytechnic Institute. These are classes and the thesis associated with obtaining a master's degree.

At the bottom of the chart are other miscellaneous activities in which this member was able to participate. These included the Corporate Entry Leadership Conference, two interviewing workshops, a workshop on career planning, a project leadership course, two conferences on artificial intelligence, and the GE Software Engineering Conference.

Figure 1: A typical STP member's activities

created in an attempt to improve software engineering training, and this section describes how we believe the STP meets this objective.

4.1 Depth and Breadth of Program

The Software Technology Program provides the depth and breadth in software engineering training that is lacking in other education programs. The introductory (nine-week course) projects, three one-year projects, and projects associated with obtaining a master's degree give members exposure to many different types of applications, allowing them to use various software engineering methodologies. The issue of academic ***book learning*** versus ***industrial practicality*** is addressed by stressing cohesion between graduate courses and the year-long projects. The underlying theories taught in courses are better understood by applying them to specific areas outside the course context. When courses are taken that are unrelated to a year-long project, the project can still benefit by the addition of a new technology. For example, one program member applied the concepts taught in a "Non-Textual Computing Environments" class to a knowledge representation project at work. The project benefited because the course-inspired ***graphical*** approach was different than the approach that otherwise would have been used.

Exposure to methodologies and techniques that members may not be using in their own projects is facilitated through close interaction with the other program members—both during the nine-week course and throughout the three one-year projects. The intensity of the course load during the nine-week course (often demanding up to 70 hours per week) fosters a tight relationship within each new group. This close-knit relationship makes each project group aware of what the other groups have accomplished, what problems they have encountered, and what methodologies they have used. After the nine-week course is over, this established infrastructure continues to be an asset to the program members. Whereas competition inherent in most academic environments often prohibits students from getting exposure to other students' work, this is not a problem in the STP. The cohesion of the group fosters interaction both in the courses taken at RPI and in the year-long projects at the Center. Consequently, members get a greater benefit from the RPI course work and their productivity at the Research Center is increased.

Because the program is in a research environment, the program member has an opportunity to work in many diverse fields. A typical range of projects for a program member might include an interactive robot simulation package, a graphical programming environment for object-oriented paradigms, and tools for natural language understanding. In this series of projects, methodologies associated with simulation programming, object-oriented programming, and artificial intelligence programming would all be used. The year-long projects are of significant size to provide exposure to all phases of the software engineering life cycle, and they are of adequate length to eliminate the major inadequacies of most software engineering training with respect to limited duration. This variety of projects, combined with the pursuit of a master's degree, imbues a theoretical education with the practicality required by industry. Because of the coupling between the student's courses and project work, there is a cross-fertilization of ideas that increases both personal productivity and the value of the education.

4.2 Multiple Roles for Program Participants

Each program member is given the opportunity to play roles other than software developer, including team leader, review participant, and software maintainer. The first of these roles, team leadership, is a critical component in a software project [10]. Program members gain team leadership experience in three ways: during the nine-week course, team leadership positions are rotated so that each individual assumes this role for a period of time; many program members have the opportunity to be team leaders on their respective one-year projects; and because of the STP team groupings, most third-year members are responsible for leading their teams.

Another necessary role of the software engineer is to be an effective reviewer of colleagues' work; reviews are often management's only method for evaluating the progress of a project [11]. The program imparts experience, both as a software review participant and as a review leader, through STP teams that review each document as it is developed.

Because maintenance is the longest and most expensive part of the software engineering life cycle, the software engineer must learn to play the role of maintainer. Program members are given the responsibility for answering questions and addressing problems associated with all software produced by them even after they have moved to a new project. This approach discourages software engineers from thinking that they are finished with code upon delivery [16].

Finally, program members assume roles that improve the program itself. They interview future program candidates, teach mini-seminars to other program members and Center employees, manage STP-related activities, and provide feedback to the program. Allowing the individuals to assume so many diverse roles is an opportunity that only an industrial institution can provide, and it is responsible for broadening the employee in a way a university cannot.

4.3 Abundant Supply of Resources

Because the STP is located at a research center, each program member is exposed to a wide variety of hardware and software tools. Hardware resources include machines from DEC, IBM, Sun, Symbolics, Apollo, AT&T, Hewlett Packard, Texas Instruments, Evans & Sutherland, Apple, Xerox, and access to Cray supercomputers. In addition to the systems software that accompanies these machines, a wide variety of applications software is available. This list includes publishing software, object-oriented environments, graphics packages, several varieties of programming languages, configuration management tools, knowledge engineering tools, and many others. The Research Center participates in many beta-tests for software vendors, ensuring that program members are exposed to the latest developments in the software arena. The plethora of software and hardware resources, however, does not alone insure that an employee will become adept at using them.

Because STP members have a strong technical motivation from their one-year projects and their RPI classes, they have the desire (and the opportunity) to learn how to use many of these resources during their three year training. The result will be a software engineer who is knowledgeable about many computing environments.

4.4 Communication and Management Skills Development

A key goal of the program is to develop well-rounded software professionals who can do more than produce software. This involves not only exposure to new concepts, but written and oral communication of one's ideas as well. Technical papers are the main channel through which new developments in a field are shared, and program members are strongly encouraged to write papers for journals and conferences. Time is allocated so that much of this task can be done during the working day. Program members attend technical conferences to support interaction and to establish channels of communication with other professionals in the field.

Presentation of one's work to management or to other engineers can often mean the difference between the continuation or elimination of a project. The business presentation course (integrated into the nine-week software engineering course) provides instruction and practice on how to deliver effective presentations on both technical and nontechnical subjects. Throughout their three-year tenure, program members give many presentations to technical staff and management concerning the status of their work, and to RPI classes concerning the theoretical topics being studied.

Software management skills such as project formulation, resource allocation, budgeting, evaluation, and other management issues are taught to program members through internal company courses (e.g., the GE Project Leadership Course, which is taken by all third-year STP members) and courses offered as part of their master's degrees (e.g., RPI's "R & D Management" course, which is a suggested course for program members). This instruction is important—even if the individual will not assume a management position—because it gives a better understanding of the overall software production process. It also allows the software engineer to understand the viewpoint of the manager, which is vital in developing effective communication with upper-level management. The opportunity to practice such concepts is not usually provided by a university.

4.5 Technology Transfer Support

While basic scientific research is generally transferred by *paper* (through articles, books, and conferences), engineering technology is primarily transferred by *people* (through prolonged personal contact, training, and teamwork). There is consistent evidence that "technology transfer results from individual, personal interactions and technology is most effectively transferred by transferring people with the appropriate knowledge and skills."[1] One way this is accomplished is when program graduates take positions in company components. They take with them three years of substantial project experience, a balance of industrial and academic learning, and a wide variety of training in both software engineering and other aspects of computer science. Ideally, a program member may transition to a component with one of his projects, allowing a dual transfer of technology. Graduates may also take with them useful tools developed at the Research Center or recommendations to acquire them.

Since the nine-week course gives new members an introduction to software engineering principles, each year-long project derives benefits from having a software engineer apply these principles. This provides a level of expertise often lacking in a research environment. Often a program member is the first or only group member with training in software engineering, and possibly the only member with training in computer science. Conversely, beneficial technology transfer can occur from the group to the software engineer. Such a transfer of advances in computer science (e.g., the latest computer graphics algorithms) is common, but technologies within software engineering may be transferred as well (e.g., object-oriented design techniques).

Particular attention is devoted to ensuring that program members have free access to the information that is available. The matrix management structure of the program, as well as the significant portion of time spent in program activities (reviews, classes, social events, etc.), keeps members from being isolated in their projects. Because members are in a training program that is independent of the mainstream promotion system and are expected to transition at the end of their tenure, the competitive environment found in similar circumstances is eliminated. The amount of time that members spend together and the willingness and openness with which they help each other lead to a phenomenon we term *technology osmosis*: the unstructured assimilation of knowledge through prolonged contact. A strong *infrastructure* exists among the group. Software utilities are freely exchanged in a forum that was organized by the program members, and new programs are rapidly brought into use because software developers view the program as an excellent group with which to perform beta testing.

This leads to the second important solution to the technology transfer problem: the creation of *technological gatekeepers*. While transferring people is the best method for a one-shot transfer of technology, continuing transfer is better accomplished through a network of technological gatekeepers. These technology liaisons should straddle organizational boundaries; speak the languages of computer scientists, engineers, and management; keep connections with each other; have a broad range of related interests; and be near their scientific communities (through attending conferences, seminars, etc.) [1],[13]. The program infrastructure, including graduates of the program, precisely meets these qualities and thus provides a continuing source of technology transfer even (and perhaps more important) after graduates have left the program.

5 Unsolved Problems

Admittedly, the STP does not solve all of the problems of software engineering education. In light of the material that we have presented, there are two problem classifications: those specific to the Software Technology Program and those inherent in software engineering education.

We can identify three problems specific to the program. First, the Research Center loses some of its best software engineers after their three-year tenure has ended. Although these people are replaced by newer members, the experience of the more mature members is purged from the Research Center and transitioned to other company components. Another problem is that the structure of such a training program would become infeasible with a large group of participants. The overhead and complexity of managing the STP would become far too great, and some of the infrastructure now inherent in the program would be lost. As it is currently structured, it is doubtful that more than fifteen new members per year could be managed effectively, a difficulty that precludes such a program as a widespread solution to software engineering education deficiencies. Another problem involves the relationship between the university and the program. While a coupling between RPI and the program exists, the STP has not worked with the university to alter its curricula to better suit the needs of the program. Though the STP receives important benefits through ties with RPI, the program has not yet exerted its influence in promoting a greater emphasis on software engineering in the RPI curricula.

Two fundamental problems of software engineering education, neither of which has a simple solution, need attention. First, most software engineering education occurs too late in the individual's training. It would be desirable to have a similar training experience at the undergraduate level (possibly through multiple internships or co-op programs), while the engineer is still forming basic skills. By beginning such training early, the software engineering frame of mind would be an integral part of computer programming. Second, some problems with technology transfer are not dealt with sufficiently. One crucial missing component is the education and training of upper-level management in the needs for software engineering, so that technology transfer meets with acceptance, both in the *perception* of the need (does management believe it is necessary?) and the *actuality* of the methods used (do these tools solve the problem?)[2]. These problems need to be solved before software engineering can become pervasive in everyday software production.

6 Conclusion

The Software Technology Program addresses a majority of the broad issues facing industrial software engineering educators today. By providing the basic education that lasts a sufficient amount of time, incorporating realistic projects and balancing both theoretical and practical learning, problems specifically inherent to software engineering education are addressed. Allowing members to play all the roles in the process, avoiding a narrow corporate view, and teaching the related communications and managerial skills, provides talents that are often overlooked in similar curricula. Finally, by establishing avenues for technology transfer through transferring people and building a lasting infrastructure, a program such as the Software Technology Program can become the cornerstone of a corporate-wide strategic plan for software engineering education. These concepts can be applied not only to software engineering education but to other areas of engineering education as well.

The STP member is able to combine the theoretical background provided by RPI and the practical experience gained at the Research Center. Other skills, including communication, management, and leadership abilities, are developed and exercised in both the academic and the industrial environments. Because of the holistic interaction between academia and industry, the program members benefit more than they would from experiencing both worlds independently, and this is why the Software Technology Program produces a synergy of industrial and academic education.

Acknowledgments

We are grateful to David E. Priest, Peter M. Meenan, George Wise, and Barbara J. Vivier for their invaluable suggestions and corrections.

References

[1] P. A. Abetti and R. W. Stuart, "Entrepreneurship and technology transfer: key factors in the inovation process," Lally Management Center Working Paper, Rensselaer Polytechnic Institute, Troy, NY 12180, 1985.

[2] M. R. Barbacci, "The Software Engineering Institute: bridging practice and potential," *IEEE Software*, vol. 2, no. 6, pp. 4–21, November 1985.

[3] T. Booth, et al., "Design education in computer science and engineering," *IEEE Computer*, vol. 19, no. 6, pp. 20–26, June 1986.

[4] L. M. Branscomb, "IBM and U.S. universities — an evolving partnership," *IEEE Trans. Ed.*, vol. E-29, no. 2, pp. 69–77, May 1986.

[5] S. N. Busenburg and W. C. Tam, "An academic program providing realistic training in software engineering," *Comm. of the ACM*, vol. 22 no. 6, pp. 341–345, June 1979.

[6] R. J. Joenck and E. C. Jones, Jr., "Joint special issue on developing the ability to communicate," *IEEE Trans. Ed.*, vol. E-27, no. 3, September 1984.

[7] J. P. McGill, "The software engineering shortage: a third choice," *IEEE Trans. on Soft. Eng.*, vol. SE-10, no. 1, pp. 42–49, January 1984.

[8] H. D. Mills, "Software engineering education," *Proc. IEEE*, vol. 68, no. 9, pp. 1158–1162, September 1980.

[9] W. Myers, "MCC: Planning the software revolution," *IEEE Software*, vol. 2, no. 6, pp. 68–73, November 1985.

[10] S. J. Pratt, "Software engineering and educational support environments," *University Computing*, vol. 8, pp. 42–45, 1986.

[11] R. S. Pressman, *Software Engineering: A Practitioner's Approach*, New York, NY: McGraw-Hill, pp. 26, 1982.

[12] J. B. Quinn and J. A. Mueller, "Transferring research results to operations," in *Readings in the Management of Innovation*, M. Tushman and W. L. Moore, Eds. Boston, MA: Pitman, pp. 60–83, 1982.

[13] "Software Engineering Institute organizational and technical overview," Documentation Services, Software Engineering Institute, CMU, Pittsburgh, PA 15213, 1985.

[14] B. C. Twiss, ***Managing Technological Innovation***, 2nd ed. New York, NY: Longman, pp. 176–205, 1980.

[15] "Wang Institute of Graduate Studies master of software engineering program description and bulletin," Wang Institute of Graduate Studies, School of Information Technology, Tyng Road, Tyngsboro, MA 01879, 1984.

[16] M. R. Woodward and K. C. Mander, "On software engineering education: experiences with the software hut game," *IEEE Trans. on Ed.* , vol. E-25, no. 1, pp. 10-14, February 1982.

IAI CORPORATE SOFTWARE ENGINEERING TRAINING & EDUCATION PROGRAM

Jonah Z. Lavi(Loeb), Moshe I. Ben Porat, Amram Ben-David

ISRAEL AIRCRAFT INDUSTRIES
BEN GURION AIRPORT, ISRAEL

Abstract

ISRAEL AIRCRAFT INDUSTRIES has developed a comprehensive educational program in software engineering. Goals of the program include: the retraining of college graduates to become software engineers with specializations in one of three application areas; (Data Processing, Embedded Computer Systems on CAD/CAM systems); and enhancement of the knowledge of currently practicing software engineers. The program is centered around three distinct full-time courses of study having an average duration of 7 months. The training program also includes a large number of short courses and seminars. The company is currently planning a M.Sc. program in embedded computer systems and software engineering in cooperation with one of the universities in Israel.

This paper describes the needs leading to the development of such an extensive program, the objectives and the structure of the various courses, the students, the training center staff, the educational computer laboratories, and the lessons learned.

INTRODUCTION

The activities and the products of Israel Aircraft Industries (IAI) are highly computerized. Most of the products (Aircraft, Missile boats, Missiles, C^3I systems) include embedded computer systems, or are built as embedded computer systems (ECS). The analysis, engineering, and development of these products is strongly supported by extensive CAD/CAM programs. Also, the daily management of the corporation in the areas of finance, stores, production and manpower is supported by very large data processing systems (DP). Most of the software incorporated in IAI products and large portions of the CAD/CAM and DP software is developed in-house by IAI software engineers.

The demand for software engineers to develop of this diversified software is increasing daily and the necessary manpower is not available. The competition for manpower on the market is increasing and universities do not supply enough qualified engineers. Furthermore, newly graduated computer scientists lack the necessary software engineering skills and the necessary application domain training. Also, most of the currently employed programmers and systems analysts lack thorough education in the modern systems and software engineering technologies necessary for the development of complex software systems. As a result, many systems are insufficiently analyzed and inadequately designed. This causes delays in the completion of projects and unnecessary expenses. These difficulties forced the company, like other companies (MCGI84), to develop within the corporate training center a large program for the training of software engineers. The program is divided into two major parts: training of new software engineers and enhancing the knowledge of practicing software engineers and programmers.

In the deliberations leading to the development of the IAI training programs, it was realized that the background and education of various software engineers should be different, depending on the types of products to be developed. Every software developer needs a general education in software engineering and in some of the underlying computer science theories. This knowledge, however, is not sufficient for the development of diversified software products. IAI and other's experiences show that an increasing portion of software development activities are in the systems requirements analysis and testing phases. Performing these activities requires comprehensive applications domain know-how (BEND84, SIMP82, SPEN84, WARN82) and familiarity with the methods used in the requirements analysis and testing in the specific domains: ECS, CAD/CAM & DP. Furthermore, the computerized systems and the programming languages and tools used in the development of software in each of the domains are different. Therefore it was decided:

a. to develop three distinct retraining programs (full time, 6 to 8 months duration) tailored to the corporate software development needs in each of the ECS, CAD/CAM & DP domains.

b. to provide the basic application domain knowledge of the participants by hiring college graduates with the necessary previous education, e.g. engineers participating in the ECS software engineering course should have, preferably, a first degree in physics or electronics. Participants in the CAD/CAM software engineering course, should have preferably, a background in aeronautical, mechanical or electronic engineering depending on the class of CAD programs they are developing. Participants in the DP software engineering course should preferably have a background in economics, finance or industrial engineering.

The corporate educational programs for currently employed engineers are composed of many courses and seminars. IAI has realized, like similar organizations in the U.S.A., that an equivalent of a first degree augmented by retraining programs is not sufficient to provide the staff needed for the development of modern engineering systems in general, (BAUC82) and in particular for software systems. IAI is therefore supporting the part time graduate education of many of its engineers and is currently negotiating the development of a special M.Sc. program in embedded computer systems and software engineering with universities in Israel.

The training programs provide engineers with basic knowledge in software engineering and computer science. This is not sufficient. To improve software development productivity, they must gain extensive experience in a particular application area. Therefore, it is not recommended, by the authors, to transfer software engineers from one major application domain to another. The efficient development of software requires application domain specialization. As in electronic engineering, where each engineer specializes in a particular area such as radar, communications, or Electronic Warfare (EW), software engineers also have to specialize in particular application domains. Such specialization is also required to advance within the company where the natural promotion path is within specialized project areas.

This paper describes the objectives and structure of the major IAI software engineering programs, demonstrates the uniqueness of each of the specialized courses, and provides brief information about the students, the training staff and its background. Finally it describes the educational computer training laboratories and some of the lessons learned.

THE IAI TRAINING PROGRAM

The IAI program retrains college graduates to become software engineers. It is centered around three major basic courses. Each course is conducted once every year or two. The courses are run as full-time courses, 9 hours a day, five days a week with 20 to 25 participants each. The three courses are:

1. Software engineering for embedded computer systems (1000 hours)

2. Programming of DP systems (960)

3. CAD/CAM Software engineering (1030 to 1120 hours)

These courses are augmented by a 465 hours part time DP systems analysis course, the planned M.Sc. program in embedded computer systems and software engineering, and a large number of enrichment courses and seminars in topics such as software management, software requirements analysis, configuration management, microprocessor software development, real-time operating systems, Ada, and computer graphics.

Overall Objectives and Design of the Retraining Courses

Objectives of the three major retraining programs are that the participants will be able to:

1. Perform necessary software development activities at various phases of the lifecycle from requirements analysis to integration and testing and during maintenance.

2. use the software engineering methods and tools applicable in the respective

application domain.

3. obtain "hands on" experience.

4. work in software development teams.

The specific objectives and content of each of the retraining programs are derived from the overall objectives by a professional steering committee set up for each program. These objectives are currently being adjusted according to detailed job analysis made for each branch of specialization using a methodology developed at the training center (KEDE85).

One of the major objectives of the programs is the development of a coherent software engineering philosophy to be imposed throughout the courses. The accomplishment of this objective is difficult since the courses are taught by so many different instructors, who come with various backgrounds and experiences and who have not all been subjected to a thorough modern software engineering education. The training center staff together with corporate R&D staff try to develop and to impose such an approach but have not yet succeeded as much as they desire. This problem is being addressed continuously and will be remedied with time as the courses are continuously improved and redeveloped. More details about the approach use in the development of one of the courses, the ECS course, are described in a previous paper by the authors (BEND84).

The detailed structure of each of the programs is entirely different and is tailored to the needs of each of the domains. The objectives and structure of the courses are described in the following paragraphs.

The DP Courses

The DP courses are the oldest in the company and were conducted long before people had learned about software engineering. Their structure is therefore different from the more recently developed courses in ECS and CAD/CAM software. The DP training program is currently divided into two parts: a basic programming course (960 hours, 7 months, full-time) and an advanced systems analysis course for the graduates of the basic course (465 hours, 8 months, part-time). Most of the modern software engineering concepts, methods and tools for requirements analysis are taught in the advanced course.

The philosophy behind this separation is well established in the IAI DP community where most of its software engineers are trained first in software programming and testing emphasizing modern structured programming techniques. Following this course they work as programmers for two or three years to become proficient in programming and testing. Only after they have received the necessary programming experience are they sent to the more advanced systems analysis course. Systems analysis, requirements definition, and negotiations with customers are performed by systems analysts, while the junior software engineers are not expected to analyze application problems or to discuss them with customers.

The specific educational objectives of the basic DP programming course are based on this philosophy. It is expected that the graduate of the program will be able to:

1. write structured programs in the IBM assembly language.

2. write structured scientific programs in a higher order language (Fortran).

3. write structured commercial and management programs in a higher order language (COBOL).

4. integrate subprograms written in assembly language and in a higher order languages into a complete program.

5. debug software using available methods and tools.

6. document software according to IAI standards.

The structure of the course is described in Table 1. As can be seen, strong emphasis is placed on IBM tools and languages since most of the IAI DP applications are run on IBM machines. Many hours in this course are also devoted to the study of IBM assembly language. This was regarded as necessary since some of the course graduates are placed in the DP Center's Systems groups. This subject should be eliminated in the future and be given later as an enhancement course only to those needing it. FORTRAN is taught in order to widen the scope of knowledge of the participants and allow them to use it in writing scientific programs when it is demanded by the application or organization.

The complementary course to the DP programming course is the DP system analysis course which, as mentioned, is given to experienced graduates of the basic course. It is expected that the graduates of this course will be able to:

1. Survey and analyze existing DP systems, describe their problems and propose objectives for improved or new systems. The analysis should include functional decomposition of the system and hierarchical decomposition of existing data bases (manual or computerized).

2. Analyze the requirements and prepare the specifications for new or improved software systems, considering the system objectives and constraints, functional decomposition of the new system, hierarchical decomposition of the data bases, and the use of existing and new equipment and software packages.

3. Conduct feasibility studies and evaluate technical and operational alternatives including the evaluation of existing commercial software packages.

4. Design new systems using current software engineering methodologies.

5. Use all the available software development tools (e.g. PSL/PSA) in the various phases of the development lifecycle and document the developed software following IAI standards.

In distinction from the other retraining courses, this course is taught part-time to practicing engineers, 14 hours per week. The duration of the systems analysis course is approximately 8 months (33 weeks).

The structure of the course is given in Table II.

As can be seen from Table II strong emphasis is placed on topics, such as structured analysis (DEMA79) and software design techniques and tools. As a prerequisite to the requirements analysis course the students are given a course on DP in the organization. This course stresses the description of the organizations and their structure, human factors in the organization, and interviewing techniques. A section is devoted to technologies such as data communications and microcomputer usage in DP. Little emphasis is placed on software testing since a good course on this subject has not yet been developed in the company. Such a course will be incorporated in future programs and will also be taught as one of the enhancement courses.

The ECS Course

The first program which was designed to incorporate an overall software engineering approach was the Embedded Computer Systems Software Engineering course. The developers of this course felt that the participants should be exposed, from the beginning of their training, to all the activities performed along the entire software lifecycle. This was based on our experience that these engineers, even the junior ones, are spending a large amount of their time on requirements analysis, testing and integration.

The educational objectives of the ECS course are to provide participants with the basic knowledge required for development and maintenance of an embedded computer system's software component. It is expected that the course graduate will be able to:

1. Analyze the specifications of simple embedded systems and their software components, check for completeness, and enhance the specifications as necessary for software design.

2. Design a simple software module in accordance with modern approaches in software design. The design should meet given specifications and should account for the constraints imposed by the computer hardware and its interfaces. The software design activities included are:

   - explanation of the software system architecture which contains the developed module.

   - design of the software module according to the principles of structured and object oriented design.(MYER78, PARN72, LISK72, BOOC83).

   - description of the design in a program design language.

   - design of the necessary data structures.

   - analysis of hardware-software tradeoffs and their impact on the design of data formats in the hardware interfaces.

3. Write structured programs, read them, and explain them. Writing of software includes:

   - writing of assembly language programs (8085/8086...)

   - writing mathematical and real-time programs for mini and microcomputers in higher order languages (PASCAL, FORTRAN, PL/M).

   - integrating subprograms written in assembly and high-order languages.

   - integrating programs with a real-time operating system (e.g., RMX86).

4. Debug programs and integrate them with the hardware using debugging tools available in the company.

5. Document software according to company standards.

6. Work in software development teams.

7. Understand commercial and engineering literature describing software, computer hardware, and interface equipment.

The structure of the ECS course is presented in Table III.

An early version of the ECS course is described and analyzed in detail elsewhere (BEND84). As can be seen in Table III, strong emphasis is placed on the study of microcomputer architecture, interfacing, and programming. Even though most of the embedded computer programs in the company are still written (due to practical engineering considerations) in Fortran, it was found very beneficial to first teach the students Pascal as an example of a structured language. This actually saved time in introducing good programming techniques. The operating systems courses stress the real-time aspects.

Strong emphasis is placed on software engineering in this program. Systems and software requirements analysis is taught using a methodology developed at IAI (LAVI84), and the object oriented approach is stressed in the software design course. Based on the experience of the first offering of the ECS program, the guided analysis of an existing project was added. It covers all phases of the lifecycle. The guided project is taught before the final student project. More emphasis should be placed on ECS software testing. This will be accomplished in future offerings of this program. It is felt that the methodologies taught in specification analysis and software design are sufficient. However, we have not yet reached the desired methodological consistency between these courses to assure a smooth transition between the specification and design phases.

The CAD/CAM Course

The most recently developed program is for CAD/CAM software engineering (KOIF84).

The basic philosophy and objectives of this course are similar to those of the ECS course. It is expected that its graduates will be able to develop a small complete CAD/CAM program starting with the requirements analysis phase and proceeding through all the development phases up to the final integration and testing, using the large set of CAD tools available within the company.

The structure and content of the program are, however, very different from the ECS program, as can be seen in Tables IV, V and VI. The CAD/CAM program is divided into two main sections: a basic program taken by all the participants (Table IV) and advanced specialization programs. The areas of specialization of the students are determined before the beginning of the course when they are assigned to the various departments in the company. Students who are assigned to CAD specialize in computational geometry and numerical design methods (Table V) while students who are assigned to CAM specialize in the use of computers in manufacturing, numerical controlled machines and robotics (Table VI). Even this division is not sufficient and students who are assigned to Electronics CAD get additional training in that area.

The climax of the CAD/CAM course, as in the other courses, is the final project which is done in groups of 2 to 3. This project is intended to expose students to the development and integration of an entire program. Here they get the opportunity to apply and integrate the various subjects they have studied, from the definition of requirements up to the integration of a complete program.

Short Courses and Seminars

Many software engineers currently working in the company lack knowledge in the newly developing topics in computer science, software engineering, and application areas. Therefore, it was necessary to develop a complete battery of short courses and seminars with an average duration of 50 to 100 hours each. Many of these courses are derivatives of the major retraining courses described in the previous sections. The list of courses includes, for example, subjects such as: microprocessors, requirements analysis, computer graphics, Ada, artificial intelligence, software management and software configuration management. It is impossible to list within this paper all the courses which are given. It is important to stress however, that these short courses and seminars are mostly tailored to unique populations according to the specialization domains of the participants. This is necessary since it is expected that all short courses will include a large amount of exercises and "hands-on" experience. Such exercises have to be tailored around examples with which both the particular groups of students and instructors are familiar.

The M.Sc. Program in Embedded Computer Systems and Software Engineering

As mentioned previously, it is realized that a Bachelors degree augmented by retraining courses and short seminars does not provide a sufficient education in software engineering (BRUC82). The complexity and the size of engineering systems in general, of software systems in particular, and of application domain problems are increasing daily. The company is therefore supporting the participation of many of its employees in graduate studies in the local universities in areas where suitable programs are available. Such graduate programs are not available today in embedded computer systems and software engineering, or in general systems engineering. It was therefore decided to develop M.Sc. programs in these areas hoping that they will later become regular academic programs. The first program being developed is the M.Sc. program in embedded computer systems and software engineering.

Major emphasis in this program will be placed on the analysis and design of multicomputer systems and their software. This is of utmost importance today, as most of the modern embedded systems are designed as multicomputer systems.

The program is intended for practicing software and systems engineers active in the development of embedded computer systems. Some of them will naturally be graduates of our retraining programs. It is expected that graduates of the program will be able to:

1. Identify potential applications of embedded computer systems.

2. Analyze the requirements of complicated multi-computer embedded systems and specify their performance.

3. Specify the computational and communication hardware and their interfaces with the environment.

4. Specify and analyze software requirements.

5. Design hardware systems and associated software.

6. Verify and validate the designs.

7. Integrate and test the systems.

8. Manage the development of complicated embedded computer systems projects.

It is expected that the basic required course in the program will be:

1. Architecture of modern computational systems (including multicomputer systems, parallel computers and computer communications).

2. Formal methods in the analysis of general systems, computerized systems, and their software.

3. Modern programming methods.

4. Analysis of embedded systems.

5. Software engineering.

6. Management of embedded computer system projects.

7. Analysis (not design) of linear, stochastic and sampled data control systems.

8. Discrete and continuous simulation and rapid prototyping.

Additional elective courses are recommended. The following are suggested:

1. Introduction to Artificial Intelligence.

2. Expert systems.

3. Introduction to VSLI design.

4. Design of man-machine systems.

5. Real-time operating systems.

6. Data bases for real time systems.

7. Communication networks

8. Operations Research.

The total number of courses to be taken will be based on the academic requirements of the university that offers the program.

The basic structure of the program is based on the MSE program of the School of Information Technology of The Wang Institute of Graduate Studies (FAIR85). However, it is augmented to include general systems issues, embedded computer systems issues and multicomputer system analysis and design.

THE STUDENTS

This section briefly describes the methods used to recruit students for the three major full-time retraining programs. Two patterns of student-recruiting are used. For most of the courses students are recruited from outside the company through ads in the newspapers, while for one course students were recruited internally. The experiment to recruit employees internally was a failure, since managers tried to retain the most qualified engineers and were reluctant to send them to a six months full-time retraining course and possible transfer to other departments. Therefore, it was decided that in the future students for all retraining courses will be recruited from the outside. Some exception will be made to this ruling.

The students recruited for the retraining courses are required to sign up for 5-years with the company after the completion of the course. The graduates thus guarantee that they are going to stay with the company and that they will not search for employment with other competing firms after completing the courses.

As mentioned earlier, all the students are university graduates. Originally, it was preferred to hire students with no previous computing experience since it was found to be difficult to change their programming habits and teach them the development of programs according to modern software engineering techniques. This rule was relaxed prior to the most recent offering of the courses when the company recruited students with previous programming knowledge, including computer science graduates, and retrained them to become software engineers in the various application domains.

The selection of students for each of the courses is a very complicated process. Normally, around 800 candidates responded to the IAI ads in the newspapers. The first selection is made using their curriculum vitae and their application letters.

Those candidates who are regarded as potential candidates for the course are invited for basic written aptitude tests. Those who pass these tests are invited to oral and written psychometric tests. Special batteries of test were developed by the corporate testing department. These test are designed to evaluate both their personality and their cognitive qualities. Special emphasis is placed on detecting the ability of the candidates to work in teams and their potential ability to advance and become group leaders. These tests also predict very successfully the ability of the candidates to pass the courses and their ability to be absorbed successfully in the departments within the company. These tests are not regarded to be sufficient, however, and each of the successful applicants is invited for an additional personal interview with a committee whose members are the course manager, a representative of the DP, ECS or CAD/CAM group (depending on the type of course), the corporate manpower department, and an industrial psychologist.

Many issues associated with the type of students and their adaptation to the intensive course program are described in a previous paper by the authors (BEND84). It would be of interest to perform a more detailed statistical analysis of the patterns of absorption of the graduates within the corporation, but such a study has not as yet been conducted.

THE IAI TRAINING STAFF

Most of the programs are tailored according to the industrial needs of the corporation in the development of qualified engineers for particular application domains. Development of the courses requires staff experienced in software engineering and in the various application domains. Many of the necessary subjects are not taught in the universities around IAI, and some of the subjects are based on the advanced methodologies and tools developed within IAI. Little assistance can be obtained currently from the neighboring university staff and other institutions for the retraining programs. Furthermore, it is expected that all instructors practice software engineering while teaching, in order to assure continuous updating of their knowledge and experience. Some of the instructors are IAI engineers who develop and practice the new methodologies, and who are interested in teaching and are willing to spend the necessary additional time beyond their regular activities and responsibilities. Other instructors are employed directly, full-time, by the IAI Training Center. It is expected that they will work part time in various IAI software engineering departments developing software for real projects. Thus they gain and maintain the necessary experience and also have the opportunity to introduce new technologies and try them out in the field. Unfortunately, there are some difficulties in finding suitable projects for the training staff.

Development of new training programs, updating the old ones, and updating of the training staff also requires continuous cooperation and assistance of the corporate R&D department, the corporate CAD/CAM project and the corporate DP center. This continuous cooperation provides the major stimuli for evaluation of the programs and of the training center's staff.

A major objective of the training center is to improve the image of its staff, to upgrade the level of its instructors and to build up their reputation. It is therefore planned that the instructors will not only work on projects but that they will consult with various corporate departments. This job enrichment of the instructors is needed to attract more qualified and ambitious staff, since the major difficulty in further development of the courses is the lack of sufficient qualified instructors in the training center.

It is expected that it will be easier to recruit necessary university staff for the new M.Sc. program as many of the courses are by now established academic courses. However, it is expected that it will be difficult to recruit university staff for the development of the new courses in embedded computer systems engineering which are not given currently in any of the universities and which will have to be developed especially for this new program.

IAI COMPUTER TRAINING LABORATORIES

Basic Needs

A basic requirement of the training programs is that the students obtain sufficient "hands-on" experience in the training center laboratories during the courses. These laboratories have to serve the needs of the three major retraining programs (DP, ECS, CAD/CAM). Further, they also have to serve all of the short enrichment courses and seminars (such as programming courses, microcomputer courses, operating system courses, requirements analysis courses, computer graphics and the use of CAD/CAM tools and programs).

Each of the laboratories has to provide services for a regular size class, normally between 20 to 24 participants. To obtain optimal results the students are divided into groups of two; thus, each laboratory has to have at least twelve identical workstations. These workstations should be compatible or identical, if possible, to the stations which the students are going to use after the completion of the courses, thus reducing the time they need after graduation to adapt to the corporate working environment.

Different software development domains in the company use different computers. Data processing activities are mainly based on IBM equipment. CDC and VAX machines and special graphic terminals are used in CAD/CAM activities. Embedded systems were formally developed around a military version of the Data General Eclipse computers and currently around INTEL microprocessors, MIL-STD 1750A based computers, and VAX machines. It is desired that the students become familiar with the host and target computers used in their application domains, and therefore the respective training laboratories must be built around the described equipment.

The Development of the Laboratories

The first data processing courses, which are the oldest in the company, were conducted at the facilities of an outside contractor and no special laboratories were built for them in the company. Only towards the end of the 70's, when the embedded computer courses were developed did the company realize the need for educational computer laboratories. The first ECS laboratory facilities were very modest. They consisted of a microcomputer laboratory based on twelve INTEL-SDK-like microprocessors, and eleven terminals were connected to a very small Data General Eclipse computer (128K memory, two small disks, five Mbyte each and some backup equipment). This lab was run experimentally during the debugging phase of the basic course modules. Naturally it was found that the equipment was not sufficient for this type of course. Furthermore, using this laboratory configuration, software developed for the INTEL microprocessors had to be loaded into the workstation (SDK) in machine language. As a result of this experience, the computer configuration was increased, and advanced operating system was installed and tape drives were added. Also a direct connection was established between the microprocessor working stations and the microcomputer laboratory which allowed the use of a cross assembler hosted on the Data General equipment and down-loading the code directly to the microprocessor workstation. This configuration was used during the first embedded computer software engineering course.

In spite of the expansion of the laboratory, it was discovered during the course that the facilities were not adequate and that the response time was too slow. Also, it was impossible to run real-time operating systems experiments using this configuration because during such experiments the computer could be assigned, at most, only to two pairs of students; one using it in foreground mode and the second in background mode. Thus, it was necessary to schedule the students to run the operating system experiments till 12 o'clock at night. In spite of these difficulties, the course was completed successfully and the company realized the need and importance of expanded educational laboratories. At that time, it was also decided to run the data processing courses within the IAI training center and to improve the microprocessor laboratories. As a result, the DG Eclipse computer was once more expanded, and a data processing laboratory and a microprocessor emulation station were added.

This configuration supported most of the activities until it was decided to develop the CAD/CAM course. At that time it was decided to enhance the laboratories. An additional budget of $850,000 was approved. The current configuration of the laboratories is:

1. A computing center built around a enhanced VAX-11/780 computer including hardware floating point accelerator, 8 Mbytes of memory, 3 fast disc drives with one half Gbytes total storage, two unibusses for improved I/O and a 285 LPM line printer. The computing center also includes the old DG Eclipse computer.

2. A software development laboratory including 12 VT-131 terminals and a line printer.

3. A DP laboratory with 12 terminals connected to the old DG Eclipse computer emulating IBM equipment standards with a RSX-70 emulation program and connected to the corporate IBM main frame.

4. A Graphics Laboratory including 12 high resolution 19" black and white graphic terminals and a high resolution black and white plotter.

5. A microcomputer development laboratory including 3 INTEL MDS series IV workstations, one INTEL MDS series III, 8 VT-220 terminals connected to it through 8 ISIS cluster boards in a Ethernet network manager by an Intel network manager, with common resources of an 84 Mbyte disc drive and a stream tape-cassette. This lab allows the concurrent work of 12 teams as long as no hardware is needed. For hardware emulation only 3 teams can work concurrently on the MDS series IV stations connected to three I ^{2} ICE 86, one I ^{2} ICE 286 and two ICE 51.

6. A real-time laboratory including 4 Intel System-310 built around an iAPX-286 processor and running under the Intel RMX 86 real-time operating system. These systems can be used as host multiuser development stations as well as dedicated target systems.

7. Five courseware development stations in the rooms of the instructors.

This configuration still does not provide the necessary computing power, connectivity, and efficiency. An upgrade of computing power will be achieved soon by the addition of a MicroVaxII and two Data General MV-2000 computers.

LESSONS LEARNED AND RECOMMENDATIONS

A comprehensive corporate software engineering program was presented in this paper. Many lessons have been learned and many conclusions have been reached during the development and running of this ambitious program.

1. The program provides an excellent solution to some of the software engineering personnel needs of the corporation. The graduates have been well absorbed and they develop software in various corporate plants and departments. However, the program has not solved the shortage of manpower with 5 to 7 years experience, which is lacking everywhere.

2. The training of engineers who can develop software efficiently and effectively requires the development of unique programs in each application domain: DP, ECS and CAD/CAM. Sometimes it is even necessary to develop subprograms dedicated to particular specializations within these domains.

3. Improving the effectiveness and productivity of software engineers requires that they specialize in particular application areas and that they not be transferred from one domain to another.

4. In spite of the similar objectives of the various programs and the similarity between some of the subjects taught in all of them, it was found necessary to redevelop these subjects for each application domain. Only very few subjects can be developed and taught without modifications in all courses. These subjects include for example programming languages, data structures, data bases and operating systems.

5. The success of the training program and related seminars depends strongly on:

a. Continuous cooperation between the staff of the training center and the staff of R&D groups responsible for the development of corporate methodologies and tools.

b. Detailed specification of course objectives and thorough preparation of educational material for each of the subjects taught in the courses.

c. Continuous updating of the courses based on lessons learned and technological advancements.

d. The development of dedicated instructors who are up-to-date and experienced in the use of modern software engineering tools and techniques.

e. The careful selection of students through a very elaborate screening process.

f. The availability of elaborate educational computer laboratories equipped with machines, workstations and tools similar to those used throughout the corporation.

The success of the training center in introducing modern software engineering techniques requires not only the training of engineers but also requires a very large promotional and educational effort to overcome the natural resistance of the old-timers to the modern methodologies and tools. Some of this resistance is overcome by the participation of representatives of leading development groups in the steering committees developing the courses.

The software engineering training program presented in this paper is among the largest of such programs run in industrial corporations. Naturally, the program does not meet all the expectations of the people who are developing and running it. The success of the program has however proven the basic assumptions made prior to its initiation. It is the current objective of all those responsible for the program to evaluate once more the structure and content of the programs, to develop more basic modules that can be taught in all application domains, and to assure that modern software engineering principles are used and taught in each of the subjects within the entire program.

REFERENCES

BEND84 Ben David, A., et al, "An Industrial Software Engineering Retraining Course", IEEE TSE Vol-10, No. 6. November 1984.

BOOC83 Booch, G, "Object Oriented Design", in Tutorial on Software Design Techniques by Freeman & Wasserman, IEEE Computer Society 1983.

BRUC82 Bruce, J.D., et al, "Lifelong Corporate Education", Massachusetts Institute of Technology, October 1982.

DEMA79 Demarco, J., "Structured Analysis and Systems Specifications", Prentice Hall, 1979.

FAIR85 Fairley, R., "Core Course Documentation, Masters Degree Program in Software Engineering", School of Information Technology, Wang Institute of Graduate Studies, Tyngsboro, Ma., 1985.

KEDE85 Kedem, A., Smilansky, J., "An Alternative to ISD in the Development of Training Packages for the Lavi Fighter Aircraft", Proceedings of the 7th Interservice/Industry Training Equipment Conference, November 1985.

KOIF84 Koifman, J., Katz, E., "CAD/CAM Engineering Course, Summary and Conclusions", The Proceedings of SIXTH Conference of the Israel Society For CAD/CAM (ITIM), November 1984.

LAVI84 Lavi (Loeb), J.Z., "A Systems Engineering Approach to Software Engineering", Proceedings of the Software Process Workshop, Egham, U.K., IEEE Computer Society, February 1984.

LISK72 Liskov, B.H., "A Design Methodology for Reliable Software Systems", Proceedings, Fall Joint Computer Conference, AFIPS, 1972 p.67.

MCGI84 McGill, J.P., "The Software Engineering Shortage: A Third Choice", IEEE TSE Vol. 10, No. 1, January 1984.

MYER78 Myers, G.J., "Composite/Structured Design", Van Nostrand Reinhold Co. New York, N.Y., 1978.

PARN72 Parnas, D.L., "On the Criteria to be Used in Decomposing Systems into Modules", Communications of the ACM, December 1972.

SIMP82 Simpson, C.L., Bettinger, C.O., "Are Computer Science Degrees Necessary in Business DP?", Journal of Systems Management, April 1982, pp 29-33.

SPEN84 Spencer, D.E., "A Proposed Curriculum for Aerospace Programmers", Communications of the ACM, Vol. 27, No. 4, April 1984, p. 283.

WARN82 Warner, W.P., Nance, R.E., "The Development of Software Engineers: A View from the User", National Computer Conference, 1982 pp 293-299.

TABLE I - THE DP BASIC SOFTWARE ENGINEERING COURSE STRUCTURE

Subject	Hours
GENERAL - 30 hours	
Enrichment Lectures	30
COMPUTER HARDWARE & INTERFACING - 65 hours	
Digital Circuits and Logic	25
Introduction to Computers	40
COMPUTER LANGUAGES & OPERATING SYSTEMS - 550 hours	
IBM Assembly Languages	150
FORTRAN	70
COBOL	230
File Organization	40
Introduction to Operating Systems, Data Bases and Communications	30
IBM JCL	30
ADVANCED TOOLS AND DATA BASES - 175 hours	
Programming IBM Data Bases	35
Screens (MFS-Message Format Services)	20
Report Generators	40
Application Generators	40
Debugging Tools	20
Use of existing software packages	20
SOFTWARE ENGINEERING - 60 hours	
Introduction to Software Engineering	60
PROJECTS	80
Total course hours	960
Course weeks (7 hours per day)	137

TABLE II - DP SYSTEMS ANALYSIS COURSE
COURSE STRUCTURE

SUBJECT	Hours
DP IN THE ORGANIZATION	40
DP TECHNOLOGIES - 95 hours	
Data Communications	35
Data Bases	30
Microcomputer Applications in DP	15
Application Generators	15
SOFTWARE ENGINEERING - 145 hours	
DP Requirements Analysis Methods and Tools	95
Software Design Methods and Tools	25
Management Techniques & Tools	25
ENRICHMENT LECTURES	15
FINAL PROJECT	170
Total Course Hours	465
Course Weeks (14 hours per week)	33

TABLE III - EMBEDDED COMPUTER SYSTEMS SOFTWARE
ENGINEERING COURSE
COURSE STRUCTURE

Subject	Hours
GENERAL - 60 Hours	
Typing + Edit	25
Introduction and Enrichment Lectures	35
COMPUTER HARDWARE AND INTERFACING - 250 hours	
Digital Electronic Circuits and Logic	45
Introduction to Micro-computers	45

TABLE III (continued)

Introduction to Micro-computers Interfacing	50
Data Communication	50
Introduction to the Intel iAPX86 components family	60
HIGHER ORDER LANGUAGES & OPERATING SYSTEMS - 285 HOURS	
PASCAL (as a structured language)	55
FORTRAN	65
Introduction to PL/M	25
Data Structures	50
Operating Systems and RMX86	90
SOFTWARE ENGINEERING - 165 hours	
Requirements Analysis	90
Software Design	50
Software Testing and Quality Assurance	25
PROJECTS - 240 hours	
Assembly Language Project	40
Guided Analysis of an Existing Project	50
Final Project	150
Total course hours	1000
Course days (7 hours per day)	142

TABLE IV - CAD/CAM SOFTWARE ENGINEERING COURSE - DETAILED STRUCTURE OF BASIC PROGRAM

Subject	Hours
GENERAL - 50 HOURS	
Typing	12
Enrichment Lectures	38
COMPUTER HARDWARE & INTERFACING - 165 Hours	
Digital Circuits & Logic	40

TABLE IV (continued)

Introduction to Computers (VAX & CDC)	50
Introduction to Microprocessors	35
Graphic Hardware	25
Computer Communications	15
COMPUTER LANGUAGES, OPERATING SYSTEMS & DATA BASES - 300 hours	
FORTRAN 77	75
Data Structures & File Management	70
Introduction to Operating systems	25
Introduction to Data Bases in CAD/CAM	130
SOFTWARE ENGINEERING & SOFTWARE TOOLS - 70 hours	
Introduction to Software Engineering	35
Designing CAD Programs	35
INTRODUCTION TO CAD/CAM - 190 hours	
Introduction to CAD/CAM & its IAI Application	65
Development of Graphic Programs	70
Man-Machine-Interface Techniques and Algorithms	55
FINAL PROJECT	135
Total Basic Program Course Hours	910
Course days (7 hours per day)	130

TABLE V - CAD/CAM SOFTWARE ENGINEERING COURSE
SUPPLEMENTARY SPECIALIZATION IN CAD

Subject	Hours
Basic Computational Geometry	70
Computational Geometry Workshop	30
Numerical Design Methods	20
Total hours	120

TABLE VI - CAD/CAM SOFTWARE ENGINEERING COURSE, SUPPLEMENTARY SPECIALIZATION IN CAM

Subject	Hours
Computers in Manufacturing	25
Numerical Controlled Machines and Post Processors	85
Industrial Robotics	45
Group Technology	15
Data Transfer Techniques (Design to Manufacturing)	20
Total hours	190

TABLE VII - NUMBER OF PARTICIPANTS IN THE RETRAINING COURSES

Year	Data Processing	DP System Analysis	Embedded Computer System S/W Eng.	CAD/CAM S/W Eng.
1975	16	-	-	-
1976	15	-	-	-
1977	18	-	-	-
1978	18	-	-	-
1979	17	-	-	-
1980	18	-	-	-
1981	17	-	19	-
1982	18	-	-	24
1983	20	-	22	-
1984	21	22	-	25
1985	19	26	23	-

SOFTWARE ENGINEERING: INDUSTRY MEETS ACADEMIA

R. A. Radice and R. W. Phillips

Rensselaer Polytechnic Institute and
International Business Machines Corporation

ABSTRACT

Software Engineering education stands at a turning point as industry continues to assert the need for more of an industry perspective in the education of software engineers and computer scientists. A two-semester course sequence in Software Engineering, taught at Rensselaer Polytechnic Institute is attempting to meet that demand by balancing theory and practice in an education environment which simulates industrial development of Software Engineering tools. Prevalent methodologies across the software life cycle are addressed, alternatives are assessed, and preferences are designated as the courses progress through the life cycle. The projects are assigned to teams and are directly related to automating parts of software production. Case studies are used on a weekly basis to reinforce concepts and to explore alternatives. An essential set of software engineering process principles serves as the foundation for this teaching approach. The students, while taxed with a demanding work load, have indicated that the approach is highly rewarding in the graduate education program.

I. INTRODUCTION

When we began to teach Software Engineering at Rensselaer Polytechnic Institute (RPI) we set three goals for ourselves. First, that the course would honestly model the life cycle of program production from an industrial perspective. Second, the courses as structured and taught would be significantly different from the typical approach to teaching software engineering. This was not to suggest that we believed we were the only ones to have thought of or to have used the approach which we shall shortly define, but we certainly were not aware when we started of anyone using the same approach. Later, we learned of Berzins, Gray, and Naumann at the University of Minnesota who have a similar, though different, approach [1]. Finally, perhaps in our naivete, we wanted our two semester course to become a model in academia and industry. This latter could only be accomplished if we maintained a steady stream of feedback from the students, RPI, and ourselves. For the latter we fortunately had the advantage of observing each other for many of the lectures, case studies, and class discussions.

It is now three years since we started, and in keeping with our goals of developing a model approach to teaching Software Engineering and of maintaining feedback, it is appropriate to now document our experiences in order to communicate with a larger audience of Software Engineering educators.

We hope and anticipate that readers of this article will provide comments, both pro and con, to us, for ultimately we do want the best course for our students.

Briefly, our combined backgrounds cover over 55 years in the software industry. Although specifically this is with IBM, we have over the last ten years been involved with assessment of the state of Software Engineering throughout the worldwide industry. While our backgrounds are with IBM, our opinions as stated in this paper are our own and do not necessarily represent those of IBM.

II. HOW THIS COURSE CAME TO BE

In November 1983, Ron Radice was contacted by Herb Freeman, then of RPI, now chairing the Computer Science Department at Rutgers, asking if he would consider teaching as adjunct associate professor for RPI's two semester graduate course in Software Engineering. As with many opportunities which present themselves, this one came at a time when a commitment to be available every week for fifteen weeks each semester simply was not possible because of business needs to travel, but the offer was of much interest. After resolving with RPI that the problem of being available every week could be addressed with two adjuncts teaching the courses, the only question remaining was who would be interested and could do an excellent job of rounding out the courses. Dick Phillips was the obvious answer for many reasons. And so in partnership we committed to ourselves and to RPI that we would be available to teach the two semester course sequence in Software Engineering.

We added a constraint of teaching on Monday nights only, to allow us added flexibility for business travel during the week which was a frequent necessity. Teaching on one night of each week meant that we would be engaged with the students for three hours of class. This in itself was taxing to both us and the students initially, but over time seems to have worked quite successfully and indeed offers advantages to the students as well.

We started teaching with the second of the two-semester sequence. Our plans were to have the first semester begin with the initial stage of the software life cycle, to complete a "first release" of a project by the end of the semester, to test and enhance the project by the end of the second semester using a different team of students than those who had developed the initial project in semester one. Since all this was not achievable, we taught the full life cycle of software engineering alternatives in methodologies from Requirements through Systems Test. We succeeded on many counts, but we probably subjected our students to an exceedingly time consuming and demanding semester. Their input and feedback was fully integrated into our next version of the courses and helped us to create a better course sequence.

In September 1984, we began the first two-semester sequence. In a number of ways our approach was still too demanding for the students and, as it turned out, for us also. Semester One had 57 students enrolled. We were both excited by the turnout and concerned when we realized we could not get to know all of these students as well as we would like. We were well aware that the intensity of the course as we would teach it demanded that we establish a good relationship with each team and each student. Due to the large class we succeeded with some, but failed with others. This was our disappointment, and we resolved to limit the class to no more than thirty students in the future. We were still working out some details in style and approach during these two semesters of Fall 1984 /Spring 1985, all of which were integrated into the Fall 1985/Spring 1986 sequence. If subsequent student feedback is to be a judge, we indeed corrected many of our initial problems, and the Fall 1985/Spring 1986 sequence was more of a success than the previous sequence.

As our goal is to continue to evolve the course through feedback, and early indications are that Fall 1986/Spring 1987 will be yet a better sequence for our students.

III. COURSE OBJECTIVES

First, we intend that the students leave the course with an understanding of the prevalent Software Engineering methodologies which exist across the development life cycle. While we do not intend that this be a survey course, we do present alternatives to each methodology. In all cases we made strong recommendations for preferred alternatives that are at the leading edge in industry today and which show evidence of having significant positive impact on quality, productivity or schedules.

Second, we intend to prepare the students for industry or at a minimum give the students a practical view of what industry is doing and what is expected of computer science/software engineering graduates who enter industry. This does not imply that we are trying to fully address the issue of professionalism, but we do agree that some changes need to be made to the predominant approach to preparing students entering the software industry, and we believe we have a role in that re-direction. This issue was hit on rather smartly in a quote from James Martin in Curt Hartog's article *Of Commerce and Academia*. Martin said,

> I think many of the top people in computing at the present time are extremely dismayed by what's happening in the computer science schools. I was at an important facility of one of the world's largest computer manufacturers recently, and the general manager of that facility commented that he would, literally, never hire a computer science graduate, that's an indication of the extent to which the computer science departments are perceived to be out of date [2].

In striving toward this objective, we have not dwelt heavily, and certainly not exclusively, on the theory behind the Software Engineering methodologies; rather we have sought a tuned balance between theory and practice, where practice takes the focus.

Third, we intend that the student after leaving our courses remember the principles of Software Engineering process and that these principles are carried on into the work and careers of each student whether in industry or academia. This objective requires that we give clear focus during the two semesters to process and process control in software as it exists today and the direction it is taking in industry. It is intended that the student will leave with an understanding of how projects and products can be controlled through process to achieve higher quality, higher productivity, and improved schedules. We will talk more on these principles in the next section.

Fourth, we intend that the student get a full life cycle view of software production. This life cycle view is based on the ETVX model of process definition [3]. The life cycle not only runs from the Requirements Stage through ship to the customer, but includes a maintenance and enhancement release. As a result of the ETVX paradigm emphasis, we take time in each process stage to focus on and ensure the use of validation methods relevant to each task during the life cycle.

Fifth, we want the student to learn to continuously re-evaluate software projects in terms of both Software Engineering and software economics. We get the students to struggle with the practicality of building a zero defect product and the cost trade-offs for doing so.

Sixth, we want the students to individually learn how to think through a software problem and to know how to assess assumptions, alternatives and trade-offs in the problem.

Seventh, we want the student to learn why data is essential to improving the state of Software Engineering. We focus on data from a three tiered perspective of maturation along the Software Engineering evolution path: Data gathering is the first step, which can then lead to good data analysis, which in turn can lead to good goal setting to manage quality, productivity and schedules.

Eighth, we intend that the student's input and feedback provide for a better course for those after them.

Ninth, we want the students to become excited about the potentials through Software Engineering and software process. We even hope that the student will have fun during these two semesters.

Tenth, we have intended that our teaching methods be fully integrated towards supporting the previous nine objectives. In our approach, we require that the class be broken up into teams, which will be assigned a project which is related to automating software engineering practices, tasks, and methodologies. We require the students to keep a project workbook, which reflects the full life cycle work and evolution of their project. We support the evolution of the project with case studies, which are intended to focus the student on particular problems in Software Engineering. The class functions as a hypothetical software corporate body named the RADLIPS Corporation, which is our way of setting the stage for management/employee dialogues throughout the project life.

IV. SOFTWARE ENGINEERING PROCESS PRINCIPLES

We believe that if Software Engineering is to advance rapidly as a discipline it requires a set of principles to guide the direction of the profession. We believe that these principles which are drawn from our work at IBM include the following: [3], [4]

1. The process of software production must be formally defined.
2. The process must be actively, continually, and consistently managed to achieve consistently improving quality and increasing productivity.
3. The process must be decomposed into stages. Each stage must be decomposed into tasks, each of which has an entry criteria, validation mechanism, and exit criteria.
4. Each work item exiting from a task must be validated before proceeding into another task as input.
5. Data capture, analysis, which includes feedback, and goal setting are essential for improving both the product and the process. Periodic process assessments must be planned and executed to monitor effectiveness.
6. Procedures must be established to certify product quality and implement any necessary corrective actions as they may be needed.
7. Problems with the product or process must be recorded and analyzed for cause, effect, and improvement. This is to be done both from a statistical assessment and from a defect extinction perspective [5].
8. Changes to the product or process must be controlled. They must be recorded, tracked and evaluated for effectiveness.
9. The software production process must be concerned with not only the development perspective, but must include the perspectives of testing, publications and related material, build and integration, marketing and service, and process management. The overall product is composed of all these perspectives.

In net, these principles support our belief that a quality process is a necessary ingredient to achieve a quality product.

V. STUDENT BACKGROUNDS

RPI has both an **Electrical, Computer, and Systems Engineering Department** and a **Computer Science Department** offering courses related to software. Students in our course are pursuing degrees in Computer Engineering and Science through both departments in about equal numbers.

The following is a profile of the students that have enrolled in this course.

Statistics

- Approximately sixty-five percent of those taking the course are engaged in Masters programs; about 30 percent are pursuing the Doctorate degree, and about five percent have been undergraduates with sufficient experience and skill to be admitted to the course.
- About 20 percent of the students that have taken this course are women.
- About one-third to one-half of all students that have taken the course are citizens of Asian, Middle Eastern, or Latin American countries.
- About one-third are currently employed as programmers and analysts in industry, government or the military.

Skills And Experience Levels

During the first session of the semester, a questionnaire is completed by the students to survey individual background, experiences, skills, interests, and goals in taking the course.

- Of the one third employed, most commute to the campus from their regular work locations at least twice weekly for this course. (One evening for the weekly lecture session and at least one evening or weekend trip for a team meeting, or to work on campus with various computing facilities).
- All have had experience in coding a program, either through prior academic studies or in a work environment.

- Most are familiar with step-wise refinement principles, but few are familiar with structured programming constructs at a working level.
- A few, (less than half), have had experience designing a program from a given set of high level specifications.
- A handful (about 20 percent) have used specific design notations, such as pseudocode.
- Almost none are familiar with data abstraction as a fundamental design methodology.
- Almost none have had experience in defining program user requirements or in project planning.
- None are familiar with formatted high level requirements and specification languages or techniques, such as PSL/PSA, SADT, SREM.

Selection Criteria

The course, in its current state of evolution, has a limited enrollment of 30 students per semester, and therefore the students are screened based on need to take the course and suitable academic background. Students wanting the course to only gain an introduction to the subject of Software Engineering are advised not to take this course, but to seek a survey type course in the subject instead. This leaves those who have already begun channeling their studies and careers toward software engineering or computer science, and who seriously want to become practitioners in the software development process. Within this set of students, further screening is done on the basis of the need for the two-semester sequence as a specific requirement for a student's particular degree program.

VI. COURSE MODULES AND TOPICS

The course is conducted in two 15-week semesters, each having a unique scope and emphasis. Lectures are conducted once a week for three hours each. A large-scale software development environment is simulated by means of team projects and case studies. The two semesters constitute a sequence, and completion of the first semester, or its equivalent, is prerequisite to taking the second.

First Semester

In terms of the software life cycle model previously described, the first semester encompasses the stages defined for Requirements, Design, Coding, and Unit Testing.

Emphasis during this semester is on techniques and disciplines for defining a product technical strategy, collecting and prioritizing user requirements, validating the requirements against prospective users, writing program specifications, dividing a large-scale development project into workable subparts, transforming the requirements to high-level design specifications, subsequently to low-level design and finally to code.

Some of the theory, techniques and disciplines taught during this semester include use of a formatted entity-relation language for defining requirements and high-level specifications, validation of requirements through user reviews, use of various design notations such as pseudocode, use of rigorous Inspection techniques for validating design against requirements and code against design.

Some of the topics for the first semester are:

- Software Engineering History And Outlook
- Introduction To The Software Development Process
- Requirements Engineering Methodology
- On Formalism In Specifications
- An ER-based Model For Requirements And High Level Specifications
- Planning The Project
- Team Dynamics

- Project Notebook Purpose And Structure
- Design Overview
- Bridging Requirements To Design
- Design Methodologies
- Software Human Factors
- User Documentation
- Design And Code Inspection Methodology
- Use Of Structured Programming Constructs
- Introduction To Unit Testing

Second Semester

The second semester encompasses all formal test stages, shipment to users for operation, and servicing of the product in use.

In addition to testing methodologies, the second semester emphasizes 1) many of the control and management aspects of the development and software service process, 2) the causes and prevention of problems associated with inheriting "old code" from prior developers (simulated in the classroom by inheriting the project developed by other teams during the prior semester), 3) the collection, analysis and feedback of data to manage and improve the process, 4) factors thought to affect the users' perception of product quality, 5) a set of criteria for evaluating the effectiveness of a software development process, and 6) finally, a technique for applying this set of criteria to a given process (their own) and making improvements.

Some of the topics for the second semester are:

- Evaluating Inherited Program Materials
- Causes And Prevention Of "Old Code" Problems
- Software Re-usability And Re-use
- Software Metrics

- Program Estimating
- Error Cause Analysis
- Overview Of Testing Process
- Test Planning
- Unit Test Methods
- Function Test Methods
- System Test Methods
- Configuration Management
- Software Packaging And Distribution
- Managing The Process And People
- Legal And Business Aspects Of Programming
- Some Factors Affecting User Perceived Quality
- Typical Process Problems And Solutions
- A Programming Process Evaluation Technique
- Improving A Development Process

VI. COURSE PROJECTS

The course centers around a set of development projects, each performed by a small team of students. Each project forms component of an integrated system of Software Engineering tools. During the course, each team will:

- Define the requirements for its component and how it fits into the whole product system
- Validate the requirements defined against prospective users (the rest of the class and the professors)
- Design the component
- Validate the design against the defined requirements
- Write a Users' Guide
- Implement the component
- Validate the implementation against the design and human factors
- Write a test plan

- Validate the test plan
- Write the test cases and test scenarios
- Validate the test cases and test scenarios
- Write a Service Manual
- Formally test the component
- Ship the completed component to users (the rest of the class)
- Service the component

The Target Product

The target product is a "Software Developer's Environment," comprised of an integrated set of tools that support software development tasks throughout the entire development life cycle.

The important reason for choosing a Software Developer's Environment as the target product and not some other equally challenging type of software product is that to adequately define the requirements and high level design for such an offering, the students must define how to automate the very Software Engineering process being taught in the course. This sort of "recursive learning" frequently surfaces some interesting Software Engineering issues and questions on the part of the students. For example, to decide on how permissive or aggressive a particular design tool should be in enforcing agreed to local design conventions or practices, the student must address the issue of freedom to innovate versus regimentation in the prospective user's design environment.

Available Projects

The class is divided into teams discussed in the next section. Each team develops a separate component of the Software Developer's Environment.

Over the past three years, ten or more projects have evolved from which the students can choose. Tested and documented program packages also exist for many of the projects from past classes, to be picked up and enhanced with new function by teams in the incoming class.

The assortment of projects from which to currently choose is:

- Formatted Language Analyzer for requirements and high-level design specifications.
- Specification Language-To-Design Language Translator
- Graphic Design Environment
- Static Design Analyzer
- Automatic Code Generator
- Code and Module Design Complexity Analyzer
- Code Inspection Verifier
- Test Case Generator
- Old-Code Restructuring Tool
- Code Reverse-Engineering Tool
- Process Metrics And Management System

Initial Requirements Input

During the first session of the first semester, the students are given a brief discussion of the market needs for a "Software Developers Environment" and a description of the above possible component parts. They are then formed into initial teams and asked to report back to the class in about thirty minutes with answers to two questions:

1. Which of the above components would the team prefer to develop during the semester and why?
2. What types of additional questions will have to be answered to complete the definition of requirements for the chosen component?

Team questions and concerns with project requirements are then discussed in class, using responses to questions to help bound and keep the requirements definitions on track. Few direct answers are volunteered, however. Instead, most questions are redirected into class discussions of the issues that would be involved, and the assumptions that might have to be made about user needs for the proposed Software Developers Environment, such that satisfactory statements of the requirements could be derived. The student teams are charged with continuing the exercise outside of class, and to return for the next session with a set of answers to their initial set of questions, a list of supporting assumptions, and a list of further questions that in turn must be answered to proceed further with the requirements definition process.

This approach marks a significant departure from the initial expectations of most students. In prior classes, or work environments to this point in their careers, assignments have been considerably more defined and bounded. The apparent purpose for the approach is to get the student involved at the outset in a "life-like" requirements definition process. However, from the educator's standpoint, the more important benefit is that it forces the student to begin formulating some key working concepts about the Software Engineering process itself, which is the very process being taught in this course. This "recursive" theme is maintained throughout the course by means of case studies and other project work designed to challenge the students' thought process.

An observation frequently reported by the students at the end of the course is that the approach forced them to think for themselves, as well as solve problems as teams, more than any other course or work experience in the past.

VII. PROJECT TEAMS

Teams of three to five individuals are about the optimum size for this particular course. Many students commute a considerable distance from their place of regular employment to the university campus, and since the course relies heavily on outside work on a team basis, students that have proximity to each other in their work locations are, if possible, placed on the same team.

An attempt is also made within these constraints, to distribute individuals with prior project experience equitably among the teams.

Organization

Rather than preassign contrived organization and individual roles within each team, we believe it is a more effective and true-to-life if the roles are allowed to evolve naturally, in response to the team tasks at hand and individual skills and interests. As in most well run, professional organizations, this form of natural selection tends to build teamwork and capitalize on particular strengths of each individual.

Dynamics

About midway through a semester, problems begin to surface in some of the teams regarding individual roles and team work. For example, a team member may lack experience in presenting and "selling" ideas to the group, and upon failure to obtain instant acceptance of an idea may withdraw and start a redundant splinter activity to "show" the group that the idea is better than the current approach. Some individuals over-commit to the team and never seem to complete agreed-to tasks on time, while others seem able to handle all agreed to tasks and more. Some individuals are more comfortable at coding than designing, or at planning the project than executing it, or at testing and debugging than at specifying a test plan, and so on. When we recognize the need to discuss team problems during the semester, a lecture is inserted on "Team Dynamics." Questions are discussed in class about how individual strengths can be capitalized on for the growth of the individual and benefit of the team. For example, should all individuals strive to become highly capable in all tasks on the team? When might team work stifle creativity, and when might it promote creativity through synergism? How can one present technical ideas effectively? What do you do when your idea is disagreed with? When might individual splinter efforts be beneficial and when might they not?

Many of the students are appreciative of this discussion and it has an immediate and visible effect on enhancing teamwork for their project. It also has given them valuable future insight into software development teams in a typical industrial environment.

VIII. PROJECT WORKBOOK

A workbook is required for each team. The workbook is the project management tool for the project and must contain the following information at a minimum:

1. PROJECT PLANNING
    a. Product size projections at the requirements and each design stage, actuals at the coding stage.
    b. Development person hours, planned and actual, by process activity through all process stages.
    c. Schedule Checkpoints
2. DEVELOPMENT PROCESS AND PRACTICES
    a. Brief description of planned process stages and validation steps through test.
    b. Team assignments and activity log
    c. Meeting minutes and duration
    d. Defect reporting procedures
    e. Design Change Request procedures
    f. Design Change tracking log.
    g. Retention and control procedures for design materials
3. PRODUCT VALIDATION RESULTS
    a. Major and Minor defects found during all inspections
    b. Errors found during each test stage
    c. Results of Usability/Installability Walkthroughs
4. DEVELOPMENT WORK ITEMS
    a. Most current Requirements and Product Level Design material
    b. Most current Component Level Design material
    c. Most current Module Level Design material
    d. Most current Code Listings
    e. All other work items resulting from Case Studies

5. PROCESS DATA FOR ANALYSIS AT END OF SEMESTER

a. Interim versions of all design documentation having reader comments, critiques, professors' comments, etc.
b. Old and revised size estimates at each design stage, and reasons for variance.
c. Rationale for variance between planned and actual person hours for each activity.
d. Rationale for variance between planned and actual calendar checkpoints for each activity.
e. Number of Design Change Requests initiated at each stage.
f. For each Inspection held, the number of person hours for:

   - Preparation
   - The Inspection session
   - Resulting rework

g. For each defect discovered during inspections and the testing stages:

   - The Process Stage in which the defect was introduced.
   - The inspection or test activity in which it was detected.
   - An estimate of the earliest Inspection or test activity in which the defect could theoretically have been detected.

IX. CASE STUDIES

In business management schools the case study method provides for a discussion of real life situations that business executives have faced. The situation, relevant information and facts are given, and the student is asked to evaluate the case under review and to come to his own conclusion. We have drawn from the successful history of business case studies as a vehicle to help our teaching of software engineering and Software Engineering process principles.

Our case studies are usually assigned to coincide with a lecture which has been given and is tied to a checkpoint in the project life cycle evolution. The case is to be analyzed by each team assigned to the course project. We stress that it is important that each team arrive at it own position on each case. Their positions may vary substantially based on the project assigned to the team. This leads to broader views than what each project might teach by itself.

At the next class meeting the case is discussed. Sometimes each or selected teams are asked to present their position. Other times the case is discussed as a general topic with the entire class and is led by one of us. In either event the purpose is to explore all aspects of the case situation before reaching any conclusion. It is not our objective to say what or who is right or wrong, rather we want discussion to explore alternatives and foster thinking about the alternatives to a preferred solution. At the summary we may state the pros and cons of each position presented during the discussion.

The following is a list and synopsis of each case study we used in our last two-semester sequence. Case studies One through 12 were used in Semester One, and 13 through 24 were used in Semester Two.

1. **Initial Requirements for Class Project**

   The student teams are given an overview of the Software Developers Environment and asked to formulate an initial set of requirements for their team's component. They must also describe assumptions made about the portion of the Software Engineering process that their component is to automate, and a list of questions that must be answered to complete the requirements process. This case study is the student's initial exposure to the type of problem solving and communication techniques that will be propagated throughout the course.

2. **Definition of Project Processes**

   The students are asked to define the process they believe they will follow during the course. The definition should be based on their previous experience in school or at work. The intent is to show how much of their attitude and viewpoint changes by the end of the semester.

3. **Code Inspection**

   A real-life example is given to the class with design specifications and a coding implementation. The teams are asked to inspect the code for errors, list and categorize the errors, and to keep data on their inspection and preparation rate. Their findings are compared to the set of finite errors "planted" in the implementation and optimal preparation and inspection rates.

4. **Human Factors**

The students are asked to do a human factors task assessment for their project from three major categories for their defined users; a) user effort to learn or relearn each task, b) effort to perform each task, and c) the effort of experiencing errors while performing each task. Each team presents their conclusions.

5. **Formalizing Requirements**

This is a three-part case study coinciding with the Requirements Engineering lectures in which a systematic method for transforming user requirements into a high-level design is taught. The final output of the case study for each team's component is an initial "Requirements and High Level Design Specification" written in a formatted, entity-relation language developed for the course, called "A Specification Language" (ASL)."

6. **Project Planning**

Component teams are given a planning structure (the Project Notebook outline) and asked to formalize their project plan with respect to schedules, size estimates, projected quality level, etc. The case study also requires the team to establish and document their process for defect reporting and tracking, design change control, and collection of other essential data for process management and future analysis.

7. **The Requirements to Design Bridge**

The teams are asked to complete their product level of design based on balancing the defined requirements with the resources and time they have available. As the projects are all too big to be completed in one rewrite, they must make decisions on what to restrict or select as necessary for Release 1. The ground rule is that they must have a working functional product subset in Release 1.

8. **Design Methodology Comparison**

The teams are asked to select which design methodology best fits their problem/project. They can pick from any specific approaches in Function Flow, Data Flow, Data Structure or Object oriented methodologies. They must make their case as to which is best for their problem/project. Each team presents their conclusions.

9. **Abstract Data Types**

The teams are asked to select an example design problem and express the solution as an ADT. Each team presents and discusses their example with the class.

10. **Object Oriented Design**

Regardless of which design methodology the team may have selected they are asked to develop a solution that is object oriented for at least part of their low level design. They are asked to discuss their problems in doing this if they had not started with an object orientation initially.

11. **The Users Guide**

Each team is to develop a users guide for their project, to distribute it to the other teams, and to solicit input for changes. The guides are discussed in class.

12. **Project Post Mortem**

Data collected during the semester is analyzed to determine how improvements could be made in program sizing methodology, defect detection efficiency, and error prevention. In this case study, the students gain an initial experience in using their own data for improving their process.

13. **The Grass is Greener in the Other Project's Yard**

This is the first case study in semester two, and projects and teams will have been shifted. That is, teams will be working on different projects than those they completed in semester one, and the team composition may be different. These new teams are asked to evaluate the product and project they inherit for testing and enhancement from a technical perspective with respect to Release 1.

14. **Comprehensive Test Plan**

Teams are asked to develop an overall test plan and strategy for their component, based upon preceding lectures on the types of testing employed in the Unit Test, Function Test, and System Test stages. Schedules and resources planned for each stage are included. Emphasis is placed on defining proper entry and exit criteria for each stage.

15. **Unit Test Plan**

This is a detailed plan to achieve adequate path coverage during Unit Test. Planned tests are described in detail, along with a rationale for their use.

16. **When do You Stop Testing?**

The students are asked to define a set of test cases which are derived from Cause and Effect Graphs, to determine the degrees of exposure as test cases are eliminated from the set, to compare the overlap between Unit

Test and Function Test, and to define a criteria for determining when testing would be complete for their project.

17. **Release 2 Content**

This case study marks the completion of a series of Requirements Engineering steps that have taken place in each team since the beginning of the semester; all teams have become "users" of all other teams' Release 1 components. Each team has collected requirements for Release 2 from their users and a set of requirements has been selected for implementation based upon trade-offs between user needs, resource and time available for the semester. Each team presents their planned content for Release 2 and rationale for the selection to the users (the class).

18. **User Documentation**

Teams are required to begin developing user documentation as soon as requirements and high-level design activities are complete for Release 2. This is to maintain focus on the user's view during the design stages of the product.

19. **Metrics**

Each team is asked to compile various complexity and quality metrics on their project in Release 2. They are then asked to make recommendations based on these assessments. The teams present their findings.

20. **Error Cause Analysis** (Or to ERR is Human, to PREVENT is Divine)

The teams are asked to assess ten errors they have found during testing this semester, to determine the primary cause of each error, and to verify the cause with the team that made the error in the environment under which the product was developed during Release 1. Each team presents their findings to the class.

21. **Quality Trade-offs**

A simple cost/value model is used to illustrate relationships between investing in better development, better testing, or better service to achieve a specified defect level when "old code" is being enhanced and shipped.

22. **Process Control through Data** (or One and One Make Two)

The students are given a real life product situation with process data over three releases of a product. The students must make a recommendation for the third release which is in progress in this case study. Should the project plan be changed? Why? How?

23. **Process Evaluation**

A technique is employed for gathering information about their own process during the semester, deriving quantitative scores for process effectiveness based on evaluation of the information, and identifying areas for improvement in their own process.

24. **Project Post Mortem**

This case study represents the culmination of experiences during the Second Semester, both in quantitative and subjective terms. In addition to the process parameters used in the First Semester Post Mortem, this case study includes results of analyzing the information on process effectiveness gathered from the previous case study.

X. GRADING CRITERIA

Since we had decided to break the class into teams, we recognized that grading an individual becomes more difficult. We could have defaulted to grading each individual based on the team evaluation, but decided that this method had some inequities. On a team of four students, if one student does not contribute equally, or in fact contributed significantly less than the others, then one of two undesirable situations can exist. Either the individual drags down the team more, or the individual gets a free ride. Neither of these were acceptable to us. We recognized that these would be isolated cases, but decided that the problem itself and not the degree of the problem had to be addressed.

We elected, therefore, to combine a mixture of grading criteria. A mid-term examination would be given and would account for 30 percent of the grade. Case studies and the project in conjunction with the project notebook would each account for 30 percent, and class participation would be considered the final 10 percent.

Thus, the individual in this scenario is in direct control of 40 percent of his grade, while the team effort accounted for 60 percent. Within the team assignment on case studies and the project, we asked that each work item be accounted for by both individual and team effort. This enabled us to discern which students were contributing equally to the team effort. In the cases where an individual was either driving the team or was dragging behind, we would account for the difference in a weighted team score by individual student.

In only two instances, over three years, have individual team members come to us to suggest that another team member was dragging their team down. These are difficult situations and in some sense these teams work in an artificial environment, as the team is together for only 15 weeks. This is hardly enough time for a team to become fully integrated working together towards a successful project completion. The two incidents, while of real importance to us, stand counterposed by all the other teams which did function together under very trying circumstances. In net the team approach can have some problems at times with individual grading. When stressed with high volumes of work, teamwork can break down, but in the overwhelming number of cases we have experienced teams working together well for graduate level projects.

In our first two semesters, we gave final examinations as well as mid-terms. We have since dropped the finals as they seemed to make little difference in grade scores, and only caused the students to go to a higher level of stress at the end of the course with studies, which, in turn, tended to diminish the completion of their projects.

We fully believe that having the students complete the project offers more value than a final exam. This value is particularly keen when the students early in the semester express clear doubts about being able to finish the project as well as they would like.

XI. TEXTS USED OVER TIME

We used the following texts, in successive semesters, as the course evolved:

1. M. L. Shooman, *Software Engineering,* McGraw Hill (1983). [5]
2. R. W. Jensen and C. C. Tonies, *Software Engineering,* Prentice Hall (1979). [6]
3. M. W. Evans, P. Piazza, and J. B. Dolkas, *Principles of Productive Software Management,* Wiley (1983). [7]
4. R. S. Pressman, *Software Engineering: A Practitioner's Approach,* McGraw-Hill (1982). [8]

These are just a few of the text books covering "Software Engineering." Of the ones we used, each focused on a few Software Engineering aspects, but no single text covered the subject entirely to our needs. Consequently, the formal texts were supplemented with the additional publications:

1. *Classics in Software Engineering,* Yourdon Press. [9]
2. *Selected Reprints In Software,* IEEE Press. [10]

3. T. S. Chow, *Tutorial: Software Quality Assurance: A Practical Approach,* [11]

4. E. Miller and W. E. Howden, *Tutorial: Software Testing And Validation Techniques* [12]

A number of additional suggested readings were also included during the course.

Student Criticisms Of Current Texts

Periodically, the students were asked for feedback on the applicability and effectiveness of the reading assignments to the current lecture and project work. More formal feedback on the text and supplemental publications was also obtained by means of a course evaluation questionnaire

The critiques received on the various text books identified two basic problems: one or two of the text books focused too narrowly on only a few aspects of Software Engineering (for example on software reliability assurance, or on project management), while one or two others covered the Software Engineering spectrum quite well, but remained a little too theoretical or abstract for the student to relate to the pragmatics of the class project, and in many cases, actual work experiences.

Deciding To Write Our Own Text:

As stated earlier, one of our principle objectives is to evolve this Software Engineering course into a model for both industry and academia. Essential to achieving this goal is to package the information such that it can be systematically presented and applied by current practitioners in industry, as well as taught effectively in an academic environment by others.

A series of text books is planned as a partial answer to this goal. The first is currently under development for publication by Prentice-Hall in 1987. It covers topics of the first semester under the title "Software Engineering: An

Industrial Approach, Volume 1." To assist those who will teach it as a formal graduate level course, publication of a supplemental teaching guide and a book of case studies used in the course is also being considered.

XII. SUPPORT ENVIRONMENT:

The support environment at our university relevant to these projects consists of an IBM 3081 running an operating system called "Michigan Terminal System," SUN terminals for graphics, and an array of personal computers. The host system is used by most of the students for project documentation and communication. Some students who are employed full time in jobs campus use their the local facilities for this work. Most coding is done in PASCAL, and in recent semesters, implementation and testing has migrated almost exclusively to the personal computer, the most popular combination being Turbo PASCAL on the IBM PC.

XIII. TEACHER-STUDENT RELATIONSHIP

The fact that the two of us and many of the students in the course are employed full time, and at distant locations, presents a unique challenge; especially in a course such as ours where project work makes continual student-teacher feedback essential. As mentioned previously, class sessions are held one night per week for three hours. Time is allocated at the beginning of each session to survey the teams for general problems and inhibitors to their project work. Problems unique to a given team are handled either by team consultations with the us after class, or by making an appointment for a consulting session before class on the following week. Such consulting sessions usually take one-half to one hour. Students are encouraged to contact us by telephone during the week also, which they often do. And finally, feedback is facilitated by requiring that each Case Study result be handed in, usually at the class session for the following week. This enables us to annotate comments and return them to the teams the following week.

To ensure maximum continuity between teacher and student, we have since the outset placed a requirement on ourselves to both attend all class sessions, at least to the extent that our individual business travel schedules permit, and to require that the Teaching Assistant (TA) attend all lectures in their entirety as well. The reason for this is to remain as involved with the students as possible under these circumstances. Since one of our goals is to become equally proficient in presenting each other's lectures, it provides an opportunity to learn each other's material. It also provides us with many chances to critique each other's presentation skills and subject matter, thus increasing the rate at which we have been able to polish and fine-tune the course.

Even with all the above precautions, practices and steps, problems have still arisen in staying on top of all student project work and problems all the time. This was particularly brought to the foreground during the Fall 1984 semester when over 60 students enrolled, 57 of whom stayed through to completion of the semester. The sheer volume of work items requiring our critique, the evaluation and grading of finished work and examinations, and of the needed team consultations was overwhelming and detracted severely from our ability to perfect the approach we were evolving and still deliver top quality education. For this reason, we set a limit of 30 students for future classes.

XIV. STUDENT FEEDBACK

Feedback on student opinion about the course is obtained at the end of each semester by means of both a formal survey administered by the university, and a less formal survey specific to this course, which we administered.

Formal University Survey:

The university survey uses a series of questions stated as a positive characteristic of the course, and the student is asked to record whether he or she "strongly agrees" with the statement, "agrees," "disagrees," or "strongly disagrees."

The survey statements are:

1. The course objectives have been clearly stated.
2. There is consistency between the objectives and what is being taught.
3. The reading assignments have aided the learning process.
4. The writing assignments have aided the learning process.
5. The level of difficulty is reasonable.
6. The amount of work required is reasonable.
7. The pace at which material is covered is reasonable.
8. The grading criteria have been clearly stated.
9. The tests and quizzes, etc. are fair.
10. The test, quizzes, etc., are useful learning experiences.
11. The course format is appropriate to the subject matter.
12. The course has logical organization and continuity.
13. The course encourages students to think for themselves.
14. The course has significantly increased your knowledge and skills in the subject area.
15. The subject matter is relevant to your education goals.

Student responses have been overwhelmingly favorable in most of the above categories over the semesters, except in the areas of reading assignments (Question 3), the amount of work (Question 6), clarity of grading criteria (Question 8), and the degree to which tests aid learning (Question 10).

A question is also included that asks the student to record on a scale of 4 to 0, whether he or she rates the overall course as "one of the best," "above average," "average," "below average," or "one of the worst." On a scale of 4 to 0, with 4 being the highest, the overall scores for the succession of semesters is:

- Software Engineering II, Spring 1984--3.13
- Software Engineering I, Fall 1984--2.07*
- Software Engineering II, Spring 1985--3.50
- Software Engineering I, Fall 1985--2.75
- Software Engineering II, Spring 1986--3.85
- Software Engineering I, Fall 1986--Not available at this this writing

*This was the class with 57 students.

Our Own Survey

An additional survey specific to the course is also administered at mid-term and at the end of each semester. The survey asks for an evaluation of each lecture module and each case study as to whether the topic or case study should receive more emphasis, receive less emphasis, be kept the same, or be dropped from the course. This has provided valuable feedback making it possible to "fine tune" the course much more rapidly.

In addition, the survey asks for opinions on other aspects of the course. Consistently given a high rating by the students each semester has been:

- The challenge of the course
- The extent to which the course has aided the students' learning process
- The extent to which the course has encouraged the students to think for themselves

Feedback from the last two semesters also indicates high ratings on course organization.

Frequently rated low or of concern, and therefore areas in which continual improvement has been sought, are:

- The amount of workload in the course
- The difficulty of examinations and limited value as an aid to learning
- The value of the text books and reading assignments relative to this course

An additional question is included in the survey that asks to what extent prior courses in this discipline have prepared the student for this course. Of concern is that in each semester the majority of answers have consistently been "could have done much more." Examples are lack of prior knowledge of basic Structured Programming constructs, of the use of modern design notations such as pseudocode, familiarity with data abstraction as a fundamental design technique, and knowledge of program specification techniques and formatted specification languages.

Write-in comments are also welcomed in the survey. Some excerpts that characterize the feedback from the most recent semester are:

- "The course is excellent! The workload is unbelievable!,"
- "The workload was far too much....,"
- "This course has easily been the best taught, most interesting of any I've taken in my seven years at RPI.,"
- "Perhaps a more scaled-down project could achieve the same result with less time required.,"
- "This course should only be considered by students seriously interested in Software Engineering methodologies and practices. P.S. to the interested student, this course is invaluable and beyond compare."

XV. WHAT WE LEARNED OVER THE SEMESTERS

Overall, we have learned that this type of teaching approach has proved to be of immense value in the eyes of most students who have taken it. We have also learned that to successfully apply this type of project-oriented approach, the maximum manageable size of the class is only about 30 students.

From a professional education standpoint, we have been careful not to turn the course project into a "how to" course rather than as a vehicle to challenge original thinking so needed in the profession.

According to repeated feedback from students, a key ingredient in the success of this approach seems to be the teaching a variety of Software Engineering approaches, and in involving the student in a life-like set of "situations" for which a number of possible Software Engineering alternatives seem equally viable at first, and from which they must choose the better approach based upon a disciplined problem solving technique.

XVI. CONCLUSIONS

We have tried to bring an industry perspective into an academic graduate two-semester course sequence in Software Engineering. We believe we have successfully accomplished this meeting of industry in academia. We have been working to improve our approach for two and half years. We hope that we will get feedback from our peers across the worldwide area of Software Engineering education that will help to improve the course even further. We believe we are achieving the objectives set forth initially, and that the students are receiving something valuable relative to actual industrial requirements for Software Engineering professionals, and that this approach is different from what they have been offered heretofore by more typical current-day courses. We anticipate that the Software Engineering Process Principles which serve as the foundation of our approach in teaching this course, as well as our work in industry, will remain with each student we have had in our classes. We hope that what we have set out to accomplish, what we have experienced, and what we have documented can indeed serve as a model for other Software Engineering course sequences.

XVII. ACKNOWLEDGEMENTS

We wish to thank RPI for giving us the opportunity to teach at their Institute and for allowing us the leeway to shape this course sequence as we felt it should be. We wish to thank IBM for supporting our efforts at RPI, for occasionally we did have to juggle priorities.

REFERENCES

[1] Berzins, Gray, and Naumann, "Abstraction Based Software Development," CACM, Volume 29, Number 5, May 1986, p. 402.

[2] Hartog, Curt, "Of Commerce and Academia," DATAMATION, September 1985, p. 68.

[3] Radice, Roth, O'Hara, and Ciarfella, "A Programming Process Architecture," IBM Systems Journal, Vol. 24, No. 2, 1985, p. 79.

[4] Humphrey, W.S., "The IBM Large-Systems Software Development Process: Objectives and Direction," IBM Systems Journal, Vol. 24, No. 2, 1985, p. 76.

[5] M. L. Shooman, "Software Engineering," McGraw Hill (1983).

[6] R. W. Jensen and C. C. Tonies, "Software Engineering," Prentice Hall (1979).

[7] M. W. Evans, P. Piazza, and J. B. Dolkas, "Principles Of Productive Software Management," Wiley (1983)

[8] R. S. Pressman, "Software Engineering: A Practitioner's Approach," McGraw-Hill (1982).

[9] "Classics In Software Engineering," Yourdon Press (1983).

[10] "Selected Reprints In Software, Second Edition," IEEE Computer Society Press (1984).

[11] T. S. Chow, "Tutorial: Software Quality Assurance: A Practical Approach," IEEE Computer Society Press, (January 1985).

[12] E. Miller and W. E. Howden, "Tutorial: Software Testing And Validation Techniques (2nd Edition)," IEEE Computer Society Press, (November, 1981).

The Computer Science Education Program at AT&T Bell Laboratories, Merrimack Valley

J. C. Cleaveland
R. W. MacDonald

AT&T Bell Laboratories

ABSTRACT

A *Computer Science Education Program* was designed to produce software engineers at AT&T Bell Laboratories, Merrimack Valley. This provided an opportunity to those who wanted to change careers or become more formally trained in software engineering and computer science. The program help ease the technology shift towards software and provided AT&T with skilled software engineers who were already familiar with the transmission system products. There was a deliberate tailoring of the program to meet the needs of this AT&T location. The paper provides an overview of the design, development, and results of the program, including the curriculum, administration, costs, and rewards.

1. Introduction

Over the last few years, AT&T Bell Laboratories at Merrimack Valley has been experiencing a sizable growth in software development activity. The Merrimack Valley Laboratories designs and develops digital terminals and systems for voice and data transmission, microwave radio systems, guided digital transmission systems, and provides computer-aided design of systems, circuits, and components. With the availability of powerful yet inexpensive microprocessors the use of software for systems control and operations became widespread. In the last 5 years, Merrimack Valley has experienced more than a 10 fold increase in the number of software developers who are actively developing, or supporting the development of, software primarily for embedded microprocessors.

When referring to this "growth," one is actually noting the shift in technologies that are required to implement the products under development. Such shifts in technology need to be accompanied by shifts in the technical skill mix of development and support staff. In 1983 management concluded that Merrimack Valley would require many more software engineers based upon the projected growth in software needs. We realized that no single solution would provide all the required software expertise. We expected that a large number of people would obtain software education outside the company in formal programs, and we expected to hire some software engineers. We also felt that special educational opportunities in software would be required at Merrimack Valley to supplement the individual courses then available. A software education task force was formed to propose curricula and methods of implementation to help individuals develop their software backgrounds. Much of the current software development activity was being carried out by staff members who were previously engaged in other areas of engineering, such as mechanical and electrical engineering. It was for these individuals, and the additional engineers who should be developing expertise in software, that the Computer Science Education Program was developed.

The program was designed during the Summer of 1983, and approved in Fall 1983. During the Spring of 1984, "ramp-up" courses were provided for those who wished to take the program but did not meet prerequisites. The program started with 32 people in Fall 1984 and finished with 20 in May 1986.

A number of significant advantages of having an in-house program were realized. These advantages included many of those previously reported[1]. These included:

1. The students were mature, motivated, and experienced. They had been with the company for an average of ten years prior to joining the program. Students were motivated by a desire to learn, not grades.

2. The courses were slanted directly towards our specific needs. All courses used the C and UNIX[1] computing environment. After covering the basics

such as good programming practices, data structures, discrete mathematics, the program emphasized software engineering and operating systems concepts, the two most important ingredients in many of our software development projects.

3. Many courses could be taught by experienced in-house instructors. These instructors could make the course material more appealing by relating it to specific work in Bell Laboratories. Specific Bell Labs tools, techniques, and methods could be naturally incorporated into the courses. Project work was coordinated acrosss several courses which provided an opportunity to experience the practice of software engineering that paralleled software project work on transmission products.

4. The students have become more valuable employees, because they now have software skills and unlike newly hired software engineers, they have considerable experience and detailed knowledge of our products.

5. An in-house program was convenient to many students. Students could take a complete education program without having to go to a college or university, attend classes that may require commuting time, work on foreign computer environments, and become entangled in considerable amount of red tape. No degree was awarded, but almost all of our students already had a Master's degree, and a second one was not a high priority.

2. Process

A task force of eight interested MTS (Member of Technical Staff) and technical supervisors were formed to evaluate possible education directions and draft a

1. UNIX is a trademark of AT&T Bell Laboratories.

proposal for meeting the identified needs. This Software/Firmware Education Task Force included the authors of this paper. To start the process, the task force reviewed the prior software engineering and computer science offerings at Merrimack Valley (locally taught courses, corporate offerings, university videotape, etc.). Also reviewed were the recommended curricula of the IEEE [2], [3], [4], [5], [6], [7], and the ACM [8], [9], [10], [11]. By surveying recently graduated technical employees, the task force developed a composite view of the typical programming backgrounds of non-computer scientists. The efforts of other AT&T Bell Laboratories locations, notably Whippany[12] and Columbus[13], were studied. Over a period of six months, the committee arrived at a consensus view of our target population, objectives, curriculum, format of presentation, and recommendations.

3. Committee Report

After considering the various alternatives, the committee recommended that a serious education program be offered over two years to about twenty-five MTS starting in September, 1984. The details of this program are given in section 5 of this paper. The goal of this effort was:

> to produce software developers, operating at the MTS level, who can engineer, design and develop the software and firmware components of future Transmission Products.

In more detail, individuals who successfully complete this education sequence should (Paraphrased from [8], page 149):

1. be able to design and code software in a reasonable amount of time that works correctly, is well documented, and is readable;
2. be able to determine whether or not they have produced a reasonably efficient and well organized software product;
3. know what general types of problems are amenable to computer solution

and the various tools necessary for solving such problems;

4. be able to assess the implications of work performed either as an individual or as a member of a team;
5. understand computer architecture and operating system concepts; and
6. be prepared to pursue in-depth development in one or more application areas and further education in software engineering and computer science.

Meeting this goal, with a carefully managed impact on the participants' personal lives and work in progress, were the criteria for success for this education program.

4. Target Population

There was a large diversity of needs in software education at Merrimack Valley. Similarly, there was a large number of possible vehicles for addressing these needs. The Software/Firmware Education Task Force decided to limit its scope to MTS level software engineering and computer science skills. In general, we chose not to address the software education needs of our associate technical populations through this program. Nor did we cover the development of software project management skills for our management population[2].

The profile of a typical participant was an experienced MTS with a Master's Degree or Doctorate in a technical area other than Computer Science (or the equivalent in experience). He or she would have worked in other engineering disciplines, and had been assuming, or would be assuming, assignments in software or firmware development. They had already met the prerequisites for

2. This is not to say that managers who wanted to learn software engineering and computer science were excluded from the program. The skills needed to *manage* software projects had to be developed outside this program. See also [14].

the program or they were readily able to master them during the rampup period that preceeded the formal course sequence.

Most of our staff of software developers matched this description in 1983. They were talented individuals with a history of success in other engineering disciplines who were then involved in some aspect of software development for embedded microprocessors. Out of necessity, many had already begun developing software without a knowledge of the foundations of software engineering or computer science. Formal training was generally limited to one to three programming courses in the use of UNIX and programming in C. A well designed program was needed to provide these people with the knowledge to correct any mismatch between their existing skills and experience, and their future assignments.

5. Computer Science Education Program

The computer science education program was a two year program with two semesters per year and two courses per semester. It was aimed at the MTS population wishing to migrate to software engineering or computer engineering. This serious, in-house, non-degree program operated at near a graduate level pace and produced quality software engineering and computer science expertise.

5.1 Admittance to the program

As noted above, the program was developed primarily for the AT&T Bell Laboratories Merrimack Valley MTS population who were interested in shifting from other technical disciplines towards software engineering and computer science. Exceptions were made for non-MTS employees. Admittance depended on satisfying the prerequisites and the approval of management. A simple application form was used to determine whether the prerequisites were met. All 32 applicants who met these requirements were admitted to the program. This was seven more than we had planned, but as we expected, attrition eventually lowered the number. Twenty-two students started the second semester; of these, all but two completed the program.

The prerequisites were satisfied by the students by taking preliminary courses or by having equivalent knowledge and experience. The prerequisites were:

1. C and UNIX experience. Some knowledge of and experience with the UNIX operating system and the C programming language was required. This could be satisfied by courses as long as they were accompanied or followed by work on a non-trivial software project.

2. Computer organization. Knowledge of the basic concepts of assembly language, machine language, stored programs, memory, number and character representation, interrupts and input/output, basics of Boolean logic was required.

3. Mathematics background. Some knowledge and experience in mathematics equivalent to that learned in calculus, linear algebra and probability. It was familiarity with mathematical methods and logic that was important rather than specific knowledge in a mathematical area. This prerequisite was already met by most MTS.

The Spring before the program began we offered a *ramp-up* course that covered the material of the first two prerequisites. Eight of the 20 graduates took this ramp-up course.

We wanted all students in the program to take all the courses, so we did not offer any advance placement; however, we did make an exception that gave two students permission to skip a course. In other cases, we encouraged the stronger students to become graders.

5.2 The Curriculum

The curriculum was carefully chosen based on the expected software needs of AT&T Bell Laboratories Merrimack Valley. The prerequisites assured a uniform starting place for serious study and work in software engineering. For each 15 week course the student was expected to spend the following amount of effort and time (per week per course):

1. 3 hours class time (during working hours)
2. 3 hours of class work (during working hours)
3. 3 hours of class work (at home)

This means the student was expected to add one hour of personal time for every two hours of education at work. Because two classes were offered at a time, the student was expected to spend 12 out of 40 work hours on the program, and an additional 6 hours a week at home. Since there were 4 semesters of 15 weeks a piece, each student was expected to spend about 720 work hours spread over two years. Combined with the 360 hours at home, means that each student was expected to devote 1080 hours to the education program. In reality students spent more than the allocated time on education at home, and less at work. We attribute this primarily to two reasons:

1. Students were still highly motivated to make significant contributions to their *real* work.
2. Homework assignments sometimes took longer than instructors anticipated.

The chosen curriculum was an accelerated version of the undergraduate curriculum sanctioned by the Association of Computing Machinery[8]. The chosen curriculum can also be viewed as an introductory graduate curriculum in computer science. It was tailored to meet the anticipated software engineering needs at Merrimack Valley. This tailoring primarily involved an emphasis on software, software engineering, large software projects for embedded microprocessors, operating systems, and systems programming.

The curriculum also emphasized project work. This implied a fair amount of work outside the classroom requiring computing facilities. The curriculum was also designed to accommodate one and two year plans. People finishing one year would have the background for programming, and those finishing two years would have a good background in software engineering. As expected almost all students took the program for two years; two students stopped at the end of one year.

A detailed description of the curriculum is given in appendix A. The course titles were:

First Year - First Semester
1. Accelerated Discrete Mathematics and Formal Methods in Computer Science
2. Programming Discipline

First Year - Second Semester
3. Computer Architectures
4. Data Structures, Algorithms and Abstractions

Second Year - First Semester
5. Operating Systems
6. Software Engineering

Second Year - Second Semester
7a. Grammars, Languages, and Translation
7b. Database Systems
8a. Expert System Technology
8b. Design of Software Tools and Programming Environments
8c. Compiler Construction Techniques
8d. Independent Study

Each course in the last semester lasted seven weeks, and the student could choose any two of the courses 8a-d. Two students chose 8d (Computer Graphics and Computer Science Theory). Originally, we had combined courses 3 and 5 into a two course sequence in computer architectures and operating systems.

We found that no outside instructors were willing to commit to a course that far in advance. There were also few instructors that were willing to teach such a combination. We therefore changed the curriculum to have separate courses.

Unlike a university environment wherein courses are continually being offered to students with unknown backgrounds, this program offered the opportunity for a more closely coordinated curriculum. Material offered during later courses could truly build upon the work of previous semesters. Since the same set of students took each class, the instructors knew what was previously taught. This program thus offered the unusual opportunity for a well planned and coordinated set of classes that could be more meaningful than the equivalent set of classes at the university. For example, as mentioned earlier, the software engineering course (6) and the operating systems course (5) shared the same class project. The project was to build an operating system, based on XINU[15]. Operating system principles, project requirements, architecture and design were handled by the operating systems class. Project management, software engineering principles, software tools and environment were handled by the software engineering class. Such a project was much more substantial than any single class could have offered. The software engineering class had a non-trivial project to manage, and the operating systems class could devote time to technical details rather than project details.

5.3 Other Students

In addition to CSEP students, we felt there would be persons who would like to take one or two specific courses. We had to decide whether to allow non-CSEP employees to take single courses from the program. We were concerned that many non-CSEP students might negativly alter the class atmosphere. Non-CSEP students would not have the same release time, and they might not have had the same background such as the previous CSEP courses. Although controversial, we finally decided to open up the CSEP courses to the general population. We had contingency plans if too many people signed up, such as offering a parallel course, or videotaping. On average we had about 5-10 non-CSEP people in each course, which was acceptable after the first semester.

6. Administering the Program

The program was administered in-house by Bell Labs, and about half the classes were taught by Bell Labs personnel. The various roles and their responsibilities were:

Students

learned and worked with other students and instructors.

Instructors

taught, assigned and administered class work, co-ordinate with other classes.

Graders

graded homework and helped students. In many cases, stronger students volunteered to become graders.

Angels

helped both the instructor and students. Angels made sure the course ran smoothly and acted as a buffer between students and instructors. Angels are particularly important for outside instructors, but were also useful for in-house instructors. The course angel worked with both students and instructors when course workloads were felt to be excessive.

The *curriculum coordinator*

obtained instructors for courses, aided the instructor in textbook selection, course content, and coordination with other courses and instructors, computing facilities, and software; the curriculum coordinator also had overall responsibility for curriculum implementation.

The *program coordinator*

was responsible for admittance procedures, withdrawals, rooms, taping of lectures, textbook ordering, and aided the curriculum coordinator and instructors.

The *education committee*

was active in the implementation of the program and during the first year of operation. It defined the program goals, procedures, and obtained management support for the program.

Initially we had thought we would videotape all lectures, but we changed our policy to videotape only upon request. If students anticipated missing class, a request to videotape the class could be made.

Regular in-depth feedback on each class was important to keep the program on track. About a third of the way through each semester, a detailed survey was given in each class so that adjustments in teaching style, content, or pace could be made. During the first semester it was important to keep weekly track of the time students spent on class work, so that adjustments to homework or the pace of the class could be made to meet our target of 6 hours of class work per week per class. It was important that the right pace be established early so that we would not lose students early in the program due to unreasonable homework demands. Also an electronic newsletter was established to provide timely communication among all CSEP participants.

We developed grading guidelines that we distributed to students and instructors. Portions of the original guidelines were changed as circumstances became clearer. We allowed numeric or letter grading on individual assignments, but the course grade could either be complete or incomplete.

Incompletes were not recorded. We found however that giving grades on individual assignments increased the stress factor for some students so we eventually corrected homework and gave very few scores. In many classes, end of the semester self-assessment exams were given. The course guidelines contained the following information:

1. Reading, study, homework, exams and projects should average about six hours of work outside of class per week.

2. Homework, exams and projects should be turned in to the instructor on time either on paper or by electronic mail.

3. It is preferable to have homework and exams returned as soon as possible to students. The instructor (or grader) should grade all work within two weeks of the due date and returned to students.

4. Since the first priority of this program is learning, students are encouraged to help each other and work together. Unless explicitly stated by the instructor all students may obtain help from fellow students on all homework and projects.

5. Individual student grades are considered private information and may not be communicated beyond the grader, instructor and student without the student's permission. Class curves and grade summaries may be public if individual grades cannot be identified.

6. At the end of each class, the instructor must make a list of students that completed the course and send this list to the program coordinator. There are two potential reasons for not completing a course: 1) not enough work turned in for grading (minimal amount is to be determined by the instructor), 2) work turned in is not up to the minimum standards (also determined by the instructor). Instructors have the responsibility of

informing students that they are not performing up to standards.

7. Completion of the computer science program is defined as completing at least seven of the eight courses.

This may seem like a very lax method of giving an educational program. There was little to show on paper how well students were doing, and little incentive or reward for doing well. This did not turn out to be a problem for us because the students in the program were motivated. They identified themselves rather than being chosen, and they were eager to learn their newly chosen field. For many the program represented a career change. In the long run performance reviews depend indirectly on how well they learned and can apply course material and concepts.

7. Rewards

Beyond the intrinsic reward of increased knowledge, we felt that active, enthusiastic management support of the program, and of the participants, would be crucial to attracting and retaining students. This support included recognition that the students, in-house instructors and program administrators would have less time to dedicate to other work assignments. This was taken into account during performance review. No direct benefit or loss was attributed to the student during performance review for participating in the program, but it was noted that the student was working through a challenging educational program. It was hoped, of course, that a student's overall performance will improve by application of the knowledge and experience gained.

We felt that active and ongoing encouragement of the student's effort by direct supervision and higher level management was needed. For example, at the end of the first year, we had a formal luncheon with students and their management. In addition to released time, support took the form of providing quality computing facilities and laboratory equipment for students to use in completing their assignments. Terminals at home and dedicated computer facilities were needed to ease the impact on personal time and provide additional opportunity for experimentation.

Upon finishing the program students and managers should know that an education program of significant merit and effort has been completed. A certificate of completion accompanied by a gift was presented to each participant by their executive director and noted in the employee's permanent record. A "graduation luncheon" for all students, their spouses, and directors was held to celebrate this achievement.

8. Costs

The purpose of this section is to outline the costs associated with offering this education program. It serves to foster an understanding of the importance that was placed on preparing our staff for the critical technologies needed in our product development. The costs of offering corporate education programs are frequently not noted. The costs associated with education are maintenance dollars that are spent in caring for and upgrading our investment in our research and development capability.

The largest cost component of this program was the loaded salaries of the students. For all of the students that participated in the program, time spent in class and on homework at work accounted for more than ninety percent of the program cost. The second largest cost component was the cost for instructors and curriculum coordinators. Six of the courses were taught by outside instructors from local universities. There was a variation in the cost of outside instructors; some of the more expensive instructors were among the best prepared and the highest rated. Compared to the cost of the overall program, the additional cost for these high quality instructors was insignificant. Administrative costs in the Education Center, the provision of computing facilities, materials, textbooks, and supplies, make up the remainder of the costs. The potential cost figures were modelled before the program was proposed and approved.

9. Summary

The need for a shift in technical skill mix at AT&T Bell Laboratories Merrimack Valley was clearly identified by upper management. A one-time mechanism for accommodating this need was proposed, approved and executed. The vehicle was a quality in-house program in software engineering and computer science that spanned two years. The cost of the program, particularly in terms of loaded salary was identified at the outset. Students were granted release time but also had to devote a considerable amount of personal time to their education. This effort was an investment in the futures of the individual technical contributors and the viability of the product line. The talent at Merrimack Valley coupled with the unique education possibilities that this cohesive course sequence offered resulted in an exciting learning atmosphere.

10. Acknowledgements

There were many people who participated in the design and administration of the program, either as members of the task force, or as members of the education committee, including Alma Healey (Program coordinator), Tom Wetmore, Jim Oberst, Bob Snicer, Ken Kretch, Bill Burdette, Kathy Luther, Steve Collins, and Bob DeMarco. We also thank the reviewers for their time and effort.

REFERENCES

1. James P. McGill, "The Software Engineering Shortage: A Third Choice", IEEE Transactions on Software Engineering, Vol. SE-10, No. 1, Jan. 1984.

2. W. Fletcher, "The Digital Logic Subject Area," Computer Vol. 10, No. 12, December 1977, pp. 72-74.

3. O. Garcia, "Computer Organization and Architecture and the Laboratory Sequence," Computer Vol. 10, No. 12, December 1977, pp. 76-90.

4. D. Rine, D. Pessel and S. Ghosh, "The Software Engineering Subject Area," Computer Vol. 10, No. 12, December 1977, pp. 97-105.

5. B. H. Barnes, et. al., "Theory in Computer Science and Engineering Curriculum: Why, What, When and Where," Computer Vol. 10, No. 12, December 1977, pp. 106-108.

6. J. T. Cain, "The Computer Science and Engineering Core Curriculum," Computer Vol. 10, No. 12, December 1977, pp. 109-113.

7. M. E. Sloan, "Evaluation Model Curriculum in Computer Science and Engineering," Computer Vol. 10, No. 12, December 1977, pp. 114-120.

8. R.H.Austing et. al., "Curriculum '78, Recommendations for the Undergraduate Program in Computer Science," Communications of the ACM, March 1979, Vol. 22, No. 3, pp. 147-166.

9. K.I. Magel, et. al., "Recommendations for Master's Level Programs in Computer Science," Communications of the ACM, Vol. 24, No. 3, March 1981.

10. S.N. Busenberg and W.C.Tam, "An Academic Program Providing Realistic Training in Software Engineering," Communications of the ACM, Vol. 22, No. 6, June 1979.

11. G.L.Engel, "A Comparison of the ACM/CCCS and the IEEE/CSE Model Curriculum Subcommittee Recommendations," Computer Vol. 10, No. 12, December 1977, pp. 121-123.

12. R. Hirderliter and S. D. Shapiro, "A Program of Continuing Education in Applied Computer Science," *Computer*, Vol. , No. 10, October 1981.

13. Internal correspondence concerning the Columbus Computer Science Education Series.

14. L.B.Robertson, and G.A.Secor, "Effective Management of Software Development.", AT&T Technical Journal, Vol. 65, Issue 2, March-April 1986.

15. Douglas Comer, Operating System Design: The XINU Approach, Prentice-Hall, 1984.

Appendix A: Course Descriptions

1. Accelerated Discrete Math and Formal Methods in Computer Science

   Logic, set theory. Combinatorics, probability. Algebraic structures, groups, finite fields. Graphs, lattices and Boolean algebra. Introduction to formal languages and finite state automata. Homework will include some programming assignments.

2. Programming Discipline

   Introduction to the software life cycle with emphasis on unit design, coding, and testing. Algorithm development. Structured programming, modularity, stepwise refinement. Top-down and bottom-up design. Information hiding. Coding style and documentation. Design for maintenance and portability. Introduction to basic programming language structures and languages other than C. Homework will include extensive programming assignments.

3. Computer Architecture

   Processor architecture, instruction sets, addressing modes, microprogramming, virtual machines. Memory organization and management, addressing, swapping, virtual memory, hierarchy of storage media. Protection features, pipelining, distributed systems, advanced computer architectures, novel computer architectures.

4. Data Structures, Algorithms, and Abstractions

   Design and analysis of algorithms and data structures. Arrays, stacks, queues, lists, trees, graphs, etc. Sorting and searching. File organization. Dynamic storage allocation. Recursion, data abstraction and procedural abstraction. Homework will include extensive programming assignments.

5. Operating Systems

   Process control, concurrent processes, resource sharing, interprocess communication. Scheduling, load control, thrashing. Input/output processing, buffers, controllers, device drivers, interrupt structures, memory management, and file systems. Homework will include a large programming project.

6. Software Engineering

   In depth study of the software life cycle. Methodologies, reviews, software metrics, quality assurance. Documentation. Introduction to project planning, organization, and management. Homework assignments will be coordinated with the programming project in course 5.

7. Topics in Computer Science I

   7A) Grammars, Languages, and Translation

   This course provides an introduction to grammars, languages, and translation. Both regular expressions and context-free grammars, and the languages that they describe, will be covered. Grammar-based recognition and parsing of strings from regular and context-free languages will be included. Syntax-directed translation will be introduced. Interesting class projects will be assigned which use the YACC(1) and LEX(1) tools (no prior knowledge of tools required).

7B) Database Systems

This course covers database system facilities; the relational data model; query languages; QUEL, relational algebra, and host language embeddings; data independence; views, integrity and authorization; logical database design; the network and hierarchical data models; database system implementation; access methods, query optimization, distributed database systems.

8. Topics in Computer Science II (Choose any two of the following)

8A) Expert System Techonology

This course introduces the basic concepts of expert system technology, focusing on logic programming. Topics to be discussed include search, representation and use of knowledge, approaches to designing expert systems, existing successful expert system applications, and a methodology for applying software engineering techniques to the production of expert systems. Two representation and programming models, rule-based programming (OPS5, Prolog, OPS83) and object-based programming (FLAVORS, SMALLTALK, Objective-C), will be presented. Knowledge of engineering skills will be discussed and compared with traditional systems analysis and design. In particular, techniques for choosing experts, determining the appropriate role for experts and interviewing experts are included.

8B) Design of Software Tools and Programming Environments

A project-oriented course in the design and development of software tools and programming environments. Class topics will include integrated tool sets, application generators, human factors, and a review of current tools and their faults. Each person or group of people will select a course project and make in-class presentations of their problem, solution, and tool design and development.

8C) Compiler Construction Techniques

This course will introduce the student to the techniques used in building compilers for high level languaegs, such as C, PASCAL and Ada. Topics will include: organization and management of symbol tables, type checking, intermediate language design, code generation and run time support environment. The emphasis is on pragmatic issues and examples will be chosen from working compilers. The student is assumed to be familiar with parsing techniques.

8D) Independent Study

Arranged with a mentor of your choice.

FORMAL EDUCATION WITHIN THE SOFTWARE LIFE CYCLE

Dr. Nancy Hall, IBM Federal Systems Division

John Miklos, IBM Federal Systems Division

ABSTRACT

Approximately ten years ago, the Federal Systems Division of IBM initiated a software engineering program to train all software professions in current topics being taught in the leading universities. Thus began an extensive program that is still in operation today. Initial results demonstrated that the quality and reliability of the FSD software product was greatly enhanced. This paper describes the education program and documents some of the initial results that indicate the success of the education program.

1. Introduction

The Federal Systems Division (FSD) of IBM has supported the federal government on key contracts for over 25 years. These projects can be characterized as being long term, large scale contracts consisting of significant hardware and software development and integration. In the mid-70's these projects provided IBM FSD with the opportunity to create large scale systems that were not being done anywhere else in the corporation. The division had thereby gained a large amount of experience in this area while future work was increasing in size and complexity. This trend indicated that traditional software development approaches needed to be refined and understood by all professionals in order for the division to remain successful.

To solve this problem FSD recognized the need to put more rigor into the software development process. Some leading software professionals, notably Harlan Mills, recognized the division had a significant population of programmers with a great deal of practical experience but were unaware of new software engineering concepts being taught in the leading universities. Mills recommended initiating a software engineering program that would train all professionals in FSD in these ideas; thus began an extensive program that is still in operation today.

This paper provides an overview of the FSD education program and the software development methodology, particularly the basic concepts that are central to the division's education program. Historically, it will describe the initial FSD education program and how it has been extended to include all aspects of software development including management and testing concerns. A major focus for all classes is the FSD life cycle for a software project; this paper defines that life cycle and the relationship between those activities and each class. In addition, it will describe a new emphasis in FSD on the Ada language and how this new programming environment will impact future FSD projects. This paper will also explain a seminar program conducted by education that continues to focus on software methodologies and extend the lessons in the classes to the practical arena

2. Phase I Class Offerings

The education program was organized around two major concepts. First, there was a well known base of technical material that the FSD population needed to understand. Secondly, and perhaps more importantly, the division had a number of "experts" in developing large software systems whose expertise could help future projects. Therefore, the solution was to attack the problem in two ways:

1. Create a set of standards and practices that would be a base for all future projects. This was accomplished by having the FSD "experts" Document their approach to developing large software systems in a manual called the "FSD Standards and Practices" (Figure 1).

2. Create a set of classes to teach the new software concepts and organize them around the Standard and Practices. In doing this the classes could

emphasize the technical material and give practical help in running new projects. The classes that were taught through 1984 included:

a. Systematic Programming Workshop (SPW) which was the basic class that all FSD programmers attended. This class discussed basic concepts such as stepwise refinement, control structures, verification techniques, and abstractions. The class designed individual procedures using the model of a mathematical function.

b. Systematic Design Workshop (SDW) which extended the ideas of SPW by defining a state machine model for data abstractions and using it to present design, refinement, and verification methods.

c. Advanced Design Workshop (ADW) which extended the concepts of SPW/SDW by presenting an enhanced state machine model for designing asynchronous systems.

d. Software Management Workshop (SMW) which presented management models and methods for software development.

The objective of this program was to educate all programming professionals in SPW and to have the experienced software engineers attend SDW and ADW. In addition, all software managers plus the lead technical staff should attend the management class.

3. Phase II (1984 Course Evaluation)

In 1984, a major revision of the program was undertaken. Practically, all the FSD programmers had attended SPW and nearly 40% had attended SDW. A smaller number of students attended ADW (perhaps 10%) but this included a majority of the division's lead designers. FSD projects were reporting an increase in quality and productivity with the increased use of the software engineering standards and methodology. Continuing the education program was worthwhile but the classes should have reflected changes that were happening within FSD and the general programming environment such as:

- New FSD programs (such as FAA) had significant reliability requirements.

- New hires were joining the division who were very knowledgeable in software engineering methodology.

- There was an increasing need to train software subcontractors in the use of this methodology.

- There was an increasing need to relate the power of the Ada language to the design concepts stressed in the training program.

- The IBM Corporation had adopted the FSD education program and was now teaching that methodology to all IBM programmers. A course called Software Engineering Workshop (SEW) was developed that taught the SPW/SDW material in a single 2 week format at the Software Engineering Institute (SEI) in New York.

It was time to take a fresh approach to education; emphasize concepts that were working, summarize those points that were obvious, and introduce subjects that might be new and beneficial. All this needed to be done while still focusing on the practices that provided overall direction to FSD project development.

To address this situation, the Software Engineering Education department (SEEd) was established in October, 1984 and chartered with 3 primary goals:

1. To provide consistent software education to the entire division.

2. To establish a pool of consultants at each of the FSD sites that will help transfer the FSD technology to actual software development projects.

3. To provide education that will blend the FSD practices and technology with the Ada language.

The education staff consists of instructors from many of the major FSD sites who are responsible for conducting classes throughout the division. The education department keeps in close touch with SEI to gain insight into new software approaches being presented in the corporation. There are currently eight instructors, all accredited as SEI instructors, and an administrator in the FSD Software Engineering education department.

4. FSD Environment

A. IBM FSD Software Life Cycle

To really understand the FSD education program one needs to understand the FSD Practices and the life cycle that the program addresses. Figure 2 is the life cycle model of the software engineering process defined within the context of a typical FSD environment of concurrent hardware/software system development. The software life cycle organizes all work into seven activities. There are five development activities (system definition, software design, software development, software system test, and system/acceptance test) that takes the system from its initial conception to user acceptance. In addition, the operational support activity provides post-acceptance support and the general support activity spans the entire life cycle. These 7 activities are further divided into 26 subactivities or work components that provide more detail of the work involved.

Thirteen of these work components (Figure 3) show how a developing software system proceeds from definition to system acceptance. These 13 work components are classified as either design or test components. Progress down the left-hand side is made by stepwise refining the system through the sequence of design work components leading to Program Development. Progress up the right-hand side is made by integrating and testing the system through the sequence of test work components leading to an accepted system.

A fundamental relationship among the 13 work components is that each set of test work components corresponds to a set of design work components indicated by the dotted lines in Figure 3. Software integration is carried out according to the software design; software system test is conducted against the software specifications. Thus, the success criterion for each test work component is the responsiveness of the software implementation to the corresponding design work component.

In addition, the success criteria for each test work component are defined during the corresponding design work component. Thus, there is a determination of system acceptance test specifications with system specifications, system integration plans with system design, software test specifications with software specifications, and software integration plans with software design.

B. Life Cycle Application

Figure 3 is a basic model illustrating the sequence of steps by which system requirements are transformed into a physical system. Variations in individual projects are accommodated by properly applying and interpreting this basic model. In a hardware/software system development, Levels 1 and 2 result in a decomposition of the system into hardware and software elements, and their eventual integration and acceptance as a complete system. Levels 3 and 4 result in the implementation of the software elements, and typically have a hardware counterpart that results in a concurrent implementation of hardware elements.

Further decomposition of the system into multiple software products may take place at levels 2, 3, and 4. Thus, there may be many concurrent software implementations, each of which is progressing through its own life cycle from the point of decomposition to the point of integration.

Decomposition of the system into lower-level elements, whether occurring at the system or software levels, results in the creation of interfaces that are documented and controlled to ensure successful integration. Each element created by such a decomposition may be viewed as following its own parallel path of life cycle tasks. Its specification includes the interfaces defined by the decomposition as well as the allocated function, and its life cycle path retains its identity until the point at which the element is integrated with some other element.

Figure 3 depicts the ideal flow of a developing system through a sequence of Software Life Cycle work components, without explicitly considering perturbations caused by changes of requirements or the discovery of errors. As a result of such perturbations, previously completed work products may be extended or modified.

5. FSD Software Engineering Education

The SEEd classes were developed to support software activities at various phases of the FSD Software Life Cycle. In 1978, the focus was on detailed design activities as identified in the SPW, SDW, and ADW classes. The plan in 1984 was to enhance these existing classes and to add additional classes to address life cycle activities that were not covered. Additional classes would include a testing workshop dealing with unit and system testing, a software engineering class emphasizing the Ada language, and a class on system architecture. These classes and their intended audiences are shown in Table I. In addition to the software engineering courses taught by FSD instructors, there are computer science courses taught by university consultants.

More recently, design of an Ada curriculum has become an important topic. A candidate Ada curriculum is shown in Table II. Although some of the courses are currently being taught, the curriculum as a whole is under development.

In the last year and a half the education department has conducted 43 classes and trained approximately 950 students. These classes were taught at all FSD locations with the majority of classes in Gaithersburg and Bethesda, Maryland.

5.1. Class Offerings

The current list of classes offered by SEEd includes:

a). SOFTWARE ENGINEERING WORKSHOP (SEW) is a two week class that replaces the SPW/SDW classes. The workshop goals are to increase the student's ability to maintain intellectual control over software complexity and to encourage personal development and professionalism within the software community.

The first week deals with pure procedures, using the model of a mathematical function. All designs in SEW are expressed in PDL/Ada, an Ada based design language. The class defines a basis set of 8 control structures that are used to design all procedures. Stepwise refinement describes a methodical way to design starting with one intended function or assignment statement and continually replacing it with a structure from the basis set. Correctness is addressed by providing a verification method for each structure in the basis set.

The second week of SEW deals primarily with the subject of data and its refinement. The material is divided into three major topics; specifications, design, and proof of design correctness. A new model (state machine) extends the function model to include state or retained data, thus providing it with a memory.

SEW stresses the need to express two views of the module, one for the user and one for the designer. The user's view is achieved through the use of data abstraction in a specification that describes "what" the proposed module will do and hides the lower level details of design. All transitions (behavior and interfaces) are fully defined in terms of an abstract model for the state data.

Data is the main driver for the next step of refinement. Once the designer selects a concrete data structure for the design, the intended functions are rewritten in terms of the new data format.

The final step is to verify the design. The verification lecture gives students an insight into the mathematical process of correctness plus a set of informal questions that can be asked during a design inspection.

SEW has a case study to specify and design a management system for a county library. The case study teams must create a formal specification and at least one level of design from a set of high level requirements.

Much of the material in the SEW class is discussed in greater detail in the book

"Structured Programming" by Linger, Mills, and Witt (19) which is distributed to students.

b). ADVANCED DESIGN WORKSHOP (ADW) extends the modular design methodology taught in SEW to concurrent systems. It begins by identifying the problems unique to concurrent design and introducing an extension to the state machine model that stresses data encapsulation, coherence and stability.

The ADW model consists of three components, called Application, Control Services, and Hardware Services. Applications programs compute the information required by the client without regard for the potential interference of other executing programs. Control Services include run-time services such as creation of address space, inter-module communication, and non-interfering access to common data. Control Services intercepts program invocations, embeds the parameters in messages, sends the messages to the addressed module, and returns output parameters to the invoker. The Applications programs appear to Control Services as a network of modules. Hardware Services are concerned with presenting a "friendly" representation of the physical hardware being used. They are not concerned with the network of programs communicating between different memories; they are only concerned with the execution of one or more processors executing in a single memory. ADW provides students with both an understanding of the problems and an appreciation of the importance of safety and correctness in concurrent design. A variety of approaches to the design of safe, correct, concurrent systems is explored. A case study is included to reinforce the ideas and to give initial experience putting them into practice.

The primary focus of the course is on the Application and its interface with Control Services. The basic unit of design for Application programs is the module, which encapsulates persistent data. Programs are expected to terminate, and modules remain dormant until invocation. The network view facilitates distributed processing; however, undisciplined invocations can lead to deadlock. Methods for avoiding deadlock, management of data stability, data coherence, and task precedence are discussed in the course.

ADW addresses material found in a technical report by B. Witt, which served as the basis for two published papers, (24) (25), and other reading from the literature on concurrency (3), (7), (11), (20). This workshop is currently being extended to include high-level architecture considerations for system decomposition.

c). SOFTWARE MANAGEMENT WORKSHOP (SMW) is organized around the FSD life cycle and a Manage to Objectives (MTO) approach. The MTO approach satisfies three sets of objectives (cost, schedule, and product) through continuous planning, monitoring, and replanning as the project evolves. The management decisions that are made depend upon the relative priorities of the three sets of objectives to obtain optimal performance against them.

SMW has a model of the management process (Fig. 4) consisting of 2 planning processes (analysis and synthesis) and a supervision process. These three processes are embedded in a software environment that is unique to a project and location. The workshop spends nearly 80% of the time on the planning process and only briefly deals with supervision; this decision is based on experienced management's comments that supervision is well known and performed reasonably well while the planning activities tend to be less well understood and practiced.

The analysis process of planning provides 3 orientations for managers. A product orientation encourages managers to gain intellectual control of their project by identifying all known work products in a work breakdown structure. The schedule orientation defines key dependencies and major milestones which will provide a skeleton of a project's overall schedule. The cost orientation discusses top down or bottom up estimating and references the book "The Mythical man Month" (12).

The synthesis process uses knowledge from the analysis process to build a set of plans and controls for schedules, cost, and products. Cost controls are centered around the earned value concept. This term and its place in the FSD accounting system is defined, and various conservative methods of claiming earned value are discussed. Schedule controls primarily deal with the software development plan and the need to identify clear and precise milestones. The product controls concentrate on computer resources, the development resources, and the need for a strong software architect.

Supervision includes comparing actual measurements to planned values to determine the health of the project. Early detection of problems is critical to the success of a project because it permits a wider range of management options. Early visibility is provided through management reviews, technical inspections, and cost/schedule measurements.

Approximately 33% of the class consists of a case study where students have an opportunity to apply the SMW concepts.

Many of the SMW concepts are discussed in the book "The Program Development Process" by J.D. Aron (4).

d). SOFTWARE TESTING WORKSHOP (STW) is a workshop describing the role of testing in the FSD life cycle. The testing workshop focuses on development testing and system testing with proper testing tools applied to each area.

Development testing looks at the unit and integration testing done initially by the development programmers. STW discusses three levels of test coverage. CO coverage means that every instruction has been executed in the program at least once and CI coverage means each segment (code from one predicate to the next) is exercised at least once. The third level of unit test coverage is path coverage. Complete path coverage is impossible particularly when loops are present. Therefore, a compromise (called Ct coverage) is used with the assumption that one path through each loop closely approximates total path coverage. STW concludes that a coverage between Cl and Ct is recommended as the minimal acceptable unit test criterion and other levels of testing beyond unit testing are needed.

Integration testing is the second level of development testing. Incremental integration testing is stressed when the individual modules are joined together in increments and tested before other modules or units are added.

System testing should be done by an independent testing organization that views the system as a user. Four approaches to system testing are introduced with special emphasis placed on the cause-effect graphing technique. Testing tools are introduced in class with the objective of encouraging students to use and understand categories of tools, particularly those that are available at their location.

The class ends by discussing project planning and estimating issues relating to software testing problems and achieving software quality. A case study is introduced to reinforce many of the lecture principles. STW discusses many topics found in text books by Beizer (6) and Myers (21).

e). SOFTWARE ENGINERING WITH ADA (SEA) is a 40 hour workshop that focuses on the design of software systems with particular emphasis on the application of Ada language facilities to support software engineering. SEA is not intended to be an Ada language class, but a software engineering class that extends the basic concepts taught in SEW.

The major objectives of SEA are:

1. To be able to decompose a software system into modules using an Object-Oriented development (OOD) technique, and record the design using PDL/Ada.

2. To recognize the goals and principles of software engineering and describe how the following features of Ada support these principles and goals: packages, separate compilation, separation of specifications from bodies, strong typing, exceptions, generics, and tasking.

3. To be able to specify and refine designs using packages, generics, subprograms, exceptions, and tasking.

A design produced using the OOD process can be represented as having several layers, each layer at a decreasing level of abstraction. Connections between successive layers are viewed as refinements; that is, the modules that are specified in one layer are refined or implemented in terms of modules that are specified in the next lower layer. Modules are described in terms of the operations that are exported and the description of the state data that is encapsulated within the module.

SEA participants have ample opportunity to exercise the OOD process in a Case Study project. The Case Study exercise consists of three activities: Software Architecture, Subsystem Design, and Modular Design.

The class is built around a number of recent articles and books that are referenced in the workshop. (1), (2), (5), (9), (10), (13), (14), (15), (16), (22), (23), (24), and (25).

5.2. University Classes

f). INTERACTIVE SYSTEMS DESIGN (ISD) is a three day class taught by visiting college professors (principally Dr. Ben Shneiderman and Dr. Rex Hartson). This course discusses the relative merits of design alternatives such as menu selection and command languages for specific users and applications. Interactive issues such as user anxiety, response time, on-line aids and error handling are discussed and a management plan is presented that emphasizes human factors. Dialog management (theory, model and tools) is presented as an integral part of the software engineering problem. This course provides recent research results in the design and evaluation of interactive systems.

g). COMPUTER SCIENCE TECHNIQUES (CST) is a one week class taught by college professors. This class expands and builds upon the ideas presented in SEW. Mathematical logic, graph theory, finite state machines, efficiency measures and notations, representation of advanced data types, and verification of pre and post conditions are covered in this course. This course requires a higher level of mathematical maturity because CST emphasizes theory more than method and is highly analytical.

h). SCIENCE OF PROGRAMMING is an experimental course taught by Professor David Gries of Cornell University, based on the material in his book(17). This class introduces a theory of correctness and uses it to develop programs from formal specifications. The theory is reinforced by developing 30-40 algorithms during the week.

6. Consultation

Starting the last quarter of 1985, the SEEd began hosting a series of meetings for experienced lead designers and programmers from multiple FSD business areas. The objectives for these round table meetings are:

- Share the experiences gained from developing software systems in FSD, with the goal of better application of methods, better designs and new insights.

- Refine the concept of a "common vision" for FSD software design methodology.

- Foster discussions about the essential elements, objectives, theoretical basis, and practical basis of software design.

- Discuss SEW concepts aimed at producing error-free software.

Benefits are foreseen from a regular exchange of ideas related to software design, software management, and software testing.

7. Conclusion

Beginning in the early 1980's, a few large software system programs (software systems that contained more than a million lines of high level source code) at FSD began design and development using the standards and methodology taught in the division's software engineering training program. The initial results demonstrated that the quality of the FSD software product was greatly enhanced. Some of the measured results and/or conclusions were (18):

- The rate of documented errors was relatively low as compared to other large scale systems.

- The error corrections were localized to a few modules. One system reported that the average number of modules changed per error was 1.9.

- The number of fixes that did not resolve the errors was low, perhaps in the 5% range.

- The number of fixes that introduced new errors was also very small, perhaps less than 1%.

This trend has been very encouraging. While the initial goal was to improve productivity, FSD has seen that the quality of our software has greatly improved. More subjectively, it appears that the software systems have improved in other ways such as:

- The software systems appear more manageable; there are more opportunities to gain early insight into the quality of the product and to take corrective actions.

- The classes provide a common software vocabulary for programmers throughout the division.

- More programmers identify with the software development approach and can provide alternatives to management for addressing problems.

All of these aspects indicate the success of the education program. By expanding the education classes and emphasizing the total FSD life cycle, the division expects more improvements in the areas of quality and productivity.

The transition from the software engineering program to the current SEEd organization has been driven by marked success in FSD software developments traceable to the divisions training program. Now, SEEd endeavors to maintain the momentum and extend the influence and contributions of software education. The continuing review of trends and developments, use of the proven, and exploration into the new, including input from consultants, round table discussions, and management and student feedback will be resources for this goal.

References

1. Abbot, R.J., "Program Design by Informal English Descriptions", *Communications of the ACM*, Vol.26, No.11, November 1983, pp. 882-894.

2. American National Standards Institute, Ada Programming Language, ANSI/MIL-STD 1815A, Washington, D.C., Government Printing Office, 1983.

3. Andrews, G.R., "Synchronizing Resources", *ACM Transactions on Programming Languages and Systems*, Vol.3, No.4, October 1981, pp. 405-430.

4. Aron, J.D., The Program Development Process, The Programming Team, Part II, Addison-Wesley, 1983.

5. Barnes, J.G.P., Programming In Ada, 2nd. Ed., Addison-Wesley, 1984.

6. Beizer, Boris, Software Testing Techniques, Van Nostrand Reinhold, 1983.

7. Birrell, A.D. and Nelson, B.J., "Implementing Remote Procedure Call", *ACM Transactions on Computer Systems*, Vol.2, No.1, February 1984, pp. 39-59.

8. Boehm, B.W., Software Engineering Economics, Prentice-Hall, 1981.

9. Booch, G., "Object-Oriented Development", *IEEE Transactions on Software Engineering*, Vol.12, No.2, February 1986, pp. 211-221.

10. Booch, G., Software Engineering with Ada, Benjamin/Cummings, 1983.

11. Brinch-Hansen, P., "Distributive Process: A Concurrent Programming Concept", *Communications of the ACM*, Vol.21, No.11, November 1978, pp. 934-941.

12. Brooks, F.P., Jr., The Mythical Man-Month, Addison-Wesley, 1975.

13. Brosgol, B.M., "Tutorial on Exception Handling in Ada", *Proceedings of the 1986 Washington Ada Symposium, DC SIGAda*, 1986.

14. Burns, A., Concurrent Programming in Ada, Cambridge University Press, 1985.

15. Cohen, N.H., "Tasks on Abstraction Mechanisms", *Ada Letters*, Vol.5, No.3-6, November-December 1985, pp. 30-44.

16. Gehani, N., Ada: Concurrent Programming, Prentice-Hall, 1984.

17. Gries, D., The Science of Programming, Springer-Verlag, 1981.

18. Jordano, A.J., "DSM Software Architecture and Development", *FSD Technical Directions*, Vol.10, No.3, 1984.

19. Linger, R.C., Mills, H.D. and Witt, B.I., Structured Programming, Theory and Practice, Addison-Wesley, 1979.

20. Liskov, B., "On Linguistic Support for Distributed Programs", *IEEE Transactions on Software Engineering*, Vol.SE-8, No.3, May 1982, pp. 203-210.

21. Myers, G.J., The Art of Software Testing, Wiley-Interscience, 1979.

22. Parnas, D.L., "On the Criteria to be Used in Decomposing a System into Modules", *Communications of the ACM*, Vol.15, No.12, December 1972, pp. 131-136.

23. Ross, D.T., Goodenough, J.B., and Irvine, C.A., "Software Engineering: Process, Principles, and Goals", *IEEE Computer*, Vol.8, No.5, May 1975.

24. Witt, B.I., "Parallelism, Pipelines, and Partitions, Variations on Communicating Modules", *IEEE Computer*, Vol.18, No.2, February 1985, pp. 105-112.

25. Witt, B.I., "Communicating Modules: A Software Design Model for Concurrent Distributive Systems", *IEEE Computer*, Vol.18, No.1, January 1985, pp. 67-77.

Acknowledgments

We would like to thank Sam Schappelle and Dr. Mei-Cheng Hu for their involvement in the writing of this paper, particularly their inputs to the SEA and STW sections.

ORGANIZATION OF THE FSD SOFTWARE ENGINEERING PRACTICES

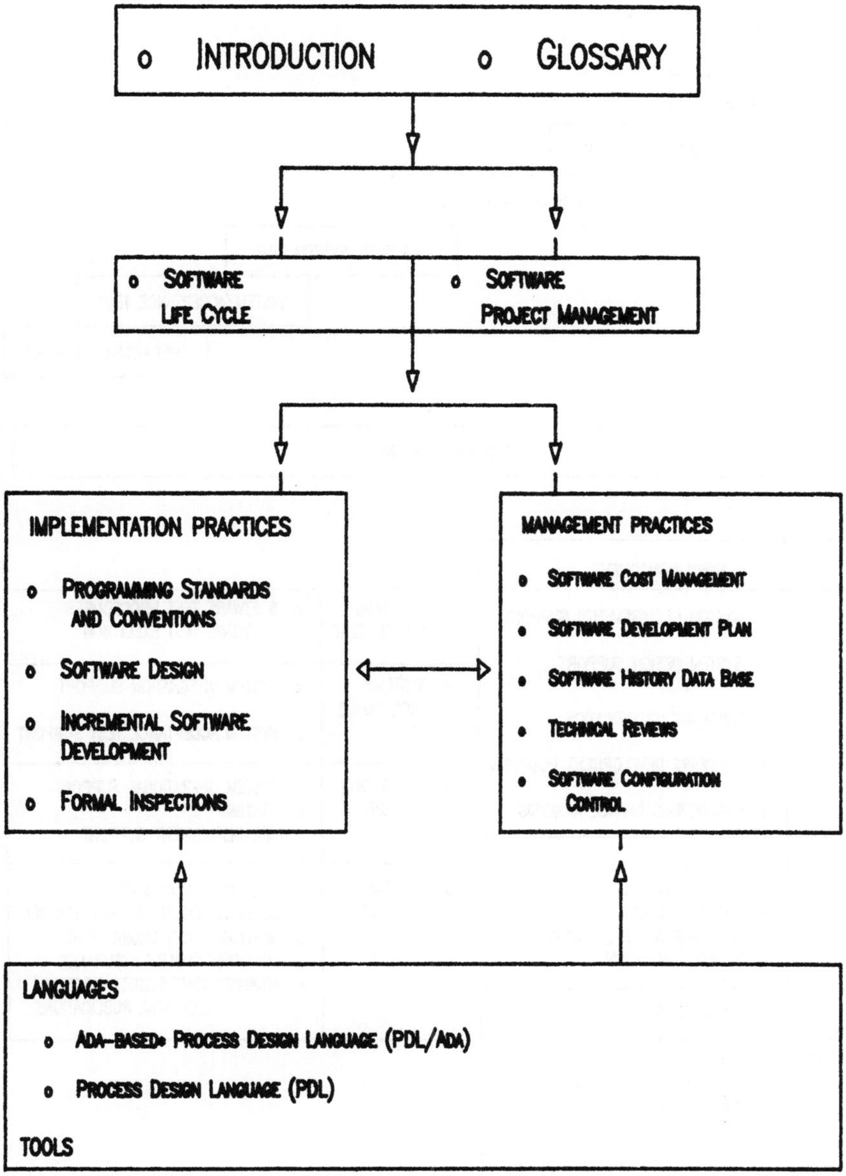

* ADA IS A REGISTERED TRADEMARK OF THE U.S. GOVERNMENT, ADA JOINT PROGRAM OFFICE

FIG. 1

THE BASIC LIFE CYCLE

LIFE CYCLE ACTIVITIES

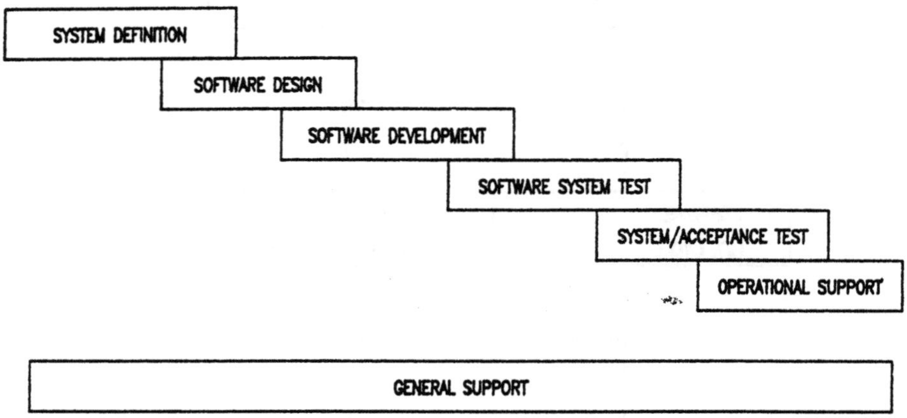

ACTIVITY	WORK COMPONENT
o SYSTEM DEFINITION	o SYSTEM REQUIREMENTS SUPPORT o SYSTEM DESIGN SUPPORT o SOFTWARE SPECIFICATION o SOFTWARE DEVELOPMENT PLANNING o ENGINEERING CHANGE ANALYSIS
o SOFTWARE DESIGN	o FUNCTIONAL DESIGN o INTEGRATION PLANNING o PROGRAM DESIGN o SOFTWARE TOOLS DEFINITION o DESIGN EVALUATION
o SOFTWARE DEVELOPMENT	o PROGRAM DEVELOPMENT o UNIT TESTING o INTEGRATION TESTING o PROBLEM ANALYSIS AND CORRECTION
o SOFTWARE SYSTEM TEST	o SOFTWARE TEST PROCEDURES o SOFTWARE TEST EXECUTION
o SYSTEM/ ACCEPTANCE TEST	o SYSTEM INTEGRATION SUPPORT o SYSTEM ACCEPTANCE TEST SUPPORT
o OPERATIONAL SUPPORT	o SYSTEM OPERATIONAL SUPPORT o TRAINING o SITE DEPLOYMENT SUPPORT
o GENERAL SUPPORT	o PROJECT MANAGEMENT o SOFTWARE CONFIGURATION CONTROL o SOFTWARE COST ENGINEERING o SOFTWARE QUALITY ASSURANCE o ADMINISTRATIVE SYSTEM CENTERS/ TECHNICAL PUBLICATIONS

FIG. 2

DESIGN – TEST RELATIONSHIPS

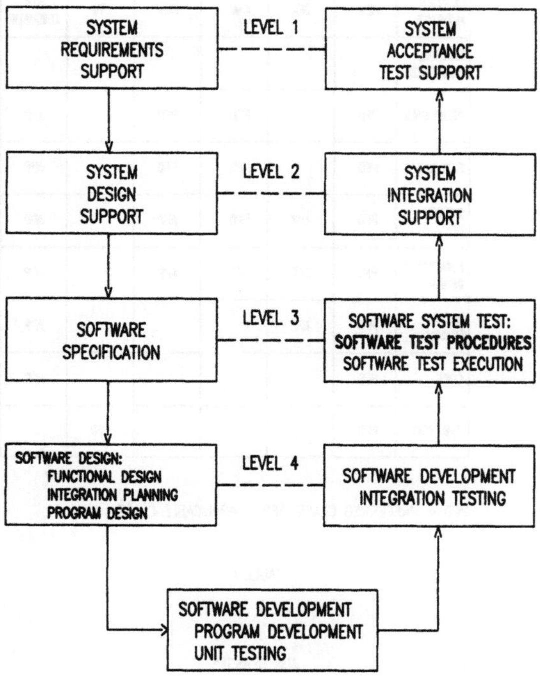

FIG. 3

A MODEL OF MANAGEMENT ACTIVITY

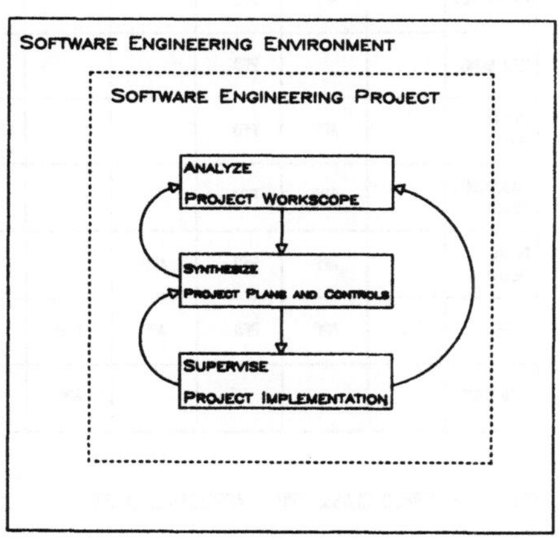

FIG. 4

S/W ENGINEERING CLASSES

CLASSES AUDIENCE	SEW	SEA	SAW	SMW	STW	STW OVERVIEW
GENERAL AWARENESS						
PROPOSALS	PFD		PFD	PFD		APP
S/W MGMT	PFD		APP	PFD		APP
SYSTEM DEF.	PFD	APP	PFD	APP		APP
FUNCTIONAL DESIGN	PFD	PFD	APP	APP		APP
DETAIL DESIGN	PFD	APP				APP
CODE	PFD					APP
S/W TEST	PFD				PFD	

PFD - PREFERRED CLASS; APP - APPLICABLE CLASS

TABLE I

ADA CLASSES

CLASSES AUDIENCE	BASIC ADA	INTRO TO ADA	SEA	ADVANCED TOPICS	ADA EXTERNALS	ADA INTERNALS
GENERAL AWARENESS		PFD	PFD			
PROPOSALS		APP	PFD			
S/W MGMT			PFD			
SYSTEM DEF.		APP	PFD			PFD
FUNCTIONAL DESIGN		APP	PFD			PFD
DETAIL DESIGN		APP	PFD	APP		PFD
CODE	PFD	APP	PFD	APP	PFD	
S/W TEST					APP	

PFD - PREFERRED CLASS; APP - APPLICABLE CLASS

TABLE II

THE CHALLENGE OF TECHNOLOGY TRANSFER

John E. Gibson, IBM Federal Systems Division
Vicki K. Heilig, IBM Federal Systems Division

ABSTRACT

Because of the increasingly complex nature of the work undertaken by Federal Systems Division of IBM, a software engineering curriculum was initiated to train all programmers in the division's practices for developing high-quality software. These practices were selected from the best academic and industrial experience available and they were documented to ensure their consistent application across the division's wide range of projects. While the division had great success in developing the classes, teaching them and measuring the student's ability to understand and use the concepts, the challenge of their usefulness was whether the technology could be transferred to the working environment. To speed this transfer and to exchange ideas and experiences associated with using the technology in the field, a Software Engineering Forum was defined and conducted to aid lead designers and programmers in sharing information about experiences gained and technology learned. They also aided the Software Engineering Education Department in making assessments about the practicality and usefulness of te concepts, tools, and technologies taught by the department.

1. INTRODUCTION

Traditionally, Federal Systems Division (FSD) of IBM has been involved in providing specialized technology in both hardware and software to the United States government. Because these activities usually dealt with large complex, long term systems both in development and use, the division recognized that the latest state-of-the-art technology should be understood and applied by all the programmers in the division, if the division were to remain competitive. Leading this drive for modern software development practices was Dr. Harlan Mills.

His work in the academic environment, coupled with his knowledge of the practical experience being accrued by the 2000+ programmers in FSD, led him to the conclusion that more systematic, mathematical rigor was needed in the software development process. Additionally, Dr. Mills convinced then Division President, John Jackson, that all programmers in the division should be trained in the new practices. To meet this goal the division developed and implemented a series of software engineering classes to educate the entire programming population.

All 2000+ programmers attended the basic class in the series, the Systematic Programming Workshop (SPW). Some 800+ key designers in the division attended a more advanced Systematic Design Workshop (SDW). In 1982, these two FSD classes were combined into a two-week Software Engineering Workshop (SEW) by the Software Engineering Institute, IBM Corporation, New York City. (The course is currently being offered to programmers throughout the corporation.) Other courses that have added rigor to the software development process are: Advanced Design Workshop (ADW), Software Management Workshop (SMW), Software Testing Workshop (STW), Software Engineering with Ada[1] (SEA, Interactive Systems Design (ISD), and Computer Science Techniques (CST). The technology itself is discussed in references (1), (2), (3), (4), (5), (6), (7), (8), (9), (10), (11), (12), (13), (14), (15).

Once this technology has been mastered in the classroom, the challenge is to transfer the techniques and concepts to the practical environment where new, bigger, and more complex problems of software development are on the rise. This paper will describe the Software Engineering Forum, FSD's vehicle for spreading the use of the technology in the field. Included in the description will be a discussion of its incorporation, its definition, its execution, and its benefits.

[1]Ada is a registered trademark of the U.S. Government, Ada Joint Program Office

2. THE NEED FOR TECHNOLOGY TRANSFER

After programmers and engineers have attended Software Engineering classes, they return to their projects where tailored interpretations of the core methodology are employed. There the fundamental ideas are internalized through practice, and te methodology is refined and extended. This leads to diversity and evolutionary enhancements to the techniques. In-the-field adaptation addresses the problems of scaling the technology up to handle extremely large (1.5 million source lines of code) software systems, of adjusting the terminology and software design components to match changing government standards, and of incorporating the use of tools (e.g., library management, architecture definition, and others).

Some technology transfers locally through established channels such as Software Engineering Councils (staffed by software executives) or through internal publications. Some of the advances made by each project are transferred by informal conversations between friends or by chance when personnel rotate among projects. In addition to these channels, the Software Engineering Education Department of the Federal Systems Division has created a Software Engineering Forum to offer an avenue of direct technology transfer between software technology experts on a regular organized basis.

The following sections will examine Forum objectives, method of formation, synopses of early meetings and conclusions.

3. FORUM OBJECTIVES

The objectives of the Forum are:

- To share design experiences gained from developing software systems in FSD, with the goal of better application of methods, better designs and new insights.
- To refine the concept of a "common vision" for FSD software design methodology.

- To foster discussions about the essential elements, objectives, theoretical basis, and practical basis of software design.
- To discuss Software Engineering Workshop (SEW) concepts aimed at producing error-free software.

4. METHOD OF FORMATION

To identify representatives to the Forum, the first invitation letters were sent to Software Development Mangers in the Federal Systems Divisions. This process helped to inform the managers who lead software organizations of the formation of the Forum and to get them to commit to sending a representative. The invitation letter stated that the attendees should be programmers who:

- have been actively engaged in software design for at least four years with IBM
- are graduates of SEW (or Systematic Design Workshop, an earlier version of SEW)
- are non-management technical leaders who influence or establish software development practices in their areas.

Because the invitations went to different functional areas, attendees nominated had diverse backgrounds with experience over different projects, customers, system sizes, etc. These differing viewpoints allowed most facets of software design, software management and software testing to be addressed. The originators of the Forum stressed that the frequency of the meetings would depend on the software community's response to the first meeting. While the first meeting was attended by programmers, it was suggested that some future meetings could include software managers.

At the first Forum, the attendees planned for short, focused meetings (two hours) to allow each meeting to have a theme. It was also decided that the participants would have a rotating responsibility for taking minutes and distributing them, and that the participants themselves would help choose the topics for discussion. The Forum guidelines for conducting the meetings included scheduling meetings every one to two months.

The Software Engineering Education Department's role was to organize and coordinate the meetings, to speak on the technology or obtain other speakers from throughout the Division, to disseminate information about the Forums and other related meetings, to conduct seminars for the various projects, and to provide consultation about the technology as the projects requested it.

From the first meeting in October, 1985, the regular exchange of ideas in the monthly Forum has increased the flow of information about software design, management, testing and tools used in the local Washington Metropolitan area within FSD. Even people from different areas of the same project are sharing ideas about tools that have a common usability.

5. MEETING SYNOPSES

In the FSD Forum the topics presented were of interest and use across projects. Listed below is a synopsis of some sample presentations discussed in the Forums.

- The benefits and deficiencies of our formal design methodology have been expressed over the course of several meetings. Benefits include: a) designs are necessary for learning one's way into a solution to a software system (the idea that design is part of a continuum to code), b) designs are needed to maintain intellectual control over a large, complex software system (essential for coordinating the efforts of a hundred or more people), c) designs are needed by people new to a project (assuming design records abstractions at several levels of detail). Deficiencies were also noted: a) designs become too detailed and are no easier to read than code, b) retaining designs adds an additional level of maintenance that contracts don't provide for, c) minimal number of tools were available to compensate for the increase in text processing and symbol processing that formal designs entail.

- Formal designs recorded in an Ada based Program Design Language are generally large and relatively slow reading. Their strong points are precision and completeness. They don't make good view foils for customer presentations. For Preliminary Design Reviews (PDR) and Critical Design

Reviews (CDR), graphical abstractions of system design are more appropriate and faster to comprehend. At one meeting we discussed the problems of customer reviews and shared ways of graphically depicting the designs. An interesting point arose concerning these customer reviews: even though design graphics are created for formal meetings, the customers are insisting that the complete design be reviewed by their staffs prior to or subsequent to the PDRs and CDRs. This means that now we must produce and support two forms of recording system design and must be prepared to answer questions about both forms.

- Designs are generally recorded as state machines at the highest level of abstraction. We often try to decompose a system into a small number (say six if possible, but as many as necessary) of these software components. If the system is not interrupt-driven and is composed of components that may run concurrently but don't interact with one another, fairly straightforward hierarchies and networks are sufficient to describe a system. At one meeting, two people from FSD Headquarters reported on their special, one-year assignment to apply the methodologies to a distributed processing system. The architecture needed for this system was significantly different from the architecture most Forum members were familiar with. They devised two basic components called "storage objects" and "task objectives." These had some of the attributes of functions and state machines, our usual software models, but were significantly different because of the triggering and blocking mechanisms built into the data objects. The system architecture was a graph with data objects and task objects as nodes.

- Our Program Design Language is based on Ada (PDL/Ada), but until very recently, our implementation has been in JOVIAL, PL/I, or assembler. Using PDL/Ada for design can lead to problems when translating Ada to a target language. The primary difficulty occurs with data structures because Ada supports more complex structures and imposes fewer restrictions than the target language. To preclude these difficulties, projects often document the structures allowed in their implementation language and then supply guidelines for PDL/Ada data structures that can be translated to the target structures, i.e., design options are restricted. Ada has closed control structures (IF, WHILE and other structures are terminated with an ENDIF or ENDLOOP), but some target languages do not, e.g., JOVIAL. In addition, JOVIAL and other languages require a BEGIN-END keyword pair for a sequence of statements and Ada does not. One project in Gaithersburg took an approach that was the converse of the usual. They modified their target language to make it look more Ada-like. They accomplished this, using the DEFINE capability of JOVIAL. The subsequent translation of PDL/Ada to JOVIAL produced code that was easier to visually compare to its design, was less subject to translation errors, and had fewer data structure restrictions imposed on the designs.

The Forum members hear technology information as described above first-hand and are able to report it back to high level software management. This forges a direct connection for technology transfer that is short, direct and quick. The ultimate success of the Forum approach depends on team effort (project representatives, project managers and education department).

Each must encourage and support one another. Third-level managers, in particular, play a key role. They hold the technology resources and they strongly influence the level of participation of their representatives. We urged management to encourage representatives to share project technology and to ask for minutes of the proceedings of each Forum.

In addition to disseminating information to the individual FSD projects, the Forum has also been very beneficial to the Software Engineering Education Department because the topics discussed have included:

- What concepts/tools/technologies are being used on the projects?
- Which are valuable and/or practical, which are not?
- Which are used in total, which are used partially?
- Which are easy to use as taught, which are difficult?

Because most FSD projects have Federal government customers, their development activities and work products are similar. These include system definition, software design and development, system/acceptance test, tools, and design language (PDL/Ada). Lessons learned on one project are then directly applicable to another project. The Forum speeds information about these lessons to each project as well as serving to aid the education department to determine the success and failures of the technology.

6. CONCLUSIONS

The Forum discussions have helped the developers and teachers of the technology decide what we as a division have learned now that we have applied the technology on projects. The Forum is a place for analyzing and advertising the successes and the failures. Some discussions include reasons for discarding parts of the technology because applications were unique, and the standard technology did not apply. However, for the Software Engineering Education Department, the major benefit of the Forum has been to "measure the water" where the use of the technology is concerned and to compare what is taught against the application of the technology. This will allow us to enhance, stress, improve, de-emphasize or change the technology as deemed appropriate in our environment and it provides us a standardized, formal avenue for disseminating the technology to the projects throughout the division. Because of the word-of-mouth endorsements of the success of the Forums, other divisions within IBM are adopting the concept for use in their environments where work components and products are more diverse than those of FSD.

References

1. Aron, J.D., "The Program Development Process, The Programming Team, Part III", Addison Wesley, 1983.

2. Barnes, J.G.P., Programming in Ada, 2nd Ed., Reading, Mass., Addison Wesley, 1984.

3. Beizer, Boris, Software Testing Techniques, Van Nostrand Reinhold, 1983.

4. Birrell, A.D. and Nelson, B.J., "Implementing Remote Procedure Call", *ACM Transactions on Computer Systems*, Vol. 2, No. 1, February 1984, pp 39-59.

5. Boehm, Barry W., Software Engineering Economics, Prentice Hall, 1981.

6. Booch, G., "Object-Oriented Development", *IEEE Transactions on Software Engineering*, 12:2, February, 1986, pp 211-221.

7. Booch, G., Software Engineering with Ada, Menlo Park, California: Benjamin/Cummings, 1983.

8. Brinch-Hansen, P., "Distributive Process: A Concurrent Programming Concept", *CACM*, vol. 21, No. 11, November 1978, pp 934-941.

9. Brooks, Frederick P., Jr., The Mythical Man-Month, Addison-Wesley, 1975.

10. Jordano, Anthony J., "DSM Software Architecture and Development", *FSD Technical Directions*, Vol. 10, No. 3, 1984.

11. Linger, R.C., Mills. H.D., Witt, B.I., Structured Programming, Theory and Practice, Addison-Wesley, 1979.

12. Myers, Glenford J., The Art of Software Testing, Wiley Interscience, 1979.

13. Parnas, D.L., "On the Criteria to be Used in Decomposing a System into Modules", *Communications of the ACM*, 15:12, December, 1972, pp 131-136.

14. Witt, B.I., "Parallelism, Pipelines, and Partitions, Variations on Communicating Modules", *IEEE Computer*, Vol. 18, No. 2, February, 1985, pp 105-112.

15. Witt, B.I., "Communicating Modules: A Software Design Model for Concurrent Distributive Systems", *IEEE Computer*, Vol. 18, No. 1, January, 1985, pp 67-77.

SECTION III

PANEL SESSIONS

Section III consists of two Parts that contain edited transcripts of two panel sessions and the associated question/answer sessions. The first panel, contained in Part 1, presents four models of industrial/academic interfaces in software engineering education. Part 2 contains the edited transcript of a panel session on the role of Ada in software engineering education.

SECTION III

PART 1

FOUR MODELS OF INDUSTRY/ACADEMIA INTERFACES

Part 1 contains the edited transcript of a panel session and the associated question/answer session on industry/academia interfaces in software engineering education. The panelists were Mark Ardis of Wang Institute, Jonah Lavi of the Israel Aircraft Industry, William Lively of Texas A&M University, and Doug Politi of General Electric. Priscilla Fowler of SEI was chair of the panel. The panelists' remarks are based on their papers, which are contained in Section II, Parts 3 & 4.

Panel Session on Four Models of Industry/Academia Interface

Priscilla Fowler: I'm happy to be organizing the panel entitled "Four Models of Industry/Academia Interface." I think that both industry and academia have made pretty significant contributions to software engineering education. However, I think if you added up all the students who have become practitioners, who have gone through Continuing Education Programs or Retraining-type programs at IBM, AT&T, Boeing Computer Services, Hewlett-Packard and Digital, you would probably give the academic people a run for their money, in terms of actual completions through the program and the generation of people doing software engineering. Until recently, many companies not only offered their own courses, but wrote their own texts and designed their own curriculum. Only recently, we have begun to see software engineering courses commonly offered with a few degree programs.

This is a shift toward a much more collaborative approach between academia and industry, for teaching software engineers. There is a significant relationship between a local industry community and an academic institution, or between a local university and a collection of industries. For instance, the Beltway Bandits have had a lot to do with what the University of Maryland teaches. Route 128 has a lot to do with what Wang Institute has taught.

I'd like to point out where the key elements and threads are. You must try to learn through your own Industrial Training Programs, how to set them up or improve them.

Mark Ardis: I'd like to talk about Wang Institute's Master's of Software Engineering Program. First, I'd like to acknowledge my colleagues and full-time faculty members of Wang Institute.

Wang Institute is a very cooperative environment, which I think is very unusual. I will explain how that cooperation has helped us evolve, and try to point out the unique aspects of the program.

In talking about Wang Institute, I usually explain how it is different from Wang Laboratories. Wang Institute is a fully accredited, independent graduate institution, which has been funded largely by Dr. An Wang. Recently, he decided he could no longer support us. Because he is no longer our benefactor, we are going out of business.

There are six required courses in our program: Formal Methods, Programming Methods, Software Engineering Methods, Computer Systems Architecture, and two management courses; one is called Management Concepts, and the other is called Software Project Management. Students must also complete two project courses. Each project course takes a semester to complete. Each has three to seven students in it. In addition, we have traditional, technical, or management electives, in either computer science or business areas. Each student takes three of those.

I'd like to elaborate on each of the aforementioned courses. Formal Methods is a theory course. It has sometimes been called, "boot camp at Wang Institute." It's too much theory, but it's supposed to be all the computer science theory a software engineer needs to know, in one semester. The most important part of it happens to be the first three lines, verification, abstraction, and specification. Those three concepts are taught with success because they introduce many more concepts and notation that get used later on in the curriculum. The formal language theory and the analysis of algorithms are prerequisite topics that students need, although they aren't as necessary as the first three topics. Programming Methods and Software Engineering Methods are two courses that are frequently packaged together in a software engineering course, in a computer science department. The division is that Programming Methods stresses what an individual does, whereas Software Engineering Methods stresses what groups do together. Thus, Programming Methods consists of coding, debugging and testing, and Software Engineering Methods consist of requirements analysis, specification, and high level design.

The Computing Systems Architecture Course has changed over the years, but it's somewhere between a traditional operating systems course and a traditional computer architecture course. In fact, we have offered either one of those two courses, to satisfy this requirement. The management courses try to do two things. First, the Management Concepts Course is based on management appreciation. Many of our students have technical backgrounds and have never taken a management course before. Their problem is trying to understand what managers do, why they get paid so much money, and what their overall value is worth. A lot of management concepts raise simple organizational issues and organizational structures. Furthermore, management concepts introduce accounting, finance, marketing, and behavior modification. Incidentally, we've had students walk out of lectures in this course. They were so outraged by behavior modification, for example. There are a lot of projects going on at the Institute, all the time. Hence, just about every course has a project hidden inside.

These courses are related to one another in that they both have prerequisites to the program. We have courses, as prerequisites to the program, that are the kinds of courses you would see in a traditional, undergraduate Computer Science Program, such as discrete mathematics, high level languages, data structures, and assembly language. We also require at least one year of work experience. Those prerequisites lead into the required courses, and it is evident that there is a relationship between the courses that have methods. Thus, Formal Methods leads to Programming Methods, which leads to Software Engineering Methods.

Students actually take the courses during the three consecutive semesters, if they are full-time students. Therefore, they must take Formal Methods and Programming Methods during the same semester. We have worked very hard to make sure that the prerequisite structures still apply. Furthermore, there are other courses that are related to one another, that are not violated. Hence, a typical scenario for a full-time student, is to take four courses in the first semester, four in the second, and three in the summer semester.

Trying to describe the average student is risky, because actually, our students are quite unique. However, the average student is about 30 years old and has about five years of work experience. Most students are employed by computer manufacturers or software houses in the Boston area. 128 is a fertile hunting ground for this kind of program; the current class comes from 20 different companies. Some of our students are international; we've had students from Columbia, Brazil, Switzerland, India, China, and Australia. Hence, the student body is quite diverse.

We have a significant problem trying to make this very heterogeneous group of people work together. However, we succeed in doing so. The current class is roughly half full-time and half part-time. The part-time students work in the local Boston area and they take one or two courses a semester. All of our courses are in the afternoon. Therefore, students are usually able to get time off from work. They usually have some kind of flexible hour arrangement. About half of the full-time students are teaching assistants and/or research assistants. The other students are full-time sponsored. That is, their company has paid for them to go to school full-time, for one year.

What do we have to offer these students? Resourses are a critical issue; we don't have enough of them. We have a fair amount of hardware. We have a 785 VAX and a 750 VAX, currently running on Unix. In addition, we have a Wang VS 100 that we have been using for word processing, although that's become less and less popular, since we have so many PC's. Even though we have a lot of computer horsepower around, it is still not enough. We don't have any work stations, but we do have a lot of software. We have standard compilers and text editors, and we have tried very hard to bring lots of other tools into our environment.

Currently, we have 10 faculty members. Additionally, we have a great staff, which has made life bearable. We have a nice computer center, consisting of six full-time computer center employees, and several student operators. They support primarily the academic side , as well as the administrative side. We have a library staff of four, which has helped us in on line searches and tool searches. A couple of students always work as faculty technical staff. Typically, we hire them after they graduate. Finally, we have four faculty secretaries. Thus, I've been very happy with the support, except for the hardware.

Curriculum is largely due to Dick Fairley and has been modified and endorsed by the National Academic Advisory Committee. This is a group of academics and industrialists who come to the institute once or twice a year to help us out and to make sure that we're on track. Every semester, a very comprehensive course notebook is created, which contains all of the lecture material, readings, homeworks, and exams. Hence, it is easy to work from previous faculty member's experiences, and we review every course before it is offered. The instructor sends out the syllabus for the new semester, so that everybody can look at it and make sure that changes that should have been made from last semester, really have been made. Finally, we've had some comprehensive evaluations, where the faculty has, as a group, looked over all the courses and made some modification and written a final report.

A problem seems to exist with students who have come full-time, thus disrupting their careers. How do you get prople to quit a job, where they are advancing, to go to school? Well, you have to compress the program into one year or they won't do it.

What about students who are narrow but deep? We've had a lot of them. You need something like the immigration course. We had a prerequisite structure, but the only way that you can find out about it is by talking to people. We had oral admissions exams; they are very time consuming.

What about conflicts with work? We insisted that our courses would never be taught at night. Most of our students have a type A personality. They can't stand to do poorly in anything. But, when they're given a course that requires 12 to 15 hours of work outside of class every week, and they are trying to work full-time, there is definitely going to be a conflict. Therefore, we insist at the oral admissions exam, that students bring this point up with their manager and tell him or her that they are serious about going to school.

How do you make sure that methods really get applied? We taught the fundamentals of one course, practiced them in another course, and practiced them again in a project course. By having an integrated curriculum, we could do that. It worked very well.

What about communication and teamwork? We have a lot of projects, not just the project courses, but projects within the courses. A lot of role playing goes on; in a typical project course, four students may play up to 12 different roles. The change in perspective is important for them. The nicest thing we had was a great student- faculty ratio of about six to one. We deliberately kept enrollment down and we brought in lots of adjunct and visiting faculty.

Craig Cleaveland: Given the fact that you had your angel, sole source cost of the program, you paint a very rosy picture, in terms of resources that you have the student- faculty ratio, et cetera. Is it possible that such an institute will arise elsewhere?

Mark Ardis: I think it is a significant problem and I don't know the solution. We thought long and hard about this when we heard that we were going out of business. A lot of the cost of our program had to do with the fact that we were a start-up, and we were isolated. Moreover, we had no economy of scale. For example, we did not live in a university environment, where there was already a library. Nevertheless, it will never be a profitable institution if it's a Master's Level Program, because master's level students are only there one year and there aren't enough of them to bring in enough tuition. I really don't know the answer. We were developing a Ph.D. Program in Software Engineering and we thought that that might help out.

Norm Gibbs: I heard a recent comment that that was a truly noble experiment for a master's degree education, but somehow got caught up with the traditional university value system. In other words, it started to move toward a Ph.D. program. Did you feel closer to the university system than to the industrial system?

Mark Ardis: Well, I think that faculty and career path is a problem. It's difficult to attract faculty who are interested in doing research, unless you have Ph.D. students. This poses a significant problem. What we found was that people who were interested in doing research, could only do so much with master's level students. They were frustrated because they could only get so much out of master's level students, and then they were gone. It became very difficult to have continuity. The model we were adopting, was to hire people. We had hired programmers to work on projects and provide the continuity. However, that wasn't enough. Therefore, I think that if you're interested in doing research, you've got to have a Ph.D. program. If you don't have an environment where you encourage research in software engineering, it's difficult to compete with other universities. There are so many rewards for doing research, that are recognized outside of the institute.

Norm Gibbs: I'm afraid I formulated my question unclearly. What I was really trying to get at was that if you had stayed in business, you would have ended up looking exactly like a lot of other places, even though you started out significantly different. You went out of business because it was such a unique experiment in education, although you were drifting toward becoming a typical research university.

Mark Ardis: We clearly had a vision that we were to be still very unique, even with a Ph.D. program. First of all, the whole concept of software engineering is a separate discipline from computer science. I think we saw ourselves as being somewhere between management and computer science. For example, we have members of our faculty who have management degrees, as opposed to technical degrees.

Secondly, we always thought the Ph.D. program assisted the Master's level program, and that the Professional Degree Program would always be a major part of the Wang Institute. That is, we thought that the research done in the Ph.D. program would lead to better tools and methods, which we could teach in the Master's Level Program. However, we never thought of the Ph.D. program as eclipsing the Master's Program.

Dick Fairley: It's also true that we were able to set our own reward structure, because we did not live in a large university environment. Thus, the Ph.D. program would always have been kept in proper perspective. People would have continued to be rewarded for being good teachers. In a larger university environment, it's a very serious question, of whether or not you could attract the kind of people and run the kind of program you want, and still compete on the grounds that other people in the university are competing on. However, we were unique in the sense that we didn't have that larger structure.

Jonah Lavi: I'll discuss the IAI–Israel Aircraft Industries experience in the training of software engineers. IAI is a large company, which employs about 20,000 people. One of our main businesses is the development of embedded systems such as avionics, missiles, and missile boats. In addition to software for these systems, we develop software for our CAD–CAM work, data processing activity, and scientific computing activities.

We set up our own training programs because the demand for software engineers was large and we could not find the software engineers we needed in the market. The universities only trained small numbers of computer scientists, without any software engineering background. Their graduates could not, for example, handle embedded computer projects without further elaborate training. We felt that computer scientists, who come to the industry, don't have the necessary application background. If you want to develop embedded systems, you should have some previous background, either in electrical engineering, mechanical engineering, or physics. If you want to develop business systems, you should have some background in business or industrial engineering. If you want to develop CAD–CAM software, you should have a background either in aeronautical engineering or in mechanical engineering. Hence, we felt that in order to develop good software engineers, people should first have a degree in an application area and only then learn software engineering, superimposed on the previous background.

In the beginning, we tried to develop the embedded computer software engineering program together with the local universities. We had long discussions with them. But they wanted academic freedom in the development. This didn't suit our needs, so we had no other choice but to develop our own program.

The development of such a program was supported by the large training center of Israel Aircraft Industries which trains employees and customers in a wide range of technical areas. In the computer systems domain, we had lots of experience running courses. We had an ADP programmer's retraining program which was tought for several years. So, we had the basic background to start our own training program in embedded computer software engineering. As soon as we recognized the need, we set up a steering committee to develop the program. Basically, we handled the development like good software engineers. First we wrote the job requirements of embedded computer systems software engineers. Later, we developed the top level design of the program. Then, we detailed the design. Once we outlined the program, we realized that we had to develop some basic new courses. We developed them very slowly. We couldn't develop all of the courses at once. Therefore, we concentrated on some basic courses. In the development of the program, we also realized that if you want to educate software engineers, you have to train them according to a coherent philosophy. It is, however, very difficult to develop such a coherent philosophy in software engineering since you don't use the same methods and tools in all the courses and phases of development. The types of tools or methods which are used depend on the type of problem you are facing. The value of a coherent approach to the students is that they will be able to understand and remember the basic approaches without going back to textbooks all the time.

Strong emphasis is placed in the training program on exercises, hands on experiments in the laboratories, and project work. Consequently, this required the building of very elaborate laboratories for various aspects of software development for both mini and microcomputers. In each training program, the students were also assigned at least two projects. The pattern which we adopted in the development of the embedded systems course, was later also followed in the development of the CAD-CAM software engineering program which fulfilled similar corporate needs.

Currently, we have three basic software engineering retraining programs: the ADP training program, the embedded computer systems program, and the CAD–CAM program. The duration of each retraining program is about 1,000 hours.

We recruited the students for the first embedded computer software engineering retraining course from inside the company. This was not very successful, because managers did not allow their good subordinates to leave for seven months. For the following courses, all of the students were recruited through ads in the newspapers. For the last course, we again took some people from inside the company. This worked out very well.

What are the advantages of having an in–house industrial training program? The programs were developed in order to meet urgent developmental needs of the company. In those programs, we were able to incorporate the experience gained on real projects. The programs are very intensive and concentrated. The program thus solved pressing and immediate needs of the company. Moreover, whenever we have the need for the training of people in a new domain we can set up a program in a similar way based on the experience we accumulated.

Naturally, there are also disadvantages. Training programs within the company are no substitute for a university education. We don't teach background courses, computer science and other basic engineering courses. Our students get only their basic retraining in these programs. They should strive in the future to obtain a Master's degree and augment their training. We feel that a Master's degree is quite mandatory these days in software engineering. Many of the jobs we are doing and systems we are developing, are very complex. Therefore, we are not competing in this area with the universities, but augmenting their education programs whenever it is necessary.

Currently, larger numbers of software engineers are available, and there is no immediate need to run additional embedded computer systems software engineering retraining programs. We feel that, at the moment, it is more important to upgrade the skills of our working engineers. Therefore, we decided to set up a series of enhancement courses.

The enhancement program is an embedded computer systems engineering program rather than a pure software engineering program. We feel that setting up a systems engineering program that teaches all aspects of computer systems engineering is more important than another software engineering program. The reason is that all of our systems are multi–level and multi–computer systems. Therefore, all the software and systems people have to be familiar with all aspects: hardware, software, and communications.

The enhancement program we are currently setting up is described in Table 1. It addresses different classes of populations; embedded computer systems project managers, embedded computer systems engineers, software project managers, software engineers, and QA engineers.

I would like to give a brief explanation on the in–house enhancement program described in Table 1. We are currently teaching a basic requirements analysis course, which should be taken by the entire population of systems engineers. We feel that requirements analysis is the most important course to be taught, since this activity constitutes 20 to 30 percent of every project. We are also preparing an advanced requirements analysis course, which is going to be taught to a more limited population. We are currently preparing an introductory software design course, to be taught to systems development managers and analysts. The development of this course is difficult since with managers, we have to discuss software designs, using drawings and not PDL's. They are not a suitable tool to discuss software designs with managers. So, we have to learn how to represent software designs to managers in a way that they can understand and discuss. We are preparing this course, which should be taught within a few months, even if we have not yet solved all the problems.

In the enhancement program, we are teaching a course on software design with Ada, which deals with sequential programs. The problem is that it is too long; it lasts 15 days. We are preparing a second software design course dealing with parallel programs. We teach a real–time operating systems course, which lasts five days. As can be seen, we already have an entire set of basic courses, in the enhancement program and we are developing additional courses now.

One course which was requested was a course on embedded computer system integration. We don't know yet how to teach it. As a first step, we had some discussion on how to approach system integration problems with experienced project engineers. Based on that, we will develop the course. It is a very difficult course to develop, since there are no available textbooks.

Additional retraining demands have come up recently and this time in the AI area. Therefore, we set up an AI training program. We decided

TABLE I

Enhancement Courses in Embedded Computer Systems Engineering IAI Planned Training Paths

Population Subject	Days	ECS Project Managers	ECS Systems Engineers	ECS Software Project Managers	ECS Software Engineers	ECS QA Engineers
Basic Requirements Analysis	5	*	*	*	*	*
Advanced Requirements Analysis	5		*	*	*	
Introduction to Software Design	5	*	*			
Software Design with ADA part 1	15			*	*	*
Software Design with ADA part 2	8			*	*	*
Introduction to Real Time O/S	1	*	*			
R/T O/S Workshop	5			*	*	
ECS Project Management	5	*		*		
Multi Computer System Design	5	*	*	*	*	
Introduction to AI	5	*	*	*	*	
Introduction to ECS CM	1	*	*	*	*	*
Introduction to ECS QA	1	*	*	*	*	
QA Workshop	10					*
System Development Final Project Workshop	5	*	*			
Software Development Final Project Workshop	5			*	*	

TABLE II

AI Enhancement Courses
New Program - April 1987

Population / Subject	Managers	Systems Engineers	AI Programmers
Introduction to AI	X	X	X
Introduction to AI Languages		X	X
Introduction to Expert Systems	X	X	X
Expert System Design		X	X
Introduction to Computerized Vision		X	X
Planning		X	X
Natural Languages		?	X
Robotics	?	X	X
All Other Courses			X

that we need enhancement courses for many of our engineers in the AI area. We developed a program described in Table 2. Some of the courses have already been taught; the introduction to Artificial Intelligence and AI languages. The course on expert systems is currently being developed.

I would like to summarize some of the lessons we have learned. The software engineering retraining programs proved to be an excellent solution to some of the corporate personnel needs. Effective training requires unique programs for people in different application areas such as data processing, embedded computer systems, and CAD–CAM. There is a need for specialization in application areas. People in the software business are not transportable from one application area to another, even in a domain such as embedded computer software engineering. Each engineer has to specialize in an application area. Finally, I would like to say that the success of the retraining programs is due to very thorough preparation and to good cooperation between the training center staff and all the other departments in the company.

Ernie Bauder: I noticed the emphasis on retraining, as well as the conclusion in the lessons learned, regarding the selection of employees. I wonder how much choice you really have in retraining people. My experience is that you always get the "dogs" from other disciplines. If they can't succeed in that other discipline, why should they succeed in software engineering?

Jonah Lavi: In our first training course, we got people from inside IAI; we did not get the best because people sent us whoever they could get rid of. Therefore, we made the decision to hire candidates from the outside, in the following training courses. With regard to the enhancement courses, it is no problem to get good people, as long as the courses are no longer than a week. However, for a retraining program, which lasts half a year, it is very difficult to get good people from within the company. I believe that we should get a mix in the future, anyway.

Ernie Bauder: What do you do with the "dogs?"

Jonah Lavi: This is a problem. Even if we take outside people, we may find out that we've missed, in some cases, in spite of the very strong screening process we have used. In the last course, we had at least one student, whom I was teaching, who turned out to be a poor student. I'm sorry we didn't do more student evaluations in the middle of the course. He was fired after being with the company for a year and a half.

Ernie Bauder: Is failure in your program sufficient grounds for dismissing a person from your company?

Jonah Lavi: Definitely. If someone who was hired for the retraining program is not doing well, you can throw him out in the middle of the course with no problem.

Ernie Bauder: Out on the street or back where he came from?

Jonah Lavi: If he comes from the outside, you have no obligation. But, if he comes from within the company, he goes back to the department he came from.

William Lively: The model that we wanted to talk about, relates to our program and our interface with industry. Our program at Texas A&M University has 800 undergraduate students, 150 graduate students, and 40 Ph.D. students. There has been a considerable decline in our program, in terms of undergraduate students. Two years ago, we had 1400. Now we have 800. Hopefully, we got rid of the high attrition rate, in the elimination of those students. I suspect that we still graduate the same number of undergraduate students, but are more efficient in the utilization of out resources.

Our curriculum is very broad based in software and hardware, with emphasis on software engineering and AI. It covers standard languages, architecture systems, and data bases. We teach an undergraduate course in artificial intelligence, which might make us somewhat unique. There is an undergraduate course in software engineering. We have specialties in graphics, vision, and so on.

At the graduate level, we have four areas of concentration and a fairly flexible, graduate program. Students are only required to take one course from each of the following areas: theoretical computing, AI and cognitive modeling, computer systems and networks, and software systems. Of course, we have some specialty areas such as vision, graphics, computer math, and simulation.

Among the software engineering courses available to undergraduates, there is a senior level course which attempts to cover the basic concepts associated with the software life cycle. These concepts include techniques such as requirements analysis, specification design, implementation testing, and emphasis on user interfaces, because they are becoming much more important in the software systems that we are building today. We usually have about 250 students per year, who are involved in our undergraduate

Software Engineering course. Basically, it has just been based on principles. The projects course and the undergraduate course really need to be strengthened by making some necessary changes.

There are three graduate courses, all related to software engineering. Advanced Software Engineering is a course which assumes that you've had the undergraduate course as a prerequisite. It covers such topics as software development environments. We make some attempt to look at methodologies, for evaluation and selection. We talk about topics of rapid prototyping and reusability. This course is a project based course. Thus, the students will have the opportunity to apply those principles and techniques that they have learned concurrently in the graduate course. We teach about 60 students per year, the Advanced Software Engineering course, at the graduate level.

A second course which has recently been added, is Software Models and Metrics. Here, we look at life cycle models, complexity models, reliability models, and cost estimation models. Additionally, we try to see if we can quantify some aspects of the software development process, which is a very important area. One of the things that does not occur very rapidly, is the transfer of technology to industry. The argument has been made that if we can quantify various techniques and show the productivity associated with the techniques, we might be able to enhance that transfer.

A new course, which we just taught for the first time last summer, called AI Applications in Software Engineering, involves topics such as AI development, automatic programming transformation systems, and knowledge based assistance. What we are really looking at, in terms of AI Application, deals with knowledge representation, knowledge acquisition and knowledge explanation. Can we really do these activities, in relation to the software development process? We taught this course for the first time last summer.

At the International Conference on Software Engineering, one of the participants gave a presentation on AI on software engineering and made the comment that he felt like AI had not really contributed to the field of software engineering, at this point in time. Hence, we may be in a little trouble teaching this course.

We want our graduates to have a firm computer science foundation, obviously good programming skills, analysis skills, design skills, and appreciation of the major software development problems, and determining requirements, which is one of the major problems. We want them to be able to go out and readily assist industry in developing software. From the reports that we get back on our students, we can conclude that they are certainly able to do this.

Some very simplistic things, but very consistent with what we want our students to do, is certainly to be flexible, able to learn, able to solve problems, and able to communicate. Clearly everybody wants their students to do that.

Communications is a major problem, for which I have no solution. Have you ever been in an environment where somebody communicated something to you and you didn't understand it, but you didn't ask them what they were saying to you? I feel this is the experience in a lot of communication problems.

Will students always be asking themselves, as they are developing software, "Where am I going from here? Why am I going there? How am I going to get there?" We hope that our graduate program would use an analytical approach to working with software systems.

The economic base for Texas has always been oil, which is sort of catastrophic for us right now. There is a major emphasis in the state for technology to be the economic base, and I think that software engineering plays a major role in that activity. So, part of our impetus, as a land grant university, is to respond to that.

In terms of program evolution, we started in 1975. We developed our first graduate course in software engineering, and closely associated with that, a graduate projects course. It was not until 1983 that we developed an undergraduate course in software engineering. In 1985, we developed the models and metrics course, and last summer, we started teaching a course on AI and software engineering.

I would say that our evolving program has tracked evolving technology. The development of programming languages has moved to the development of programming environments, which has moved to the development of software. Incidentally, I think the software development environments parallel the Ada efforts, the Stone Man efforts and the Method Man efforts, including the efforts that DoD has been involved in.

One of our facilities that has been very beneficial to the faculty and students is our Laboratory for Software Research. Formed in 1983, it provides a focus for research in student development projects, and provides a structure for the faculty and students to get together. We have regular seminar series, led by different faculty members. There are about seven or eight faculty members who work within the laboratory. We've been able to get small grants for students, through the auspices of the laboratory and some larger grants, for multiple faculty and students.

We have had projects with IBM, Texas Instruments, and Lockheed Missile and Space. In some cases, we have worked for free and in other cases, they have paid us. These activites have been a special blessing to our university. We have a very strong alumni from Texas A&M, who have managed to rise rather high in management. They seem to enjoy coming back to their Alma Mater and interacting with us, even to the extent of providing fairly nice research funding.

A particular interaction that was important, was out of a course that we taught last summer in AI and software engineering. In this particular course, a number of the Lockheed engineers came and shared with us the problems associated with the development of the Express System, which is a very large, sophisticated software development environment. The students consequently formed a team that worked on a prototype model for this environment. They also were involved in some literature study. All 15 students had an opportunity to review their projects with the Lockheed engineers.

One clear benefit is that it has provided funding for some of our students. The Air Force has provided funding for some of their retired employees, who have gone back. Thus, we've been very successful in getting funding.

The experience on real, large scale systems has been valuable for our students. What this involvement does, is allow the students to see where industry is, what's going on in the industrial environment, and what the role is that management is playing. We've taught a number of concepts in our software engineering courses, within a "baptismal environment." That has no religious connotation. "Baptismal" is a Greek word which simply means to be totally identified with something. We'd like for our students to be thoroughly developed in a project.

The one-man project has an autonomy aspect, so the group dynamics do not appear. But, it allows the students to build confidence. Competition and cooperation were both a result of the Lockheed contract. They did compete, to see who could develop systems with a higher quality. But they also cooperated with one another; there were good group dynamics.

Of course, one of the questions you always ask when you do a project is, "How well do you really adhere to the software engineering techniques that you previously learned? If you don't adhere to those techniques, see what happens." The students have the opportunity to view those sorts of things.

One of those things that came out of this course, is the real need for something called a life cycle artifact data management system. We really need to capture the corporate history of the development of software projects, and we pay the price, when we fail to do that.

Express is an evolving system environment. Students get the opportunity to see how the requirements are dynamic, because we don't really understand the system that we want. They had an opportunity to observe the failures that occur, due to various constraints, problems, systems, and people in industry. There is the benefit from one-to-one industry interface. Our students work on a one-to-one basis with software engineers, at Lockheed, in the particular case that I've been talking about.

In summary, the experience that the students have gained has been very beneficial. The scope of the interaction between the university and industry should be defined very clearly. If they are going to give us a fairly sizable sum of money, they tend to dictate the schedules and the activities. Clearly, you don't want to be involved in developing production systems for industry. One might think, "Well naturally, that won't happen." But sometimes, it's surprising how you sort of slip on their critical path. I don't think that you want to do that, by any means.

Our students have benefited from their involvement with industry. They get an opportunity to see what industry is like. Industry gets an opportunity to see what they're like. For future employment, this is very beneficial.

Dave Haddad: Has there been any research benefit to your faculty as a result of the cooperation with Lockheed?

William Lively: Yes, I certainly think so, in terms of the AI activities in software engineering. It certainly hasn't been proven that AI provides viable answers. Therefore, there's an opportunity to investigate various AI techniques in software development. I certainly think that that's been the case for the faculty.

Joel Schnoor: I am concerned about the GE Software Technology Program. Imagine a manager besieged by a software crisis: "Help! Help! What am I going to do? I have all this software that has to be created. All of my existing software needs maintenance and none of it has been developed with software engineering techniques. What am I going to do?"

The manager decides to hire some help: "I think I'll hire some help. Loraine, can you bring me some resumes of computer science candidates? Millions of them? Well, how about those with software engineering training? Only two?"

Now, this clearly introduces a problem in software engineering education. Most computer science graduates have no software engineering training. Any such training that does occur, usually occurs too late in the individual's curricula, so that a sufficient appreciation of software technology is not gained.

Another problem arises during the interview: "Well, that's a mighty fine stack of documentation you have there. What is it? You mean that's a design document for a bubble sort? Well, in school, did you have any real life projects? All of your assignments were canned problems? Well, what are you doing with this project now? You mean you're going to just throw this all away?"

Because of the brevity of most training programs in academia or industry, the amount of documentation produced for a project is disproportionate to the size of the project. Also, because most projects are canned, they are just thrown away and therefore, they are not created with maintenance in mind. They are not maintainable.

So, the manager decides that the individual needs on the job training. This creates other problems. Introducing the general: "Forget the training! He's needed on the front lines now!"

Industry often sacrifices the education of the individual, because of real life schedules and deadlines. Industry often overstresses practicality, tossing theory to the wind. On the other hand, academia may cover a broad range of methodologies, but it usually doesn't cover enough, in great detail.

There exists another problem. The manager overhears a presentation given by one of the software engineers: "This is the worst presentation I've ever heard! It's terrible! Can't my software engineers do anything but sit in a corner and code?" Most software engineers are not well versed in communication skills, interview skills, and leadership skills, and very few of them have any experience on large scale team projects.

Finally, the last straw: "This is incredible! My software engineers all have the attitude of hear no evil, speak no evil. They don't communicate with each other. I'm trying to bring software engineering into an R & D environment and I don't know how to do it. We have all this software we're creating, we have to ship out to the masses, to the rest of the company. I don't know what to do. I need help. I have impending deadlines."

Then, one morning, two A.M., while the manager is logged on at home working, all the problems become crystal clear: "Oh my goodness, the problems have become crystal clear. There is a positive curriculum. There is not enough software engineering training at the university level. Most projects are so small that the documentation is too large, the projects are thrown away and there is no maintenance done. There is a dichotomy of institutional objectives. Stress is a practicality. Academia doesn't stress enough practicality. There is a lack of breadth. My software engineers aren't getting training in other areas, such as communication. There is a deficiency of technology transfer. We have to spread software engineering to the masses. But how am I going to approach these problems?"

Then, the manager has the Epiphany: "Eureka! I've got it! I have got it! I will create a program which covers a broad range of software engineering methodology, provides experience in a variety of areas, and gives the individual a graduate level degree. This program will be a synergy; a synergy of industrial and academic education. I will call it the Software Technology Program." With that, the manager rips open his shirt and becomes Captain Synergy.

Doug Politi: The Software Technology Program is centered at General Electric's Corporate and Research and Development Center, in Schenectady, New York. It's a three-year locational program with 30 people. It was designed with the following objectives: to provide high quality software engineering leaders for our company's components, and to distribute software engineering within the research center where it is located and throughout the company.

It begins with an intense eight-week software training course, with theory being taught by Roger Pressman and the practicality being understood by applying this theory to real world projects at the center, with a team of three other people. At the same time, they are taking effective business presentation courses and many seminars, explaining the resources and uses of resources at the center.

The rotational part of the program begins when each year the program member chooses a new project, from a wide variety of application areas: artificial intelligence, computer simulation, graphics, real-time control, factory automation and so on. He then tries to integrate that while pursuing his Master's degree at Rennsalaer Polytechnic Institute, RPI, so that the two are combined.

When the person graduates from the program, he will take with him the technology, the tools and the software engineering training he has received to the company components.

The program provides both deep and broad software engineering training. It does this by teaching multiple methodologies: object oriented design, data flow design, rapid prototyping, not only in the eight-week course, but in the year-long projects, as well and the theory being taught at Rennsalaer Polytechnic Institute.

Because the center is so diverse and there are such a wide veriety of application areas and because we rotate each year, to a new project, we get to work in new application areas. Moreover, we get to see how the software engineering is applied to those different applications. We also try to integrate RPI course work with work that we are doing at the center. This is particularily evident with work that we are doing for our thesis. The Master's requirements indicate that we do a thesis and we try to integrate it, so that the thesis is being done, in conjunction with one of the year long projects. A friend of mine took theory that he learned in an expert systems course at RPI, and applied it to the work he was doing on a project for designing aircraft engine compressors.

You not only get exposure to the projects you're working on and the application areas you're working on, but exposure to the projects of the other 30 STP's and how software engineering was applied successfully and unsuccessfully to each of those projects.

Because each of the programs is of significant enough size—multiple year, multiple person projects—you get to see the reality and practicality of applying software engineering, and not applying software engineering to those applications. Unlike most software engineering training, where the role of software developer is stressed, the Software Technology Program allows the STP to play multiple roles. To "play multiple roles," is a joke. It wasn't my idea.

When I was an undergraduate, we used to talk about the three G's: get it going, get it graded, get it gone. Throw your project out when it's done. Software maintenance is not understood and the importance of software engineering to maintenance is not understood. That's not true in the program. Even after you leave one of your rotational assignments, you are held responsible for coming back and helping those projects, if there are problems.

To understand these next two points, of team leader and review participant, one must understand how we structured the program itself. We have tried to take independent but related projects and group them together. For instance, we have an artificial intelligence group, where three people, working on the projects of causal reasoning, reasoning with uncertainty and diagnostic expert systems. These are different projects, but they are related. So, we group them together, so they can review each other's documents, because they are knowledgeable about the related subject area. Each of them get to play the role of review participant, but the third year STP will get the opportunity to be the team leader and worry about organizational issues, associated with that team.

Because we each try to better the program and put more into the program, we can take on as much responsibility as we want. We can teach courses, teach mini seminars, bring people in for seminars, organize the summer course, and so on. Thus, we get a wide spectrum of roles we can play.

Because we are located at the research center, we have an abundant supply of resources. We are also just south of Saratoga Raceway and we have an abundant supply of race horses. Hence, the richness of the environment is important to the program.

In terms of hardware, we have around 30 VAX, 1000 PC's, 125 Suns, Simbolics, and links to Cray computers. Because the center is so diverse, there's a wide range of software tools that are needed. Because we are on the leading edge of many of these application areas, the center tends to be a good site for test releases on new software and liveware, as we saw before. We not only get to work with the Ph.D.'s at the center, but with professors at RPI, as well. The important point to notice, however, is that we are getting the motivation and encouragement to learn the hardware and software we may not otherwise get, from RPI. They are giving us assignments and project work in these courses which, in conjunction with the resources we have at the center, help us to get a better grasp on the material which is being taught to us. Moreover, we'll be learning new hardware and software, we might not otherwise have time for.

An important point to consider is that we are not just trying to provide software engineering training, but we are trying to train software engineers. This can't be done effectively, unless you try to provide communication, management, and leadership skills. This includes such activities as writing technical papers, attending conferences, delivering presentations, and learning and practicing leadership skills. When the new program members enter this program, they take a corporate entry leadership conference. Before they leave, they take a week long project leadership conference. We take an R & D management course or it is suggested that we take an R & D management course at RPI. But we get to apply all of this, while we are doing work at the center.

But teaching software engineering to 30 people each year, or training software engineering people each year, isn't enough. We have to justify the expense of this and we have to be able to transfer the technology of the program, through one of the terms that we call "technology osmosis" to people other than the 30 people who were involved.

We must justify the expense of the program. Justifying it, by saying we trained 30 people, isn't enough. We can look at transferring the technology to both software engineering and the application technology, at three levels. At the most global level, we say the corporation. How are we going to transfer the technology to the corporation? Well, each year, the graduates of the program go to different company components. They take with them, not only the software engineering training that they've had, but the experience of working with different applications, different hardware, and software tools.

Now, at a more localized level, at the research center, we have to transfer information, software engineering, to research types, who tend not to be overly concerned about software engineering. But at the same time, there's research being done in software engineering, in certain parts of the center, and we have to spread that information throughout the center, as well.

At an even more localized area, within the group itself, within the STP program, Software Technology Program, itself, we have technology osmosis, which we consider an informal communication; it's a spreading of the information about other people's applications, and about course work being done at RPI. You have this informal communication at lunchtime, and parties and such.

Not only do you have to build this technology transfer structure, you have to preserve it. You have a lasting infrastructure for technology transfer. Consequently, the graduates of the program become what we call "technological gatekeepers." When they go to the company components, they then become a gatekeeper, because they've kept ties to us. Thus, the information taught at the research center goes through them to their company components. It is not only technological information and application areas being done at the center, but course work being done at RPI, as well.

So, very quickly, Captain Synergy did not save the day totally. There are some unsolved problems which are specific to the Software Technology Program, and those more fundamental to software engineers each year. As we finally ramp them up to be most productive, they graduate and we send them to the company components. That's good for the components. It's not necessarily good for the research center.

Because the program is limited in size, it cannot really be considered a universal solution to software engineering education. We need a tighter coupling with RPI. We currently have a passive role. We say, "These are the courses that are being offered there. Good. Take them to best suit your needs," instead of saying, "These are the courses we want at RPI. Why don't we sit down and decide what you're going to help teach for our people?"

At a more global level, we still consider most software engineering occurring too late. We want to see it at the undergraduate level. Furthermore, we have to train upper level management. They still aren't necessarily aware of the need for software engineering and the effects of not having software engineering.

The program is both deep and broad; broad in the sense that you learn multiple methodologies, and deep in the sense that you get to apply these for an extended period of time. You get to play multiple technical roles: researcher, software developer, maintainer, review participant, team leader, etc. You have an abundant supply of resources and the motivation to learn how to use them. We try to teach well-rounded individuals the skills involved in communication, technology, management, and leadership. We have built an infrastructure to transfer this information to the masses.

Dick Fairley: I'm glad to see that the program didn't crush your sense of humor, as too often occurs in graduate education. What happens when you leave the nest and go out to the operating divisions of the company? How are you received in those divisions and how do you feel, being shoved out of the nest and losing your support systems, in the new environment?

Doug Politi: I feel like I'm getting shoved out. It used to be that the three-year program got extended into at least a four year program, because they didn't want to leave the research center. It's a nice area, and we are ready to move onto our next stage, and take on something new.

As far as our reception in the components, one of our problems has been that General Electric is a very big company, with a lot of components and a lot of software work going on. But we are used to working on various state of the art software projects. One of the problems we've had, is identifying those real, leading edge pockets. However, we are starting to do that now. I think our reception has been very good.

Gary Ford: You used the word "theory." I had a little problem when I heard "theory" and "Roger Pressman" in the same sentence. I'm wondering if you could explain how the word "theory" was used in your discussion and give us an idea of whether theory is the opposite of practical or it has some other meaning, with respect to your program.

Doug Politi: I am using the term "theory" to reflect on software engineering.

Priscilla Fowler: Where do these people end up downstream, maybe not as soon as they get out, but a few years later? What's happening to them? Do they lose the impetus of their software engineering education? Do they end up buying into whatever the corporation is doing or do they manage to actually cause change to take place within the environments they work?

Jonah Lavi: The students start on various projects. Although we teach lots of programming, most of the students start with small projects or requirements analysis, since that's one of the major activities in the company. The students move on, becoming responsible for projects. They have been very successful.

Priscilla Fowler: Is that different than the responsibility of other people within the company, who are doing software projects? Are they turning out significantly different?

Jonah Lavi: I think that they are better.

Keith Decker: They tend to enter project teams as members of software project teams, in these very high tech areas of General Electric. Now, what we've seen happen, is a little hard to say, because our program is barely five years old, as it is.

Priscilla Fowler: So far, GE sees enough of a pay-off, to keep funding it?

Keith Decker: So far. But it is still very young.

Mark Ardis: I think a lot of our students come in at the point where they are getting pressed into project leadership roles. When they go out, they tend to lead projects. I don't know whether they are significantly better or worse than if they had not come. I'd like to think that they would be better off if we haven't been around long enough, to know what happens to these people five years later. But some of them act as change agents. They feel as if they have a mission. One went to work for an AI firm. One went to Medical School, and another went on to pursue a Ph.D. in Computer Science.

William Lively: Most of our students go to places like TI, Lockheed, General Dynamics, and a few of the oil companies. Most students go into programmer analyst-type positions. Others become part of a project and frequently, within five years, move into graduate roles.

Priscilla Fowler: Do you have any feedback from those Texas A&M alumni or other sources, that would indicate that your graduates are more desirable than a computer science graduate?

William Lively: At one time we had an Industrial Advisory Committee, which dissolved. However, from seven or eight years ago, that was the indication that we had.

Priscilla Fowler: They've already addressed the changing demands for their programs. So, I'd like to ask them now, what would you do differently, if you had to do it all over again? What do you think that Dave (Besemer) would do differently?

Keith Decker: First of all, Dave had a difficult time answering this question. One thing he would have liked or he would like, is to have more help managing the program. With 30 people, it's getting on the edge of too much for one person to handle, even with all the help that we provide.

Secondly, early on, there was a decision to teach the eight-week software engineering course off site; this turned out to be a really bad idea. Hence, we would stress that the immigration course idea is good, and it should be held on site, where they will have access to all of the tools and people that they are going to use throughout their training.

Mark Ardis: Well obviously, we would like a wider base of financial support. We made a lot of mistakes, but I think we learned from them. I think we reached a point where we really felt like we were doing all the right things.

William Lively: I guess we'd lobby for the development of the SEI, a little bit sooner, in terms of benefiting for that. Certainly, I think that that's going to be important.

After listening to some of the comments on our project, I think we need to have a stronger project course and sructure it better. There are a lot of ideas that have come out of this discussion in the last two days.

Jonah Lavi: I don't think that we would have done anything different. The basic structure of the course is good. Also, the process used in the development of the course, was the natural way of developing a good training course. You can't speed things up in this business. Maybe there is one thing we would have changed; we would have tried to get some teachers who had more industrial experience. But that is something which you cannot always control. It's not always easy to get experienced teachers. There is a lot of experience needed by techers in a training program. I think the IBM experience that we heard about this morning is a different approach to it. It's very important to get people with lots of experience to train the people.

Priscilla Fowler: I would just like to underline what Jonah and Al Pietrasanta have said and that is, to set something like this up, to make something that's going to last for awhile and produce a quality product, meaning a good software engineer requires a number of years and a lot of hard soliciting and fund raising, before you can get executives to buy into it. They don't pop up overnight. Therefore, I would suggest that you keep patience in mind.

Jonah Lavi: The problem in the company was not so much to get the funding for it, but that it takes a good two years to prepare a program like this. People told me at the time, "Get the program started within a few months," and I refused. We have followed up on what happened to the training program at General Dynamics. They set up a program within five months. They taught ten different courses over half a year, and every week a different person came into the course, teching only one subject for a week. The next week, another teacher came to teach. Naturally, the students never got an integrated approach, from the beginning to the end. I don't think the course was very successful. Moreover, they lost most of the people, later on in the program.

Thus, the clue of preparing a training program is to really do it well, like any other software engineering project. You have to really plan it and do it slowly. There are no miracles in this business.

Priscilla Fowler: Is there a future for this? We are going to continually need sources of software engineering, that are based in industry. Will the universities ultimately supply enough of these folks, like they do now, of mechanical engineers and chemical engineers? Do you see a continuing need? Do the industry people think they are going to continue to have to do this?

Jonah Lavi: I definitely would prefer not to run that many training programs in the company, because it is a very expensive proposition. To run and develop such courses with 25 people costs probably something like three quarters of a million dollars. It's very expensive. So, I would prefer to recruit people from the universities. In order to be able to hire those engineers that we really need now in our company, there must be a change in the universities. They need to set up a program in computer systems engineering. I think this type of a program can be set up for undergraduates, graduates, and Ph.D.'s.

Now, I might go even a step further. The systems we are developing are so complex, and we need more and more people with a Master's degree or a Ph.D., to deal with real industrial development problems. A Ph.D. degree is not a luxury in industrial development today.

Keith Decker: I think that we would still see the need at GE, maybe not so much any more for software engineering, but to back up a little bit. It's part of GE's corporate culture, that half of the people that join the General Electric Company from the undergraduate level enter through a training program, as opposed to direct hires. It's part of the way that GE works; they want people to have a chance to try out different things, to find out what they want to do, before they start locking themselves into a position. Even if the people coming out were the most excellent software engineers in the world, there would still be this very useful purpose for the program.

William Lively: We produce Ph.D.'s in software engineering, out of our program and there seems to be a demand for it. I guess the number that we have produced has not been that high, because we have a broad curriculum. But we have produced Ph.D.'s that have gone to General Dynamics and to Sandia.

I certainly think there is a future for software engineering as a field. We are going to keep building very complex systems, which are going to require this type of activity.

Mark Ardis: Wang Institute was planning a Ph.D. program. We had two models. One was a traditional Ph.D., similar to a technical Ph.D., to do research in software engineering. We thought that there was a need for that. The second model, similar to an advanced practitioner, was an M.D. degree.

Keith Decker: Speaking from GE's point of view, there is work being done in software engineering, at the research center, and of course, there are no such people with these backgrounds. It seems that if they continued to feel that they should be active in that area, they would like to see people with that kind of background.

Jonah Lavi: If I could recruit another two Ph.D.'s to my group, I would recruit them today. But I can't find them. I need them, because the problems that we are facing are very, very difficult. There are many, many problems which we are faced with, everyday. We have to apply new techniques to solve new problems and I think they should be solved by Ph.D.'s. I prefer Ph.D.'s, because they have the ability to do this job. I feel there is a tremendous need for them today.

Mark Ardis: Is there a future in software engineering, as a field? I think software engineering has an identity crises. If you ask two people for their opinion on what software engineering is, you'll get three or four answers. Moreover, that's not just faculty that you are asking; that's anybody. So, I think that there is an identity crisis and whether we get beyond that, is the answer to the question.

If software engineering can somehow coalesce and become an identifiable field, then I think it has a future. But until that happens, it's undetermined, in my view.

Jonah Lavi: I would say software engineering has no future, but computer systems engineering, has a future. You have to train engineers to do the job, the engineering job, and they have to get the engineering training. Again, it should be a computer system engineering program, in which people have to learn, among other things, modeling of physical systems. It's very similar, for example, to control engineering. The first thing the control engineer learns, is to model physical systems. No attention has been given to the actual problem of modeling of systems in most computer science curricula. However, computer programs are basically control programs of some other things. If you are not able to model the physical systems, industrial systems, or commercial systems, you won't be able to engineer the software for it. Therefore, you have to look at that entire field, as an engineering field and all aspects of it; that is the future.

William Lively: I think there is a future in software engineering, as soon as we define what it is. Clearly, there are going to be complex software systems. We are going to need to do some engineering.

Keith Decker: Software engineering education for executives is a problem. One of the ways we've tried to address it at the center, is by holding three to five-day seminars, for management, on requirements analysis and software planning, etc. I've heard of other ways to address that problem. I have a friend who used to be a manager at Xerox and apparently, all Xerox management takes a five-day software management course, even if they don't manage software. I think that that is a great step. But, it's hard to get an entire company to do something like that.

Jonah Lavi: I think that there is a definite need to give courses in software engineering to executives. The question is how to build them, what to show them, and how to demonstrate the problems. One problem is to present the structure of the software in a way which management can understand. If we would be able to do that better, we would have an easier time presenting material to managers. That seems like a very important area, which could help us explain software problems to managers.

William Lively: I think that there are many companies whose executives are not nearly as enlightened as GE's. I think that knowledge about new techniques and methodologies and so forth, is really necessary. The studies on technology transfer indicate that we are really not doing a very good job in industry, as a whole. So, I think that education is necessary.

Mark Ardis: I guess I'd feel a little pompous, telling an executive that he really ought to take my course. But we did have some positive experiences with high level managers participating in our program. Their experience was that it's important for executives to participate in continuing education, all throughout their careers. For software engineering, the problem is packaging. We don't know how to package the material, to make it attractive to them. Thus, we have to work on that, if we want them to take our courses.

Questions and Answers on The Industry/Academia Panel

Priscilla Fowler: We'll take questions from the floor now.

Gail Sailer: This is a little bit of a different thrust. Jonah talked about the five–year commitment of the students in the program. The RPI students didn't really address whether there was a commitment back to GE, and I know that Wang doesn't really encourage interviewing with their students, as they are going through the program. Is there a commitment back to the corporation that either sponsors them or GE, and is upper management afraid of raiding, so that they would not sponsor such a program?

Keith Decker: No, there is no commitment at GE, after three years. However, I think that there is that fear, but you just try to work with it—you just have to try to keep on top of it.

Gail Sailer: Do most people go back and stay for awhile?

Keith Decker: We are nine for 12, which isn't bad.

Mark Ardis: At Wang Institute, we do prohibit recruiting of corporately sponsored students, so that companies can feel secure that their employees will be loyal. I don't know what the data is, in terms of how many of them go back, but we had very positive relations with companies that were sending students every year, on a continuing basis and even increasing the number.

Ernie Bauder: I have an observation that might be of interest. I just completed reviewing about 30 applicants from high school for scholarships, which I also did about five years ago.

Interestingly enough, out of the 30 applicants, all in the top 15 percent of the class, only one said he was going into computer science. Five years ago, it was about 50 percent. Almost all of them, with the exception of two or three, had extensive computer programming courses and other software engineering–like courses at their high school. All of them looked through computer science, at some application, like astronomy, biochemistry, or some other hard science. The computer is a tool that they are using to look at some other career.

Priscilla Fowler: Would the panel like to comment?

Keith Decker: I don't know whether it matters or not, but when I started out, I wanted to be an astrophysicist, so I was in the Physics Department for a year. Sometimes in high school, different things look more interesting; then, you go to college and get experience with other things and your views change.

Jonah Lavi: I think one problem is that people learn only programming in high schools, and not anything about how to solve problems. Many of the high school programs are a waste of time because they don't teach the students how to solve problems. I think the students have the wrong picture about what's going on.

Steve Woffinden: Is there a future in software engineering? When we look at job titles, we see a variety. But until recently, we rarely saw "the software engineer." Do you see the job of Software Engineer evolving and becoming a specific sort of job or is it just software engineering, referring only to principles that allow us to develop good software?

Mark Ardis: In the Boston area, a "software engineer" is a euphemism for a well–paid programmer. There has been an inflation of terminology, but, to my knowledge, not the corresponding requirement for upgrading skills.

Jonah Lavi: There is one problem with the so called "software engineers." Most of them stay as programmers and they are not getting the chance to move up to project management. Most system project managers have come from the hardware side. I think there should be a tremendous effort being made, to change the image, so that more people, in all management levels, should come from a software engineering background. It is going to make a big change in the development of projects.

Mark Ardis: I want to disagree with that. Our experience was that we had a lot of people who were technically very competent, getting pushed into management, and they didn't like it.

Jonah Lavi: It's a problem that they don't like it, because they don't appreciate its importance. But there's a tremendous need for it.

Keith Decker: There seems to be a shortage of managers, who have had a software background, versus a hardware background.

Larry Morell: Is there any possibility of getting some of the materials that the panel members have used, distributed to the Software Engineering Institute?

Mark Ardis: We would like to get our curriculum at Wang out to the public and I think some efforts are already underway.

Dick Fairley: We collected a large body of material and archived it and shipped a copy to SEI. So, all of the course notebooks, for the past five years, all of the course syllabi, all of our tech reports are somewhere at SEI.

Charlie Martin: I have a question with reference to the future of software engineering, because it seems to me that part of the problem is that software engineering has two futures, and we need to split them. On one side, there are the techniques of software engineering, which ought to become part of computer literacy: commenting your code, writing correct code, and so on. On the other hand, there are real problems in software engineering: the mathematical properties of large codes, large configuration management systems, efficiency of algorithms, and so forth.

Does anyone else see it that way, and if so, are we orienting software engineering teaching the right way?

Mark Ardis: Tony Hoare describes software development as being a craft these days, as opposed to a science. I think that that's part of what you were saying. I think there is very much that element in a lot of what we are teaching.

Charlie Martin: Let me take one more, quick cut. The idea that I'm trying to stress is that the craft part should eventually become a requirement for anybody who uses computers, because people are starting to write programs themselves: for example, the biomedical people that I deal with are writing their own programs. Our problem is to teach them to do it right. But on the other side, somebody has got to build the new tools and has to do the software engineering of software engineering.

Gary Ford: I want to ask about another kind of industry–academia interface that may have quite a bit of value. Because the artifacts and the processes that we study in software engineering, unlike the other sciences or engineering, are not tangible and small scale, we cannot study them in the laboratory. Is there a way that you could develop some kind of mechanism for university faculty to get into industry, for sabbaticals or for summers, to get realistic experience and to conduct experiments? On the other hand, is there any way for us to get the best people from industry, to come to universities, on a sabbatical of perhaps a year, and do some teaching and share their experience with university faculty?

William Lively: We have a very good relationship with industry and we have talked about Summer Development Programs for faculty, where they would go and work with industry, to try to interface with them better, to try and learn more about what they are doing and also to facilitate technology transfers. So, I think what you're suggesting is certainly viable and hopefully, in the state of Texas, we have a mechanism where we can do that.

Mark Ardis: I think one problem with that is the reward structure. Several of our faculty consult in local industry and thus, keep in touch with real problems. The problem is, how do you reward people, within a traditional academic environment, for doing something which isn't necessarily academically respectable?

Keith Decker: We have the same kind of problem, although not necessarily with software engineering, in the fact that a lot of people at the Research and Development Center are associate faculty at RPI and a lot of RPI professors consult at the Research Center, although there haven't been any particular experiments being done with the program yet.

Jonah Lavi: I think that in projects like ours, we should get university professors to come and consult, and something good will come out of it. It's a beginning. Many of the people here have not met Professor David Havel, who has developed the statecharts, together with us, at Israel Aircraft. The first time I asked him to come to consult, he refused. It took several years, until I got him on a real project. I think that he finally found out that the real industrial problems are very meaningful and he got a lot of academic results from working with industry. So, I think that it is a two– way street, between academia and industry, and I think that industry should get many more people from academia, to do work on the real problems.

Priscilla Fowler: It looks like about one third of the audience is from industry, two–thirds from academia. I would suggest you all take advantage of the rest of the time at the conference to mingle and compare notes and think about the answers to some of these questions yourselves.

John Brackett: There was very little discussion, among the other panelists, on what I regard as the most interesting point of this session, from Jonah Lavi, about the need for computer system engineering, rather than purely software engineering. Over the last couple of weeks, as part of preparing a course I'm giving this summer on requirements analysis for real–time systems, I visited three, large aerospace companies. In all cases, people who "think they need to know software engineering," are really doing system engineering, hardware–software trade–offs and understanding what software and hardware together can do. The point he made, is that there is not a future for software engineering, but only for computer system engineering. This seems to have been bypassed by the rest of the panel. I would just like to see if the rest of the panel would like to come back to that.

William Lively: Let me just comment that at Texas A&M, we are currently developing a Computer Engineering Program. We are changing the name of our Department, to Computer Science and Engineering. So, we definately see the need for such activities.

Mark Ardis: I guess I agree that there is a future in computer systems engineering. But I think that the problem is that there are a lot of problems where the fundamental obstacle seems to be in getting the software to work, and that is why they tend to view it as a software problem. The software engineers get asked to do a lot of things that are not traditionally software engineering tasks. So, that may be the state of the industry or it may just be the state of our knowledge.

Keith Decker: I'd also agree, that computer systems engineering is very important. In fact, actually there are two or three paths that people follow, when they get their Master's at RPI. One is strict computer science and the other is computer systems engineering. But for different types of people, depending upon the applications they are interested in, they might not be interested in a systems engineering approach, although many are.

Priscilla Fowler: I would like to say "thank you" to all my panelists and especially to the guys from GE, who enlivened the late afternoon's sluggishness. Thank you all very much.

SECTION III

PART 2

ADA IN SOFTWARE ENGINEERING EDUCATION

Part 2 of Section III contains the edited transcript of a panel session and the associated question/answer session on the role of Ada in software engineering education. The panelists were Ben Brosgol of Alsys, Larry Druffel of SEI, Robert Firth of SEI, Nico Habermann of Carnegie–Mellon University, and David Lamb of Queens University. Norm Gibbs of SEI was chair of the panel. Nico Habermann was interviewed by Jim Tomayko of Wichita State University. The interview was videotaped and presented to the conference attendees.

Panel Session on Ada in Education

Norm Gibbs: The first question I would like to ask refers to the goals of computer science education and software engineering education. Because these goals differ, what is the proper role of Ada in each?

Larry Druffel: I think that there's an implied question in the selection of a language for either computer science or software engineering in an educational institution. I think it's reflective of the tension that exists between the need to educate and the need to prepare students for the real world. Every engineering school I've ever been associated with has grappled with the issue of preparing people to get a job or preparing people to think. The first responsibility is to prepare by providing the basic education. The educator has a customer – his student. That student has to make it in his other market, the job market.

Now, I'll by analogy say that when I studied at the University of Illinois, about the time that the transistor was designed and developed, we learned about transistors. It didn't fundamentally change the concept that we had to learn. We still learned about things like amplifiers, oscillators and that sort of thing. But the way that we designed them changed considerably because we were designing with transistors, instead of with tubes. Today, of course, nobody in his right mind would teach students to design with tubes.

But back in that day, that wasn't so clear. University of Illinois was a little bit ahead of some of the other schools. The point is, we actually had to learn some different physics. We had to be a little bit more aware of the duality theories. But the fundamental concepts were the same. The engineering department chose to teach us about transistors, so that we could be more effective in the job market.

Fundamentally, I believe that you first have to make the decision in favor of being able to support the educational activities. But you can't do that, being blind to your students' marketability. So, I just wanted to present the question that was implied and perhaps get some comments before I finish answering the question that was answered.

Ben Brosgol: It's always useful to start by defining one's terms. At the risk of oversimplifying, I will claim that software engineering focuses on the process of software development rather than on the end result of that process, while computer science deals more broadly with the issues surrounding the behavior of that end product.

In a computer science curriculum, it would be a mistake to use one, single language. Anyone majoring in computer science must have an understanding of several languages—I would hope at least Pascal, Ada, Algol 60, Lisp, Snobol, Cobol, and some assembly language—with the mastery of at least two or three. Even people who are not computer science concentrators, who just want to learn something about programming, should still have exposure to more than one.

For training in software engineering, on the other hand, I do not see a compelling reason to use any language other than Ada. There are several reasons for my stating this. First, Ada was designed as a real language, not a research language, with software engineering principles built in from the start. It therefore has the necessary functionality, or, in some cases, lacks features that interfere with good programming practice. Second, Ada has received more attention than any other language in the area of design methods, a subject that belongs in any software engineering curriculum. Object–Oriented Design, a fairly popular technique, works with Ada. So do some other methods based on graphical representations of the design, such as the one that Ray Buhr talked about earlier, or the PAMELA method devised by George Cherry. Producing a design that maps well to the key features of the implementation language is a fundamental issue in software engineering, and Ada with its packages, generics, and tasks, provides the best example of a target language that can exploit good design techniques.

Since Ada has sometimes been overly "hyped," we should keep in mind that there are areas of computer science in which it is not appropriate. For example, it's not the best language for describing harware register transfers; nor would I want to have Ada as the sample language for which students must produce a compiler in a one–semester course in compiler construction.

On the other hand, a very interesting course in computer science would be a study of the rationale of the design of Ada. When you look back on the language's history, the design process was fascinating. Decisions were faced, and trade-offs were made; it was the most ambitious attempt ever made at truly engineering a language. I believe that the actual Ada design rationale document, written by Jean Ichbiah, will be available soon. This should be a good basis for a one-semester course.

David Lamb: I want to talk about training versus education. There's a perception that engineering programs have more of a training component to them than computer science programs. I don't think that's true. I've been involved in writing a software engineering textbook and I've spoken with several engineers about what's involved in engineering. They typically say that engineering really means applying principles to solve problems and expecting the technology to change every five years—you learn this year's technology in order to have something to work with. However, one needs to concentrate on the fundamental principles and know how to use those principles in order to solve problems. Don't get bound to any particular technology. Engineering programs concentrate on teaching people to think as much as computer science programs do. It's just that the kind of thinking is slightly different. Engineers solve problems. Computer scientists are in a funny position. People haven't yet developed the perception of the proper role. Many people who go through undergraduate computer science programs really ought to be going through undergraduate computer software engineering programs, except there are not very many. I think that many computer engineering programs are more heavily hardware oriented than what should be involved with software engineering.

In both programs the role of Ada in education is like the role of any other piece of technology. It's like the role of the vacuum tubes or the transistors in electrical engineering 30 years ago. It's a particular piece of technology that you'll use. What you really care about is the principles that underly the technology. The language has some particular embodiment of those principles. But really, the principles are what matter.

I disagree with Larry about how important Ada is in getting people and interviewers excited about the job market. The interviewers get excited about seeing a senior level project course, because they care about people having worked, as well as students having worked with other students. Most interviewers want to know, "Did the students learn things that will help them, that will make them flexible enough to adapt to my company? Did they learn how to work with other people? Did they learn some of the principles that we use?" I don't think that many interviewers are all that excited about any particular language.

Robert Firth: I have spent ten years teaching various things about computers. During that time, I had the good fortune to participate in developing three new courses, varying in length from simple six-week courses to a fifteen-month Master's course. My colleagues and I worried about what we were trying to teach and how we were trying to teach it. In courses where we were consciously teaching software engineering, I think there was no such thing as individuals writing programs. There were projects that had to be written by teams of three to eight people. I think this is one of the key points – software engineering is building artifacts. It is building things of significant size and for some external purpose. It's not just proving that you know how to code a bubble sort in Pascal. It is demonstrating that you understand how five people can build a message switching system in a week.

The original purpose of programming languages was for software engineering. It was for building artifacts that served some realistic purpose. The programming languages used in the real world (Fortran, Cobol, and now Ada) were designed with that intention. They were designed to be vehicles for software engineers to communicate with each other and with the computing engine. Therefore, if I were teaching a software engineering course, I would use Ada as the vehicle because it is the most modern technology we have, for all its faults and virtues. When teaching engineers, you need to teach them with state of the art tools because when they graduate, they will be solving state of the art problems. Therefore, the role of Ada is to be the vehicle that engineers use to learn principles, to practice their skills, and above all, to get experience in the creation of realistic programs and systems.

What we were trying to teach in computer science, however, were concepts, such as Ada types, addresses, control flow, the difference between random access memory and random access backing store, communications protocols, and finite state machines. Things like the Von Neumann memory is a very helpful concept that you have to get across to your students.

There are some languages that are good at this and some that are not. In the past couple of weeks I have followed a fascinating discussion (on the electronic media) about the meaning of pointers in C. The great majority of the comments betray a fundamental lack of understanding of the basic concept of what a pointer is and what an address is. I somehow feel that if I were told to teach people what addresses and pointers are, I wouldn't do it that way. Indeed, when we did that we used a systems language, not C. We used assembly code to get the point across. Thus, for computer science, and for teaching concepts, you need to use languages that expose those concepts, free from the sort of accretions that all large scale programming languages require. I would use Ada to teach those concepts that Ada embodies better than any other language, but not to teach concepts where I think the structure of Ada disguises the fundamental principles or has wrapped up the fundamental principles in engineering practice (to the extent that you can no longer isolate them). For instance, I can use Ada to teach data structures or to teach the principles of modular programming. I would not use Ada to teach some aspects of systems programming, such as memory management and device handling. I certainly would not use Ada to teach numerical programming because it is too far away from the principles of the target machine.

Therefore, in software engineering the role of the programming language is as a tool, the single best tool available for training the engineer. In computer science, a programming language is a pedagogical device. It's a way of explaining concepts. I think you have to use several because each language has specific concepts that it illustrates well, and other concepts that it doesn't illustrate so well.

Jim Tomayko: The goals of computer science education and of software engineering education are different. What is the proper role of Ada in each?

Nico Habermann: I think there are certain things that computer science and software engineering have in common. In other respects, they differ. What they have in common is that both make use of data abstraction, modularity, and other concepts, upon which programming is based. They differ where the computer science community is interested more in the analysis of languages, analyzing programming concepts, and comparing languages. Computer science is interested more in how, for example, programming concepts are reflected in program languages. For software engineering, however, the interest is more in how the language allows the programmer to express the programs that he wants to write.

I think that Ada has a role to play. Ada is conservative by computer science standards in reflecting the results of the software engineering research that went on in the 1970's, but is important in practice, because it addresses the problems of the software engineer by supporting the programming concepts directly in a computer language.

Norm Gibbs: The second question considers only the early courses in an undergraduate computer science program. Many of you are probably feeling either implicit or explicit pressure to answer the question about the role of Ada in beginning courses. The next question for the panel has two parts: In what ways is Ada a better vehicle than Pascal or Modula-2 for teaching the elementary concepts of programming? Second, Pascal was designed to be a teaching language; Ada was designed to be a language for professional software engineers developing large, real-time embedded systems. Isn't it inappropriate to try to force Ada into a role (as a teaching language) for which it was not intended?

Ben Brosgol: Let me give a brief comparison of Ada versus Pascal and point out places where Ada is better for teaching introductory programming concepts. One example is the way the two languages treat arrays. Arrays in Ada can be dynamic; in Pascal, the restriction that arrays be static can make it clumsy to express what would otherwise be a simple program. In the area of formal parameters, although Pascal has been generalized to allow one–dimensional unconstrained arrays (using the Ada term), I was not able to find in the standard an allowance for multi–dimensional unconstrained array formal parameters. Thus general vector processing in Pascal is permitted, but apparently not general matrix processing. Both are equally supported by Ada.

Type equivalence, an important concept for novice programmers to grasp, is simpler in Ada than in Pascal. In case you thought that Pascal was easy, let me read a couple of lines from the Pascal language standard on conformability and conformant types (Section 11.3.4): "An array type T (with a single index type) is said to be *conformable* with a conformant array schema S (with a single index type specification) if all of the following conditions are true. Let I represent the ordinal type identifier of the index type specification of S..." It then goes on with four fairly dense sentences, as to what that all means.

In Ada, type equivalence is much simpler. Two types are the same if and only if they have the same name. Thus there are basic parts of the language, namely what a data type means, where Ada presents significant simplicity.

Pascal has some artificial limitations; for example, functions cannot return values from structured types. In Ada, there is no such restriction; the language is at once more powerful and more simple than Pascal.

There are several places in Pascal where the syntax is quite clumsy; for example, there is a problem with dangling "else" clauses, and the semicolon–as–separator rule has some subtleties. Ada corrects these problems.

Students learning how to program should, at some point, be introduced to the issues surrounding concurrency: synchronization, mutual exclusion, and so on. There is nothing in Pascal in this area; Ada, on the other hand, contains a tasking facility that serves as a useful vehicle for instruction on these topics.

The Ada package concept can be taught to new prgrammers as an effective modularization feature. It is absent from Pascal.

Most of the comments that I made concerning Pascal apply also to Modula 2. Now, Modula 2 does have a kind of tasking facility, but its model (namely, coroutines) is much more restrictive than what Ada provides. Also, in Modula 2, identifiers are case sensitive: ALPHA, Alpha, and alpha are all regarded as different. This was not a good language design decision.

In response to the second part of the question—whether adopting Ada for teaching is a misuse because of its original intent as a language for real–time systems—it is worth noting that languages are often used in ways far from their original intent. Pascal is probably a prime example of this. It was designed solely for educational use, but it is currently being used in many other kinds of environments. Simula was designed for simulation, but its class concept—perhaps the first example of data abstraction in a programming language—gave it broader applicability. Cobol and Fortran have been used to write compilers.

Ada was indeed designed for real–time applications. However, if you look back at the requirements, the vast majority are not specific to real–time embedded systems, but are rather for a general–purpose language embodying sound software engineering principles. I think if you were to ask the authors of the language requirements documents, they would concur that it was in fact their intent that Ada be used not just for real–time applications, but also for tool development and general–purpose programming. So it is not accurate to regard Ada as just a real–time language.

I do not think it is a misuse of Ada to put it in a university classroom environment. In sponsoring the design of Ada, the DoD intended it to be taught and used at universities. Certainly the academic community has been involved with Ada from the earliest days, in commenting on the requirements, consulting during the design, and participating in the language's review. Several faculty members and graduate students at Carnegie–Mellon were involved in this process. So, Ada is not foreign to the university environment, and it has the necessary features to make it effective as a teaching language.

David Lamb: When teaching the introductory programming courses, we have a lot of trouble simply getting students to understand anything about how computers work and how to do the very fundamental things in programming. There's a real need to not confuse the students with things that are currently beyond them. I'll agree that many of the things being said are true concerning areas in which Ada is a better language than Pascal; some things are simpler in Ada than in Pascal. There are, however, also a lot of things in Ada that get in the way of trying to teach a beginning student what's going on. Overloading, for example, is fundamental to Ada and very useful, but I despair of trying to teach even a third-year student about overloading. One doesn't try to teach overloading in an introductory course. But because it's in the language and in the compilers, students will trip over it and get confused. The beginning students really need compilers with good error recovery, good error messages, and good debugging facilities because that's where they have trouble. I think a lot of educators are seriously concerned that, while some things may be better in Ada for beginnning courses, the things you don't want to have to deal with will get in the way.

I still think that when you are concentrating on teaching, you want a language that's designed with introductory beginning students in mind.

Robert Firth: This question deals with introductory programming and data structures.

When you've got a fresh mind to teach programming to, two things are essential. First, teach the concepts in a correct and reasonable manner — they have to understand the fundamental concepts. Second, avoid problems whose explanation is beyond the scope of the course. There may be such problems in the language; such problems exist in all programming languages. But students should not have to face those problems merely to get simple programs running.

By way of example, I would never use Pascal as a teaching language. There are two problems. First, it has no facility for separate compilation. This is a fundamental mistake because it would be damaging to give someone, as their first programming language, a language that lacked the concept of separate compilation. It is misleading them in one of the absolutely vital principles of computer programming. The second problem with Pascal is that it has data structures with no means of leaving them other than falling through the bottom. This leads to such badly structured code that, once again, you are fundamentally misleading them in the manner in which you execute small pieces of algorithms.

Now let's take the other aspect — that they might trip over things. Look at the abstract data typing facilities of Modula 2 and of Ada. Both of these languages have very peculiar restrictions as to how you can build "an opaque type" or a "private type." To explain those restrictions requires a very deep understanding of how compilers work, how separate compilation and the linkage of object code works, and how the concepts of dependent compliations work, which you juust cannot explain to a first year student. Therefore, whenever they have a problem whose solution seems to imply an abstract data type, neither Modula 2 nor Ada is a really appropriate vehicle for teaching this because students have to accept on faith, restrictions that are completely incomprhensible to them.

I would choose Modula 2, rather than Ada, as a first teching vehicle. However, I believe that a subset of Ada with some of the problem areas availed from them, is probably almost as effective as Modula 2 for the first year. There are one or two areas where you should not trespass. You know if they open that chapter of the manual, you'll say, "Well, you are expecting the third year course under Professor Lamb." That's not a very nice answer to an intelligent and enthusiastic student, who wants to get ahead, but it's the best you can give them. For that reason, I would pick Modula 2 rather than Ada. They have less chance of getting into trouble if they try to venture for themselves, in additional areas of the language. These are the key points. The main concepts must be there, in a correct manner, and there must not be unreasonable stumbling blocks in the path of their first few programming exercises.

A teaching language whose sole purpose is to teach the language, is useless. The world had no use for such things. The purpose of a teaching language is to teach something else, something to which the language refers. In a beginning course, that can only be the basic concepts of what programs are and what they do. For that reason, a software engineering language, in principle, is better because it addresses the real world directly, provided the language has been constructed on sound principles. Hence, it's not inappropriate to use Ada as a teaching language, if you do so with care, and if you understand both Ada and teaching.

Larry Druffel: First of all, if you just consider the introductory courses, with some sort of abstract assumption that your students are not going to do anything else after they take those two courses, it's not at all clear to me that Ada would be the right strategy. It isn't better, if that's all you're going to do. I don't know very many such cases where you are just going to teach that first course and the students aren't going to go on.

I am intrigued with some of the notions that Ray Buhr proposed. In the early 1970's, we started teaching procedures and funtions earlier, rather than later in the course. Traditionally, we built our way up in complexity, until we finally taught the most difficult concept, which was procedures. Consequently, students left the course, usually not understanding procedures and functions and not getting that fundamental notion. So, we turned it around and said, "Let's teach that first. Let's give students building blocks and teach them to use those building blocks." We built the bodies and the procedure declarations for them and they put those together. Surprisingly, they learned procedures very well. I think that a generally understood concept in education, is that what you teach first, gets reinforced through use and therefore, the most powerful concept ought to be taught first. If you focus on the structure first, then I really think that a language like Ada is more powerful than a language like Pascal, because Ada allows you to teach those structured notions first. For instance, it isn't even inconceivable to me, that one might teach generics first. It's probably somewhat of a revolutionary notion, but particularly if the generics are already built and all you have to do is instantiate them. If the generics are fairly simple, you would teach the structural notions before you started to teach the detailed algorithmic notions.

Ada and Pascal are somewhat compatible. The fact that Ada was designed as a software engineering language does not necessarily make it incompatible with teaching it in computer science. Moreover, I feel compelled to take on this notion of subset because it is incomprehensible to me, that the educational community would be somehow constrained from subsetting the language. From the very beginning, the statements of the DoD were very clear about subsetting. It was for production purposes. The early statements actually pointed out, that for educatonal purposes, you must necessarily subset.

About 15 years ago, we spent a lot of time, for our introductory course at the Air Force Academy, subsetting Algol—a simple language. We subsetted all of the superfluous details out, so we could just teach the concepts. Then we built a little compile and go compiler, so that we could have 1300 students gobbling up a Burroughs 5500 system. You could prevent them from getting themselves in trouble by having a very simple compiler. Why can't you do that with Ada? I think it's a misreading of the question of subsetting. Therefore, I encourage anybody who wants to teach subsetting, to write a simple compile and go compiler. It's an interesting exercise for your upper-division compiler course. Make it fast. Don't let them use the features that will get them in trouble. However, don't subset away the important features.

Jim Tomayko: The next question is to consider only the early courses in an undergraduate computer science program: introductory programming and data structures. In what ways is Ada a better vehicle than Pascal or Modula 2 for teaching the elementary concepts of programming?

Nico Habermann: I would summarize that in the following way: Pascal is dated 1970 and Ada is dated 1980. This expresses the main difference between the two. Pascal is the result of a very early program language we taught in the 1960's, at a time when we weren't concerned much yet about building real systems. Therefore, software engineering ideas are not reflected in Pascal at all, whereas Ada was published in 1980, after a decade of research in software engineering. One fundamental difference between the two is modularity and another is the separation of specification, a concept not inherent in Pascal.

Jim Tomayko: How about Modula 2 then?

Nico Habermann: Well, Modula 2 is fairly close to Ada. I wouldn't make that strong of a distinction between the two. With respect to Modula 2, you can see the various results of software engineering. These are in the language directly. Thus, there is a distinction between the two.

Modula 2 has a drawback, compared to Ada, in that you can't grow with it very much. However, for early courses, there is not much difference.

One could use Modula 2 very well for introductory programming courses. But the thing that I find missing in it, is that later on in the senior years when you have to talk about real systems, Modula 2 is insufficient whereas Ada is a rich language that allows you to talk about systems.

Jim Tomayko: Well, you almost answered this, but I will ask it again. Pascal was designed to be a teaching language; Ada was designed to be a language for professional software engineers developing large, real-time embedded systems. Isn't it inappropriate to try to force Ada into a role (as a teaching language) for which it was not intended?

Nico Habermann: Absolutely not. Pascal lacks the certain things that one must teach, right from the beginning. They are the notion of modularity and the separation of specification and implementation. Neither of those concepts is in Pascal. Therefore, it is absolutely wrong to start teaching Pascal, because you teach students the wrong things. There are certain things in Ada, that I think you ought to practice right from the beginning. One of these smaller things is the initialization of variables in the declaration. This is something which supports the idea of inductive proof of programs. Everybody should be trained to program in that style—where you know you have values which may change when the program is executed. With Pascal, you can't do that. It is completely arbitrary. Hence, the programmer has to behave in a very disciplined manner, so as to make sure that he does the right thing. Pascal simply lacks the support for the basic concepts that one should teach right from the very beginning. Therefore, Ada is much better, although it is a language that has a lot of interactive features. It is absolutely necessary to try to teach Ada similar to the way in which Physics is taught. You compare the way that Physics is taught in high school with the way that mathematics is taught (starting at the bottom and building up all the time). You build up the concepts, throughout high school and one builds on top of the other. In Physics, they don't do it that way. Instead, you start out with something that covers a broad spectrum of society. You talk about the model of molecules and elementary concepts. You survey the entire field of subsets. But you don't go into too much detail. In education, don't simply go through a linear progression of knowledge. Survey the knowledge and then specialize in various areas. Build it up, in more or less layered structures.

Thus, that's what should be taught in Ada. Start with major concepts of Ada, but restrict yourself to certain things. Don't start, for example, by talking about the exception handling. Instead, begin with modularity, show how it is used, show how to build it, and demonstrate how to specify interfaces of packages, functions, and procedures, etc. Don't start with very compicated examples and procedures. The concepts, themselves, can be taught to everybody who is interested in programming. One can pick out those concepts of Ada that are suitable to a programmer. Build upon that foundation and then, go on specializing in deeper concepts.

Jim Tomayko: Consider the following proposition: There are at least four major areas of concern for educators considering using Ada in undergraduate courses. The first is the complexity of the language and the interactions of its various features. The second is the quality (including speed and user interface) and availability of appropriate textbooks using Ada. The fourth is Ada knowledge and experience of instructors.

Would students recieve a better overall educational background by using Pascal or Modula 2 in the early courses and then using Ada in advanced courses, because of the issues on the proposition above?

Nico Habermann: I already expressed a very strong opinion, that Pascal is actually no longer the right thing. I think it was the right thing in the 1970's, but it is no longer the right thing in the 1980's.

With respect to Modula versus Ada, I don't have such a strong preference for one or the other. The only thing, is that I think that one can grow in Ada, whereas you are limited in your growth with Modula 2. I think that it's actually a matter of how the material is organized. If you organize the material in the right way, then Ada is as good an introductory language as Modula 2 is. Therefore, it depends on the application of the material that we develop. If you do that right, I don't see a need for first going to Modula 2 and then to Ada. Right now, Modula 2 is not a very good alternative. I don't object to Modula 2 at all, but if we make sure that we have the right educational material, Ada is as good as Modula 2, and you can grow with it.

Now, to be specific, I do believe that there is quite a bit of complexity in Ada, particularly if you combine certain features. If you mix generics, exception handling, and tasking in your programs, you get into some very intricate things. You must organize the material very clearly.

Moreover, I think that you have to teach people certain habits of discipline before they can use these language facilities. Otherwise, users will get into trouble.

Ada compilers are really getting better now. The DEC compiler is really quite good. I believe it performs well enough, for a class of 40 students to do a class project, with no problem. From a teaching viewpoint, therefore, there are Ada compilers around that are good enough, for that purpose. That is not to say that there are no problems with compilers, but they have more to do with the really large embedded systems. Development will still go on for a while and has to go on for a while, but I don't think that education has to be concerned about that so much.

The quality of the available textbooks using Ada and the knowledge and experience of the subject are both real problems. What I've seen in general, is that textbooks have the flavor of redoing Pascal in Ada. I think that they start out by stating, "This is an assignment statement," and, "This is a while–statement," and so forth—this is all wrong. Instead, they should begin with, "This is a package, and this is the way that packages interface," and explain the difference between specification and implementation.

Another thing that I think should be done, is that we don't start with this idea of programming from scratch. What should be taught, is that students first see something like a programming system and how it is represented. From the representation, first learn things about how the interfaces are specified. Then, gradually get into modifying or improving existing software, so that they get the understanding of structure, concept, interaction, interfacing, and so on. Consequently, they can start building on top of things that are already in existence instead of starting from scratch.

Consider an architect, for example. When an architect builds a house, he already has a lot of models of how the house should be built, not only of the process, but also of the object itself, and the relative proportions and the materials. He knows all these kinds of things, which are helping him to build the house. He doesn't build it from scratch, but from models and materials that are in existence. This is something that we ought to teach to the students, right from the beginning—to program from existing knowledge and programs. Therefore, Ada is really suitable for doing that. If we write educational software packages and present those to the students, as the first thing, I think that we will teach them a completely different style of programming, which will be a lot more effective.

Availability of textbooks is a serious problem. Moreover, most people who teach Ada need help teaching programming. Ada can help a lot to turn that around if we can produce the right educational materials. I am not very concerned about compilers. I think that the problem with compilers is straightening itself out. I am concerned about the complexity, however. Thus, the quality of textbooks and the experience of instructors are my two main concerns.

Jim Tomayko: Fundamentally, what you are saying is that independently of Ada, there should be a real change in how we teach programming, and that Ada is a vehicle by which you can accomplish that change?

Nico Habermann: I think you're right. If you look at the history of programming theory, in the 1960's, we wrote one-page programs and were studying programming constructs. In the 1970's, we wrote ten-page programs that could still be handled by very simple things, such as separate compilation. Now, we are trying to build embedded systems, which are very large. Therefore, for a single programmer to sit and take a piece of paper and a pencil and write a large system, is absolutely out of the question. It's actually the wrong approach. You should proceed from the beginning, with the idea of a system. Therefore, you cannot oversee the entire thing, and you have to think about interfaces and how to use things that are not under your control. So indeed, you have to investigate the different programming styles and attitudes toward programming.

Now, Ada, I believe, is the right vehicle to support that. Ada has support in the language. That is the good thing about it.

Jim Tomayko: Do you think that currently, there are any other factors that inhibit the use of Ada in education?

Nico Habermann: There is one more and that is the availability of an environment. If you use a DEC Ada compiler, there are some tools, but not related to Ada. Therefore, in order to take this approach, one has to have a rich environment in which there is already a lot of software available. The first thing is to go back to the architect. The architect has examples how to do this. He can go to Italy and he can go to New York and look at the buildings there and study their construction. In our case, however, we teach our students by giving them a compiler. I think that we should give them software. That is not in existence currently. Therefore, it is a huge task, not a simple one. We should produce environments in which Ada packages are available to the students. These environments are more in the laboratory style, where students will find the material and things that are available for modification and building. That's the kind of thing that is also missing. So, I don't know who's going to do it, but I think that it is actually the role for the SEI, to create such environments.

Jim Tomayko: I was wondering if there are any other ways that the educational community can address some of these areas of concern, and overcome some of these problems?

Nico Habermann: It has been done by having people write textbooks as well as educational material, organize workshops. Moreover, these people can write programs for the Ada environment and build up a network community, in which people exchange ideas and make the programs available and so on. This would be the most effective way. I could see the SEI's role, to coordinate that type of work. I would think that it would be the educational community that would go in this direction and produce the necessary educational material, both in software and textbooks.

Jim Tomayko: Do you see any role of the government, aside from the SEI, of course, like AJPO?

Nico Habermann: I would say a minor role. In each of those cases, it should be a stimulating role, but not a role of a dictator, not a role of taking leadership, in the sense of prescribing people what should be used or how much of it should be used. That would be all wrong. I trust people. I think that there are a lot of talented people around. I don't think that it is necessary to tell them what to do, but to more or less make use of their talents. I still see the role as supporting, and as a catalyst, making it possible for people to do this. My priority is actually more on the style of providing funding for people to do this, than anything else. But don't tell them what to do.

David Lamb: I think there are a couple of issues that weren't on the list, that may be more important than some of the ones that were. One of the issues on the list of concerns of educators, was complexity of the language and interactions of various features. I guess that is a concern. There's another factor to it, that is not on the list, which nobody can get around. This factor is that academics are used to an idea of academic freedom; one is allowed to hold an opinion, regardless of the facts, in some situations. There are a lot of people who just do not like Ada, have not studied it much, and are not going to teach it. You are not going to convince them to teach it. Many people in the academic community treat Ada the way that they have always treated Cobol: "That is something that the DoD invented and we don't like it." Usually the business schools teach Cobol and the computer science departments do not. The same kind of thing may happen with Ada.

Now, I'm being very pejorative about my own discipline. However, to overcome this kind of prejudice, an individual instructor can teach whatever he likes in his courses. But to some extent, you've got to follow the curriculum. There's a whole pattern. You're teaching a course that is a prerequisite to other courses, so there is a lot of consensus that you need in order to build a program. If you've got a department, where half of the people want nothing to do with Ada, and one or two people want to use it, it's hard for those one or two people to influence the whole department, let alone an entire faculty. You're not going to change the introductory programming courses, without getting your entire university to agree with it, because three quarters of the university requires an introductory programming course in their programs. Therefore, there's a lot of inertia and universities are often very conservative. However, if Ada were clearly the best language to use, you would have a little more ammunition to overcome the inertia.

I think that there is a problem in education. There is a perception among educators that simplicity and elegance are important. Very few computer science educators have had a lot of experience in industry and almost none of the students have. It's hard to bring in the idea that, "You have this complex situation that you need to solve." It is difficult to deal with that, in a university context. It's not even clear that you should deal with that in a university context.

More importantly, Nico Habermann's tape said that compilers are okay now. Nico is teaching at a school where the students felt incredibly oppressed by the amount of work that they had to do. So, I think Nico is talking about a situation where educators expect to have their students put up with a lot. There isn't an Ada compiler, to the best of my knowledge, that is to Ada, what the Waterloo Fortran compiler was to Fortran, 20 years ago. There is not a compiler that is aimed at being very fast, having very good error recovery, or having very good debugging. Few industrial compilers are good enough for educational purposes. They may be validated, but they are not very useful. I've heard fairly good things about the ALSYS compiler. But the PC version requires that you have an expensive PC and that you purchase an extra board; we cannot do that in a university environment. I mention PC's because a number of universities are getting students to buy personal computers. They can run Fortran, Pascal, and

Modula on their personal computers. They are going to have to pay a lot of money to run Ada on those personal computers. Maybe that's a problem that will be solved in a few years. But it's certainly a real problem now.

Nico talked about building big environments, to help you teach; that's a big investment. Most universities are very poor and can't afford that kind of an investment. Even once it is built, it is a big investment, to start using it, if you aren't absolutely certain that it's going to work out well. At Carnegie, they have built new environments for introductory programming, because a few people were convinced that that was the right way to go. Carnegie is a fairly rich university, so they can afford to do that, whereas most of us cannot.

Robert Firth: I have a deal of trouble with this question, because these areas of concern would not necessarily be my areas of concern. The proposals to remedy them, do not seem to remedy the areas of concern. The language is complex, but life is tough and why do we pay educators to develop courses? It's not any more difficult to teach than Cobol. I have taught Cobol, and I took three months to learn it, before I attempted to start to teach it.

I think that Larry Druffel was right. You teach a carefully designed subset of the language and you lead them into the other features, in the later courses, as those features are needed.

A much harder problem is the quality of Ada compilers. We would not contemplate using an Ada compiler, until a VAX 780 could support 50 students, all programming at once. There is no way to justify a colossal investment of hardware to use a fashionable, expensive programming language, rather than a slightly less fashionable, cheap one. Compilers have a long way to go, before they reach that point.

Again, one possibility is Larry's suggestion of the university writing its own, very fast and slick subset compiler. If there is one thing that universities are rich in, it is programming effort. They have these indentured servants called graduate students, who can do this kind of thing. However, I would regard that issue as the number one obstacle to starting up an Ada course, without an extensive amount of preparation of systems software and extensive purchases of computers. I think it makes Ada courses in many colleges infeasible. I mean, teaching people to program, where they may have a 10-minute wait to get a simple program put together, is crazy.

Now, I learned programming when you hung up your paper tape in the evening and you got it back the next morning. But students today are under a great deal more pressure and they have much tighter deadlines for their course work than we had. Giving a student a deadline of one week for a programming exercise, when he is going to spend most of that time sitting and waiting for the system, is unreasonable. So, I don't know any other answer to that, other than build your own subset compiler or wait.

I won't talk about the Ada knowledge and experience of instructors. It's a perennial problem, that people who can do something other than teach, do so because gee, they like to eat. People who do nothing but teach, rapidly deteriorate because their experience becomes obsolete, at a markable rate. I noticed this when I spent more time teaching than what was appropriate.

On the question of textbooks, I'm astonished at this idea. I think that the Ada language has more and better textbooks than any other programming language. Some of the textbooks addressing Ada, at all levels of difficulty are quite superb. They are far better than the textbooks we could scrounge up if we wanted to teach C or Cobol or even Fortran, as a first language.

How can we increase the use of Ada in education, assuming that that is our objective? One way is to get better software, better support software. But I have no idea how that can be achieved, considering the number of people screaming for Ada and the small amount of softwarehouse power providing the answers. Maybe the educational community can address this concern by jointly funding some Ada development work. An unusual suggestion, that the education community should cooperate on anything. But who knows, maybe they will this time.

I think the appropriate role for the DoD and the AJPO, is to do nothing. There is no way that we will force this to happen. Indeed, it is inappropriate that we should force it to happen. Ada should be demand driven, meaning that people should teach Ada, because they feel they are going to do something valuable, by teaching Ada and not because Ada is mandated or that you can get government funding, if you teach Ada or some nonsense.

Now, AJPO should continue to participate in discussions, such as this one, and in moving information around the place and encouraging people politely, when they can. But I just do not see how funding a DoD standard Ada programming course is going to achieve anything, at all worth achieving. I guess I'm somewhat of a pessimist with regard to these issues on Ada. The things that are wrong, I don't see any quick fix for. Time and effort is probably the major answer.

Larry Druffel: I agree and disagree with Robert. First, let me comment that I remember those early days. I remember hanging up paper tape in the morning, after staying up all night and getting it back the next night.

I absolutely agree with him, in that I have a strong belief that Ada or any other technology, ought to win because of its technical merits and only because of its technical merits. If it doesn't, then it should fail. Therefore, I question the value of a mandate and I would absolutely fight one that even tried. David is right. Professors are going to do what they want to do anyway. I would discourage any such notion, in a university, even where the administrators of the university would try, if such where the case, to force a specific language on the department. I think that this is absolutely the wrong thing to do.

However, I disagree with Robert in that the AJPO should do nothing. It is the role of the AJPO to encourage the use of the language and more importantly, to remove hindrances. If there are things that are hindering its use in the academic world, then the AJPO ought to actively find ways to remove those hindrances. Here's a good case in point: If, and I believe that it is true, the education community really needs a first-class, nicely supported compiler, then the educational community ought not necessarily go out and jointly fund it. What if the educational community gets together and defines its needs and provides the specification, and we challenge industry and DoD to fund it? I think the AJPO ought to facilitate its use. Then people can make the choice, for the right reasons, because it is the best technical choice.

Ben Brosgol: The complexity of the language is manageable if you teach Ada properly. It is important, during instruction, to emphasize not just what the language is, but also why the features were developed, and how they are used. Here's an example in the area of tasking. If you try to learn the semantics of task activation by just looking at the rules, you will be completely puzzled. Does the activation come just before, or just after, the *begin*, and what difference does it make? You have to know why the rules were formulated in the manner they were, and this requires looking at the interaction with exception handling. When I have taught these subjects to students who had some previous exposure to the language, they were pleased and relieved to find that what had previously seemed to be just *ad hoc* rules in fact had a perfectly reasonable rationale.

One problem that always comes up in teaching Ada is knowing where to start. Let's face it, there is inevitably going to be some degree of magic and mystery. To do input/output, you have to instantiate a generic. You can hide this for a while from the students through carefully chosen precompiled packages, but sooner or later you'll have to confront good old TEXT_IO.INTEGER_IO and its friends.

I have taught Ada to Cobol programmers. Well, Cobol doesn't have generics but it sure has input/output, and I was not sure how well the Ada approach to I/O would be received with its "roll your own" attitude. I decided to bite the bullet on this; in the first workshop, students compiled the well-traveled generic instantiation

```
with TEXT_IO;
package INT_IO is new TEXT_IO.INTEGER_IO(integer);
```

into their libraries. So they experienced separate compilation, packages, and generic instantiations, even before they saw an *if* statement! I won't say that everyone found it intuitively obvious, but it proved to be less of a problem than I feared. Actually, I think that one of the main difficulties was the scary sounding words "instantiate" and "generic." By the end of the third week, when generics were covered in some detail, the students understood the principles behind the feature and the mechanics of what was going on.

Another way to deal with complexity is through good textbooks, and there are some excellent ones on the market. I can mention a few; be assured that these are my own opinions—I'm not getting any rebates from the authors. In the Ada course for Cobol programmers, I used Robert Clark's *Programming in Ada: a First Course*, and also, intended for those with Pascal experience, John Barnes' *Programming in Ada.* The students found both of these to be quite good. Alan Burns' *Concurrent Programming in Ada* is a nice exposition of the Ada tasking features. Grady Booch's *Software Components with Ada* and Michael Feldman's *Data Structures with Ada* are both effective texts. There are of course others, but these are the ones that I am most familiar with and have no hesitancy about recommending.

Someone asked, I think in jest, whether Ada was too complicated for computer science faculty to learn. Well, anyone teaching programming at the college level is able to learn Ada. The issue is one of attitude, not aptitude. At universities there's quite often a "not invented here" factor, and a tendency to favor home grown languages, so introducing a new language meets resistance.

I should make a few remarks about compilers. DEC VAX Ada has already been mentioned as an excellent vehicle for instruction. The Alsys Ada compiler on the PC AT has also been highly successful in classroom use. Availability is not the issue. The problem, as others have observed, is cost. Alsys Ada, I regret to say, is still a bit more expensive than Turbo Pascal. Although I don't see any magical solutions here, we can expect the same phenomenon with Ada compilers as with other software, as competitive factors and improved technology combine in yielding better products at lower prices.

What should the DoD do to promote Ada at universities? I'd like to say, "They should consider the value of having trained Ada programmers in the marketplace, and have some means to fund universities to accomplish this goal." However, I would concur that if Ada is to succeed at universities, then this should come from its technical merit rather than from DoD funding and pressure.

Dennis Ahern: I've been quite encouraged by the comments about the possibility of creating a subset of Ada, to be used for educational purposes. I think if there were such a thing and it were, in fact standardized, it would have many benefits. In particular, there could be textbooks written, that would focus on that subset. If there is going to be an effort to try to define a subset of Ada that would be useful for educational purposes, what educational group might do such a thing?

Larry Druffel: Well, I have to disagree with any notion of standardizing a subset, for two reasons. First, I think that it makes no sense in the educational environment. By building a subset or compile and go compiler, you will indeed have a convention that is the set of features you want to teach, because that is what will be supported by the compiler. But during the whole exercise of development of the language, we looked at the subsetting issues and it is extremely difficult to come up with a proper subset of the language. Secondly, everybody who teaches it will have somewhat of a different model of what's most important. Moreover, if you try to come up with a standard subset first, you constrain what the educator is going to teach and the ways in which he can present it. So, while I applaud the underlying notion behind what you said, I would really disagree with standardizing of subset, even for educational purposes. That's not to say that I'm opposed to subsetting for educational purposes.

Raymond Buhr: I am one of the early educational enthusiasts of Ada. I find myself slightly on the other side of the fence now. I've taught Ada. I've taught design with Ada. I've been faced with teaching an introductory course. I really wanted to use Ada, but I gave up, for a host of reasons. The universities that I live in, just are not ready to make that kind of a commitment. As a political expedient, Modula 2 was the only thing I saw left. I agree that Pascal is now a bad language to teach programming in, as a first language. I think universities are politically willing to accept that Modula 2 is a good language, perhaps for teaching introductory programming. Many universities are making that move. There are good, cheap compilers. I've used the Logitech compiler. It has good error messages and it has a screen editor. Unlike the Ada for the PC, it doesn't take over the machine, to become a dedicated Modula 2 machine. You just load a program in, as part of your existing environment and use all your familiar editors. As a political expedient, Modula 2 has many advantages. I would encourage people to think about that.

On the subset side, I disagree with Larry. I think you can define an Ada subset, as being the equivalent of Modula 2. Although it has some quirks such as case sensitivity, Modula 2 subset is still a perfectly rational choice.

Keith Pierce: I am interested in the existence of compilers, and I heard some contradictory answers from the panel. One person said that compilers exist now, perfectly acceptable for the educational community. Another panelist said that compilers do not exist, that can compile a short Ada program in less than 10 minutes and can support 50 students simultaneously. So, what's the answer?

Ben Brosgol: Well, there are Ada compilers available, that have compilation speeds of hundreds of lines per minute. For example, the Alsys compiler on the PC AT runs at about 200 lines per minute. On a 386-based machine, it is even faster. Obviously, this is a one-person machine. Although not all universities are scrapping their timeshared mainframes, microprocessor-based workstations are becoming more prevalent.

Norm Gibbs: I think we are misleading people, if we let them think that they can get into Ada, like they can by buying Turbo Prolog and putting it on their existing PC, without a lot of additional investment. We are not down to the Turbo level yet.

Robert Noonan: I have been using Ada since back when it was a color. At the College of William and Mary, we have been teaching Ada to upper level undergraduates since 1982. By and large, Ada for us, is a paper language. We would like to push it more widely into the curriculum. I think there's support within the faculty to do that. The problem, is that it is very difficult to do. Yes, we can mount Ada on a work station or two. Yes, we can get a couple of AT's and put Ada on them. But we cannot teach 50, 100, 200, 500 undergraduates on two or three AT's. We are stuck, particularly if we are buying memory boards. The same is true for Sun work stations or Apollo work stations; it just can't be done. You are restricted to only teaching Ada in a single section of an upper level course somewhere.

Robert Firth: One of the last things I was involved with, back in England in Military college, was selecting a vehicle for teaching Ada to undergraduates. Absolutely do not use work stations. Your undergraduates are compiling programs in a very carefully structured environment. You have provided them with extra packages; for instance, some input/output packages, so they don't have to worry about generic instantiation. Whenever you change one of these, you can't give every student his own floppy and say "Do a global recompilation of library X." They absolutely must compile on a single shared machine, with a single shared library, that you set up, as the pedagogical vehicle. Therefore, we picked DEC VAX on VMS. Whereas we can easily tolerate 50 or 60 people simultaneously compiling Fortran, we could only tolerate perhaps 7 or 8, at the most, simultaneously editing and compiling Ada. We need something like a factor of five improvement in Ada compilers, before we can contemplate major programming courses, given the resources available.

Robert Noonan: At least you have the luxury of having a VAX. We have an IBM main frame and Primes, and there are no Ada compilers for those machines. So, we are stuck using work stations or convincing the computer center to junk all the stuff it already has.

John Brackett: I believe our problem is really a general technology transfer problem. Being the first instructor on campus, to pick up Ada is not a job that I would want to be involved in. There's a technology transfer kit needed from somewhere. I happen to believe this is one of the places that the DoD or the SEI has a role.

My belief is, if anyone is ever going to teach Ada in a university, part of my technology transfer kit has to be an Ada compiler, optimized to an environment which universities have.

My main point is, when you put all the little factors together, they don't fit together. A fast compiler has to be part of the transfer kit. Exercises have to be integrated with the transfer kit. The book has to be integrated with the transfer kit. Nobody, on most campuses, wants Ada. Therefore, why should the instructor go through all the grief? I think unless somebody takes responsibility for what I call system integration of the transfer kit, not much is going to happen with Ada in universities.

John Brackett: I tend to believe that SEI is the only vehicle that might have the role to try to specify the transfer kit, with any hope of it coming about. Without it, I can't think of a good reason, even having been interested in Ada for a long time, why I would want to go through the grief of teaching the first Ada programming course on any campus.

Caroline Eastman: It's probably premature at this point to ask if Ada should be used in the high schools. But I'd like to ask if anyone on the panel would care to comment on the impact of what is being done now in the high schools on the issues raised? That is where many people get their first exposure to computer programming.

David Lamb: I'd like to try and tackle that, as I teach introductory programming. We have been involved a lot, in the last few years, talking about what the impact that increased computer programming education in high school is going to have on our introductory courses. So far, we spend as much time teaching the people who know nothing, as we do on teaching people who have had the high school courses, what they learned wrong, by learning Basic or even learning Pascal, taught by a high school instructor, who is even less qualified than some of the poorer college instructors. I don't think that there is anything in introductory computer programming courses, that couldn't be taught in high school, if you had the better, simpler language. I don't think Ada is for high schools. But the main problem with teaching, pushing programming down into the lower levels, is that there is only so far that you can go, before you start needing some discrete mathematics.

Ben Brosgol: I think that Logo would be a much better choice than

Basic. But Basic generally comes with the machine. People have to pay for Logo and unfortunately, that results in a lot of people knowing Basic.

Gary Ford: I assume that ALSYS did not set out to write a slow compiler. They probably have the compiler running as fast as reasonable, at this stage. If there were financial incentives offered by the DoD or from some other organization, what would be the feasability of your company producing a much faster compiler from your existing compiler? Would it be a whole new effort? Can you do it in six months or a year or would it take a lot longer? What is the scope of the problem?

Ben Brosgol: It would be a fairly large effort to redesign the compiler to optimize for compilation speed. Our cuurent design had as its major goals to generate highly efficient code, to allow the processing of very large programs—hundreds of thousands of lines of Ada—and to be portable to a large variety of hosts and targets. The tradeoff was in the area of compiler size and compilation speed. Reorienting the technology at this point, well, this would not be easy.

Norm Gibbs: Is your answer that you can't modify the current one, but you have to start from scratch?

Ben Brosgol: I wouldn't say start from scratch, but it would be a major effort to redesign it.

David Lamb: As I do some of my research in compiler technology, I would think that building a series of subsets of Ada is a harder problem than building the compilers that have been around so far. You've got a language subset design problem and you've got the problem of designing a family of related compilers, with different constraints. One way in which it is easier, is since they are subsets, you don't have to go through the validation suite. I think that that has been a major problem in getting usability out of some of the existing compilers.

John Brackett: I think the key point in getting from here to there involves going back to what we are trying to achieve for educational purposes. I suspect that anybody who is going to make compiler changes, other than to the front end of their compiler for the syntax of the subset language, is going to start over with totally new code generators. If you don't go to some innovative approach for picking up library units, directly into the code, you can never achieve the required speeds.

My main point is that it's 20 to 50 times harder than Watfor to build a high-speed Ada educational compiler system. No one has thought about building a total Ada compilation system, including library modules and reusable components that operate at speeds comparable to equivalent systems for other languages in the university "compile and go" environment.

Charles McKay: Having been involved with Ada, and teaching it for some time, I think that we are failing to pay adequate attention to the appropriate criteria for judging what should be in a first course. We, are all too often thinking about what has always been in a first course. That's in terms of algorithms, data structures, semantics, and syntax that are normally associated with issues of programming in the small. I'm not certain that that's what we should be doing. I don't think that we'd be doing justice to Ada, if we continue that focal point. We need to be thinking in terms of higher levels of abstraction. We also need to be thinking in terms of looking at a problem and decomposing it, in some reasonable way, so that modules and their interfaces are reasonably clear. There is an interesting availabilty of public domain reusable components in Ada. They enable us to introduce concepts of programming–in–the–large by focusing on specifications of reusable modules and their interfaces in the first course. Programming–in–the–small is facilitated by good examples embedded into the implementation part of these modules.

When Pascal came along, those of us who had managed to escape Algol, looked at Pascal in the same context of a one–semester course in which it became very obvious that you could not do your job and teach syntax. You had to deal with semantic contructs and user defined data structures. It was interesting to see that by shifting the emphasis, students still seemed capable of picking up the syntax issues. Ada came along. It is perhaps six times as large, and as complex as Pascal. We still try to teach it in a one–semester course, which is most inappropriate. The issues there really boil down to looking at fundamental issues of rationale. You can teach: "What is the problem we are trying to solve? What are the alternatives that are available to solve the problem?" Then you have the opportunity to abstract, at a much higher level and to deal with things that are more effective in todays systems.

I think it's interesting to note that the students I've had the pleasure of working with, are perfectly capable of backing up and picking up on the syntax as well as the semantic constructs.

Stuart Reges: I also work a lot with the Advance Placement Program in Computer Science. I think I'm probably the chief advocate of software engineering. I'm also interested in the question about what high school teachers should be teaching.

Should someone be trying to teach Ada concepts, if they are forced to use Pascal? Furthermore, in a data structures kind of course, should you make opaque implementations a major theme?— Given that you can't enforce it and Pascal does not enforce the opacity, but student graders can.

Ben Brosgol: Yes.

Robert Firth: Never impose a restriction that the compiler does not enforce, in a programming course. One of the most infuriating things a student can come across, is a solution that compiles, executes, gets the right answer and then gets downgraded, because he hasn't put the comments in the right margin, for example.

Stuart Reges: Are you saying that we should not be pushing in the direction of making opaque implementations?

Robert Firth: No. Absolutely not.

Ben Brosgol: I disagree. I think that it is certainly possible and appropriate to introduce software engineering principles. when teaching Pascal, even if the principles are not enforced by Pascal. Thus, I would say yes, do it.

Larry Druffel: That's what I was going to comment also. It isn't a question of, "Should I use Ada-like things?" It's a question of, "Should I teach good software engineering?" The answer is absolutely yes.

David Lamb: We actually teach abstract data types and opaque types, in the second half course, in the first year. The students absolutely hate it when you grade them on anything but the fact that the program works. But we do that anyway. We teach them how to comment and document. I think that teaching them about language restrictions is pretty much the same thing. Students will hate it but they will learn it.

Stuart Reges: Do you do that in Pascal?

David Lamb: Yes. We teach our second course in Pascal.

Brad Brown: Giving an industry point of view, Ada is not a real-time embedded system language. It doesn't work well for that. Real-time systems just don't work well with Ada. The government doesn't care. They go ahead and and impose it to us on contracts anyway. So, we at Boeing have probably already trained several hundred, maybe even several thousand people, how to program in Ada. The previous experience was Jovial. Now, we have Jovial written in Ada. But this doesn't matter. We meet our contract requirements.

I think the real issue that we are dealing with is that whether you program in Ada or program in Jovial or C, it's not the language—it's how you do it. There are places where Pascal is going to be better than Ada and places where C is better than Cobol. Thus, the real issue is software engineering, not the material we do it with.

MIX
Papier aus verantwortungsvollen Quellen
Paper from responsible sources
FSC® C105338
FSC
www.fsc.org

If you have any concerns about our products,
you can contact us on
ProductSafety@springernature.com

In case Publisher is established outside the EU,
the EU authorized representative is:
Springer Nature Customer Service Center GmbH
Europaplatz 3, 69115 Heidelberg, Germany

Printed by Libri Plureos GmbH
in Hamburg, Germany